GMAT

Data Sufficiency

Prep Course

(A Thorough Review)

JEFF KOLBY

DERRICK VAUGHN

KUNDA VAMSIDHAR

Additional educational titles from Nova Press (available at novapress.net):

➤ **GRE Prep Course** (624 pages, includes software)

   GRE Math Bible (528 pages)

➤ **GMAT Prep Course** (624 pages, includes software)

   GMAT Math Prep Course (528 pages)

➤ **Master The LSAT** (560 pages, includes software, and 2 official LSAT exams)

➤ **The MCAT Physics Book** (444 pages)

   The MCAT Biology Book (416 pages)

   The MCAT Chemistry Book (428 pages)

➤ **SAT Prep Course** (640 pages, includes software)

   SAT Math Bible (480 pages)

➤ **Law School Basics:** A Preview of Law School and Legal Reasoning (224 pages)

➤ **Vocabulary 4000:** The 4000 Words Essential for an Educated Vocabulary (160 pages)

ISBN: 1–889057–54–1

GMAT is a registered trademark of the Graduate Management Admission Council, which was not involved in the production of, and does not endorse, this book.

11659 Mayfield Avenue
Los Angeles, CA 90049
Phone: 1-800-949-6175
E-mail: info@novapress.net
Website: www.novapress.net

ABOUT THIS BOOK

If you don't have a pencil in your hand, get one now! Don't just read this book – Write on it, study it, scrutinize it! In short, for the next four weeks, this book should be a part of your life. When you have finished the book, it should be marked-up, dog-eared, tattered and torn.

Although Data Sufficiency questions are difficult, they are *very* learnable. This is not to say that the Data Sufficiency section is "beatable." There is no bag of tricks that will show you how to master it overnight. You probably have already realized this. Some books, nevertheless, offer "inside stuff" or "tricks" which they claim will enable you to beat the section. These include declaring that answer-choices C, or E are more likely to be correct than choices A, B, or D. This tactic, like most of its type, does not work. It is offered to give the student the feeling that he or she is getting the scoop on the test.

The Data Sufficiency section cannot be "beaten." But it can be mastered—through hard work, analytical thought, and by training yourself to think like a test writer. Many of the exercises in this book are designed to prompt you to think like a test writer.

We will discuss all the mathematical and logical concepts you need to handle Data Sufficiency questions. The multiple-choice format is also discussed to make understanding the Data Sufficiency format easier.

Typically, you do not need to actually solve a Data Sufficiency problem in order to answer the question. You just need to determine whether a definitive answer is possible. This book teaches you how to do that and how to do it with confidence.

CONTENTS

ORIENTATION

Format of the Math Section

The Math section consists of 37 questions and is 75 minutes long. The questions come in two formats: *Data Sufficiency* and *Multiple-choice*. Typically, one-third of the Math section consists of Data Sufficiency questions.

How to Decide whether You Need This Book?

Considering the competition for business school, even a single lower percentile score on the GMAT can knock you out of contention for the school of your choice. If you need to improve your chances of getting into a better school, then you need this book.

Even people good at multiple-choice problems often struggle with Data Sufficiency problems. This book shows you how to treat Data Sufficiency problems like Multiple-choice problems through paradigms. So, if you are good at the Multiple-choice and not at Data Sufficiency, the paradigms discussed in this book will help you apply the skills from multiple-choice problems to Data Sufficiency problems.

Format of the book

Part I introduces the Data Sufficiency question and the typical formats in which these problems appear.

Part II presents strategies for attacking Data Sufficiency questions.

Part III presents a review of GMAT math that applies to both Data Sufficiency questions and Multiple-choice questions.

Directions and Reference Material

The directions for Data Sufficiency questions are rather complicated. Before reading any further, take some time to learn the directions cold. Some of the wording in the directions below has been changed from the GMAT to make it clearer. You should never have to look at the instructions during the test.

<u>Directions:</u> Each of the following Data Sufficiency problems contains a question followed by two statements, numbered (1) and (2). You need not solve the problem; rather you must decide whether the information given is <u>sufficient</u> to solve the problem.

The correct answer to a question is

> A   if statement (1) ALONE is sufficient to answer the question but statement (2) alone is not sufficient;
>
> B   if statement (2) ALONE is sufficient to answer the question but statement (1) alone is not sufficient;
>
> C   if the two statements TAKEN TOGETHER are sufficient to answer the question, but NEITHER statement ALONE is sufficient;
>
> D   if EACH statement ALONE is sufficient to answer the question;
>
> E   if the two statements TAKEN TOGETHER are still NOT sufficient to answer the question.

<u>Numbers:</u> Only real numbers are used. That is, there are no complex numbers.

<u>Drawings:</u> A figure accompanying a data sufficiency question will conform to the information given in the question, but may conflict with the information given in statements (1) and (2).

You can assume that a line that appears straight is straight and that angle measures cannot be zero.

You can assume that the relative positions of points, angles, and objects are as shown.

All drawings lie in a plane unless stated otherwise.

<u>Example:</u>

In $\triangle ABC$ to the right, what is the value of y ?

(1) $AB = AC$

(2) $x = 30$

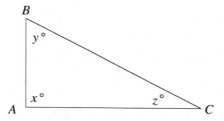

Explanation: By statement (1), $\triangle ABC$ is isosceles. Hence, its base angles are equal: $y = z$. Since the angle sum of a triangle is 180°, we get $x + y + z = 180$. Replacing z with y in this equation and then simplifying yields $x + 2y = 180$. Since statement (1) does not give a value for x, we cannot determine the value of y from statement (1) alone. By statement (2), $x = 30$. Hence, $x + y + z = 180$ becomes $30 + y + z = 180$, or $y + z = 150$. Since statement (2) does not give a value for z, we cannot determine the value of y from statement (2) alone. However, using both statements in combination, we can find both x and z and therefore y. Hence, the answer is C.

Notice in the above example that the triangle appears to be a right triangle. However, that cannot be assumed: angle A may be 89° or 91°, we can't tell from the drawing. **You must be very careful not to assume any more than what is explicitly given in a Data Sufficiency problem.**

Reference Information

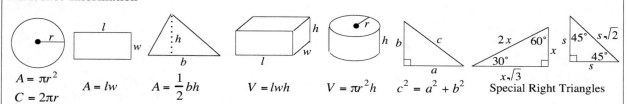

$A = \pi r^2$

$C = 2\pi r$

$A = lw$

$A = \dfrac{1}{2}bh$

$V = lwh$

$V = \pi r^2 h$

$c^2 = a^2 + b^2$

Special Right Triangles

The number of degrees of arc in a circle is 360.
The sum of the measures in degrees of the angles of a triangle is 180.

Although this reference material can be handy, be sure you know it well so that you do not waste time looking it up during the test.

Part One

Understanding Data Sufficiency

Introduction

Data Sufficiency questions test quantitative reasoning ability through an unusual set of directions. Generally, data sufficiency problems require much less calculating (and sometimes no calculating) than do multiple-choice problems, but they are trickier.

A math problem can be presented in many formats, such as, multiple-choice, problem solving, quantitative comparison, etc. Data Sufficiency is just one such format. But there is much to learn about the format. The discussion originates from the peculiar set of directions for the format, which we will discuss shortly. For now, it's important to know that this format is trickier than all the other formats because it involves both logic and math. Because of the involvement of logic, many general strategies come into the picture. All these general strategies are discussed in detail in this chapter and the next. By the end of the second chapter, you will be well versed in the Data Sufficiency format. But unless you have very strong math skills, you might still find these problems challenging. The remaining chapters of the book focus on general math skills.

Before proceeding, note this crucial point:

Multiple-choice problems are about solving, while Data Sufficiency problems are generally limited to determining whether a solution exists. So, in Data Sufficiency problems, we usually skip the step of actually solving the problem. We will see that this advantage makes Data Sufficiency problems easier.

Grammar of Data Sufficiency Problems

➤ A Data Sufficiency problem looks like:

Question Setup?

(1) Statement (A)

(2) Statement (B)

 Note the difference between the phrases "a problem" and "a question setup" used in this book. *A problem* refers to the question setup and its two statements.

For example,

If $x + y = 10$, is $x = 4$?

(1) y is not 6.

(2) y is 4.

Here, "If $x + y = 10$, is $x = 4$?" is the question setup, and "y is not 6" and "y is 4" are the statements. "A problem" means the Question Setup, Statement (1), and Statement (2) together.

➤ Let's use the example above to demonstrate certain concepts about a Data Sufficiency problem:

- A problem refers to exactly one system (hidden or revealed). The question setup and the statements focus this system. For example, in the problem above, "$x + y = 10$" is the system that the question setup and the statements refer to. The system is not always explicitly stated in the problem. Sometimes, it's not given, and we call it hidden or implied.

- Any description of the system (like "$x + y = 10$") is a property of the system. Statements are also the properties of the system, since they describe or constrain the system. In the above problem, "$x + y = 10$," "y is not 6," and "y is 4" are the properties of the system "$x + y = 10$." These are the known properties (confirmed properties) of the system. There are unknown properties also. For example, we do not know the value of x in the question setup. Here, x is an unknown property, and "Is $x = 4$?" is also an unknown property, which equals either Yes or No, or True or False.

- Known properties, for example, "$y = 1$," "x is not 3," and "x is 4." reveal certain facts. For example, "Is $x = 4$?" "what is x?" "$x + 2$" expect certain facts to be answered. The value of x is not yet known, so x is an unknown property and $x + 2$ is as well. Until we calculate the value of the unknown property, we consider the property unknown. Once calculated, we consider it a known property.

- We can generalize to say, any Math problem is made up of only known and unknown properties, and the problem generally asks to determine at least one unknown property. We view a Math problem as a collection of known and unknown properties. Here's an example:

Example: If $(a - b)(a + b) = 7 \times 13$, then what are the values of a, b and $a - b$?

$(a - b)(a + b) = 7 \times 13$

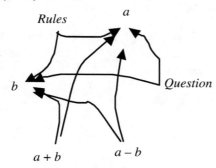

Here, the arrows refer to dependencies. For example, the unknown property called the question depends on knowing a, and b, the property $a + b$ depends on the properties a, and b, and so on. Rules are also properties. For example, the rule in the figure above binds a and b.

- A question setup contains at least one unknown property (That's what makes it a question setup).

- The statements are merely the known properties of the system, which act as means to find the unknown properties. Statements are generally chosen to be clues or facts about the system to be used to determine the system. The statements can also be viewed as constraints on the system.

- **Finally, let's Break-up a Data Sufficiency problem using the following table:**

	Known Properties	Unknown Properties
The Question Setup	*Can Have*	*At least one*
Statement(s)	Is what Statement is made up of.	None

Example: If $x + y + z = 6$, then do any two of the three numbers x, y, and z sum to 3?

    (1) x, y, and z are three different positive integers.

    (2) x, y, and z are consecutive integers.

The break–up of the problem looks like this:

	Known Properties	Unknown Properties
Question Setup	$x + y + z = 6$	x, y, and z are unknown properties. We do not know their values.
		Question equals "Do any two of the three numbers x, y, and z sum to 3?" The expected answer is either Yes or No.
Statement (1)	x, y, and z are three different positive integers.	None (Statements always have only known properties)
Statement (2)	x, y, and z are consecutive integers.	None (Statements always have only known properties).

- Any known property can be a statement.

- When we are able to find all the unknown properties of the system, we have determined the entire system. Sometimes, to solve a problem, it is easy to find the system, and then the unknowns.

- As mentioned, problems are based on a system, hidden or revealed. In the two examples discussed so far, the systems, $x + y = 10$ and $x + y + z = 6$, are revealed by the questions themselves. Sometimes, the system is hidden as in the following example:

Example: If (x, y) is a point on a line, then what is the value of x when y is 1?

     (1) x is 2 when y is 0.

     (2) x is 0 when y is 2.

- The system is not directly given here. The question is about a *hidden* system: the line $x + y = 2$.

- The statements must support the system, since they are the properties of the system. For example, here, you can check that the points $(2, 0)$ and $(0, 2)$ satisfy the equation of the line. This is to say, the points satisfy the question setup, and the statements together, which are merely the collection of the known and the unknown properties of the system.

- In the process of solving the problems, sometimes, we find the unknowns first, and then the system; and sometimes, we find the system first and then the unknowns.

- If statements are sufficient to evaluate the unknown property, called the question, then we have data sufficiency.

- We so far treated statements as known properties. We will now treat the known properties as constraints. The perspective is referred to as the Constrain Paradigm. Let's start with an example.

Example: Every time x increases (decreases) by a particular value, y decreases (increases) by two times that value (*this is the system description*). What is the value of x when y is 3?

     (1) When y is 1, $x = 3$.

     (2) When y is 2, $x = 1$.

- Statements (1) and (2) above are constraints that limit the system. For example, the shape of the hidden system in the problem (question setup) is $x + 2y = c$. So, the system varies with c. In other words, in order to fix (determine) the system, we need to know the value of c. Substituting either statement in the equation $x + 2y = c$ yields 5 for the value of c. Therefore, the statements constrain the system from being any other system but $x + 2y = 5$. Thus, we can say the statements are the constraints that fix the system. If not sufficient, they may fail to constrain.

- In the above example, initially, the system $x + 2y = c$ could be any system such as $x + 2y = 1$, $x + 2y = 1.5$, or $x + 2y = 5.6$, etc. Now, either statement — (1) or (2) — prevents the line from being any line other than $x + 2y = 5$ (Since when y is 1, $x = 3$, we have $c = x + 2y = 3 + 2(1) = 5$).

- In the above example, $x + 2y = 5$ is the system, and the points $(1, 2)$ and $(3, 1)$ given in the two statements are just two instances of the system. Instances are properties of the system.

- If a system is completely determined (for example, in the above problem when c is calculated, we determined that the system is $x + 2y = 5$), we can answer any detail about the system. We can find the instance in Statement (1) or Statement (2) or some other instance.

- Sometimes, the system is generic. For example, $x + 2y = 5$ is a generic system, and there are multiple instances of the system. The points (1, 2) and (3, 1) are instances of the system. Another example is a triangle with a fixed base and fixed altitude moving on the base. In this case, the area of the triangle, $1/2 \cdot base \cdot height$, remains constant. But, the perimeter isn't constant. So, we say the system is hanging on the property base: with the height fixed, the area is automatically fixed. We have seen that we do not always need to find a fixed system to answer for a particular unknown property. Sometimes, a generic solution will do.

- If we are able to find the fixed system in a problem, instead of a generic one, we have data sufficiency regardless of what is asked about the system. So, we can know the area of a fixed triangle, the perimeter of a fixed triangle, etc. This is the Constructability Check, which we will discuss in the Geometry chapter.

- If we are only able to find a generic system, check whether for each instance the unknown property, called the *question*, has a single value. If yes, the data is sufficient. If the value varies, the data is insufficient. Regardless of the instance that follows from the system $x + 2y = 5$, the value of $x/2 + y$ is always 2.5. So, if we are asked to find what is $x/2 + y$, we have sufficient data. If instead, we are asked to find what is $x + y$, the answer varies with the instance (with the value of y). Hence, we have insufficient data. Another example is the angle made by a circular arc is constant regardless of the point on the arc where the angle is measured.

 ➤ **A *plausible set* is the set of all elements that a property can take.**

Here are a few examples:

Example: If we specify that x is 4, then the plausible set for x is {4}.

Example: If we say x is not 3, then the plausible set for x is the set of all numbers other than 3.

Example: If we say x is an even number, then the plausible set for x is $\{\dots, -4, -2, 0, 2, 4, \dots\}$.

Example: For the question "Is x equal to 4?", the plausibility set is {Yes, No} — Yes when x is 4, and No when x is not 4. Arranging the detail correspondingly, the plausibility set of x is {4, Every number other than 4} for the plausibility set of the question being {Yes, No}.

Now, what is the precise distinction between Data Sufficiency and Data Insufficiency?

Data is said to be sufficient if the plausibility set for the question setup has a single element (exactly one answer). Data is said to be insufficient if the plausibility set for the question setup has more than one element (more than one answer).

You will not see problems where there are no elements in the plausibility set (no answer). This means the system being referred to by the problem is invalid. Such problems are not presented on the GMAT.

➢   Based on this, the answering system for Data Sufficiency problems is

The correct answer is

○	A	If Statement (1) ALONE is sufficient to answer the question but Statement (2) alone is not sufficient;
○	B	If Statement (2) ALONE is sufficient to answer the question but Statement (1) alone is not sufficient;
○	C	If the two statements TAKEN TOGETHER are sufficient to answer the question but neither statement alone is sufficient;
○	D	If EACH statement ALONE is sufficient to answer the question;
○	E	If the two statements TAKEN TOGETHER are still NOT sufficient to answer the question.

➢   **What type of problems are invalid and won't be asked on the GMAT?**

The following two types of problems cannot be asked:

✖ **I. A problem in which the question setup alone is sufficient will not be given.**

The reason is simple. Because then, the solution is possible without any statements and there is no answer-choice to choose for the scenario. The kind of problem is as silly as this:

"If x equals 4, then what is x?"

A few other examples:

"If $x + y = 5$ and $y = 1$, is $x = 4$?" (By substitution, we get $x = 4$.)

"If $x + y = 5$ and $y = 1$, is x not 4?" (By substitution, we get x is 4.)

✖ **II. Problems involving invalid systems will not be given.**

Example 1 (Invalid):   If $x + y = 5$, what is x ?

(1) $x = 4$

(2) $y = 2$

If x equals 4 and y equals 2, then $x + y = 6 \neq 5$. So, there won't be any system in which $x + y$ equals 5, while x equals 4 and y equals 2. So, the system used in the problem (Question plus the two statements) is invalid and THE GMAT takes care not to ask such questions.

In other words, an invalid system is one where certain properties violate other properties of the system. For example, here, any two of the properties "$x = 4$," "$y = 2$," and "$x + y = 5$" are violated by the third property.

Let's look at another example of an invalid Data Sufficiency problem:

✖ **Example 2 (Invalid):**   Does Set $A = \{2, 3\}$?

    (1) A is the set of all odd prime numbers greater than 1.

    (2) A is the set of all odd prime numbers less than 5.

Observe that statements (1) and (2) contradict each other: (1) says A is set of all odd primes greater than 1, while (2) denies A contains odd primes greater than or equal to 5. This will never occur on a GMAT Data Sufficiency problem.

➤ Constraint Paradigm

Consider the problem

    What is x?

Here, x is free to take any value: 1, 1.2, 3, or 15, ... , or any other real number. So, the plausibility set of x is the set of all real numbers.

Now, consider the problem

    If $x + y = 5$, then what is x?

Here, x can also be any number, but bound by the constraint $x + y = 5$. Since y is not given, x is still free to take any value.

Now, consider the problem

    If $x + y = 5$, then what is x?

    (1) $|y| = 2$

The statement $|y| = 2$ says y is +2 or y is –2. So, the plausibility set of y is $\{2, -2\}$. If y is 2, on substitution, $x + y = 5$ forces x to be 3; and if y is –2, then $x + y = 5$ forces x to be 7. Thus, the plausibility set of x is now pared down to just two numbers: $\{3, 7\}$. Thus, the possible values of x have been constrained to a much smaller set. Thus, we see that Statement (1) $|y| = 2$ acts as a constraint on the system.

Summary: **All Properties are also Constraints.** So, the statements can be treated by either paradigm: Properties or as Constraints.

➤ **Constraints either make the plausibility set of the question smaller or keep it as is. They never make the plausibility set larger. Here is an example, where the plausibility set is unchanged by the constraints (statements).**

    If $x + y = 5$, then what is x?

    (1) $y = 2$

    (2) $2x = 10 - 2y$

Dividing Statement (2) by 2 yields $x = 5 - y$. Substituting this in the equation $x + y = 5$ yields $5 - y + y = 5$, or $5 = 5$. This is a known fact, and does not need the statement to prove it. Hence, the statement does not constrain the system any further. This means the plausibility set has not been decreased. Such a statement is moot: the statement is not sufficient or more precisely not required.

• **Any statement that is not required is insufficient.**

➤   Now, let's express the answering system for Data Sufficiency problems in the constraining paradigm:

The correct answer is

    ○   A   If Statement (1) ALONE constrains the question to a single answer but Statement (2) alone does not (constrain the question to a single value);

    ○   B   If Statement (2) ALONE constrains the question to a single answer but Statement (1) alone not (constrain the question to a single value);

    ○   C   If the two statements TAKEN TOGETHER constrain the question to a single answer but neither statement alone does;

    ○   D   EACH statement ALONE can constrain the question to a single answer;

    ○   E   If the two statements TAKEN TOGETHER still DO NOT constrain the question to a single answer.

Examples for each of the above choices is shown below:

Choice A Correct: What is x?

(1) $x + 1 = 2$ which answers the question as $x = 1$; Statement sufficient.

(2) $|x| = 1$ which answers the question as $x = 1$ or -1; Statement not sufficient.

Choice B Correct: What is x?

(1) $|x| = 1$ which answers the question as $x = 1$ or -1; Statement not sufficient.

(2) $x + 1 = 2$ which answers the question as $x = 1$; Statement sufficient.

Choice D Correct: What is x?

(1) $x + 1 = 2$ which answers the question as $x = 1$; Statement sufficient.

(2) $x + 3 = 4$ which answers the question as $x = 1$; Statement sufficient.

Either statement is sufficient.

Choice C Correct: What is x?

(1) x is negative: which answers the question as any number that is negative; Statement not sufficient.

(2) $|x| = 1$ which answers the question as $x = 1$ or -1; Statement not sufficient.

Common solution is $x = -1$; The statements sufficient only together.

Choice E Correct: What is x?

(1) $x + 2$ is positive   which answers the question as $x > -2$; Statement not sufficient.

(2) $|x| = 1$ is positive   which answers the question as $x = -1$ or 1; Statement not sufficient.

Together still say, x could be -1 or 1. The statements together not sufficient.

If there is only one solution, data is sufficient; and if more than one solution, data is not sufficient.

Invalid Problem Types:

✖ You will not see problems where there are no solutions. These kinds of problems are considered over-constrained or invalid. A blank plausibility set for the question setup is never possible.

✖ You will not see problems where the question alone is sufficient.

➢ **Degree of Freedom Paradigm**

Before discussing the paradigm, let's discuss what *degree of freedom* means.

➢ Suppose we have the system

$x + y + z = 4$

- Suppose the question is "What is x?" Let's find the degree of freedom of the system for x. Subtracting y and z from both sides of the equation yields $x = 4 - y - z$. This equation says that x depends on the variables y and z. So, as the values of the variables y and z change x changes. So, the degree of freedom of x is 2, which means that x is two variables away from its value being fixed. In other words, we would need at least the values of y and z to calculate the value of x. In other words, we say, x is dependent on the 2 variables. Now, suppose you add a rule, say, $y = 1$. Substituting yields $x = 4 - y - z = 4 - 1 - z = 3 - z$. Now, x is dependent on only z, so its degree of freedom has been decreased to 1.

- Suppose the question is "What is $y + z$?" Let's evaluate $y + z$. Subtracting x from both sides of the equation $x + y + z = 4$ yields $y + z = 4 - x$. So, the value of $y + z$ depends only on x. So, the degree of freedom of $y + z$ is 1.

- Suppose the rule is $x^2 = 4 - y - z$. Here, given y and z (say, given the rules $y = 1$ and $z = 1$, substituting in the equation $x^2 = 4 - y - z$ yields $x^2 = 4 - 1 - 1$, or $x^2 = 2$, or $x = +\sqrt{2}$ or $-\sqrt{2}$), we would have two solutions possible for x. Therefore, we need another rule like x is positive or x is negative so that the exact value of x is determined. So, the degree of freedom of x from the equation $x^2 = 4 - y - z$ is 3. Hence, x is 3 bits of information away from being determined. Same is the case with the quadratic expression in x: $x^2 = 4x - y - z$. For the same reason, linear equations are said to have degree 1, and quadratic equations are said to have degree 2. Now, the rules are merely constraints. Adding constraints reduces the degree of freedom; in general, by one degree per constraint.

- If $x = 4 - (y + z)$, then you may be tempted to treat $y + z$ as a single variable, say s, and say that the degree of freedom is 1 (s alone), but this is incorrect. The equation $x = 4 - (y + z)$ clearly indicates y and z are two separately varying variables.

- Suppose $x = 4 - y - z$ and $x = 2 + p$. Here, the degree of freedom of x is only 1 (p alone).

- Suppose we have a system in two variables, x and y. The degree of freedom must be 2. The system is changed (played) by the two variables. Now, suppose we have a constraint like $x + y = 5$. Subtracting y from both sides yields $x = 5 - y$. Thus, x is dependent on y; and for each value of y, we automatically have the value of x decided (fixed) by the rule. We say x and y are one-to-one with each other, meaning that one value of y yields exactly one value of x, and one value of x yields exactly one value of y. Effectively, it is equivalent to say, the system is now dependent on a single variable (x or y alone). Hence, the degree of freedom is 1. Thus, the degree of freedom decreases by 1 (x or y) for one rule (constraint) and stands at 1. In general, the degree of freedom decreases by 1 per constraint. In other words, earlier, we had to choose both x and y to fix the system, so the degree was 2. Now, we need to choose only one of them (x or y), and the other variable will be automatically fixed (evaluated) and the system is fixed. So, to fix the system, we need to know (or fix) only one of x and y.

- Suppose we have a system in two variables x and y, and we have the rule $y = x^2$. For each value of x, we have one value of y. Thus, y is one-to-one with x. But, for each single value of y, there are two values of x possible (one positive and one negative). Thus, if we consider the system as x and $y = x^2$, the degree of freedom is 1 (one set of values for x^2 for each single value of x). If we consider the system as y and $x = \sqrt{y}$, the degree of freedom is 2 (2 values of $\sqrt{y}$) for each value of y. In such cases, the degree of freedom is the minimum number that can be picked. So, the degree of freedom here is 1.

- There are exceptions to the rule that each constraint reduces the degree of freedom by 1. For example, suppose we have a constraint like $|y| = 2$. Then y could be 2 or –2. Substituting each value in the equation $x + y = 5$ yields $x = 3$ or 7. So, y is not fixed, and correspondingly x is not fixed. So, the constraint fails to reduce the degree of freedom. Although there are exceptions to the rule, the degree of freedom method of solving Data Sufficiency problems is very effective.

- In conclusion, when the degree of freedom is reduced to zero, we have a single solution for the question setup and the corresponding data [Statement (1) plus the Question setup or Statement (2) plus the Question setup or all together] used is sufficient.

➤ Now, let's discuss the answering system for Data Sufficiency problems in the Degree of Freedom Paradigm:

The correct answer is

     ○ A   With Question plus Statement (1) ALONE, degree of freedom is zero but with Question plus Statement (2) ALONE, it is not.

     ○ B   With Question plus Statement (2) ALONE, degree of freedom is zero but with Question plus Statement (1) ALONE, it is not.

     ○ C   With the Question plus the two statements TAKEN TOGETHER, degree of freedom in the sense of the question is zero but not with the Question plus either statement alone.

     ○ D   With the Question plus either statement ALONE, the degree of freedom in the sense of the question is zero.

     ○ E   With the Question plus the two statements TAKEN TOGETHER, the degree of freedom in the sense of the question is not zero.

A few examples in Data Sufficiency order: *question alone sufficient* **(not shown below) – D—A, B—C—E:**

Example for Choice *D*: What is *x*? The degree of freedom here is 1.

(1) $x + 1 = 2$ which answers the question as $x = 1$. This reduces the DOF to $1 - 1 = 0$.

(2) $x + 3 = 4$ which answers the question as $x = 1$. This reduces the DOF to $1 - 1 = 0$.

Either statement is sufficient.

Example for Choice *A*: What is *x*? The degree of freedom here is 1.

(1) $x + 1 = 2$ which answers the question as $x = 1$. The rule is linear and the DOF reduces to $1 - 1 = 0$.

(2) $|x| = 1$ which answers the question as $x = 1$ or -1. The statement fails to reduce the degree of freedom by 1 because *x* has two possible values from the statement.

Example for Choice *B*: What is *x*? The degree of freedom here is 1.

(1) $|x| = 1$ which answers the question as $x = 1$ or -1. The statement fails to reduce the degree of freedom by 1 because *x* has two possible values from the statement.

(2) $x + 1 = 2$ which answers the question as $x = 1$. The rule is linear and the DOF reduces to $1 - 1 = 0$.

Example for Choice *C*: What is *x*? The degree of freedom here is 1.

(1) *x* is negative: which answers the question as any number that is negative. The statement fails to reduce the degree of freedom by 1 because *x* has two possible values from the statement.

(2) $|x| = 1$:   which answers the question as $x = 1$ or -1. The statement fails to reduce the degree of freedom by 1 because *x* has two possible values from the statement.

Common solution is $x = -1$. This reduces the DOF to $1 - 1 = 0$.

Example for Choice *E*: What is *x*? The degree of freedom here is 1.

(1) $x + 2$ is positive: which answers the question as $x > -2$. The statement fails to reduce the degree of freedom by 1 because *x* has two possible values from the statement.

(2) $|x| = 1$ is positive: which answers the question as $x = -1$ or 1. The statement fails to reduce the degree of freedom by 1 because *x* has two possible values from the statement.

Both together still say *x* could be -1 or 1. The statements together fail to reduce the degree of freedom by 1 because *x* has two possible values from the statement.

➤ **Example of an invalid problem where the Question Setup alone is sufficient:**

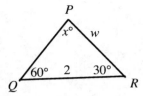

What is the perimeter of ΔPQR?

(1) $x = 90$

(2) $w = 1$

This is an invalid data sufficiency problem since the question (the figure in the question) alone yields the answer and therefore the statements are not required. Such questions are suitable for multiple-choice questions and never for Data Sufficiency.

➤ **Another example of "Question Alone Sufficient" type of invalid problem:**

Is $\sqrt{\dfrac{1}{n^2 + 2}}$ an integer?

(1) n is an integer.

(2) n is a multiple of 3.

$\sqrt{\dfrac{1}{n^2 + 2}}$ is not an integer any value of n, so we don't need any info [Statement (1) or (2)] to determine this. A problem of the type will not be given on the GMAT.

➤ **Example of an invalid problem because of an Unrealistic System:**

Is Set $A = \{2, 3\}$?

(1) A is the set of all odd prime numbers greater than 1.

(2) A is the set of all odd prime numbers less than 5.

Statement (1) says A is the set of *all* odd prime numbers greater than 1, while Statement (2) says A is the set of all the odd prime numbers less than 5. If (1) has to be believed, A equals $\{3, 5, \ldots\}$; and if (2) has to be believed, A equals $\{3\}$. We have a contradiction and therefore the system is invalid. This is not a valid data sufficiency problem. Such problems are not asked on THE GMAT.

Generally, a multiple-choice problem fixes a system to degree zero, but the question in a data sufficiency problem never fixes the degree of freedom to degree zero. The format keeps the system hanging with a degree of freedom of at least one. Hence, the properties of the system aren't fixed with the question alone.

➢ **Safe Assumptions About All Data Sufficiency Problems**

We have discussed that all Data Sufficiency problems are based on a particular realistic system, so the question setup and the statements support a central system. They do not contradict each other. The system determined by the Question Setup plus Statement (1) is in congruence with Statement (2).

Example: What is the value of n given the equation $23 - 9 + n = 2 + s$?

　　　　(1)　$s = 14$

　　　　(2)　$n/s = 1/7$

If Statement (1) is used [$23 - 9 + n = 2 + s$, or $23 - 9 + n = 2 + 14$, or $n = 2$, so $n/s = 2/14 = 1/7$], n/s would equal 1/7. So, the statements are in congruence with each other and the question setup. This type of problem is valid for the GMAT.

➢ **Data Sufficiency Answers can be tabulated as**

Here ✓ means sufficient, and ✗ means not sufficient.

Statement 1	Statement 2	Answer
✓	✗	A
✗	✓	B
✓	✓	D
✗	✗	Statement (1) and Statement (2) together

Statement (1) and Statement (2) together	Answer
✓	C
✗	E

➤ **Flow Chart for Solving Data Sufficiency Problems**

Strategy This flow chart indicates the order of steps to take to solve a Data Sufficiency problem.

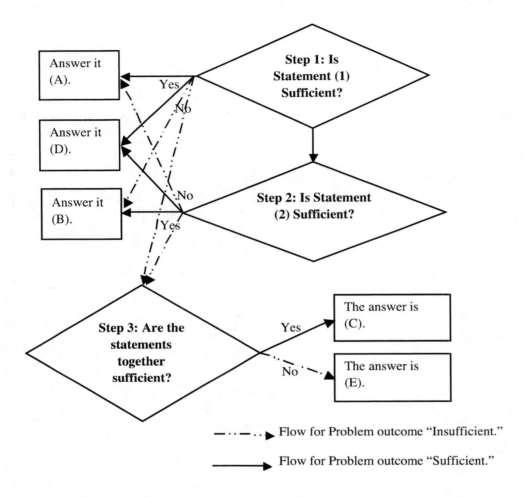

As shown in the flow chart, there are three steps involved in answering a Data Sufficiency problem. But, neither of the first two steps have precedence over the other. So, Step 1 and Step 2 can be interchanged in the sequence of analyzing. That is, either of the following sequences can be followed:

Step 1 → Step 2 → Step 3   or   Step 2 → Step 1 → Step 3

The first two steps are mandatory for any Data Sufficiency problem, and Step 3 is followed only when these mandatory steps fail to determine data sufficiency. In other words, when neither of the first two steps (1) and (2) is sufficient, Step 3 is followed.

Data Sufficiency Order: We will call the order "*question alone sufficient–* D—A, B – C – E" or the equivalent "*question alone sufficient–* D—B, A – C – E" as the data sufficiency order. In the order, —A, B— means that A and B have equal precedence. So, the order means the same as *question alone sufficient–* D—B, A – C – E.

➢ **Let's study the choices in the Data Sufficiency order:** *question alone* **sufficient — D — A, B — C — E:**

The correct answer is

A Problem solving question. (For example, a multiple-choice problem.)

If $x + y + z = 6$, $y = 1$, and $z = 2$, then what is x?

(A) 1

(B) 2

(C) 3

Substituting $y = 1$ and $z = 2$ in $x + y + z = 6$ yields $x + 1 + 2 = 6$, or $x = 6 - 1 - 2 = 3$. No extra detail required to evaluate x unlike in Data Sufficiency where statements are needed.

A

If $x + y + z = 6$ and $y = 1$, then what is x?

(1) $z = 2$

(2) x is even.

Substituting $y = 1$ in $x + y + z = 6$ yields $x + 1 + z = 6$, or $x + z = 6 - 1 = 5$.

Step 1: Statement (1) alone: Substituting $z = 2$ in $x + z = 5$ yields $x + 2 = 5$, or $x = 5 - 2 = 3$. The plausible set for x is {3}, which has a single element. The statement is sufficient.

Step 2: Statement (2) alone: x is even. There are many even numbers. So, the plausible set of x is {… –4, –2, 0, 2, 4, …}. Since there is more than one element, the data is insufficient.

The answer is (A).

B

If $x + y + z = 6$ and $y = 1$, then what is x?

(1) x is even.

(2) $z = 2$

Here, the statements are just swapped. By the same explanation as above, Statement (2) is sufficient, while Statement (1) is not. So, the answer is (B).

D   If $x + y + z = 6$ and $y = 1$, then what is x?

(1) $x - z = 1$

(2) $z = 2$

Substituting $y = 1$ in $x + y + z = 6$ yields $x + 1 + z = 6$, or $x + z = 6 - 1 = 5$.

Step 1: Statement (1) alone: Adding $x - z = 1$ from the statement to $x + z = 5$ yields $x - z + x + z = 1 + 5$, or $2x = 6$, or $x = 6/2 = 3$. The statement is sufficient.

Step 2: Statement (2) alone: Substituting $z = 2$ in $x + z = 5$ yields $x + 2 = 5$, or $x = 5 - 2 = 3$. The plausible set of x is {3}, which has a single element. The statement is sufficient.

The answer is (D).

C   If $x + y + z = 6$, then what is x?

(1) $y = 1$

(2) $z = 2$

Step 1: $x + y + z = 6$ can be simplified to $x = 6 - y - z$. Substituting $y = 1$ yields $x = 6 - y - z = 6 - 1 - z = 5 - z$. Now, if z is 1, then $x = 5 - z = 5 - 1 = 4$. If z is 2, $x = 5 - y = 5 - 2 = 3$. Thus, the plausible set of z is {…, 1, 2, …} for which the corresponding plausible set of x is {…, 4, 3, …}. There is more than one element in the plausible set of x and therefore the statement alone is *not* sufficient.

Step 2: Just like Statement (1), this statement is also insufficient. Let's see why. Subtracting y and z from the equation $x + y + z = 6$ yields $x = 6 - y - z$. Since y and z are not known, x cannot be known. The statement is not sufficient.

Step 3: The statements together: Substituting $y = 1$ and $z = 2$ in $x + y + z = 6$ yields $x + 1 + 2 = 6$, or $x = 6 - 1 - 2 = 3$, which is a unique value for x. So, the statements together are sufficient.

Let's analyze in other manner. Given $y = 1$, $x + y + z = 6$ becomes $x + 1 + z = 6$, or $x + z = 6 - 1 = 5$. Subtracting z, we get $x = 6 - z$. Therefore, x has a one-to-one relation with z, meaning that one value of z yields exactly one value of x. We know x is one-to-one with z from Statement (1), and we know z has only one value (= 2) from Statement (2). Because of the one-to-one relation of x with z, x will have a single value. In other words, the plausible set for x has a single element. Together the statements are sufficient, and the answer is (C).

E   What is x?

(1) $x + y + z = 6$

(2) $y = 1$

Step 1: Statement (1) not sufficient.

Step 2: Statement (2) not sufficient.

Step 3: The statements together: on substituting $y = 1$ in $x + y + z = 6$, we get $x + 1 + z = 6$, or $x + z = 6 - 1 = 5$. Since z is not known, x is not known. The plausibility set of z is $\{\ldots, 1, 2, \ldots\}$, and the plausibility set of x is $\{\ldots, 3, 4, \ldots\}$. There is more than one element in the plausibility set of the question and the statement is not sufficient.

In the above examples, the equations $x + y + z = 6$, $y = 1$, and $z = 2$ are all constraints. From the top of the table through the bottom, the constraints are stripped one by one and as a consequence the answer descends the order *question alone sufficient*– D—A, B —C—E, which is the same as *question alone sufficient*– D—B, A—C—E. That's what happens as the question setup is *de-constrained* also called *relaxed*. We will quite often reference this point.

Strategy

Two-column Convention: One column doesn't know the other, just as one statement doesn't know the other. So, analyze each statement in independent columns.

The convention looks like:

Analyze the question setup alone here in the common area above the columns. The derivations here are common to the statements and can be used in either statement (either column).

Statement (1) here	Statement (2) here
Region to analyze Statement (1) plus the question and the derivations. *YOUR WORK FOR STATEMENT (1) Alone HERE!*	Region to analyze Statement (2) plus the question and the derivations. *YOUR WORK FOR STATEMENT (2) Alone HERE!*
Note: Do not know Statement (2) or its derivation here.	Note: Do not know Statement (1) or its derivation here.

Here is the place to work with the statements together.

This structure indicates that statements are tested separately; and when neither alone is found sufficient, they are then tested together.

An example is shown below.

➢ **Example:**   If x is positive, what is x?

     (1) x is even.

     (2) x is prime.

Analysis of the question setup that will be used in both statements: Here, we note that x is positive.

Statement (1): x is even.	Statement (2): x is prime.
Statement (1) and question setup known here, not Statement (2).	Statement (2) and question setup known here, not Statement (1).
Here, we do not know x is prime. For example, *we do not know x is not 4, but here we know x is not 3.*	Here, we do not know x is even. For example, *we do not know that x is not 3, but we know x is not 4.*
Here, we know the question setup, so we know x is positive.	Here, we know the question setup, so we know x is positive.

Here, we analyze the statements together: From the statements together we have that x is even, prime, and positive, and there is only such number: 2. Hence, the statements together are sufficient.

While practicing the problems, always use the 2-column convention. The explanations for many problems in the book are provided through the convention.

Strategy

No precedence is given to statements (1) or (2), each has equal priority.

In the Data Sufficiency Problems, no priority is given to Statement (1) or to Statement (2).

Suppose the answer to the problem below is (A).

What is x?

(1) $x - 1 = 0$

(2) $x > 0$

Then the answer to the problem below with just the statements swapped is (B).

What is x?

(1) $x > 0$

(2) $x - 1 = 0$

Watch out!

Statements must be initially treated separately. [Statement (1) alone and Statement (2) alone first; If needed, Statements (1) and (2) together next.]. Separate column treatment means

Do not apply the details or derivations from one statement to the other.

During Step (1) and Step (2), treat each column separately.

In Step (3), treat the columns together.

This is the 2-column strategy.

You may want to cover up one statement (column) with your had while analyzing the other.

Strategy

<u>**Summary: Standard strategy for answering a Data Sufficiency problems.**</u>

➢   Collect all the possible answers that Statement (1) allows for the question.

➢   If it allows only a single value, then data is sufficient. If it allows more than one value, then data is insufficient.

➢   There is never a case in a valid Data Sufficiency question when no answer is allowed.

➢   Do the same with Statement (2).

➢   If neither statement is individually sufficient, then check the statements together.

Types of Questions

A Data Sufficiency question can be asked in three basic formats:

1)   Yes/No Questions

2)   Question Word Questions

3)   Choice Questions

1. Yes/No Questions

Here, the answer to the question is "Yes" or "No." The only other possible answer is "Might be or may not be."

Either "Yes" or "No" means the data is sufficient.

"Might be or may not be" means the data is insufficient. So, if the plausibility set is either {Yes} alone or {No} alone, then data is sufficient. If it is {Yes, No}, then data is insufficient.

Examples:

auxiliary verb	Subject	main verb		Answer Yes or No
Do	you	want	pizza?	No, I don't.
Can	you	swim?		Yes, I can.
Has	she	completed	post-graduation?	Yes, she has.
Did	they	leave to	the picnic ?	No, they didn't.
Exception! the verb "be" simple present and simple past				
	Is	Frieda	Indian?	Yes, she is.
	Was	Abraham	home?	No, he wasn't.

Here, the expected answers are only two: Yes or No.

2. Question Word Questions

Question word	auxiliary verb	subject	main verb		Answer Information
Where	do	you	live?		In Mexico.
When	will	you	have	dinner?	At 8pm.
Who	did	she	meet?		She met Katrina.
Why	hasn't	Paulo	done	it?	Because she can't.
Exception! verb be simple present and simple past					
Where		is	Mumbai?		In India.
How		was	she?		Fine

Here, the answer to the question is "information." The information expected is never an expression such as $m + n$ or $2m + 1$. It is always a numeric value. So, if the plausibility set has a single element, data is sufficient. If there is more than one element in the plausibility set, data is insufficient.

3. Choice Questions

auxiliary verb	subject	main verb		OR		Answer In the question
Do	you	**want**	tea	or	coffee?	Coffee, please.
Will	we	**meet**	Rodrigo	or	Romario?	Rodrigo.
Did	she	**go**	to Mexico	or	Alaska?	She went to Alaska.
Exception! verb **be** simple present and simple past						
	Is	your car	white	or	black?	It's White.
	Were	there	$15	or	$50?	$15.

For Choice Questions, the answer to the question is "in the question." So, if the plausibility set is exactly one of the choices, data is sufficient. If it is more than one choice, data is insufficient.

Logic of Data Sufficiency Problems

The general principles for solving the data sufficiency problems are fundamentally rooted in transformation of the problem. Usually, the transformation is aimed at reducing the problem to a simpler and more understandable form. There are rules on how to do the transformations. To understand the process better, let's analyze a few examples. A Yes/No type of problem is taken. The possible outcomes of any data sufficiency problem are two in number: *Data Sufficient* or *Data Insufficient*. Equivalents in the form of an investigative agency problem (a verbal problem) have been given for comparison by analogy (The replies are equivalents of statements in the data sufficiency problem).

➢ **Example:**

Is $x = 3$?	Investigative Agency Query: Is he Aaron?
(1) $x - 3 = 0$	Approver reply: (1) By identity, he is definitely Aaron.

The outcome of the question "Is $x = 3$?" is "Yes" (He is Aaron) and the outcome of the problem is "data sufficient." The problem can be transformed into other variables. Assume $t = x - 3$ and transform it into t as

Transformation:

Query Setup: Is $t = 0$?	I know from inside that Aaron's American name is Holbrooke, so in America I enquire "Is he Holbrooke?" The state of the problem and the query can always be transformed to our convenience.
Statement (1) $t = 0$	Reply (1): "He is Holbrooke."
	Equivalent investigation is
	Question Setup: Is he Holbrooke?
	Reply (1): By identity, he is Holbrooke.
	We got the info required. Now, it would be unnecessary to worry whether it's an American investigation, a Russian investigation, or a Canadian. So, the state doesn't matter as long as we have the answer.

If you transformed the problem in the example as

Is $x \neq 3$?   Query: Isn't he Aaron?

(1) $x - 3 = 0$ Reply (1): By identity, he is definitely Aaron.

If you transformed the question setup as

Is $x = 2$?   Query: Is he Ronald?

(1) $x - 3 = 0$ Reply (1): By identity, he is definitely Aaron.

The outcome of the problem hasn't changed. The outcome is still data sufficient. But, the transformation from "Is $x \neq 3$?" to "Is $x = 2$?" isn't safe because not for each case "$x \neq 3$" does x equal 2. So, a statement like $x \neq 3$ would render "not sufficient" after the transformation while with setup "Is $x \neq 3$", it is sufficient. When you want to know "Is he Ronald?", you wouldn't ask "Is he Aaron?" If you get an assertive reply (in this context, replies are given by statements) that "He is Stewart," you are done with the inquiry. But if you get a non-assertive reply (might be or may not be) like "He isn't Ronald," your investigation isn't done. You are yet to determine whether he is Aaron. That's how the transformation of the question is unsafe.

Compare the following transformation of the above problem:

Is $x = 3$?   Query: Is he Aaron?

(1) $|x| = 3$ Reply: He certainly looks like Aaron, but he could be him or his twin brother.

                  Your investigation isn't complete with this reply.

The absolute value of x is 3 when x is 3 or -3. So, x could be 3 or -3. Since we not sure whether x equals 3 or not, data is insufficient. Earlier, we had data sufficient and now, we have data insufficient. This indicates, the transformation from the earlier problem to the current problem is unsafe.

So, how do we determine whether a transformation is safe? There are guiding rules and we discuss them now.

➢ TRANSFORMATIONS AND THE RULES

There are the two basic rules for safe transformations. Transformations that are not binding are not safe. The two rules are:

Equivalence (It sure is),

and

Complementary (It sure isn't).

The rules apply between the plausible sets of the original and the transformed question setups.

We will discuss:

Rule (1): Equivalence rule is safe everywhere.

or

Rule (2): Complementary rule is safe with the question but not safe with the statements.

Let's start with exercises for practicing the drawing of the plausibility sets and gradually move to the rules:

➢ **Example 1:** I am a civilian if my rank is 3. I am army if my rank is 4. I am a senior citizen if my rank is 5. Which one of them am I?"

The plausibility set of the question setup is $\dfrac{\frac{Army}{Senior\ Citzen}}{Civilian}$ and the corresponding plausibility set of the rank is $\dfrac{\frac{4}{5}}{3}$. So, I am $\dfrac{\frac{Army}{Senior\ Citzen}}{Civilian}$ if my rank is $\dfrac{\frac{4}{5}}{3}$.

➢ **Example 2:** People in a country are designated by the ranking system: Retired civilians hold the rank 3. Army people have either rank 4 or rank 5. Peasants and retailers have rank 6. Who is Mike and what is the rank of John and Rice?

(1)   The rank of Mike is 6.

(2)   John is an army man.

(3)   Rice is a retired civilian.

The plausibility set for the designation is $\dfrac{\frac{Retired\ Civilians}{Army}}{Peasants,\ Retailers}$ and the corresponding set for the rank is $\dfrac{\frac{3}{4,5}}{6}$.

We can also map the cases as

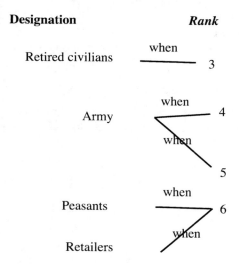

Statement (1) that the rank of Mike is 6 shortlists the plausibility set of the *rank* of Mike to $\dfrac{-}{\dfrac{-,-}{6}}$ and the

plausibility set of *designation* of Mike to $\dfrac{-}{\dfrac{-,-}{\textit{Peasants, Retailers}}}$. Since we have more than one element here

(Peasants, Retailers), Statement (1) is not sufficient to determine exactly who I am. We can test the same from maps as well by deleting all the ranks for Mike, except 6, as shown.

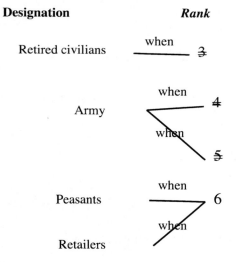

Also, delete all designations linked to deleted ranks. So, Mike could be a peasant or a retailer. We do not know. So, Statement (1) is not sufficient.

Similarly, the plausibility set of the rank of John from Statement (2) is $\dfrac{-}{Army}$ and the corresponding set

for the rank is $\dfrac{-}{4,5}$. Since we have more than one answer (4 and 5 are answers), the statement is not
$\qquad\quad\;\;\overline{}$

sufficient. Shortlist the map yourself, as we did earlier.

Rice is a retired civilian. Hence, the plausibility set reduces to $\dfrac{Retired\;Civilians}{-}$ and the corresponding

rank's plausibility set becomes $\dfrac{3}{-,-}$. Since we have single element, data is sufficient. Shortlist the map
$\qquad\qquad\qquad\qquad\qquad\qquad\quad\;\;\overline{}$

yourself as we did earlier.

➤ **Example 3:** Similarly, if we consider the plausibility set for the question setup as $\dfrac{Data\;Sufficient}{Data\;Insufficient}$,

the plausibility set for the problem is $\dfrac{A,B,C,D}{E}$ (order followed as always).

➤ **Example 4:** The plausible set of a Yes/No type of question such as "Is $x = 3$?" is {"Yes," "No"}. So,
the plausibility set of the question setup is correspondingly $\dfrac{Yes}{No}$ for the plausibility set of x being

$\dfrac{3}{All\;Numbers\;-\;\{3\}}$. Graphically, the conversion can be mapped/explained with the relation.

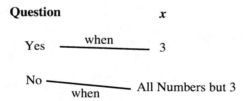

Now, let's test whether information like "x is 3" is sufficient. This eliminates all numbers but 3 from the
domain of x. From the mapping, the string "Yes"—"3" is eliminated. Hence, effectively, it eliminates "No"
from the domain of the question setup. We have only one answer and that is "Yes." So, data is sufficient.

If instead, we are given $x \neq 2$, then the answer in the domain of x is $\dfrac{3}{All\;Numbers\;-\;\{3\}-\{2\}}$, which

correspondingly maps to the question as $\dfrac{Yes}{No}$. Since there is more than one element in the plausibility set
for the question setup, we have "Data Not Sufficient."

EQUIVALNCE RULE

➤ Let's check whether the transformation of a question setup from "Is $x = 3$?" to "Is $|x| = 3$?" is safe.

The plausible set of the question "Is $x = 3$?" is $\dfrac{Yes}{No}$, and the corresponding plausible set for x is

$\dfrac{3}{All\ Numbers\ -\ \{3\}}$. The graphical representation is

Question x

Yes ———— when ———— 3

No ————————— All numbers but 3
             when

Now, suppose we transform the question as "Is $|x| = 3$?". Then $|x|$ equals 3 when x equals -3 or 3. So, the

plausibility set of the transformed question is $\dfrac{Yes}{No}$ when the plausible set of x is

$\dfrac{\{-3,3\}}{All\ Numbers - \{3\} - \{-3\}}$. Converting this to the plausible set of the question "Is $x = 3$?" yields $\dfrac{No, Yes}{No}$

("No" for -3 and all other numbers, and "Yes" for 3). This is not same as $\dfrac{No, Yes}{No}$ or one-to-one with the

original set $\dfrac{Yes}{No}$. So, the transformation isn't safe. This is to say, if you do the transformation, though not

always, you might be stumped for example in the following case:

➤ **Example 1: Original**

Is $x = 3$?

(1) $|x| = 3$

(2) x is positive.

Here, Statement (1) alone is not sufficient, and Statement (2) alone is not sufficient. The statements together are sufficient, and the answer is (C).

➤ **Example 2: Transformed**

Is $|x| = 3$?

(1) $|x| = 3$

(2) x is positive.

Here, Statement (1) alone is sufficient, Statement (2) alone is not sufficient, and the answer is (A). But the answer to the original problem is (C). That's why we call the transformation unsafe.

Thus, unsafe transformations can lead you to choose the wrong answer choice. For the transformation to be safe, the plausibility set of the original and the transformed questions must be in a one-to-one relation. This

means that the transformation of the plausibility is safe if it changes $\dfrac{Yes}{No}$ to $\dfrac{Yes}{No}$ (equivalence transformation) or from $\dfrac{Yes}{No}$ to $\dfrac{No}{Yes}$ (complementary transformation). But the transformations $\dfrac{Yes}{No}$ to

$\dfrac{Yes, No}{No}$, $\dfrac{No}{Yes}$ to $\dfrac{Yes, No}{No}$, $\dfrac{Yes}{No}$ to $\dfrac{No}{Yes, No}$ and $\dfrac{No}{Yes}$ to $\dfrac{No}{Yes, No}$ and vice versa are not safe because of

one-to-one failure (one element in the plausibility set does not point to one element in the other plausibility set).

The transformations that violate one-to-one are not safe.

➤   Just like the question setups, the statements can also be transformed. Here we have an example:

Example (3) shows this type of transformation

Is $x \neq 3$?

(1) $|x| = 3$

(2) x is positive.

Earlier we answered the problem with "Data Sufficient" by (C); and even now, we answer the problem with "Data sufficient" by (C). That's why we call the transformation safe.

COMPLEMENTARY RULE

➤   For the transformation "Is $x = 3$?" to "Is $x \neq 3$?" and vice versa, use the complementary rule. The

plausibility set for the question "Is $x = 3$?" is $\dfrac{Yes}{No}$, with the plausibility set for x being $\dfrac{All\ Numbers - \{3\}}{\{3\}}$.

For the plausibility set for x, the plausibility set for the question "Is $x = 3$?" would be $\dfrac{No}{Yes}$. So, after

transformation, Yes has transformed to only No and No has transformed into only Yes. So, one-to-one

between the question setup is satisfied. You can work out visually that the transformation $\dfrac{Yes}{No}$ to $\dfrac{No}{Yes}$ is

one-to-one. The transformation is called a Complementary transformation and is safe only for question setups, not for statements.

More examples:

➤   **Example 1:** The transformation of the question setup from "Is the non-zero integer x odd?" to "Is the non-zero integer x even?" is safe. Let's check it.

For the plausibility set of the question setup "Is x odd?", the plausibility set mapping is $\dfrac{Yes}{No} = \dfrac{Odd}{Even}$; and

for the transformed question "Is x even?", the plausibility set mapping is $\dfrac{Even}{Odd} = \dfrac{Yes}{No}$. Inverting the

mapping for the transformed question setup yields $\dfrac{Odd}{Even} = \dfrac{No}{Yes}$. Comparing this to the original mapping

$\dfrac{Yes}{No} = \dfrac{Odd}{Even}$ yields $\dfrac{Yes}{No}$ maps to $\dfrac{No}{Yes}$. Still we have one-to-one though the mapping is inverted. So, the

transformation is safe and the transformation is a complementary transformation.

➤ **Example 2:** If 0 is considered to be neither odd nor even, then is x odd?

(1) x is not even.

The plausible set for question setup is $\dfrac{Yes}{No}$ which for x is $\dfrac{Odd}{0, Even}$. Since Statement (1) says x is not even, we eliminate it. So, $\dfrac{Yes}{No} = \dfrac{Odd}{0, -}$. So, there is chance for both Yes (when x odd) and No (when x is 0). Therefore, Statement (1) is not sufficient.

➤ **Example 3:** If 0 is considered to be neither odd nor even, then is x even?

(1) x is not even.

Here, data is sufficient $\dfrac{Even}{-, -}$. The statement is sufficient.

➤ **Example 4:** Is x not an even integer?

$$\frac{Yes}{No} = \frac{\text{All Real Numbers} - \{\dots - 4, -2, 2, 4, \dots\}}{\{\dots - 3, -1, 1, 3, \dots\}}$$

➤ **Example 5:** What is x?

(1) x is not 3.

(2) x is 4.

The plausibility set of the question is the plausibility set of x, which is *All Real Numbers*. With Statement (1), the plausibility set is *All Real Numbers* – {3}, which contains not just a single number but every real number other than 3. Hence, the statement is not sufficient.

With Statement (2), the plausibility set reduces to {4}, which contains exactly one number. Hence, the statement is data sufficient.

➤ **Example 6:** Could x equal 2 or 3?

Question Setup = $\dfrac{Yes}{No}$ for $x = \dfrac{2, 3}{\text{All Numbers} - \{2, 3\}}$. The question can be transformed into an equivalent form as "Is $\left| x - \dfrac{1}{2} \right| = \dfrac{5}{2}$ or in complementary form as "Is x not equal to 2 or is x not equal to 3?"

More transformation examples:

➤ **Example 7:** "Is $2k$ an integer?" <u>can</u> be transformed to "Is $2k$ not an integer?" (By the Complementary Rule). The plausibility set for the original question is $\dfrac{Yes}{No}$ for which k is

$$\frac{\{\dots - 1.5, -1, -0.5, 0, 0.5, 1, 1.5, \dots\}}{\text{All Numbers} - \{\dots - 1.5, -1, -0.5, 0, 0.5, 1, 1.5, \dots\}}$$

➤ **Example 8:** "Is $2k$ an integer?" <u>cannot</u> be transformed to "Is k an integer?"

The plausibility set mapping for the original question is

$$\frac{Yes}{No} \text{ for } k = \frac{\{... -1.5, -1, -0.5, 0, 0.5, 1, 1.5, ...\}}{\text{All Numbers} - \{... -1.5, -1, -0.5, 0, 0.5, 1, 1.5, ...\}}$$

while the plausibility mapping for "Is k an integer?" is

$$\frac{Yes}{No} \text{ for } k = \frac{\{... -3, -2, -1, 0, 1, 2, 3, ...\}}{\text{All Numbers} - \{... -3, -2, -1, 0, 1, 2, 3, ...\}}$$

because the two mappings are not equal. In verbal terms, for $2k$ to be an integer, k need not be an integer. So, the transformation from "Is $2k$ an integer?" to "Is k an integer?" is not safe.

➤ **Example 9:** "Is k equal to half of some integer?" cannot be transformed to "Is k an integer?" The two mappings are not equal. In verbal terms, not always "k equal to half some integer" does k become an integer.

➤ **Example 10:** "Is $2k$ not an integer?" (By Complementary rule) for which $\frac{Yes}{No}$ follows for k as

$$\frac{\text{All Numbers} - \{... -1.5, -1, -0.5, 0, 0.5, 1, 1.5, ...\}}{\{... -1.5, -1, -0.5, 0, 0.5, 1, 1.5, ...\}}$$

This <u>can</u> be changed to "Is k half of some integer?" (By the Equivalence Rule). In verbal terms, whenever $2k$ is an integer, k is half the integer. So, the question transformation "Is k half of some integer?" The complementary statement is "Is k not half of some integer?" Thus, the transformation is OK. You can check the mapping of the original question setup and the transformed question setup to arrive at your conclusions.

➤ Here we do mappings for issue's we discussed above. "Is $2k$ an integer?" <u>cannot</u> be transformed to "Is k an integer?" Because not for every value of k for which $2k$ is an integer need k be an integer. In other words drawing the mapping for the original question yields $\frac{Yes}{No}$ for

$$k = \frac{\text{All Real Numbers} - \{... -1.5, -1, -0.5, 0, 0.5, 1, 1.5, ...\}}{\{... -1.5, -1, -0.5, 0, 0.5, 1, 1.5, ...\}}$$

and for the transformed question "Is k an integer?" it is

$$\frac{\text{All Real Numbers} - \{... -3, -2, -1, 0, 1, 2, 3, ...\}}{\{... -1.5, -1, -0.5, 0, 0.5, 1, 1.5, ...\}}$$

which are not equal or complementary. So, the transformation is unsafe. For the same reason, the transformation from "Is k an integer?" to "Is $2k$ an integer?" isn't safe either.

In other words, not every time $2k$ is an integer, k need be an integer. This is an equivalence failure.

➤ **Example 11:** What is $\dfrac{1}{\dfrac{b}{a}+1+\dfrac{b}{c}}$?

You can transform this to "What is $\dfrac{b}{a}+\dfrac{b}{c}$?" because given $\dfrac{b}{a}+\dfrac{b}{c}$, we know $\dfrac{1}{\dfrac{b}{a}+1+\dfrac{b}{c}}$. In other words,

each single value of $\dfrac{b}{a}+\dfrac{b}{c}$ yields just one single value for $\dfrac{1}{\dfrac{b}{a}+1+\dfrac{b}{c}}$. So, a one-to-one relation exists

between the two. Thus, the transformation is safe.

Watch out! The expression $\dfrac{1}{\dfrac{b}{a}+1+\dfrac{b}{c}}$ cannot be transformed to "What are the values of $\dfrac{b}{a}$ and $\dfrac{b}{c}$?" This is

because if we are given $\dfrac{b}{a}$ and $\dfrac{b}{c}$, then we can always calculate $\dfrac{b}{a}+\dfrac{b}{c}$, but the reverse is not true. Given

$\dfrac{b}{a}+\dfrac{b}{c}$ we cannot get both $\dfrac{b}{a}$ and $\dfrac{b}{c}$. This is called de-constraining, and we have discussed that the answer

moves down the *Data Sufficiency order* as we do the de-constraining. So, if Statement (1) was $\dfrac{b}{a}+\dfrac{b}{c}=3$,

the question "What is $\dfrac{b}{a}$ and $\dfrac{b}{c}$?" has data *not* sufficient, while the original question "What is $\dfrac{b}{a}+\dfrac{b}{c}$?" has

data sufficient. In other words, this can be explained as $\dfrac{b}{a}$ or $\dfrac{b}{c}$ are not have one-to-one with $\dfrac{b}{a}+\dfrac{b}{c}$.

Note! **Transformations must be done with likes. For example, the question "What is x?" cannot be transformed to "Is $x = 3$?" by knowing that x is rather a set of numbers and not a single number or that x is a letter.**

Part Two

Strategies for
Data Sufficiency Problems

Introduction

Having studied the data sufficiency format in depth, we will now study specific tips and strategies for these questions.

The strategies specific to Math topics are discussed in their respective chapters, which occasionally discuss format specific tips as well.

Data sufficiency problems typically require much less computing than multiple-choice problems.

The advantage of the data sufficiency format is that we do not need to actually solve the problem; we just need to determine whether there is exactly one answer.

The same problem, when presented as a multiple-choice problem, would probably need to be computed. Here is an example that is easier in the Data Sufficiency format than in the Multiple-Choice format.

Example: Consider the following two formats of the same problem.

Multiple-Choice Version: In Triangle *ABC*, if *AC* = 5 and *BC* = 4, then what is the length of *AB*?

Data Sufficiency Version: In Triangle *ABC*, what is the length of *AB*?

   (1) *BC* = 4

   (2) *AC* = 5

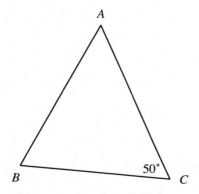

In the multiple-choice version, we are given two sides *BC* = 4 and *AC* = 5 and one angle $\angle ACB = 50°$, and we are asked to evaluate *AB*. Given the details, we can use the Law of Cosines to evaluate *AB*. [By the Law of Cosines, $AB^2 = AC^2 + BC^2 - 2AC \times BC \times \cos(\angle ACB)$.] However, The Law of Cosines is too complex for the GMAT (there is no Trigonometry on the test). So, the multiple-choice version of the problem is too complex for the GMAT.

But to solve the data sufficiency version, we just need to know that given an angle and two sides of a triangle, we can construct a unique triangle and determine any property of the triangle. Hence, *AB* can be calculated and the question answered, and we do not need to actually do the calculating. So, the data is sufficient.

Thus, in the data sufficiency version, we can skip the Law of Cosines. (In fact, we can answer the question even without knowing that a formula like the Law of Cosines exists.) In the multiple-choice format, these calculations are a must. Hence, a complex multiple-choice problem can be simple in the data sufficiency format. This is not to say that data sufficiency problems do not require any calculations. Occasionally, calculations must be done to determine whether more than one solution exists.

Note: The GMAT does not expect you to know complex math such as the Law of Cosines. The GMAT expects only knowledge of basic Algebra and Geometry. The intention of the example is merely to illustrate that even complex multiple-choice problems can become easy in the data sufficiency format.

Strategy

SUBSTITUTION (Special Cases)

Substitution is the most common strategy used in most question formats.

Problems in any format are made up of just two things:

Known Properties and Unknown Properties

We already discussed what are Known and Unknown properties.

The standard procedure when substituting is

Substitute for the unknown properties with a substitution instance.

Choose a substitution such that none of the known properties are violated.

If after substituting, the results do not violate any known properties, then the substitution instance is a feasible one.

Otherwise, it is not feasible.

Example: Does the sum $p + q + r + s$ equal 4?

(1) $(p + q)/(r + s) = 1$

(2) $p = q$ and $r = s$

First, form substitution instances.

The minimum requirement is that the substitution instance must agree with the known properties.

Suppose we choose $p = 1$, $q = 1$, $s = 1$, and $r = 1$ as the substitution. Then we must check whether it satisfies both statements (which are the known properties of the problem). By doing the check, we find that yes $(p + q)/(r + s) = (1 + 1)/(1 + 1) = 1$ and $p = q$ $(1 = 1)$ and $r = s$ $(1 = 1)$. So, we confirm this is a valid instance. Now, plugging the substitution instance into the unknown property "Is $p + q + r + s = 4$?" yields "Is $1 + 1 + 1 + 1 = 4$?" or "Is $4 = 4$?", or of course Yes.

Now, let's choose another substitution such that the known properties, which are the statements, are satisfied. Let's choose $p = 2$, $q = 2$, $s = 2$, and $r = 2$. Now, let's evaluate the unknown property "Is $p + q + r + s = 4$?" with this instance. We get "Is $p + q + r + s = 4$?" or "Is $2 + 2 + 2 + 2 = 4$?", or of course No.

Thus, we have two values possible for the unknown property called the question ("Is $p + q + r + s = 4$?"). They are Yes and No. The second substitution yielded a double case. Otherwise, it would have been tedious to check the infinitely many possible substitution instances. So, the statements together are not sufficient. The answer is (E).

- *In most problems, there are multiple substitution instances possible. To check whether each of them yields a single value for the question is tedious. Thus, using the method is tedious to answer "Data Sufficiency." But answering Data Insufficiency is easy: we just need two substitution instances to show a double case, as n the above example, for the question and we are done.*

- While analyzing Statement (1) alone, the data is the Question Setup plus Statement (1). The substitution instance must be in agreement with the data.

- While analyzing Statement (2) alone, the data is the Question Setup plus Statement (2). The substitution instance must be in agreement with the data.

- While analyzing the statements together, the data is the Question Setup plus Statement (1) plus Statement (2). The substitution instance must be in agreement with the data.

Strategy

There are two common redundancies in Data Sufficiency problems:

I. Either statement follows from the other:

Sometimes one statement plus the question setup can imply the other statement. See Example 1 below.

II. Neither statement alone seems sufficient:

Sometimes, just by looking at the problem, we can say neither statement alone is sufficient. So, we eliminate (A), (B), and (D). See Example 2 below.

Example 1: A sequence consists of the consecutive integers from 1 through m. Which number could m be 49 or 50?

    (1)   The average of the integers in the sequence is not an integer.

    (2)   The median of the integers in the sequence is not an integer.

The definition of *median* is "When a set of numbers is arranged in order of size, the *median* is the middle number. If a set contains an even number of elements, then the median is the average of the two middle elements."

For consecutive integers, the average always equals the median, whether there are an even number of consecutive integers or whether there are an odd number of them.

Check the following examples:

The average of 1, 2, 3, 4 is (1 + 2 + 3 + 4)/4 = 2.5, which is also the median.

The average of 1, 2, 3, 4, 5 is (1 + 2 + 3 + 4 + 5)/5 = 3, which is also the median.

The detail "average equals median" along with Statement (1) "<u>average</u> is not an integer" means that "<u>median</u> is not an integer" <u>also</u> which is Statement (2). This means that Statement (1) implies Statement (2).

Similarly, when we say Statement (2) "<u>median</u> is not an integer" we mean Statement (1) "<u>average</u> is not an integer" as well.

So, Statement (1) directly implies Statement (2), and likewise Statement (2) implies Statement (1). In other words, either statement follows from the other.

So, if one statement is sufficient, the other statement must also be sufficient [Here, the answer is (D)]; and if one statement is *not* sufficient, the other statement must also be *not* sufficient [Here, the answer is (E)].

In such cases, the answer is (D) or (E).

The average (= median) is not an integer only when m is odd. For example, the average and the median of 1, 2, 3 is 2, while the average and the median of 1, 2, 3, 4 is 2.5, not an integer. So, m must be odd, not even. Therefore, of the choices 49 and 50, m must be 49 only and not 50. So, we are left with a single answer, 49. The answer is (D), either statement alone is sufficient.

Example 2: What is the area of the figure *MNOPQ* ?

(1) *NOP* is an equilateral triangle.

(2) *MNPQ* is a square.

If Statement (1) is not given, Triangle *NOP* could expand upward and possess any height, and therefore the area could have any value.

If Statement (2) is not given, Rectangle *NPQM* could descend to any length downwards, and therefore the area of the rectangle could have any value.

So, the net area of the two figures cannot be determined without both statements. This eliminates choices (A), (B), and (D).

If we have a solution with the statements together, the answer is (C); if we don't have a solution with the statements together, the answer is (E).

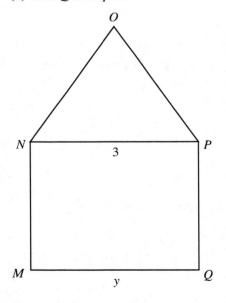

Constructability Check of the System

We studied in the first part that if we can determine a system completely, we can calculate each of its properties.

This is a great strategy. An example of this is the constructability check in geometry where the system is the given geometric figure.

It says, if we are able to draw a complete figure, we can answer any property about it. So, to determine whether we can answer the question, just test whether we can draw the figure. We can always measure a property after creating the complete drawing. See Example 1.

This technique can be applied anywhere, not just in geometry.

Sometimes a generic figure will do, and a fixed figure is not needed. See Example 2.

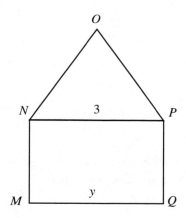

Example 1: What is the area of the figure *MNOPQ*?

(1) *MNPQ* is a square.

(2) *NOP* is an equilateral triangle.

The system (which is the figure here) effectively contains two figures: 1) the triangle, 2) the rectangle.

A triangle can be constructed given all its sides, and a rectangle can be constructed given at least two adjacent sides.

Statement (1) says that the rectangle is indeed a square. Hence, each side of the rectangle equals side *NP*, which measures 3 (from the figure). So, the rectangle can be constructed.

Statement (2) says the triangle is equilateral. Hence, each side of the triangle equals side *NP*, which measures 3 (from the figure). So, the triangle can be fully constructed touching the rectangle at *NP*.

So, we have the net system, figure, which we can use to measure any property such as area. (Note: To measure the area of any arbitrary figure, we can split the figure into small horizontal or vertical strips, then calculate the area by multiplying any two adjacent sides and then and sum all of them. Like this, any property of a system would have a means to measure given the figure or the system is fixed.) Hence, the statements are together sufficient, and the answer is (C).

Example 2: What is the area of the triangle?

(1) $AB = 5$

(2)   The altitude to AB measures 4.

With the statements together, we have the length of base AB and the height (altitude) of the triangle. So, the third vertex C is located at a distance of 4 from the base AB, as shown in the figure. But, that could be any of the multiple points on the line l that are 4 units from AB, as shown in the figure. If you thought since we do not have a fixed figure we cannot answer the question, you are mistaken. The figure shows three instances of the Point C, or in other words, three instances of the triangle ABC. For each instance, the area of the triangle is the same $1/2 \cdot base \cdot height = 1/2 \cdot 5 \cdot 4 = 10$. So, the area is 10, and we have data sufficiency. The answer is (C).

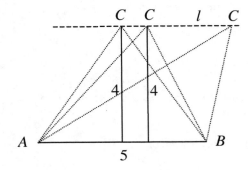

Again, not all unknown properties are fixed. For example, if instead of "What is the area?" we were asked "What is the perimeter?" we would have insufficient data because for each instance in the triangles above, the perimeter changes.

Concentrate precisely on what the question asks!

For example, if you are asked whether A equals B, then do not concentrate on whether (A is greater than B) or on whether (A is less than B).

Just try to establish that A equals B or that A does not equal B.

So if the question is

Is $x = 3$?

(1) x is not 3.

(2) x is greater than 2.

Statement (1) alone is sufficient since it says, "No, x is not 3."

Statement (2) says x may equal 3 or may not equal 3; the data is insufficient.

Hence, the answer is (A).

Strategy

Set Your Attitude towards solving Data Sufficiency right before exam! Here is the summary of the required attitude.

First, start by analyzing the question as though the statements were not given. The goal is to answer the question without using the statements (though this is not actually possible). In the process, you may determine the deficiencies of the question. You have the possibility of finding the statement(s) which could have (compensated for) the deficiencies of the question. In the process, you are expected to find statement(s) that are sufficient. The statement(s) not yet found sufficient individually have to be taken to the next steps.

Second, you need to analyze the statements individually. Do not give up analyzing a particular statement until you are certain that the statement alone would not help answer the question.

Third, if neither statement alone is sufficient, analyze whether the statements together are sufficient. Finally, unless you are certain that the statements together are not sufficient, do not answer (E).

Example: If the function "$\sqrt{}$" is defined to be the positive square root of y, then does $\sqrt{3-2x}$ equal $\sqrt{2x}+1$?

(1) $2x^2 \neq 3x + 1$

(2) $4x^2 = 6x - 1$

First: Thoroughly analyze the information in the question setup:

We must determine whether $\sqrt{3-2x}$ equals $\sqrt{2x}+1$. Squaring both expressions yields $3-2x$ and $2x+1+2\sqrt{2x}$. Subtracting $2x$ and 1 from both of these expressions yields $2-4x$ and $2\sqrt{2x}$. Squaring both yields $4+16x^2-16x$ and $8x$. Subtracting 4 from both yields $16x^2-16x$ and $8x-4$. Adding $16x$ to both yields $16x^2$ and $24x-4$. Dividing both by 4 yields $4x^2$ and $6x-1$. So, $\sqrt{3-2x}$ equals $\sqrt{2x}+1$ only when $4x^2$ equals $6x-1$. This is precisely what Statement (2) says, so the statement is sufficient. Note: Even if the statement were flatly contradicted, it would have been sufficient.

Second: Now, thoroughly analyze the statements individually.

As discussed, $\sqrt{3-2x}$ equals $\sqrt{2x}+1$ if $4x^2$ equals $6x-1$. Dividing the last two expressions by 2 yields $2x^2$ and $3x-1/2$. The inequality in Statement (1) $2x^2 \neq 3x+1$ does not violate or support the condition: $2x^2$ equals $3x-1/2$ (This means $2x^2$ may or may not equal $3x+1$ or $2x^2$ may or may not equal $3x-1/2$). So, Statement (1) does not sufficiently constrain $\sqrt{3-2x}$ either from equaling $\sqrt{2x}+1$ or not equaling it. So, the statement is not sufficient.

Third: If neither statement individually has helped, then thoroughly analyze the statements together. But, here, Statement (2) alone was sufficient, so Step 3 is not required.

The answer is (B).

Be Careful of Making Unwarranted Assumptions.

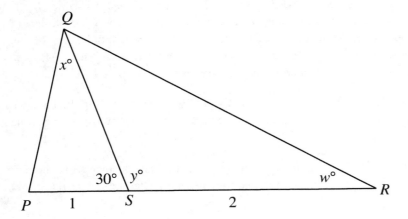

Example: What is the perimeter of $\triangle PQS$?

  (1) $x = 45$

  (2) $w = 15$

Because angle w is outside of $\triangle PQS$, it is tempting to think that angle w is not required to construct $\triangle PQS$, but it is. The second paragraph below shows that w can determine x. Hence, if Statement (1) alone can answer the question, then Statement (2) can as well.

The minimum details needed to construct a triangle are one side and two angles, *or* two sides and one angle, *or* all the three sides. In $\triangle PQS$, we have $\angle PSQ = 30°$ (from the figure) and the side $PS = 1$. So, we are short of knowing one angle or one side to construct $\triangle PQS$. Statement (1) would help with an angle in the triangle. So, Statement (1) is sufficient.

Construct line $PS = 1$. Draw an angle making 30 degrees with PS at S and name the line l. Extend the line PS 2 units further to the right of the point S to locate the point R. Now, draw another line measuring w (= 15) degrees with PR from the point R, and name the line m. So, the point of intersection of l and m is the point Q. Now, measure $\angle PQS$ to find x.

The answer is (D).

Note: The GMAT never claims figures are drawn to scale.

At least it doesn't expect you to take the scale or a protractor to do any measurements on the monitor screen, right!

But sometimes you can use a "Birds eye" view to answer a problem.

Watch out!

Be Conservative When Using Statements!

The key to success with data sufficiency problems is to use the statements very conservatively. Don't conclude *"Data not sufficient"* unless you have proven it to yourself by using the techniques presented in this book. An indicator that you aren't attentive or conservative enough while solving problems is that you are either answering (C) repeatedly or still worse (D) repeatedly. This might mean, you aren't using your math skills sufficiently or you haven't prepared yourself with the data sufficiency skills. If you have been answering (E) too frequently, it might mean you have insufficient math knowledge. The fix for this must be in the preparation stage. All this should not discourage you from answering a particular question with a single answer given you are confident enough. Answering 3 or more of 5 consecutive questions with a single answer-choice should be considered abnormal.

Example:

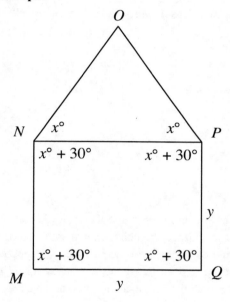

What is the perimeter of the figure *MNOPQ* ?

(1) $x = 60$

(2) $y = 3$

If you thought x and y are the only unknowns in this problem and therefore thought we need both to answer the question, you are not being conservative in using the statements.

Summing the angles of quadrilateral *MNPQ* to 360° yields

$(x + 30) + (x + 30) + (x + 30) + (x + 30) = 360$

$4x + 120 = 360$

$4x = 240$

$x = 240/4 = 60$

Thus, x is already available from the question itself (the figure can be considered as listing the properties and is part of the question itself), and therefore Statement (1) is *not* needed. Hence, Statement (1) is *not* sufficient, though it may be more accurate to say it's not required. Since $x = 60$, each angle of the quadrilateral is $x° + 30° = 60° + 30° = 90°$. Since two angles of the triangle in the figure equal $x°$, which equals $60°$, we can calculate the third angle $180° - 60° - 60° = 60°$.

We have all the angles of the figure now, but we do not have a single length. Hence, we cannot draw a unique figure, though we can draw similar figures. If we draw one figure with a particular length, we can always draw another similar figure with double the length and the same angles. The area changes, but the angles remain the same. So, knowing y could help. Since each angle in the quadrilateral is $90°$, it is a rectangle. Given any two adjacent sides in a rectangle (here MQ and PQ), the rectangle can be constructed. Now, NP equals y, being the opposite side of the rectangle. Once we have one side and two angles in a triangle, the triangle can be constructed. Hence, knowing y can help construct both the rectangle and the triangle. So, Statement (2) is sufficient, and the answer is (B).

➤ **Geometry Note: To construct a unique figure, we need at least one length. Knowing all the angles, but none of the lengths is not sufficient.**

Summary: Be conservative in using the statements.

Sometimes it is better to use intermediate expressions.

Example:

Is $n^2 + 2n$ an integer?

(1) $n^3 + 3n$ is an integer.

(2) $2n$ is an integer.

Whether $n^3 + 3n$ is an integer depends on whether n is an integer; and likewise whether $n^2 + 2n$ is an integer depends on whether n is an integer. Further, $2n$, being an integer, depends on the value of n. So, the answer to the question, and the trueness of the statements, depend on the common term n. In this scenario, n is a bridging term between the statement and the question setup. In such cases, we pick such a term as the intermediate one and analyze the statements. This problem is solved after the following note.

Mappings between the Statements and the Question (to check if we can arrive at a double case).

We know that when the plausibility set has more than one element for the question, we have data insufficiency. We also call it a double case.

Mapping is a standard technique for finding the insufficiency or the double case.

In this technique, we relate each possibility of the statement against the answer we get for the question. If we have more than one answer, we have data insufficiency.

Before proceeding to the example, note the following kinds of relations:

One-to-one between a statement and the question means each possibility of the statement yields only a single value for the question.

Many-to-one between a statement and the question means all possibilities of the statement yield one value for the question.

One-to-many between a statement and the question means each possibility of the statement yields multiple possible answers for the question.

Example: Is $x = 2$?

(1) $x > 1$

Statement (1) allows multiple values for the unknown x. For example, 1, 1.1, 1.233, ..., 2, ..., and so on. All these values yield the answer *No*, except for 2, which yields *Yes*. So, we have *many-to-one* for all x but 2, and we have *one-to-one* for 2.

Example: Is $x = 2$?

(1) x is one of the numbers from the set $\{2, 3\}$.

We have the mapping 2—Yes and 3—No. Hence, if x is 2, the answer to question is Yes; and if x is 3, the answer is No (x is not 2). Here, we have one value for one possibility. This is *one-to-one*.

Example: What is x?

(1) $|x| = 3$

Here, the plausibility set of x is $\{+3, -3\}$. This is *one-to-one* since $x = 3$ yields the answer 3 and $x = -3$ yields the answer -3.

In all this, "many" means more than one and could mean just two.

Example: If $x^2 + 2xy + y^2 = 1$, then what is x?

(1) $|y| = 3$

Here, y could be $+3$ or -3. The quadratic equation we have varies with each value of y. For each quadratic equation, we get two different values for x. So, we have a *one-to-many* relation between the statement and the question.

Now, let's solve the example.

Example: Is $n^2 + 2n$ an integer?

(1) $n^3 + 3n$ is an integer.

(2) $2n$ is an integer.

If n is an integer, then $n^2 + 2n$ is an integer. Otherwise, it is not. This means, the domain of $n^2 + 2n$, being an integer, is $\dfrac{Yes}{No}$ against the domain of n, being an integer, is $\dfrac{Yes}{No}$. Here, we have a one-to-one relation.

Similarly, if $n^3 + 3n$ is an integer, n is an integer; and if it is not, n is not integer. Here, again we have a *one-to-one* relation between the statement and the question.

Now, for $2n$ to be an integer, n need not be an integer (In other words, n may or may not be an integer when $2n$ is an integer. For example, if $2n = 4$, $n = 2$ is an integer; and if $2n = 3$, $n = 1.5$ is not an integer). This means that we have a one-to-many relation between $2n$ being an integer and n being an integer. Just for clarity, $\dfrac{Yes}{No}$ for $2n$ being an integer means $\dfrac{Yes, No}{No}$ for n being an integer. This means that the statement shows a double case with the question.

Now, let's do the mapping between the statement and the question via the intermediate expression.

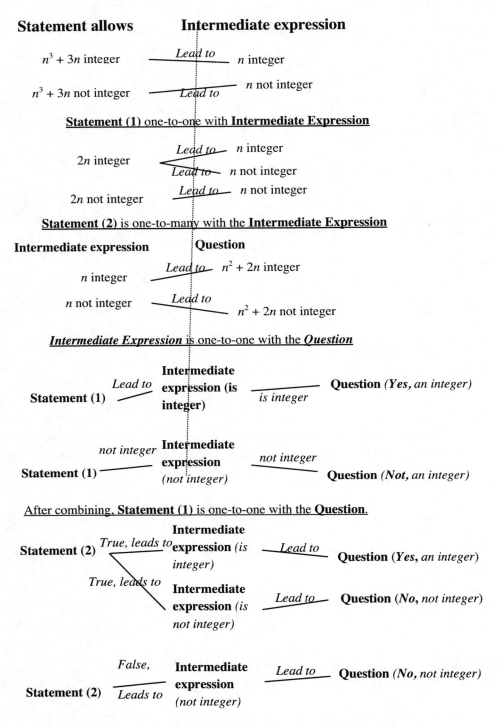

Statement allows   **Intermediate expression**

$n^3 + 3n$ integer ———— *Lead to* ———— n integer

$n^3 + 3n$ not integer ———— *Lead to* ———— n not integer

Statement (1) one-to-one with **Intermediate Expression**

2n integer ———— *Lead to* ———— n integer
            ———— *Lead to* ———— n not integer

2n not integer ———— *Lead to* ———— n not integer

Statement (2) is one-to-many with the **Intermediate Expression**

Intermediate expression   **Question**

n integer ———— *Lead to* ———— $n^2 + 2n$ integer

n not integer ———— *Lead to* ———— $n^2 + 2n$ not integer

Intermediate Expression is one-to-one with the *Question*

Statement (1) — *Lead to* — **Intermediate expression (is integer)** — *is integer* — **Question** (*Yes,* an integer)

Statement (1) — *not integer* — **Intermediate expression (not integer)** — *not integer* — **Question** (*Not,* an integer)

After combining, **Statement (1)** is one-to-one with the **Question**.

Statement (2) — *True, leads to* — **Intermediate expression** (*is integer*) — *Lead to* — **Question** (*Yes,* an integer)

— *True, leads to* — **Intermediate expression** (*is not integer*) — *Lead to* — **Question** (*No,* not integer)

Statement (2) — *False, Leads to* — **Intermediate expression** (*not integer*) — *Lead to* — **Question** (*No,* not integer)

Combining a one-to-many relationship with a one-to-one relationship
yields a new one-to-many relationship.

After listing the mappings above, following the leads of Statement (1) yields the single answer *No*, while following the leads of Statement (2) yields a double answer, *Yes* as well as *No*. So, Statement (1) alone is sufficient, and Statement (2) alone is not sufficient.

Let's find the mapping "n is not an integer" to "$n^3 + 3n$ is an integer." If the answer is *No*, the data is sufficient. Even if the answer is "Yes" alone, we have a double case and the data is *not* sufficient.

Here is the analysis to say that unless n is an integer, $n^3 + 3n$ and $n^2 + 2n$ are not integers:

Note that squaring or cubing a decimal produces a new decimal with more digits after the decimal point. Also, note that multiplying a decimal by an integer produces a new number with either fewer or equal number of digits after the decimal point. Finally, note that two numbers with an unequal number of digits after their respective decimal points would never sum to an integer. Therefore, the sum of n^3 and $3n$, which is $n^3 + 3n$, and the sum of n^2 and $2n$, which is $n^2 + 2n$, are not integers.

Here are examples of the above demonstration:

Suppose $n = 1.5$. Then, n^2 equals 2.25 and $n^3 = 1.5^3 = 3.375$ (Observe that squaring or cubing only resulted in an increase in the number of digits after decimal).

Also, $2n = 3.0$ and $3n = 4.5$. The sum of 2.25 and 3.0 is not an integer, and the sum of 1.728 and 4.5 is not an integer. So, $n^3 + 3n$ and $n^2 + 2n$ are integers only if n is an integer.

A General Case Study vs. Sufficiency:

Statement-to-*Question*

Statement		Question	Is it a double case?
One	To	One	No double case, which means data sufficient.
One	To	Many	Double case, which means data *not* sufficient.
One	To	None	Impractical case.
Many	To	One	No double case, which means data sufficient.

Transformation-to-*Question*

Transformation		Question	Is transformation Safe?
One	To	One	Yes
One	To	Many	No
One	To	None	No
Many	To	One	No

Watch out!

You must always check *One-to-One* between the original plausibility set and the transformed plausibility set. Do it with care. For instance, the following transformations are mistakenly done.

Original Problem   Transformed Problem

Example 1:

                                                               If $x - y + z = 4$, then what are the values of x, y, and z?

If $x - y + z = 4$, then what is $x - y - z$?

(1) $x = 1$

                                                                (1) $x = 1$

(2) $z = 3$

                                                                (2) $z = 3$

Why is this transformation incorrect?

Reason: To calculate $x - y - z$ it is not necessary that we know the value of each of the variables x, y, and z. So, the transformation "what is $x - y - z$?" to "What are the values of x, y, and z?" is incorrect. For example, with the changed transformation, a statement like "$x - y - z = -2$" is not sufficient, while it is sufficient with the original problem. This could be considered like un-constraining the rule "$x - y - z = -2$." In other words, the relation between the original question and the transformed question is One-to-Many (since there can be different combinations of x, y, and z that can lead to single value for $x - y - z$). Un-constraining yields One-to-Many mapping between the original and the transformed problem because of which the answer-choice (for the transformed problem) moves down the flow chart order

$$\frac{\begin{array}{c} Neither Statement \operatorname{Re}quired \\ \hline D \\ \hline A,B \end{array}}{\begin{array}{c} C \\ \hline E \end{array}}$$ relative to the answer-choice for the original problem. Here, the answer

moved from (B) to (C). The reason is that you needed to substitute both statements in the equation given in the question setup to evaluate each of the variables x, y, and z.

Now, let's change the question such that the answer moves up the flow chart (that is, to "neither statement required case"). For that, let's change the original question "If $x - y + z = 4$, then what is $x - y - z$?" to "If $x - y + z = 4$, then what is $x - y + z$ (the value of this is given in this question itself)?" So, we have a Many-to-One relation between the original question and the transformed question. This is called constraining and the effect of this is that the answer-choice (of the transformed problem) moves up the order.

$$\frac{\begin{array}{c} Neither Statement \operatorname{Re}quired \\ \hline D \\ \hline A,B \end{array}}{\begin{array}{c} C \\ \hline E \end{array}}$$. Here, the answer moved from (B) to *Neither Statement Required*.

Regardless, both the changes mentioned are incorrect.

Let's solve the original problem:

Original question: "If $x - y + z = 4$, then what is $x - y - z$?"

Here, $x - y$ can be know by substituting $z = 3$ [from Statement (2)] in the equation $x - y + z = 4$:

$$x - y + 3 = 4$$

$$x - y = 1$$

Now, $x - y - z = 1 - 3 = -2$. Here, we just needed Statement (2), and we answered it as (B).

➤ **Usually, there is more than one way to solve a problem. For example, the previous problem can be solved in the following way.**

Alternate Method: We can also solve the problem by using an intermediate expression t assigned to the expression $x - y - z$. So, $x - y - z = t$, or $x = t + y + z$. Substituting this into the given equation $x - y + z = 4$ yields

$$t + y + z - y + z = 4$$

$$t + 2z = 4$$

$$t = 4 - 2z$$

Now, it is clearer that given z, we can determine t, the required expression. So, Statement (2) alone is sufficient, and the answer is (B).

The more I expect, the less I get!

As we increase the expectation of the question setup, the answer-choice tends to drop in the

data sufficiency order: $\dfrac{\dfrac{Neither Statement\,Re\,quired}{D}}{\dfrac{A, B}{\dfrac{C}{E}}}$ and as we decrease the expectation, the

answer-choice tends to rise in the order.

Example: Which two of the three sentences — I, II, and III — must be true?

(1) I is true and exactly one of II and III is true.

(2) II is true and exactly one of I and III is true.

Statement (1):

We know that I is true. Also, exactly one of II and III is true. Effectively, Statement (1) says that exactly two of the three sentences I, II, and III is true, but it doesn't say exactly which two. So, the question is not fully answered and therefore the statement is not sufficient. The statement says only that I is true.

Statement (2):

This statement is similar to Statement (1), but with I and II exchanged. So, the derivations are similar. Thus, Statement (2) is not sufficient. The statement says only that II is true.

With the two statements together, we have that both I and II are true. We are able to determine the two true sentences, so we are done. We wrap-up saying the statements together are sufficient. The answer is (C). We don't care about III. Actually, we know that III must be false.

If we were asked "How many of I, II, and III are true?", we could not wrap at the point without taking note that III is false. Since exactly one of II and III is true and since II is true, III must be anything other than true (say false). The answer is two, and we wrap here.

Now, let's relax the question setup:

Example: Is it true that exactly two of the three sentences I, II, and III are true?

>   (1)   I is true and exactly one of I and II is true.

>   (2)   II is true and exactly one of II and III is true.

The question is relaxed compared to previous example in the sense that here we only need to find whether or not it is true that exactly two of the three sentences I, II, and III are true. In the earlier question, we were asked this plus "which two." Hence, the question setup has relatively lower expectation. Note that as we increase the expectation of the question setup, we tend to get the answer-choice lower in the order:

$$\overline{\text{Neither Statement Re}\textit{quired}}$$
$$\frac{\frac{\frac{\frac{D}{A, B}}{C}}{E}}{}$$ and as we decrease the expectation, we tend to get a rise in the order.

Statement (1) says I is true plus one of I or III is true. This means that exactly two of the sentences I, II, and III are true. The question is answered and therefore the statement is sufficient.

Statement (2) says II is true plus one of II or III is true. This means that exactly two of the sentences I, II, and III are true. The question is answered and therefore the statement is sufficient.

The answer is (D). The answer to previous question was (B). We moved up the order by decreasing the expectation.

>   ■   If the question is "What is $x + y$?", then do not test whether x and y have single solutions. It's possible that both have multiple solutions yet $x + y$ is fixed. So, focus on the question asked, not on its components.

>   ■   Real time problems (problems with variables changing with time), like the example below, are possible on the GMAT.

Example: If x and y are unequal numbers, then what is the value of $x + y$ at a particular point in time?

>   (1)   At any given time, x equals either 3 or 5.

>   (2)   At any given time, y equals either 3 or 5.

A possible mistake: With the statements together, both x and y have a double case. So, it is easy to mistakenly think that $x + y$ would also have a double case and answer (E).

The mistake is that effectively you are transforming the question to "What are x and y?" which is not in congruence (one-to-one or complementary) with the transformation rule.

Here, we do not have a unique value for either x or y (both x and y change with time). But since x and y are unequal numbers (this is given in the question), when x equals 3, y must equal 5 (then $x + y$ equals 8); and when y equals 3, x equals 5 (again $x + y$ equals 8). Either way, we have a unique value for $x + y$. So, at any given time, the system would have a single value, which is 8. Hence, data is sufficient. Also note that if you transformed the question to "What is *x* and *y*?" or "What is *x/y*?" you would yield the result data *not* sufficient. The transformations are against the one-to-one rule.

Strategy

Sample Plug-in Method.

In this method, we check whether the objects in a statement have a one-to-one relation or a many-to-one relation with the question setup. If so, the statement is sufficient. If not, the statement is *not* sufficient.

Example: In the figure, lines *AB* and *DE* are parallel. What is the value of *x* ?

(1) $y = 45$

(2) $z = 67.5$

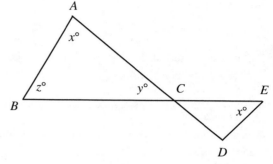

In this method, we check whether the object in the statement is one-to-one with the question setup. For example, to check data sufficiency for Statement (1) alone, we check whether a single value of *y* yields a single value for *x*.

Statement (1): Suppose $y = 30$. [Note that *y* can be different from the value given. OK. But what is the advantage of doing this? The advantage is to find if we have one-to-one between *y* (statement) and the *question*. If we have a single value for the *question* for a single *y* ($y = 30$), then we would likely have a single value for the *question* for $y = 45$. The purpose of this test is to find one-to-one. So, we know if given y = whatever, the value of the *question* can be found.] Substituting the sample in the figure yields $\angle ACB = y° = 30°$. Since *AB* and *ED* are parallel lines, the alternate interior angles, *B* and *E*, are equal $\angle B = \angle E = x$ (from the figure), and the alternate interior angles $\angle A = \angle D = x$ (from the figure). Since the angle sum of a triangle is 180°, $\angle A + \angle B + \angle ACB = 180°$; $x + x + 30° = 180°$; $2x = 150$; $x = 75$. So, we can formulate that given a valid value for *y*, we can calculate a single value for *x*. Statement (1) gives the value of *y*. So, Statement (1) is sufficient.

In other words, from above, we can derive the value of *x* given *y* alone by the means $x = (180 - y)/2$, and we can find *x* given *z* by the means $x = z$ (alternate interior angles of two parallel lines *AB* and *CD* are equal). The equation $x = z$ indicates that one value of *z* will yield only one value for *x*. Therefore, the info *z* equals whatsoever alone is also sufficient to answer the question. Hence, either statement alone is sufficient. The answer is (D).

Example: If $x^2 + 2xy + y^2 = 25$, then what is the value of $x + y$?

(1) $y = 3$

(2) $x = 2$

Substituting a particular value for y, say 2, in the equation $x^2 + 2xy + y^2 = 25$ yields

$$x^2 + 2x(2) + 2^2 = 25$$

$$(x + 2)^2 = 25$$

$$x + 2 = \pm 5$$

$$x = -2 \pm 5$$

So, for each value of y, x has two solutions and therefore $x + y$ has two solutions as well. This is a one-to-one failure between y and $x + y$ and therefore Statement (1) is not sufficient.

Similarly, there is no one-to-one relation between x and $x + y$. Hence, Statement (2) alone is not sufficient.

Given statements (1) and (2), x and y can be summed to get the value of $x + y$, so the statements together are sufficient. The answer is (C).

Sometimes, one-to-one can exist with one particular value given in the statement and not with any other value. So, be careful.

Example: If $x^2 + 3xy + y = -7$, then what is the value of $x + y$?

(1) $y = 2$

(2) $x = 3$

Substituting a particular value for y, say 1, in the equation $x^2 + 3xy + y = -7$ yields

$$x^2 + 3x(1) + 1 + 7 = 0$$

$$x^2 + 3x + 8 = 0$$

Since this is a quadratic equation, it might have 2 solutions. Hence, it is easy to mistakenly think that for a single y that the variable x will have more than one solution and therefore so does $x + y$, causing a one-to-one failure.

Substituting the value for y given in Statement (1), $y = 2$, in the equation $x^2 + 3xy + y + 7 = 0$ yields

$$x^2 + 3x(2) + 2 = -7$$

$$x^2 + 2(3)(x) + 9 = 0$$

Factoring by the perfect trinomial square formula $(a + b)^2 = a^2 + 2ab + b^2$ yields

$$(x + 3)^2 = 0$$

$$x = -3, \text{ a single solution}$$

Hence, y and x have a one-to-one relation for the specific value $y = 2$ and then x equals -3. Therefore, $x + y$ is one-to-one as well. Statement (1) is sufficient.

Substituting any value for x, say, $x = 2$ in the given equation $x^2 + 3xy + y = -7$ yields a linear equation in y and y alone (such as $2^2 + 3(2)y + y = -7$, or $4 + 6y + y = -7$). Hence, we have a single solution for y given a single x and then we get single result for $x + y$. Hence, Statement (2) alone is sufficient.

The answer is (D).

Watch out!

Example: **If $x + xy + y = -1$, then what is the value of $x + y$?**

   (1)   **$y = -1$**

   (2)   **$x = 2$**

Substituting $y = 1$ yields a linear equation that will derive a single value for x. So, x and y are one-to-one for all values. So, it is easy to mistakenly think that Statement (1) alone is sufficient.

For a particular value, $y = -1$, substitution yields

$$x + x(-1) + (-1) = -1$$

$$x - x - 1 = -1$$

$$-1 = -1$$

This is a known fact, so x could be any real number. Hence, for $y = -1$, we have a one-to-many relation between y and x; and therefore for this particular value, the data is insufficient.

Strategy

Degree of Freedom Method – Geometry

Angle Facet: To find an angle of a triangle, constructing a similar triangle is sufficient.

Side Facet: To find a side of a triangle, the exact triangle is needed.

The degree of freedom is 2 for the *angle facet*. This can be explained as follows: Because we know the rule "the sum of three angles of a triangle is 180 degrees," an angle equals 180 degrees minus the other two angles of the triangle. Hence, the angle is dependent on the other two angles, and the degree of freedom is 2.

The degree of freedom is 3 for the *side facet*. This is explained as follows: Unless we are given a *side and two angles* or *two sides and one angle* or *all three sides* of the triangle, the triangle cannot be fixed (constructed uniquely) and therefore the side cannot be measured. In any of the three cases, we need 3 variables, and therefore the degree of freedom is 3.

To find an angle, either an angle facet or a side facet helps. But, to find a side, the side facet is the only way.

Example: In the figure, lines AB and DE are parallel.
What is the value of x ?

(1) $y = 45$

(2) $z = 67.5$

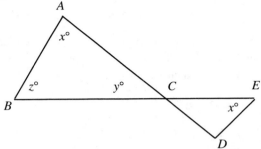

To determine the measure of angle x, we just need to draw a similar figure (angle facet), a precise figure (side facet) is not necessary. In other words, we do not need to form an exact replica (side facet) of the figure; a similar figure (angle facet) will suffice.

We have defined angle facet as the situation where we can apply the rule "The angle sum of a triangle equals 180 degrees." When we cannot apply the rule, we have a side facet.

The degree of freedom in the angle facet is 2; and in the side facet, it is 3.

The angle facet is to construct a similar triangle, and the side facet is to construct the exact triangle.

If the question asked for a side, we would need a side facet. But the question here asks for just angle x. So, we can do with either an angle facet or a side facet.

Since the lengths of none of the sides of the figure are given, we rule out using a side facet.

In the angle facet, as we know, we have the degree of freedom 2 (which means we need two rules). We have the rule $\angle B = \angle E$, or $z = x$ (since AB and DE are parallel lines, we equate the alternate interior angles). This is a different linear equation from any of the equations we already have (we have angles sum to 180 degrees), and therefore it reduces the degree of freedom by 1 (degree of freedom reduces by 1 per equation or property). Hence, the degree of freedom now is $2 - 1 = 1$. Thus, we are short one angle (by angle facet). So, we still need one more rule. At this point, we stop looking at the question and start looking at the statements because we know that we need to analyze a Question Setup in a Data Sufficiency problem only until we reduce the degree of freedom to 1. This is the minimum degree of freedom to which the question itself (without statements) can ever reduce.

Now, either statement $y = 45$ or $z = 67.5$ is a rule in the angle facet. Hence, either statement alone is sufficient, and the answer is (D).

Equation maps:

In this method, we represent each given equation as a string.

The objective of the Equation maps is not to solve the problem but to show the route to solve the problem.

Example:

$$x + y = 3$$

$$x + z = 5$$

$$x + q = 10$$

What is the value of $x + y + z + q$?

(1) $x = 2$

(2) $y = 1$

Let's list each of the three linear equations given in the system in the form of strings (one string for each equation) of the variables as shown below:

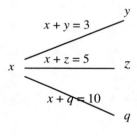

The first string, represented as $x + y = 3$, says that given x, the value of y can be calculated. Similarly, the string $x + z = 5$ says that given x, the value of z can be calculated, and the string $x + q = 10$ says that given x, the value of q can be calculated.

Let's start with Statement (1): $x = 2$. Replacing x with 2 in the map yields

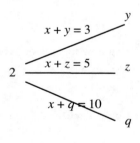

Now, in each string, there is only one unknown (y in the top string designated by $x + y = 3$, z in the middle string designated by $x + z = 5$, and q in the third string designated by $x + q = 10$).

Hence, from the first string, y can be calculated; from the second string, z can be calculated; and from the third string, q can be calculated by the shown relations.

Thus, $x + y + z + q$ can be calculated and therefore the statement is sufficient.

Though it is not necessary, let's do the calculations:

$$2 + y = 3; y = 1$$

$$2 + z = 5; z = 3$$

$$2 + q = 10; q = 8$$

So, $x + y + z + q = 2 + 1 + 3 + 8 = 12$.

Statement (2): $y = 1$

Replacing y with 1 in the map yields

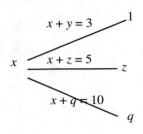

In the top string, x is the only unknown. So, x can be calculated from the relation $x + y = 3$.

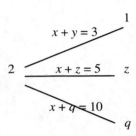

Here, we can follow Statement (1) as well. But, let's solve it independently.

In the middle string, x and z are the variables of which x is known. Hence, z is can be calculated.

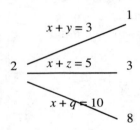

Similarly, q can be calculated. So, $x + y + z + q = 2 + 1 + 3 + 8 = 12$.

So, each term in $x + y + z + q$ is known and the sum can be calculated. In each string now there is only one unknown (y in the top string designated by $x + y = 3$, z in the middle string designated by $x + z = 5$, and q in the third string designated by $x + q = 10$).

Hence, from the first string y can be calculated, from the second string z can be calculated, and from the third string, q can be calculated by the shown relations.

So, then $x + y + z + q$ can be calculated. Hence, the statement is sufficient.

Though not necessary, let's do the calculations as well:

$$2 + y = 3; y = 1$$

$$2 + z = 5; z = 3$$

$$2 + q = 10; q = 8$$

So, $x + y + z + q = 2 + 1 + 3 + 8 = 14$.

Since we know y, the only unknown remaining in the top curve is x and can be calculated using it's relation $x + y = 3$. The result is $x = 2$.

Once we have x, we can calculate the variables z and q just as we did in Statement (1).

Hence, Statement (2) is sufficient.

The equation map for another system:

$$2x + y + 3z = 10$$

$$x + y + 2z = 12$$

$$5x + 2y + 3z = 15$$

can be drawn as shown in the figure.

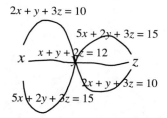

 Simple problems can be answered on the fly. But in each step, confirm that you aren't making an error.

Example: If $w \neq 0$ and $w = 2x = \sqrt{2}y$, what is the value of $w - x$?

    (1) $\dfrac{\sqrt{2}}{2}y = 2\sqrt{2}$

    (2) $\sqrt{2y} = 2\sqrt{2}$

Statement (1) $\dfrac{\sqrt{2}}{2}y = 2\sqrt{2}$ yields a unique value for y; no need to calculate.

Squaring Statement (2) $\sqrt{2y} = 2\sqrt{2}$ yields $2y = 8$, which yields a unique value for y; no need to calculate further.

Either statement alone determines the value of y. We confirm here that we aren't erring; we actually get a unique value for y. Statement (1) is already a linear equation, and squaring both sides of Statement (2) yields a linear equation in y (degree 1) in a single unknown and therefore yields a unique value for y.

Given the value of y, the equation $w = 2x = \sqrt{2}y$ uniquely determines the values of w and x. Hence, the difference $w - x$ can be calculated. Since w and x have unique values, so does the difference $w - x$. Therefore, either statement alone is sufficient, and the answer is (D).

Example: If $w \neq 0$ and $w = 2x = \sqrt{2}\,y$, what is the value of $w - x$?

(1) $\dfrac{\sqrt{2}}{2}\,y^2 = 2\sqrt{2}$

(2) $\sqrt{2y} = 2\sqrt{2}$

The degree of the equation in Statement (1) is 2. So, we get two solutions for *y* from here, and therefore we get two values each for *w* and *x*. So, we will probably get two different values for $w - x$ (We need to check whether we are erring here by actually doing the full calculations). Therefore, Statement (1) alone is not sufficient.

Statement (2): $\sqrt{2y} = 2\sqrt{2}$. Here, *y* has a single value (degree being 1). So, we get a single value each for *w* and *x* as well, and therefore a single value for $w - x$. So, Statement (2) alone is sufficient.

 Strategy

Variable Quantity Analysis.

Example: The general formula for the profit per unit of a product is defined as

The Average Selling Price per unit minus the Average Production Cost per unit

Each book was sold at the same selling price. Did the average production cost decrease with the number of books produced?

(1)   The production cost increased with the number of books produced, but the selling price of each book remained constant at $24.5.

(2)   The profit per unit from the sales of the books increased with the number of books produced.

Statement (1):

The selling price is irrelevant here. The production cost for 6 units is, of course, higher than that for 5 units. So, the statement reveals only information that can be clearly understood from the question and therefore the statement alone is not sufficient.

For example, suppose, 5 units cost $5 to produce (here, cost per unit is $5/5 = $1).

If the 6th unit costs less than $1, then the average cost per unit is lower; but if the 6th unit costs more than $1, then the average cost per unit is higher.

For example, if the 6th unit costs $0.75 (< $1), then the cost per unit decreases to $5.75/6, which is less than 1.

If the 6th unit costs $1.25 (> $1), then the cost per unit increases to $6.25/6, which is greater than $1.

This is a double case and therefore the statement is *not* sufficient.

Statement (2):

From the formula given, we have

The Profit per unit = Average Selling price of each book – the Average Production cost.

Since the selling price remained constant, suppose $24.5, the Profit per unit equals 24.5 – the Average Production cost.

The Average Production cost equals 24.5 – The Profit per unit. This equation is in its most reduced form.

The statement says that the profit per unit increases with the number of books produced, which we call the print size. So, we can term profit per unit as a variable changing with print size.

Now, any equation in its most reduced form would not have just a single variable changing with something (here, changing with print size).

For example, we have,

The Profit per unit + the Average Production cost = 24.5.

Since the Average Production cost changes with print size, Profit per unit must also change with print size such that the two again sum to 24.5. Since, Profit per unit increases with the Print size, the Average Production cost must decrease with print size so that the two again sum to 24.5.

In other words, since the Profit per unit is a function of the Average production cost, the Profit per unit must also be a function of the print size.

The Profit per unit + the Average Production cost = 24.5.

↑↓ The Average Production cost equals 24.5 – The Profit per unit ↓↑.

The Average Production cost equals 24.5 – f(print size).

The equation is such that, if f (print size) increases, the Average Production Cost decreases.

The answer to the question is "Yes. Average Production Cost decreases."

The statement is sufficient.

The answer is (B).

The Question Alone Is Never Data Sufficient.

In Data Sufficiency problems, there is no answer-choice for the case where the question alone is sufficient. So, a valid GMAT Data Sufficiency problem always needs at least one statement.

For the same reason, if both statements just reveal information contained in the question, then data is never sufficient.

Example:

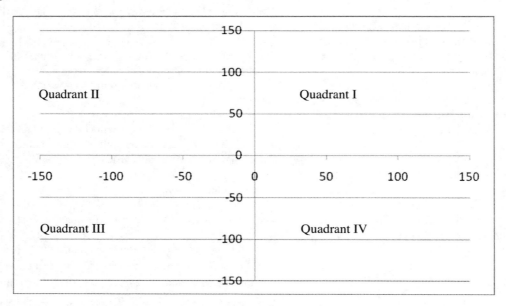

A coordinate plane is shown in the figure. A curve can be drawn using the equation $af(x) = bx - 2b$ ($ab \neq 0$). If $(1, t)$ is a point on the curve, then in which quadrant does the point lie?

(1)   The curve crosses the y-axis on its positive side.

(2)   The curve crosses the x-axis on its positive side.

Dividing the equation $af(x) = bx - 2b$ by a ($a \neq 0$ since $ab \neq 0$, so division is valid) yields

$$\frac{af(x)}{a} = \frac{bx}{a} - \frac{2b}{a}$$
$$f(x) = \frac{bx}{a} - \frac{2b}{a}$$

Substituting the point $(1, t)$ in the equation yields $t = b(1)/a - 2b/a = -b/a$. Now, if b/a is negative, t is positive and the point $(1, t)$ lies in Quadrant I; and if b/a is positive, t is negative and the point $(1, t)$ lies in Quadrant IV. So, the question can be transformed as "Is b/a negative?" or "Is b/a positive?"

Statement (1): The curve crosses the *y*-axis on its positive side.

Suppose the curve crosses the *y*-axis at the point $(0, q)$ [the *x*-coordinate is 0 where a curve crosses the *y*-axis].

The curve crosses the *y*-axis on its positive side, so *q* must be positive. Putting the point $(0, q)$ in the curve equation yields

$$q = \frac{b}{a}(0) - \frac{2b}{a}$$
$$q = -\frac{2b}{a}$$

Since we are given that this is negative, *b/a* must be positive. Hence, Statement (1) alone is sufficient. The point $(1, t)$ is in Quadrant I; Data sufficient.

Statement (2): The curve crosses the *x*-axis on its positive side.

Suppose the curve crosses the *x*-axis at the point $(p, 0)$ [the *y* coordinate is 0 where a curve crosses the *x*-axis].

The curve crosses the *x*-axis on its positive side, so *p* must be positive. Putting the point $(p, 0)$ in the curve equation yields

$$0 = \frac{bp}{a} - \frac{2b}{a}$$
$$\frac{2b}{a} = \frac{bp}{a}$$
$$2 = p$$

Since *p* is positive, the curve crosses the *x*-axis on its positive side. But this is what Statement (2) says. So, we were able to derive the statement using the question alone and therefore we can say the information in the question plus Statement (2) is equivalent to the question alone. Since this is a standard assumption we always make that the question alone is never sufficient, here, the question plus Statement (2), isn't sufficient either; Data insufficient.

The answer is (A).

➤ **One-to-One Check in the Transformations**

Example:

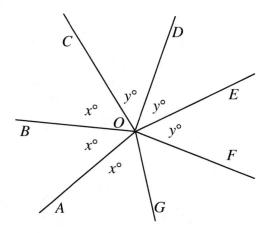

In the figure, is *x* a multiple of *y*?

(1)   ∠*BOD* measures 45°.

(2)   ∠*BOE* measures the same as the ∠*AOD*.

The transformation of the question to "What are x and y?" is incorrect. Why? Because x/y does not have a one-to-one mapping with x and y. For example, x/y is 2 when $x = 2$ and $y = 1$ and when $x = 4$ and $y = 2$.

Statement (1): $\angle BOD = 45°$.

From the figure, $\angle BOD = x + y$, so $x + y$ equals 45°. Dividing the equation $x + y = 45$ by y yields

$$x/y + 1 = 45/y$$

$x/y = 45/y - 1$, could be an integer (when $y = 5$ or 9) or may not be an integer (when 45 is not a multiple of y).

So, the statement alone is *not* sufficient.

Statement (2): $\angle BOE$ equals $\angle AOD$.

From the figure, $\angle BOE = x + 2y$ and $\angle AOD = 2x + y$. Equating the angles yields

$$x + 2y = 2x + y$$

$$y = x \qquad \text{by canceling } x + y$$

Dividing each side by y yields

$$y/y = x/y$$

$$1 = x/y$$

Hence, Statement (2) alone is sufficient.

The answer is (B).

    Mistakes:

If you did the question transformation

from

What is $4x^2$?

(1) $|2x - 2| + |2x + 2| = 4$

(2) $|3x - 1| + |3x + 1| = 6$

to

What is $2x$?

(1) $|2x - 2| + |2x + 2| = 4$

(2) $|3x - 1| + |3x + 1| = 6$

it is a mistake. Why? Check for one-to-one.

You can see that in the original problem above, either statement is sufficient, and the answer is (D). But in the transformed problem, the statements together are not sufficient. The analysis is simple and left to you. The reason is that the answer to the original problem is (D), while the answer to the transformed problem is (E).

One-to-One: The mapping from $2x$ to $4x^2$ is not one-to-one, meaning that for both different numbers for $2x$, –2 and 2, $4x^2$ equal a single number (16). This is called "many-to-one." We studied that this kind of transformation is not safe. We know that this will have the capacity of moving the answer-choices up the data sufficiency order. This means, that since we have a many-to-one relation between $2x$ and $4x^2$, the transformation "What is $4x^2$?" to "What is $2x$?" takes the value down the data sufficiency order and the transformation "What is $2x$?" to "What is $4x^2$?" takes it up the data sufficiency order.

What is $4x^2$?   What is $2x$?

(1) $2x = 2$ (1) $2x = 2$

(2) $x^2 = 1$ The answer is (D).   (2) $x^2 = 1$ The answer is (A).

Either way, the transformation's is wrong.

Similarly, the transformation from "Is x prime?" to "Is x odd?" is unsafe because not all prime numbers are odd, nor all odd numbers prime. Hence, the mapping of the set of odd numbers is not one-to-one with the set of prime numbers.

Watch out!

Don't assume that everything that appears in a problem is needed!

In the example below, it is a mistake to assume that because x and y appear in the expression that we need both x and y to evaluate the expression. This type of mistake can be avoided by using the statements very conservatively.

Example: What is the value of $\sqrt{\dfrac{x^2}{y^2}} \cdot \sqrt{\dfrac{y}{x^2}} + \sqrt{\dfrac{y^2}{x^2}} \cdot \sqrt{\dfrac{x^2}{y}}$?

(1) $x = 59$

(2) $y = 49$

$$\sqrt{\frac{x^2}{y^2}}\sqrt{\frac{y}{x^2}} + \sqrt{\frac{y^2}{x^2}}\sqrt{\frac{x^2}{y}} =$$

$$\sqrt{\frac{x^2}{y^2} \cdot \frac{y}{x^2}} + \sqrt{\frac{y^2}{x^2} \cdot \frac{x^2}{y}} =$$

$$\sqrt{\frac{1}{y}} + \sqrt{y}$$

So, given the value of y, a unique value of the expression can be determined. However, we do not have any means to determine y from x. So, Statement (2) is sufficient, and Statement (1) is unnecessary. The answer is (B).

General mistake:

If you feel one statement is sufficient while the other one appears to be out of context, then try to derive the later statement using the former. If derivable, either statement is sufficient, and the answer is (D).

Example: If x and y are two consecutive integers in the increasing order, then what is the value of $\sqrt{x} + \dfrac{1}{\sqrt{x}}$?

(1) $x = 10$

(2) $y = 11$

Since Statement (1) gives a value of x that we can use to evaluate $\sqrt{x} + \dfrac{1}{\sqrt{x}}$, the statement is sufficient.

Statement (2) gives a value of y that can determine the value of x (Since x and y are two consecutive integers in increasing order and y is 11, x must be 10). So, Statement (2) is also sufficient. The answer is (D), either statement alone is sufficient.

Method II:

The expression $\sqrt{x} + \dfrac{1}{\sqrt{x}}$ can be evaluated given x in Statement (1). Since x and y are consecutive integers in ascending order, x equals $y - 1$. So, $\sqrt{x} + \dfrac{1}{\sqrt{x}}$ equals $\sqrt{y-1} + \dfrac{1}{\sqrt{y-1}}$. The value of y is given in Statement (2). So, Statement (2) indirectly determines the value of the expression. Hence, either statement is sufficient, and the answer is (D).

General mistake:

Sometimes knowing too much can lead you astray because your confidence overrides your reasoning, leaving you to proceed with incomplete reasoning. For example, the analysis below that if you made for the example in the second figure is quite intelligent but is not complete.

The figure can be constructed by drawing the line n first, then the line m at an angle x, and then line l at an angle y. In the process, you needed both x and y. So, if you thought both statements are needed to solve and therefore the answer is (C), you are mistaken. You will see that knowing y is sufficient. The answer is (B).

Note, you need not draw n. Just draw m and then draw l relative to m at angle y. Now measure anti-clockwise angle between m and n and we are ready with the answer to the question.

Example:

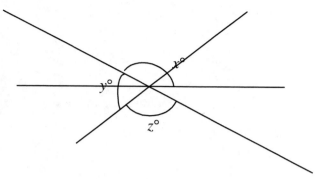

$z =$

(1) $x = 105°$

(2) $y = 122°$

Let's name the lines in the figure.

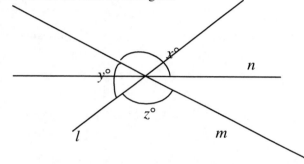

Statement (1) is not sufficient because, given x, the line l can freely rotate changing the angle z.

The answer is (B).

Strategy

We can express (transform) a question in certain variables into a question into certain other variable(s) for convenience if we have one-to-one between the original *question* and the changed *question*. For example, the question "If $x = 5 - z$, then what is x?" can be transformed to "If $x = 5 - z$, then what is z?" since we have one-to-one between x and z (meaning that one value of x yields only value of z and one value of z yields only one value of x.]

Example:

$$x + y = 3$$

$$x + z = 5$$

What is the value of x ?

(1) $y = 2$

(2) $z = 4$

Given y, the variable x can be calculated from the first equation in the system as $x = 3 - y$. Also, given z, the variable x can be calculated from the second equation in the system as $x = 5 - z$. The equations $x = 3 - y$

and $x = 5 - z$ indicate that x is one-to-one with y and one-to-one with z. Also, z is one-to-one with both x and y. Expressing this as plausibility sets for x, y, and z gives $\dfrac{\begin{array}{c}0\\\hline 1\\\hline 2\\ \vdots\\ \vdots\end{array}}{}$, and $\dfrac{\begin{array}{c}3\\\hline 2\\\hline 1\\ \vdots\\ \vdots\end{array}}{}$, and $\dfrac{\begin{array}{c}5\\\hline 4\\\hline 3\\ \vdots\\ \vdots\end{array}}{}$, respectively. There is

only one value for y and z for a single value of x. Similarly, there is only one value for x for a single y or a single value of z. So, the question can be transformed as

What is y or what is z?

(1) $y = 2$

(2) $z = 4$

Clearly, either statement alone is sufficient, and the answer is (D).

Strategy

Common solution methodology for Data Sufficiency problems with operators and functions.

First, find the domain of the arguments.

Evaluate the question for each possible set of values for the arguments within their respective domains.

Finally, check whether all the possibilities that statement(s) allow yield a single answer for the question.

If yes, we have data sufficient. If no, we have data insufficient. The following example illustrates.

Example:

a	$\overline{a}$	b	$a * b$	$a + b$
0	1	0	0	0
0	1	1	0	1
1	0	0	0	1
1	0	1	1	1

The operators '*', '+' and '⁻' are defined only on the binary numbers (0 and 1 are called binary numbers) as tabulated. If x and y are two binary numbers, then what is the value of $x * \overline{y} + y * \overline{x}$?

(1) $\overline{x} * \overline{y} = 0$

(2) $\overline{x} + \overline{y} = 1$

Step 1: Find the domain of the arguments of the operators x and y. Since they are given to be binary, clearly, the domain of both is 0 and 1.

Step 2: The possible set of values of the arguments $\{x, y\}$ are $\{0, 0\}$, $\{0, 1\}$, $\{1, 0\}$, $\{1, 1\}$.

Step 3: Evaluate the expression in the question for each of these possible values.

Let's do it in tabular form as shown below, also calculating the values of the expressions in the statements $\bar{x} * \bar{y}$ [in Statement (1)] and $\bar{x} + \bar{y}$ [in Statement (2)], and $x * \bar{y} + y * \bar{x}$ (from the question).

x	y	$\bar{x} * \bar{y}$	$\bar{x} + \bar{y}$	$x * \bar{y} + y * \bar{x}$
0	0	$\bar{0} * \bar{0} = 1 * 1 = 1$	$\bar{0} + \bar{0} = 1 + 1 = 1$	$0 * \bar{0} + 0 * \bar{0} = 0 * 1 + 0 * 1 = 0 + 0 = 0$
0	1	$\bar{0} * \bar{1} = 1 * 0 = 0$	$\bar{0} + \bar{1} = 1 + 0 = 1$	$0 * \bar{1} + 1 * \bar{0} = 0 * 0 + 1 * 1 = 0 + 1 = 1$
1	0	$\bar{1} * \bar{0} = 0 * 1 = 0$	$\bar{1} + \bar{0} = 0 + 1 = 1$	$1 * \bar{0} + 0 * \bar{1} = 1 * 1 + 0 * 0 = 1 + 0 = 1$
1	1	$\bar{1} * \bar{1} = 0 * 0 = 0$	$\bar{1} + \bar{1} = 0 + 0 = 0$	$1 * \bar{1} + 1 * \bar{1} = 1 * 0 + 1 * 0 = 0 + 0 = 0$

Step 4: We need to find the possibilities that the statements allow and check whether in each case the answer to the question has been changing or it's fixed.

Statement (1) says $\bar{x} * \bar{y} = 0$ and the cases that yield the same result are represented in rows 2, 3, and 4 only in the above table. Not in each case did the value of the expression in the question $x * \bar{y} + y * \bar{x}$ equal 0 (It equaled 0 in rows 3 and 4, and it equaled 1 in row 2). In other words, the rows that Statement (1) allows are 2, 3, and 4 and these represent the values of x and y that are permitted by the statement, and not all of these happen to be yielding the same value for the question $x * \bar{y} + y * \bar{x}$. Hence, the statement is not sufficient.

Now, the rows that Statement (2) $\bar{x} + \bar{y} = 1$ allows are 1, 2, and 3 only, and not in each of these rows did the value of the expression $x * \bar{y} + y * \bar{x}$ equal 0 (It equaled 0 in 1st row, and in 2nd and 3rd equaled 1). This is a double case and therefore Statement (2) alone is not sufficient.

Each time $\bar{x} * \bar{y}$ equals 0 and $\bar{x} + \bar{y}$ equals 1 (rows 2 and 3), $x * \bar{y} + y * \bar{x}$ equals 1. Here, we have a unique solution. Hence, the statements together are sufficient.

The answer is (C).

Strategy

Be cunning in solving data sufficiency problems.

Sometimes you might not know a particular detail in the question, but can still solve the problem.

For instance, suppose in the example below you do not know what a Fibonacci series is, and the Fibonacci series is the key to the problem.

Example: Is Set *A*, a Fibonacci series?

    (1) The *n*th term in the series *A* is given by

$$F_n = \begin{cases} 0 & \text{if } n = 0 \\ 1 & \text{if } n = 1 \\ F_{n-1} + F_{n-2} & \text{if } n > 1 \end{cases}$$

Still you can determine whether Statement (1) is sufficient (as shown below).

— After reading the next example, you should appreciate that the advantage of the data sufficiency format is that you do not actually need to know what the answer to the question is as long as you are sure that exactly one answer exists. This way, you can skip many of the calculations that are inevitable in a multiple-choice problem.

Example: Two series are said to match each other if the corresponding terms of the two series are the same. Is the set *A*, a Fibonacci series?

    (1)   The *n*th term of series *A* is given by

$$F_n = \begin{cases} 0 & \text{if } n = 0 \\ 1 & \text{if } n = 1 \\ F_{n-1} + F_{n-2} & \text{if } n > 1 \end{cases}$$

    (2)   Each term in Series *A* equals the sum of the preceding two terms just like a Fibonacci series, and a Fibonacci series has 0, 1 as the first two elements.

Two series are said to match each other if the corresponding terms of the two series are the same. The terms of a series are generally determined by using a set of initially given terms and generating the remaining terms by applying the rules to initial terms. If we are able to write down all the terms in a set, then we can compare it with some other set, say, the Fibonacci series.

We either **must** say the two series match completely (to answer the question with Yes) or say they do not match (to answer the question with No). These are the ways to say the data is sufficient. To say that the two series match, we **must** show that each corresponding element matches. To say that the two series do not match, we just need to show that at least one pair of corresponding elements do not match. That's why, in data sufficiency, determining that the answer is "No" is usually easier than determining that the answer is "Yes."

Unless we have written down each term in Series *A*, we wouldn't need the Fibonacci series for comparison with the series. When we can write the series, we certainly have the result that either *A* equals the Fibonacci series or that it doesn't. Hence, we can say data insufficient when we are not given the definition of Series

A adequately enough to write down each term in the series. If given, we can say data sufficient and determine that either *A* equals Fibonacci or it doesn't.

Statement (1): $F_n = \begin{cases} 0 & \text{if } n = 0 \\ 1 & \text{if } n = 1 \\ F_{n-1} + F_{n-2} & \text{if } n > 1 \end{cases}$

A series is said to be completely defined when both the initial values and the rules associated with the series are completely defined.

Series *A* is completely defined and therefore we can calculate each term in the series. So, we can write each term in the series as

Initial Value: $F_0 = 0$

Initial Value: $F_1 = 1$

By Rule: $F_2 = F_0 + F_1 = 0 + 1$

By Rule: $F_3 = F_1 + F_2 = 1 + 1 = 2$

...

and so on.

So, here, Series A can be completely written.

So, it can be compared with the Fibonacci series to determine whether it equals the Fibonacci or it doesn't.

We are not actually concerned whether the result is "Yes, it equals" or "No, it doesn't" as long as we are sure we are able to answer the question with one of the two statements.

So, the data is sufficient.

The statement would have been tested for data insufficiency even if the question did not explain the Fibonacci series. This is how we have devised the answer.

Statement (2): Each term in *A* equals the sum of preceding two elements just like a Fibonacci series, and a Fibonacci series has 0, 1 as the first two elements.

Let's transform the question to "Can all the terms in Series *A* be completely written down?" So, check whether the series is defined completely enough to write the series completely?"

We have the rules of the series, but we do not have the initial values of the series.

Since the rule of *A* matches the Fibonacci series, we **must** look at the initial values of the two. If the initial values of the two are the same, the sets will match. Here are some examples:

Each successive number in series *A* is greater than the preceding number by the previous number. So, the rule for *A* is: $F_n = F_{n-1} + F_{n-2}$.

Initial values: Suppose the first and the second terms in the series are 0 and 1. ($F_0 = 0$ and $F_1 = 1$, initial values like Fibonacci series)

Applying the rule, to the remaining terms yields

By Rule: $F_2 = F_0 + F_1 = 0 + 1 = 1$

By Rule: $F_3 = F_1 + F_2 = 1 + 1 = 2$

...

and so on. Here, *A* matches the Fibonacci.

But suppose the initial values were $F_0 = 1$ and $F_1 = 1$, different from Fibonacci. Then,

By Rule: $F_2 = F_0 + F_1 = 1 + 1 = 2$

By Rule: $F_3 = F_1 + F_2 = 1 + 2 = 3$

...

and so on. Here, *A* does not match the Fibonacci. We have a double case, and therefore the statement is not sufficient.

The answer is (A).

Wild Card Method (to find data sufficiency only):

- We treat statements separately.

- In this method, we treat the statement other than the one currently under analysis as a wild card and eliminate almost all the info related to the wild card.

- If, after the elimination, we are able to find the answer to the question, we have the statement under study *Data Sufficient*. If still we have multiple answers, we cannot judge as Data Insufficient. We need to do a full analysis of the statement under consideration.

- Thus, it is only a preliminary investigation technique. An example is shown below.

- The method is different from what we have been doing so far in that we are now eliminating the info related to the other statement.

Note: In Statement (1), Statement (2) is the wild card; and in Statement (2), Statement (1) is the wild card.

1	x	$x + y$
x	z	y
$x + y$	3	v

Example: In the table, if the sum of each column equals the sum of each row, then what is x ?

(1) $v = -2$

(2) $z = 1$

Statement (1): $v = -2$

Since we are testing Statement (1) alone, assume that we do not know Statement (2). That is, assume we do not know the value of z.

1	x	$x + y$
x	"Don't know"	y
$x + y$	3	v

We are given that the sum of columns and the rows is the same. Hence, we have

Rule 1: Row 1 Sum = Row 3 Sum; $1 + x + (x + y) = (x + y) + 3 + v$

Rule 2: Column 1 Sum = Column 3 Sum; $1 + x + (x + y) = (x + y) + y + v$

Rule 3: Col 1 Sum = Col 3 Sum; $1 + x + (x + y) = 1 + x + (x + y)$ [The expression on left side of the equal sign is same as the one on the right side. So, this is an understood equation.]

Effectively, we have the above two equations plus the one in Statement (1): $v = -2$. We have 3 different equations in 3 unknowns: x, y, and v. The statement is sufficient to determine x.

Statement (2): $z = 1$

Now, with the full table

1	x	$x + y$
x	z	y
$x + y$	3	v

We are given that the sum of columns and the rows is the same. Hence, we have:

Rule 1: Row 1 Sum = Row 2 Sum; $1 + x + (x + y) = x + z + y$; $z = x + 1$.

Rule 2: Row 1 Sum = Row 3 Sum; $1 + x + (x + y) = (x + y) + 3 + v$; $v = x - 2$.

Rule 3: Row 1 Sum = Col 1 Sum; $1 + x + (x + y) = 1 + x + (x + y)$. [LHS same as RHS. So, the rule is redundant.].

Rule 4: Col 1 Sum = Col 2 Sum; $1 + x + (x + y) = x + z + 3$; [Same as Rule 1. So, the rule is redundant.].

Rule 5: Col 1 Sum = Col 3 Sum; $1 + x + (x + y) = (x + y) + y + v$; $1 + x = y + v$; $v = 1 + x - y$.

Rule 6: Using Statement (1); $z = 1$.

Thus, we have a system of 4 unknowns in 4 different linear rules (Rules 1, 2, 5, and 6). So, we have a solution for each of the unknowns. So, x can be determined using the statement and therefore it is sufficient.

The answer is (D). The solution is $x = 0$, $v = -2$, $y = 3$, and $z = 1$.

Strategy

Language and Grammar are important.

The language and the grammar of the questions and statements are important and must be understood. They are important even as you write the transformed question or the statement.

Example:

$$A = \{2, 4, 7, 8\}$$

$$B = \{3, 6, 7, 8\}$$

A and *B* are two sets containing the elements shown above, and *C* is another set. If *x* is a number common in all the three sets, what is the value of *x* ?

(1)   7 is not in set *C*.

(2)   8 is in set *C*.

An element common to all three sets would also be common to any two of the sets. The common elements of the three sets *A*, *B*, and *C* are also common to the sets *A* and *B*. The set of common elements of *A* and *B* is {7, 8}.

So, by saying *x* is a common number of the three sets *A*, *B*, and *C*, we are assured of having at least one number common to all three sets, which is at least *x*.

So, *x* equals 7 or 8. The question can be transformed as "which one does *x* equal 7 or 8?" and not as "Is *x* equal to 7 or 8?" [because the former is a choice question and needs an integer type answer, here, 7 or 8; while the later is effectively a Yes/No question and is satisfied by knowing whether *x* equals either 7 or 8.] Note here that the language and the grammar are important during transformation of the question and the statements.

Statement (1):

Statement (1) says 7 is not in set *C*. So, *x* cannot be 7 (because we know that *x* is common to all three sets *A*, *B*, and *C* and therefore *x* must be in the set *C* as well, while 7 is not in set *C*.). Clearly, *x* must be 8 (because we know *x* is either 7 or 8. So, if it is not 7, it must be 8). Hence, the statement alone is sufficient.

Statement (2):

Statement (2) says 8 is in set *C*. But we do not know whether 7 is in set *C*. If 7 is in set *C*, *x* could be 7 or *x* could be 8. So, we still have two possibilities and therefore the statement alone is not sufficient.

The answer is (A), Statement (1) alone is sufficient and Statement (2) alone is not.

➤ **Tip:** A more comprehensive Statement like Statement (1) in the following example that seems to have been written with much concentration should be the one to use for determining Data Sufficiency. Statement (1) seems to be written with much interest, taking more time and effort, taking care of the exceptions such as "no element repeats in the series," etc.

One under-defined statement – One adequately defined statement:

8.   What is the mean (average) of the numbers in the series if each number in the series is different from the others?

   (1)   The 3-digit numbers that have a remainder of 3 when divided by 5 are all the elements that the series contains and no element repeats in the series.

   (2)   The series consists of all the 3-digit numbers that have a remainder of 3 when divided by 5.

The 3-digit numbers that have a remainder of 3 when divided by 5 are 103, 108, 113, …, 998.

Statement (1): The 3-digit numbers that have a remainder of 3 when divided by 5 are all the elements that the series contains and no element repeats in the series.

The numbers in the series could be only a few or all of the 3-digited numbers that have a remainder of 3 when divided by 5 listed in the set {103, 108, 113, …, 998}.

So, the mean will depend on the numbers contained in the series, which we do not know. Hence, the statement alone is *not* sufficient.

Statement (2): The series consists of all the 3-digit numbers that have a remainder of 3 when divided by 5.

Statement (2) has additional information beyond Statement (1) that the set contains all the elements from the set {103, 108, 113, …, 998} but doesn't say if it contains any other elements. So, we cannot presume that the series is 103, 108, 113, …, 998. In fact, the series is not completely defined. So, the mean cannot be calculated. The statement is *not* sufficient.

The answer is (A).

You might see problems that are merely logical, but with a mathematical context.

Example: x is one of the numbers 3 or 6. Is xy equal to 12 ?

   (1)   Exactly one of the following is true: x equals 3 or y does not equal 2.

   (2)   Exactly one of the following is true: x equals 6 or y does not equal 4.

Statement (1): Exactly one of the following is true: x equals 3 or y does not equal 2.

Case 1: $x = 3$ is true and $y \neq 2$ is false: "$y \neq 2$ is false" means that "y equals 2." Here, $xy = 3 \cdot 2 = 6 \neq 12$.

Case 2: $x = 3$ is false and $y \neq 2$ is true: "$x = 3$ is false" means x equals the only other permitted value 6. Now, xy equals 12 only if $y = 2$. But, since $y \neq 2$ is true, xy is not equal to 12 here as well.

These are the only two possible cases with the statement, and we do not have a double case. The answer is "No, $xy \neq 12$" and therefore the statement is sufficient.

Statement (2): Exactly one of the following is true: x equals 6 or y does not equal 4.

Case 1: $x = 6$ is true and $y \neq 4$ is false: "$y \neq 4$" is false means $y = 4$. Here, $xy = 6 \cdot 4 = 24$.

Case 2: $x = 6$ is false and $y \neq 4$ is true: "$x = 6$ is false" means x equals the only other permitted value 3. Now, xy could equal 12 only if y equals 4. But, here, we know $y \neq 4$. So, xy cannot equal 12.

These are the only two possible cases with the statements and we do not have a double case. The answer is "No, $xy \neq 12$" and therefore the statement is sufficient.

The answer is (D).

Example: x is one of the numbers: 3 or 6. Is xy equal to 12 ?

(1)   Either x equals 3 or y does not equal 2.

(2)   Either x equals 6 or y does not equal 4.

Note: The statement "Either A or B is true" means either A is true, or B is true, or BOTH.

Statement (1): Either x equals 3 or y does not equal 2.

Case 1: $x = 3$ is true and $y \neq 2$ is false: "$y \neq 2$ is false" means that "y equals 2." Here, $xy = 3 \cdot 2 = 6 \neq 12$.

Case 2: $x = 3$ is false and $y \neq 2$ is true: "$x = 3$ is false" means x equals the only other permitted value 6. Now, xy equals 12 only if $y = 2$. But, since $y \neq 2$ is true, xy is not equal to 12 here as well.

Case 3: Both $x = 3$ and $y \neq 2$ are true in which case $xy \neq 3 \cdot 2 = 6$. But it could equal 12. So, we have a double case and therefore the statement is not sufficient.

Statement (2): Either x equals 6 or y does not equal 4.

Case 1: $x = 6$ is true and $y \neq 4$ is false: "$y \neq 4$" is false means $y = 4$ is true. Here, $xy = 6 \cdot 4 = 24$.

Case 2: $x = 6$ is false and $y \neq 4$ is true: "$x = 6$ is false" means x equals the only other permitted value 3. Now, xy could equal 12 only if y equals 4. But, here, we know $y \neq 4$. So, xy cannot equal 12.

Case 3: Both $x = 6$ and $y \neq 4$ are true in which case, $xy \neq 6 \cdot 4 = 24$. But it could equal 12. So, we have a double case and therefore the statement is not sufficient.

Now, if Case 3 [from Statement (1)] were to be believed, then, the case plus Statement (2) yields the analysis: since $x = 3$ and $y \neq 2$ in the case, the way Statement (2) applies on this is since x not equal to 6, $y \neq 4$ must be true which means $xy \neq 3 \cdot 4 = 12$.

Now, if Case 3 [from Statement (2)] were to be believed, then the case plus Statement (1) yields the analysis: since $x = 6$ and $y \neq 4$ in the case, the way Statement (1) applies on this is since x not equal to 3, $y \neq 2$ must be true which means $xy \neq 6 \cdot 2 = 12$.

So, $xy \neq 12$. The statements together are sufficient, and the answer is (C).

Case Study Analysis

➤   The Contrapositive.

Example: If the value of p is one of the numbers 2 and 3, then is $pq \neq 6$?

(1)   If p equals 2, then q equals 3.

(2)   If q equals 3, then p equals 2.

If you thought that the statements say the same thing, you are mistaken.

The problem has to be solved by thorough case study analysis.

	$q = 2$	$q = 3$	$q = \ldots$
$p = 2$			$pq > 2 \cdot 3; pq > 6$
$p = 3$			$pq > 3 \cdot 3; pq > 6$

Statement (1): If *p* equals 2, then *q* equals 3.

Here, we have the product $pq = 2 \cdot 3 = 6$. Change the entire row $p = 2$ as shown:

	$q = 2$	$q = 3$	$q = \ldots$
$p = 2$	✘	✔	✘
$p = 3$			

But it is possible that when *q* equals 3, *p* equals 3. Here, $pq = 3 \cdot 3 = 9 \neq 6$. This can be observed from the Column $q = 3$: Row $p = 3$ being blank (blank could mean ✘ or ✔).

We have a double case and therefore the statement is not sufficient.

Statement (2): If *q* equals 3, then *p* equals 2.

Here, we have the product $pq = 2 \cdot 3 = 6$. Change the entire column $q = 3$ as shown:

	$q = 2$	$q = 3$	$q = \ldots$
$p = 2$		✔	
$p = 3$		✘	

But it is possible that when *p* equals 2, *q* equals 2 as well. Here, $pq = 2 \cdot 2 = 4 \neq 6$. This can be observed from the Column $q = 2$: Row $p = 2$ being blank (blank could mean ✘ or ✔).

We have a double case and therefore the statement is not sufficient.

With the statements together, we can superimpose the statements as

	$q = 2$	$q = 3$	$q = \ldots$
$p = 2$	✘	✔	✘
$p = 3$		✘	

Filling the table with product *pq* for each case (each cell) yields

	$q = 2$	$q = 3$	$q = \ldots$
$p = 2$	✘	✔	✘
$p = 3$	$pq = 6$	✘	$pq > 6$

In none of the possible cases ($p = 2$, $q = 3$ or $p = 3$, $q = 2$, or $p = 2$, $q > 3$) could *pq* equal 6. So, we have that $pq \neq 6$. The answer is (C).

Think outside of the Box.

Strategy Do not limit your thought process. Anything not constrained by the conditions in the problem is possible.

Example: Is *xy* equal to 12 ?

(1)   Either *x* equals 3 or *y* does not equal 2.

(2)   Either *x* equals 6 or *y* does not equal 4.

Here, *x* could be 3 and *y* could be 2 and then $xy = 6 \neq 12$.

Think outside of box: *x* is free to take any value (**including decimals**; we didn't need to use decimals in the premise of our discussion.). So, why constrain ourselves by the impression the problem gives.

x could be 2 and *y* could be 6 and here $xy = 12$. Since we have a double case, the data is not sufficient.

Example:

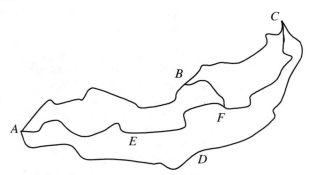

Point N The figure is not drawn to scale.

The figure shows all the available routes between stations A and C. What's the shortest route available to reach Station C from Station A?

(1) $AB < AE < AD$

(2) $BC < EC < CD$

Summing the inequalities in the two statements yields

$$AB + BC < AE + EC < AD + CD$$

$$ABC < AEC < ADC$$

Watch out!

If you answered that ABC is the shortest route of ABC, AEC, and ADC and concluded that the data is sufficient, you are mistaken. Apart from these, there is another route $ABFC$. If $BC < BF + FC$, then ABC is the shortest route. Instead, if $BC > BF + FC$ then ABC is the shortest route. We have a double case and therefore the statements together are *not* sufficient. The answer is (E).

Strategy

Trend analysis

Counting problems are sometimes best solved by Trend Analysis.

Example: Any line that joins two nonadjacent vertices of a polygon is called a diagonal. How many diagonals does the polygon P have?

(1)   If P is a polygon with m sides, then a polygon with $m + 1$ sides would have 5 diagonals more than the number of diagonals P has.

(2)   If P is a polygon with n sides, then a polygon with $n + 1$ sides would have 14 diagonals more than the number of diagonals P has.

Note: The usage of the two different variables, m and n, for a single number in the two statements is OK because each statement is independent of the other. Here, though not mentioned, m means n. We can view the information as data collected from different sources.

Statement (1): If *P* is a polygon of *m* sides, then a polygon with *m* + 1 sides would have 5 diagonals more than the number of diagonals *P* has.

A triangle is a polygon with 3 sides and has 0 diagonals.

A quadrilateral is a polygon with 4 sides and exactly 2 diagonals (a polygon with 4 sides has 2 more diagonals than a polygon with sides 3).

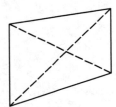

Thick lines are sides and dashed lines are diagonals.

A pentagon is a polygon with 5 sides and exactly 5 diagonals [5 – 2 = 3; A polygon with 5 sides has 3 more diagonals than a polygon with 4 sides.]

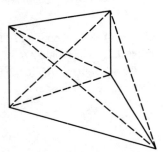

Thick lines are sides and dashed lines are diagonals.

The trend is that the difference increases continuously with the increase in the number of sides of the polygon. So, given the difference we can determine the number of sides *m* of the original polygon because it is unique. The statement is sufficient.

For a particular value of *m*, an *m* + 1 sided polygon would have 5 more diagonals than an *m* sided one. Capturing the value of *m* will determine how many diagonals the polygon has.

Thus, Statement (1) alone is sufficient to answer the question.

The answer is (D).

Statement (2): If *P* is a polygon of *n* sides, then a polygon with *n* + 1 sides would have 14 diagonals more than the number of diagonals *P* has.

As discussed in Statement (1) [though the statement has no data to carry], the number of diagonals is an (continuously) increasing function of the number of sides of the polygon. So, no two polygons of different number of sides will have same number of diagonals. So, *m* + 1, the number of sides of the polygon having 14 diagonals is unique. So, *m* + 1 has a unique value which can be calculated with given data and therefore *m* = the unique value – 1 = another unique value. Given *m*, the number of diagonals the polygon has can be calculated.

Statement (2) is sufficient.

Knowing that a unique value exists for the question isn't enough for data sufficiency unless we are in a position to calculate the unique value. Conversely, a unique value exists if only it is calculable. Otherwise, we might have multiple answers.

Watch out!   Read the problem carefully.

Example: If a and b are two consecutive integers, then what is the value of a?

> (1) $ab = 6$
>
> (2) $3^a > 1$

$a = 2$ and $b = 3$ satisfy both statements. Here, $a = 2$.

$a = 3$ and $b = 2$ satisfy both statements. Here, $a = 3$.

The same two double cases occur with Statement (2) alone as with the statements together. Hence, the statements together are *not* sufficient, and the answer is (E).

Example: If a and b are two consecutive integers, then which is smaller.

> (1) $ab = 6$
>
> (2) $3^a > 1$

Don't assume that because a is written before b that a is the first consecutive integer. b could be the first if b happens to precede a.

Statement (1): $ab = 6$

The product ab equals 6 when

> $\{a, b\} = \{-2, -3\}$ or when $\{-3, -2\}$ or when $\{2, 3\}$ or when $\{3, 2\}$

The first (smaller) number of the two consecutive numbers a and b in the respective order is

> -3 for $\{-2, -3\}$
> -3 for $\{-3, -2\}$
> 2 for $\{2, 3\}$
> 2 for $\{3, 2\}$

We have two possible answers: -2 and 2, not just one. So, we have a double case and the statement is *not* sufficient.

Statement (2): $3^a > 1$

The statement says only that a is greater than 0, which is not useful information.

Since Statement (2) says that a is positive and since b could not be negative (because then $a \cdot b =$ positive $\cdot$ negative $=$ negative $\neq 6$), a and b must equal 2 and 3 or 3 and 2, respectively. Either way, the first number is 2, so the answer is 2 (single solution). Hence, the statements together are sufficient, and the answer is (C).

The language of the question and the statements is important.

Example: There are 300 people in a conference hall. Each person is either an engineer or a professor or both or only a journalist. What is the probability that a person randomly picked from the hall is a journalist?

   (1)   There are 200 people who are an engineer or a professor.

   (2)   There are 200 people who are exclusively an engineer or a professor.

Each of the 300 people in the conference hall is an engineer or a professor or both or a journalist, so there are four categories of people:

Engineers alone

Professors alone

Engineers & Professors

Journalists alone

So, the Number of Engineers + the Number of Professors + the Number of Engineers &Professor(s) + Journalists = 300.

Now, Statement (1) presents the count of Engineers alone + Professors alone + Engineers & Professors as 200 while the count plus the Journalists alone actually equals 300. Hence, the count of Journalists alone must be 300 – 200 = 100. Hence, the probability = 100/300. The statement is sufficient.

But, Statement (2) presents only the count of Engineers alone + Professors alone as 200. Here, the count of Engineers & Professors is not known and therefore the count of Journalists cannot be calculated which means, data insufficient.

The answer is (A).

 Even if we know that a unique value exists for the question, if we cannot calculate the unique value, still data is *not* sufficient.

 Need to analyze a problem completely.

Example: In the figure, lines *l*, *m*, and *n* intersect at *O*. Is $a = 5/7$?

   (1) $x = ay$

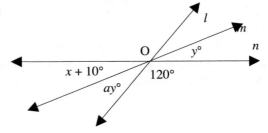

Equating vertical angles yields $y = x + 10$. Now, Statement (1) says, $x = ay$. Plugging the equation $x = ay$ into $y = x + 10$ yields $x = a(x + 10)$. Solving for x yields $x = \dfrac{10a}{1-a}$. Also, $y = x + 10 = \dfrac{10a}{1-a} + 10 = \dfrac{10a + 10 - 10a}{1-a} = \dfrac{10}{1-a}$. So, a is less than 1 since only then $\dfrac{10}{1-a}$ would be positive so that it qualifies to equal angle y as in the figure.

Now, we know that the angle made by any point on a line is 180°. Hence, the angle made by point O on line l is 180°. Hence, $120° + y° + x° = 180°$; $y + x = 60$; $\dfrac{10}{1-a} + x = 60$; $10 + x(1 - a) = 60(1 - a)$; $10 + x - ax = 60 - 60a$; $x(1 - a) = 50 - 60a$; $x = \dfrac{50 - 60a}{1-a}$. Since, $1 - a > 0$, we know, $50 - 60a$ must also be positive so that $x = \dfrac{50 - 60a}{1-a}$ is positive. Hence, $50 - 60a > 0$; $50 > 60a$; $a < 50/60 = 5/6$. So, if we thought a might be 5/7 or may not be 5/7, and there is a double case, we are mistaken. We haven't analyzed the problem completely. The following analysis is pending:

Summing the angles made by point O on line n is 180°. Hence, $120 + ay + x + 10 = 180$. Simplifying yields $ay + x = 50$. Substituting the known results $x = \dfrac{10a}{1-a}$ and $y = \dfrac{10}{1-a}$ into this equation yields $\dfrac{10a}{1-a} + \dfrac{10a}{1-a} = 50$. Hence, $2\left(\dfrac{10a}{1-a}\right) = 50$. Multiplying both sides by $(1 - a)$ yields $20a = 50(1 - a)$. Distributing the 50 yields $20a = 50 - 50a$. Adding $50a$ to both sides yields $70a = 50$. Finally, dividing both sides by 70 yields $a = 5/7$. We have a single value for a. So, the statement is sufficient.

Strategy

If the plausibility set allowed by one statement contains each element of the plausibility set of the other statement:

The later is sufficient, if the former is sufficient.

The former is *not* sufficient, if the later is *not* sufficient.

Later *not* sufficient means nothing about the former.

Former sufficient means nothing about the later.

Example: Is $x^2 > -6x - 5$?

    (1) $-5 < x < -1$

    (2) $-4 < x < -2$

First, let's find for which values of x is $x^2 > -6x - 5$?

The solution of x for the inequality $x^2 > -6x - 5$ to be true is as shown on the number line below:

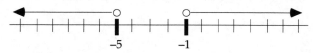

Statement (1) says $-5 < x < -1$ (Horizon for x here is -5 through -1) and for any x in the range, $x^2 > -6x - 5$ is false.

Statement (2) says $-4 < x < -2$ (Horizon for x here is -4 through -2) and for any x in the range as well, $x^2 > -6x - 5$ is false. This is even clear from Statement (1) also.

In short, since the bigger (more comprehensive) statement [Statement (1)] is sufficient, the smaller statement [Statement (2)] is sufficient.

The answer is (D).

Suppose the statements were

    (1) $-6 < x < -1$

    (2) $-4 < x < -2$

Here, as well, Statement (1) is bigger than Statement (2). But, here, in the region $-6 < x < -5$, $x^2 > -6x - 5$ is true; and in the region $-5 < x < -1$, $x^2 > -6x - 5$ is false. So, this is a double case, and Statement (1) is not sufficient.

In case, the bigger statement is not sufficient, the smaller statement must be analyzed separately. Statement (2): $-4 < x < -2$ is sure a region throughout which $x^2 > -6x - 5$ is false; Data sufficient.

The answer is (B).

Summary:

If the bigger statement is sufficient, then the smaller statement is sufficient.

If the bigger (more comprehensive) statement is not sufficient, analyze the smaller statement separately.

Though we treat statements separately, we can take clues from the other statement. Derivations of one statement can act as clues to the other statement. This is because any derivation is also a property of the unique realistic system that the problem focuses. But, since according to GMAT Data Sufficiency structure, we treat statements separately, the clues must be proven separately in the statement receiving the clue. The best way to prove a clue is to substitute it and check whether the statement is satisfied.

Here are few examples:

Example 1: Suppose one statement says or derives that the solution for z is 3 or 5. The other statement can use this as a clue. But before that, we have to check whether we have means to prove the clue. This is easily done by the feasibility test called substitution. So, we substitute for both $z = 3$ once and $z = 5$ once; see which one is feasible since we already know at least one would be feasible (lest the system wouldn't be realistic). Thus, the clues helped us save the re-evaluation.

Example 2: Suppose Statement (1) says, the *Question* = 9 alone. This comes as a clue to Statement (2). Since we know at least one clue will work, while we have only one clue, the clue must be feasible. No need to check the same. Now, the remaining job is to find solutions that Statement (2) allows apart from 9. If we have any such solution, we have a double case. Lest the statement is sufficient. Here, we save the effort of deducing *Question* = 9.

Example: If $x \neq 0$, what is x ?

(1) $\dfrac{x\left(x^5\right)^2}{x^4} = 128$

(2) $\dfrac{x\left(x^2\right)^5}{x^3} = 256$

Statement (1): $\dfrac{x\left(x^5\right)^2}{x^4} = 128$

Apply the rule $\left(x^a\right)^b = x^{ab}$ to the expression $\dfrac{x\left(x^5\right)^2}{x^4}$: $\dfrac{x \cdot x^{10}}{x^4}$

Apply the rule $x^a \cdot x^b = x^{a+b}$ to the new expression: $\dfrac{x \cdot x^{10}}{x^4} = \dfrac{x^{11}}{x^4}$

Finally, apply the rule $\dfrac{x^a}{x^b} = x^{a-b}$ to the latest expression: $\dfrac{x^{11}}{x^4} = x^{11-4} = x^7$

This says Statement (1) is true.

Statement (2): $\dfrac{x\left(x^2\right)^5}{x^3} = 256$

By similar steps as in Statement (1), we get Statement (2) is $x^8 = 256$. We can use the clue from Statement (1) that $x = 2$ [Though we use the clue in Statement (2), note that the clue is local to Statement (1) only]. So, no need to calculate it again. But, still, the exponent of x^8 is even and therefore it will have two roots (two solutions). While 2 is one solution and (that's why) x^8 equals 256 the other solution could be $x = -2$, and even then x^8 equals 256.

The answer is (A).

Watch out!

Even if we use only a small detail provided by a statement, we consider the statement used.

Watch out!

Don't be misled by seemingly easy problems. They might have an intriguing twist.

Don't be complacent. Analyze the problem to its complete end.

Start a problem by first holding your hands shielding Statement (2). So, now you have only two things: The Question Setup and Statement (1).

Next, shield Statement (1), so you now have only two things: the Question Setup and Statement (2).

If you are sure that either statement alone is sufficient, un-shield both statements (Keep the traces of the last Statement in your mind intact). Now, try to solve the problem as if it were a multiple-choice problem with (properties in) both statements included in the question.

Example 1: $\left(x - \dfrac{y}{3}\right) - \left(y - \dfrac{x}{3}\right) =$

(1) $x - y = 9$

(2) $x + y = 11$

Looking at the two simple linear equations in the statements, you might be lulled into thinking the statements together determine x and y and therefore that the statements together are required to solve the expression, especially since the expression $\left(x - \dfrac{y}{3}\right) - \left(y - \dfrac{x}{3}\right)$ is a bit complex. This happens often when you are in hurry, and since we hate exams, you will unknowingly be moving yourself into a comfort zone (which means minimizing analyzing). Then, you start seeing the problem as though both statements are required. If your hands aren't holding a pencil, this is a strong indication that you have been trying to find a comfort zone. You answered (C), while the original answer is (A), shown below. For the same reason, the transformation "What is x?" or "What is y?" is wrong.

$$\left(x - \frac{y}{3}\right) - \left(y - \frac{x}{3}\right) = x - \frac{y}{3} - y + \frac{x}{3} = \frac{4}{3}x - \frac{4}{3}y = \frac{4}{3}(x - y) = \frac{4}{3}(9) = \quad (\text{since } x - y = 9)$$

$$12$$

The answer is (A).

Example 2: The figure shows the path of a circular racetrack. What is the length of the circular arc *AB*?

(1) The full perimeter of the sector in miles is $\dfrac{\pi}{6} + 1$

(2) The net length of the two arms (straight lines) in the sector is 1.

If you thought arc *AB* equals the perimeter of full sector minus the arms and therefore answered Statement (1) minus Statement (2) and thereby concluded the statements together are required, you are mistaken.

The arms (radii) of the sector are equal in length. The net length of the two is 1. Therefore, the length of each must be 1/2.

When calculating distance, degree measure must be converted to radian measure. To convert degree measure to radian measure, multiply by the conversion factor $\dfrac{\pi}{180}$. Multiplying 60° by $\dfrac{\pi}{180}$ yields $60 \cdot \dfrac{\pi}{180} = \dfrac{\pi}{3}$. Now, the length of arc traveled by the car in moving from point A to point B is S. Plugging this information into the formula $S = R\theta$ yields $S = \dfrac{1}{2} \cdot \dfrac{\pi}{3} = \dfrac{\pi}{6}$. Now, π is a numeric constant and equals approximately 3.14. Therefore, Statement (2) alone is sufficient.

Statement (1) gives $\dfrac{\pi}{6} + 1$. Suppose the length of each arm is r. Then, the length of the two arms $= 2r$ and the length of the circular arc is the central angle $\dfrac{\pi}{3}$ times arm length r which equals $\dfrac{\pi}{3} r$. So, the net length of the two is $\dfrac{\pi}{3} r + 2r = r\left(\dfrac{\pi}{3} + 2\right)$. Statement (1) gives that this equals $\dfrac{\pi}{6} + 1$. Therefore, we have

$r\left(\dfrac{\pi}{3} + 2\right) = \dfrac{\pi}{6} + 1$, or $r = \dfrac{\dfrac{\pi}{6} + 1}{\dfrac{\pi}{3} + 2} = \dfrac{1}{2}$. Hence, the length of the arc AB equals $\dfrac{\pi}{3}$ times arm length, which is

1/2 and this equals $\dfrac{\pi}{6}$. Therefore, the statement is sufficient.

The answer is (D), either statement alone is sufficient.

Part Three

Math Review

Substitution

Substitution is a very useful technique for solving GMAT math problems, whether it is a Multiple-choice problem or a Data Sufficiency problem. It often reduces hard problems to routine ones.

All math problems consist of only *known properties* and *unknown properties*.

Here is the standard method of substitution:

> **Substitute for the unknown properties based on the known properties.**
>
> **In other words,**
>
> **Choose a set of values for the unknown properties. If all the known properties are satisfied, then the set is a valid one.**

Any set of values we choose for the unknown properties is referred to as a plug-in.

Even the rules in the problem are properties.

Whether it is a Multiple-choice problem or a Data Sufficiency problem, the standard methodology is the same.

In a multiple-choice problem, the unknown property is quite often the question and this unknown property is substituted into the answer-choices to see which one of them satisfies the rules in the problem.

Example (Multiple-choice):

If n is an even integer, which one of the following is an odd integer?

(A) n^2 (B) $\dfrac{n+1}{2}$ (C) $-2n-4$ (D) $2n^2-3$ (E) $\sqrt{n^2+2}$

Properties: n is an even integer.

Note that "n is an even integer" is a known property. The question is an unknown property. The property of (imposed on) the unknown property is that it is an odd integer. So, we **must** choose the answer-choice that is odd. Let's follow a step-by-step methodology to solve the problem:

Step 1: List the properties of the problem.

    1) The known property: n is even.

    2) The unknown property: *The question* is odd.

    3) The answer-choices: (A) n^2 (B) $\dfrac{n+1}{2}$ (C) $-2n-4$ (D) $2n^2-3$ (E) $\sqrt{n^2+2}$

Step 2: Choose a substitution that has the known properties.

The only known property is that n is even, so choose, say, $n = 2$ as a substitution.

Step 3: Now do the substitution.

The multiple-choice format says we must pick one answer-choice, so substitute $n = 2$ in the answer-choices to determine which one is odd.

Now, n^2 becomes $2^2 = 4$, which is not an odd integer. So, eliminate (A). Next, $\dfrac{n+1}{2} = \dfrac{2+1}{2} = \dfrac{3}{2}$ is not an odd integer—eliminate (B). Next, $-2n - 4 = -2 \cdot 2 - 4 = -4 - 4 = -8$ is not an odd integer—eliminate (C). Next, $2n^2 - 3 = 2(2)^2 - 3 = 2(4) - 3 = 8 - 3 = 5$ is odd and therefore the answer is possibly (D). Finally, $\sqrt{n^2+2} = \sqrt{2^2+2} = \sqrt{4+2} = \sqrt{6}$, which is not odd—eliminate (E). The answer is (D).

Step 4: If we could not arrive at a unique answer-choice, then repeat the check with another suitable plug-in. Do this until we get a unique answer-choice. This is to say, start from Step 2 again.

Whether it is a multiple-choice problem or a data sufficiency problem, the process is the same.

Example 1:   Which expression is odd $n^2 + 3$ or $n^2 + 4$?

      (1) n is an even integer.

      (2) $-2n - 4$ is an even integer.

Properties: The question "Which expression is odd $n^2 + 3$ or $n^2 + 4$?" is a property in the sense that the answer is true or false. $n^2 + 3$ and $n^2 + 4$ are properties as well in the sense that they equal some values. Each property is as well a system rule. For example, "Which expression is odd $n^2 + 3$ or $n^2 + 4$?" is true is a system rule and is a property or "Which expression is odd $n^2 + 3$ or $n^2 + 4$?" is false is a system rule and is a property. Since we do not know whether "Which expression is odd $n^2 + 3$ or $n^2 + 4$?" is true or whether it is false, it is an unknown property.

In Data Sufficiency problems, the statements are properties and each must be studied separately. Hence, we have

Statement (1): n is an even integer.

Property revealed by the statement:

n is even

Choose a substitution, for example, $n = 0$ and substitute in the answer-choices:

$n^2 + 3 = 0^2 + 3 = 3$, odd.

$n^2 + 4 = 0^2 + 4 = 4$, even.

Hence, the statement is sufficient.

Statement (2): $-2n - 4$ is an even integer.

Property revealed by the statement:

$-2n - 4$ is even

or

$-2n = 4 + \text{even} = \text{even}$

or

$n = \text{even}/2,$

which may or may not be even

Hence, we **must** choose two substitutions, one where n is odd, and one where n is even.

Choose $n = 1$ (odd) and substitute in the question:

$n^2 + 3 = 1^2 + 3 = 4$, even.

$n^2 + 4 = 1^2 + 4 = 5$, odd.

Here, $n^2 + 4$ is an odd number. This says the question is $n^2 + 4$.

Choose $n = 2$ (even) and substitute in the question:

$n^2 + 3 = 2^2 + 3 = 7$, odd.

$n^2 + 4 = 2^2 + 4 = 8$, even.

Here, $n^2 + 3$ is an odd number. This says the question is $n^2 + 3$.

We have a double case and therefore the statement is *not* sufficient.

The answer is (A).

Example 2: If n is an integer, which of the following CANNOT be an integer?

(A) $\dfrac{n-2}{2}$ (B) $\sqrt{n}$ (C) $\dfrac{2}{n+1}$ (D) $\sqrt{n^2+3}$ (E) $\sqrt{\dfrac{1}{n^2+2}}$

The only properties are

n is an integer.

The property question is not an integer.

Choose $n = 0$ according to the known properties, and substitute:

$\dfrac{n-2}{2} = \dfrac{0-2}{2} = \dfrac{-2}{2} = -1$, which is an integer. So, eliminate (A). Next, $\sqrt{n} = \sqrt{0} = 0$. Eliminate (B). Next,

$\dfrac{2}{n+1} = \dfrac{2}{0+1} = \dfrac{2}{1} = 2$. Eliminate (C). Next, $\sqrt{n^2+3} = \sqrt{0^2+3} = \sqrt{0+3} = \sqrt{3}$, which is *not* an integer—it

may be our answer. However, $\sqrt{\dfrac{1}{n^2+2}} = \sqrt{\dfrac{1}{0^2+2}} = \sqrt{\dfrac{1}{0+2}} = \sqrt{\dfrac{1}{2}}$, which is *not* an integer as well. So, we choose another number, say, 1. Then $\sqrt{n^2+3} = \sqrt{1^2+3} = \sqrt{1+3} = \sqrt{4} = 2$, which is an integer, eliminating (D). Thus, choice (E), $\sqrt{\dfrac{1}{n^2+2}}$, is the answer.

Strategy

Substitution can be done for any property in the problem, not just for a question, an answer-choice, or an unknown property; and, occasionally, it can be done for the known properties as well.

Example 3:   If $x + y + z = 6$, then do any two of the three numbers x, y, and z sum to 3?

(1) x, y, and z are three different positive integers.

(2) x, y, and z are consecutive integers.

Properties:

A) $x + y + z = 6$

B) The question setup is an unknown property of type Yes/No. So, if any two of x, y, and z sum to 3, the answer is Yes; and if they don't, the answer is No.

Statement (1): x, y, and z are three different positive integers.

Properties:

(1) $x + y + z = 6$

(2) x, y, and z are three different positive integers. Hence, $x \neq y$, $y \neq z$, and $x \neq z$.

Let x, y, and z be the different numbers, in increasing order of size. Then we have the inequality $x < y < z$.

Now, choosing a plug-in, assume $x > 1$. From the inequality, we have $y > 2$ and $z > 3$. Adding the inequalities yields $x + y + z > 6$. This violates the known property $x + y + z = 6$. Hence, the assumption $x > 1$ fails. Since x is a positive integer, x must be 1.

Next, assume $y > 2$. Then $z > 3$ and $x + y + z = 1 + y + z > 1 + 2 + 3 = 6$, so $x + y + z > 6$. This contradicts the given property $x + y + z = 6$. Hence, the assumption $y > 2$ fails (is incorrect). Since we know y is greater than x (= 1), y must be 2.

Now, substituting known values in equation $x + y + z = 6$ yields $1 + 2 + z = 6$, or $z = 3$.

No two of the three numbers 1, 2, and 3 sum to 3.

Hence, the statement is sufficient.

The answer is (D).

Statement (2): x, y, and z are consecutive integers.

Properties:

(1) $x + y + z = 6$

(2) x, y, and z are consecutive integers.

Choosing a plug-in, suppose $a + 1$, $a + 2$ and $a + 3$ are the three consecutive integers x, y, and z, respectively. Since $x + y + z = 6$, we have

$$(a + 1) + (a + 2) + (a + 3) = 6$$

$$3a + 6 = 6$$

$$3a = 0$$

$$a = 0$$

Hence, the numbers are $a + 1 = 0 + 1 = 1$, $a + 2 = 0 + 2 = 2$, and $a + 3 = 0 + 3 = 3$. Now, check whether any two of the numbers sum to 3, and answer the question with "Yes" or "No." This can be determined and therefore the statement is sufficient.

The answer is "No," no two of the numbers sum to 3.

General mistakes:

Never use unknown properties to generate a substitution.

If a question asks "Is $p + q = 0$?" and you thought this occurs only when $p = -q$ and thought that the statement satisfying the condition would be data sufficient, you might be mistaken.

Example 4:   Does $p + q = 0$?

      (1) $(p + q)(p - q) = 0$

The question reveals only the unknown property called the question setup, which equals "Yes" if $p + q = 0$ and "No" if $p + q \neq 0$.

Now, let's analyze Statement (1).

Since statements are always known properties, we can list the statement as a known property:

$$(p + q)(p - q) = 0$$

As mentioned, the following analysis is mistaken: The statement satisfies the *condition $p = -q$* (on substituting $-q$ with p in the statement, the left-hand side results in 0, which equals the right hand side.) Hence, the statement is *sufficient*. ✖ This is wrong.

The mistake occurs in using the property $p = -q$ as the criteria for choosing the substitution while $p = -q$ is still an unknown property. A substitution example need not be bound by unknown properties.

The scope of this incorrect substitution is to understand that "Since the substitution $p = -q$ worked, this is *one* possible solution." So, $p = -q$ could be true and the question setup could be "Yes." But this substitution doesn't say whether there are any other solutions not binding to $p = -q$ which is when we get the answer to the question as "No" or "False." Hence, we could have a double case, in which case the answer is *Data not sufficient*.

The solutions of the given property $(p + q)(p - q) = 0$ are $p = q$ and $p = -q$, and the value of the question $p = -q$ is true in first case and not necessarily true in the second case. So, $p = -q$ could be true, or it could be false. The statement is *not* sufficient.

Substitution can show *Data Insufficiency*, but never *Data Sufficiency*.

This is because to show *Data Insufficiency*, just two substitutions can generate a double case: One substitution to show that the question has *Value* 1, and the other to show the question has a different *Value* 2. Since we do not have a unique solution, the *data is insufficient*.

But to show *Data Sufficiency*, we **must** check all possible substitutions that can be done and show that each yields a unique value for the question. Suppose there are n unknown properties. Then a combination of each possible value of each of the n unknown properties in their respective domain is a substitution example. Now, we must confirm that all these combinations yield a single value for the question (numeric or yes/no type) to be able to say *data sufficient*. But to check the substitution against all these possible combinations is a tedious process, so the substitution method generally works better to prove *insufficiency* than *sufficiency*.

Nevertheless, much depends on the problem. Sometimes, it is easier showing *Sufficiency* than *Insufficiency*.

Before going ahead, let's discuss what are Boundary Conditions?

Boundary Conditions

These are the points at which the *trend* of a question can change. For example, for the question "Is $x > 2$?", 2 is the boundary point because while $x \leq 2$, the answer has been No and immediately after 2, the answer is Yes. This change in the trend is brought about by the boundary value 2, and the boundary is for the variable x. "$x = 2$" is the boundary condition. $x \leq 2$ on the number line is the side to which the answer is different from the answer to the other side, $x > 2$. If we are given $x + y = 3$, then the boundary condition for y is $y = 1$. Because, to the right side of $y = 1$ on the number line, x is less than 2 and to the left side, it is greater than 2. Now, let's discuss how, we can use boundary conditions for answering data sufficiency problems.

Consider a question setup

$$\text{Is } x^3 - 6x^2 + 11x - 6 > 0?$$

First, we need to find the boundary points. Boundary points are the points that can change the trend of a question. In this case, the sign of the expression. In the question "$x^3 - 6x^2 + 11x - 6 > 0$?", for example, $x^3 - 6x^2 + 11x - 6$ equals 0 when x equals 1. Now, a little before 1, say at $x = 0.99$, the expression is less than 0 (negative): $x^3 - 6x^2 + 11x - 6 = (0.99)^3 - 6(0.99)^2 + 11(0.99) - 6 = -0.020301$. And a little after 1, it is greater than 0 (positive). So, $x = 1$ is a boundary condition. Here, the boundary conditions are the roots of the equation $x^3 - 6x^2 + 11x - 6 = 0$.

There can be more than 1 boundary point. For example, $x^3 - 6x^2 + 11x - 6$ also equals 0 when $x = 2$ and $x = 3$.

Now, the trend that the expression $x^3 - 6x^2 + 11x - 6$ is positive continues to exist from $x = 1$ to $x = 2$ (root to root). After that, it is again negative until the next root , that is, to $x = 3$. Clearly, $x^3 - 6x^2 + 11x - 6$ is positive for all x greater than 3 because we do not have any roots after 3 itself. Similarly, $x^3 - 6x^2 + 11x - 6$ is negative for all x less than 1 (we have no roots less than 1).

The following graph shows how the expression $x^3 - 6x^2 + 11x - 6$ changes with x.

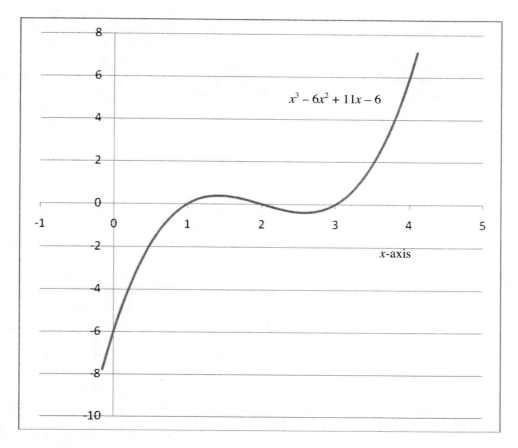

$x^3 - 6x^2 + 11x - 6$

Now, let's study the technique in more detail.

<u>Trend change between boundary conditions</u>

As we has discussed, trends can change the boundary conditions. So, if a statement's scope is completely within two adjacent boundaries, there won't be any change in the trend, which means the data is sufficient.

If a statement's scope covers more than 1 boundary condition, then clearly the trend may change. Here, we may have a double case in which case the statement is not sufficient.

Here is an example:

Example 5:   Is $x^3 - 6x^2 + 11x - 6 > 0$?

    (1) $1 < x < 2$

    (2) $1 < x < 3$

The roots of $x^3 - 6x^2 + 11x - 6 = 0$ are 1, 2, and 3, so these are the boundary points.

Statement (1): $1 < x < 2$: The region for x doesn't include even a single root. This means, there is no trend change in the region (Observe the graph above. For each point, in the region, not including 1 and 2, the expression $x^3 - 6x^2 + 11x - 6$ is positive). Hence, the statement alone is sufficient.

Statement (2): $1 < x < 3$: The region includes one root (the root 2). This says, there may be one trend change. When there is at least one trend change, we have a double case. Refer to the curve for the expression in the figure above. For the region $1 < x \le 2$, the expression is not negative and for $2 < x < 3$, it is negative. So, the statement allows one trend change, which means we have a double case. The statement is not sufficient alone.

The answer is (A).

Example 6:   Is $x^3 - 6x^2 + 11x - 6 > 0$?

      (1) $2 < x < 3$

      (2) $1 \le x < 2$

The roots of $x^3 - 6x^2 + 11x - 6 = 0$ are 1, 2, and 3, so these are the boundary points.

Statement (1) $2 < x < 3$: The region for x doesn't include even a single root. This means, there is no trend change in the region [Observe the graph above. For each point, in the region, not including 2 and 3, the expression $x^3 - 6x^2 + 11x - 6$ is negative]. Hence, the statement alone is sufficient.

Statement (2) $1 \le x < 2$: The region includes the root 1. Hence, there may be a trend change unless the question is "Is $x^3 - 6x^2 + 11x - 6 \ge 0$?" or Is "$x^3 - 6x^2 + 11x - 6 \le 0$?" Therefore, there should be one trend change, and we should have a double case. Observe that for $x = 1$, the expression equals 0 and for $1 < x < 2$, it doesn't. So, we have a double case, and the statement is not sufficient.

The answer is (A).

Example 7:   Is $x^3 - 6x^2 + 11x - 6 \le 0$?

      (1) $2 < x < 3$

      (2) $2 \le x < 3$

The roots of $x^3 - 6x^2 + 11x - 6 = 0$ are 1, 2, and 3, so these are the boundary points.

Statement (1) $2 < x < 3$: Since there are no roots in the region, there is no possibility of a double case. Therefore, the data is sufficient.

Statement (2) $2 \le x < 3$: The region includes the root 2. Now, we need to check whether the root itself causes a trend change. For that, first we need to split the region as $x = 2$ and $2 < x < 3$. For $2 < x < 3$, expression is positive and the answer to the question is No. For $x = 2$, the answer to the question is Yes. Thus, we have a trend change, which causes a double case. Therefore, the statement is not sufficient.

The answer is (A).

Example 8:   Is $x^3 - 6x^2 + 11x - 6 < 0$?

(1) $1 < x \leq 2$

(2) $2 \leq x < 3$

The roots of $x^3 - 6x^2 + 11x - 6 = 0$ are 1, 2, and 3, so these are the boundary points.

Statement (1) $1 < x \leq 2$: The only root in the region is 2. For $1 < x \leq 2$, $x^3 - 6x^2 + 11x - 6$ is zero or positive (not < 0) and therefore the answer is No. Even for $x = 2$, $x^3 - 6x^2 + 11x - 6$ is not less than 0. Therefore, the statement is sufficient.

Statement (2) $2 \leq x < 3$: The region includes only the root 2. For $x = 2$, $x^3 - 6x^2 + 11x - 6 = 0$. The answer is No. For $2 < x < 3$, $x^3 - 6x^2 + 11x - 6$ is negative. So, the answer is Yes. This is a double case and therefore the statement is *not* sufficient.

The answer is (A).

Example 9:   Is $x^2 - 10x > -20$?

(3) $3 < x < 7$

(4) $2 < x < 9$

The polynomial $x^2 - 10x + 20$ is of degree 2 (x^2 is the highest power). Hence, $x^2 - 10x + 20 = 0$ has exactly two roots since the expression $x^2 - 10x + 20$ is not a perfect square trinomial. Since it is not a perfect square trinomial, we have two different roots and again the trend changes twice (in this case, negative to positive once and positive to negative back; the roots are themselves the points where the trend changes.) So, if we have two roots, we have two trend changes.). We can tactically guess that $x^2 - 10x + 20$ is not a perfect square trinomial because if it were the expression would have a trend change from positive to zero and then back to positive. Throughout this, the answer to the question "Is $x^2 - 10x < -20$?" is unanimously No double case. This means the *question* alone is sufficient, and again the GMAT does not ask such data sufficiency questions.

Statement (1): $3 < x < 7$

For $x = 3$, $x^2 - 10x + 20 = 3^2 - 10(3) + 20 = -1$ (negative).

For $x = 4$, $x^2 - 10x + 20 = 4^2 - 10(4) + 20 = -4$ (negative).

For $x = 6$, $x^2 - 10x + 20 = 6^2 - 10(6) + 20 = -4$ (negative).

For $x = 7$, $x^2 - 10x + 20 = 7^2 - 10(7) + 20 = -1$ (negative).

For $x = 3$, the expression equals –1; and for $x = 4$, the expression equals –4. It appears that as x increases, we are moving farther from the nearest boundary point (the point where the expression equals 0).

For $x = 6$, the expression equals –4; and for $x = 7$, the expression equals –1. It appears that as x increases, we are nearing the next boundary point.

It appears that both boundary points of the system are not within the region $3 < x < 7$. So, the trend of the expression $x^2 - 10x + 20$ hasn't changed in the region. This means, $x^2 - 10x + 20$ must be less than 0 for all $3 < x < 7$.

Statement (2): $2 < x < 9$

For $x = 2$, $x^2 - 10x + 20 = 2^2 - 10(2) + 20 = 4$ (positive).

For $x = 3$, $x^2 - 10x + 20 = 3^2 - 10(3) + 20 = -1$ (negative). So, there appears to be a trend change between $x = 2$ and $x = 3$. Hence, we have one boundary point here.

For $x = 8$, $x^2 - 10x + 20 = 8^2 - 10(8) + 20 = 4$ (positive). So, there appears to be another trend change between $x = 3$ and $x = 8$. Hence, we have another boundary point here.

For $x = 9$, $x^2 - 10x + 20 = 9^2 - 10(9) + 20 = 11$ (positive).

Now, our range $2 < x < 9$ lies between the boundary points.

Hence, Statement (2) is spread across both sides of at least one boundary point and therefore we have at least two possible answers. So, the statement is not sufficient.

The answer is (A).

Problem Set A: Substitution

1. Is x equal to -1?

    (1) $|2x - 2| + |2x + 2| = 4$

    (2) $|3x - 2| + |3x + 2| = 6$

2. Is x equal to -1?

    (1) $|3x - 2| + |3x + 2| = 6$

    (2) $|x - 1| + |3x + 2| = 5$

3. Is x equal to 1?

    (1) $(3x - 2) + (3x + 2) = 6$

    (2) $x^2 + 2x = 3$

4. Is the integer k a prime number?

    (1) $k + 1$ is prime.

    (2) $k + 2$ is not prime.

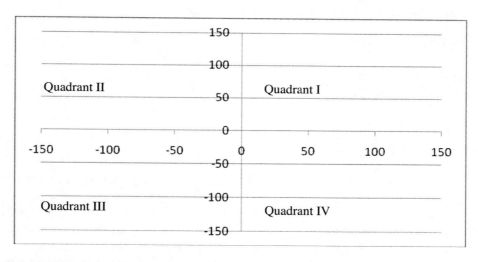

5. In which quadrant does the point (p, q) lie?

    (1) $2p + 3q = 5$

    (2) $4p - q = 7$

6. Is $x = 9$?

    (1) $x^2 - 7x - 18 = 0$

    (2) $x^2 - 10x + 9 = 0$

7. Is $x = 9$?

    (1) $x^2 - 7x - 18 = 0$

    (2) $x^2 - 10x + 10 = 0$

Answers and Solutions to Problem Set A: Substitution

1.   Is x equal to -1?

    (1) $|2x - 2| + |2x + 2| = 4$

    (2) $|3x - 2| + |3x + 2| = 6$

Substitution A:

Both statements are satisfied when $x = -1$.

$|2(-1) - 2| + |2(-1) + 2| = |-2 - 2| + |-2 + 2| = |-4| + |0| = 4 + 0 = 4$.

$|3x - 2| + |3x + 2| = |3(-1) - 2| + |3(-1) + 2| = |-3 - 2| + |-3 + 2| = |-5| + |-1| = 5 + 1 = 6$.

Substitution B:

Both statements are also satisfied when $x = 1$.

$|2(1) - 2| + |2(1) + 2| = |2 - 2| + |2 + 2| = |0| + |4| = 0 + 4 = 4$.

$|3x - 2| + |3x + 2| = |3(1) - 2| + |3(1) + 2| = |3 - 2| + |3 + 2| = |1| + |5| = 1 + 5 = 6$.

Hence, we have a double case with the statements taken together.

The answer is (E).

2.   Is x equal to -1?

    (1) $|3x - 2| + |3x + 2| = 6$

    (2) $|x - 1| + |3x + 2| = 5$

Statement (1) is satisfied when $x = -1$:

$$|3x - 2| + |3x + 2| = |3(-1) - 2| + |3(-1) + 2| = |-3 - 2| + |-3 + 2| = |-5| + |-1| = 5 + 1 = 6$$

Hence, Statement (1) supports x being -1 in the sense that "x COULD BE -1." If -1 is the only solution for x from Statement (1), then the statement is sufficient and says "Yes, x equals -1." If it has more solutions, it says "Can't say, x could be -1 or some other solution." Before trying to find other solutions, let's wait until we have also analyzed Statement (2). [This is not a breach of conservativeness. We are trying to determine whether there is a message in Statement (2) that we can pass to Statement (1). Note that it still has to be proven in Statement (1) if not already proven by it!]

Substitution shows that Statement (2) is not satisfied when $x = -1$:

$$|x - 1| + |3x + 2| = |-1 - 1| + |3(-1) + 2| = |-2| + |-1| = 2 + 1 = 3, \text{ not } 5$$

Therefore, the statement does not support x being -1. Hence, the statement says "x CANNOT equal -1." This has two points to tell. First, from the assertive reply that Statement (2) gives, Statement (2) is sufficient. Second, since the two statements must have at least one common solution (otherwise it would not be a valid problem), Statement (1) must have at least one more solution apart from -1 (which means not -1 again). This highlights the double case with Statement (1). Clearly, Statement (1) is *not* sufficient.

Strategy

Here, Statement (2) is reducing the effort of analyzing Statement (1). Had Statement (2) not told us that x is not -1, we would not have known that Statement (1) had other solutions apart from -1 unless we completely analyzed Statement (1). We could have analyzed Statement (1) without using Statement (2), but Statement (2) helped reduce the computation. We can occasionally take such inputs from one statement to the other with the sole purpose of reducing computations. But this still means we analyzed the statements separately.

The answer is (B).

3.   Is x equal to 1?

    (1) $(3x - 2) + (3x + 2) = 6$

    (2) $x^2 + 2x = 3$

Both statements satisfy the question (more precisely they are compatible with the question). The problem model in Statement (1) is a linear equation in x, so degree is 1. Hence, we expect a single solution, and $x = 1$ must be it.

Since the problem model in Statement (2) is a quadratic equation in x, the degree of the equation is 2 and we expect two solutions.[*] The solutions are either equal (here, data sufficient) or unequal (here, data insufficient because there is one more solution other than $x = 1$). Solutions are equal when the equation taken to the left side or right side yields a perfect square trinomial such as $x^2 + 2ax + a^2 = 0$ or $x^2 - 2ax + a^2 = 0$. But, subtracting 3 from both sides of $x^2 + 2x = 3$ yields $x^2 + 2x - 3 = 0$. This is not same as the corresponding perfect square trinomial form, which is $x^2 + 2x + 1 = (x + 1)^2$, and therefore we say there are two different solutions and therefore the statement is *not* sufficient.

The answer is (A).

4.   Is the integer k a prime number?

    (1) $k + 1$ is prime.

    (2) $k + 2$ is not prime.

The properties we know are

       k is an integer.

       k is an unknown property. Hence, $k + 1$ and $k + 2$ are unknown properties as well.

What do we do? Substitute for unknown properties.

Suppose $k = 2$ (chosen such that $k + 1 = 3$ is prime and $k + 2 = 4$ is not prime). Now, both statements are satisfied, and here k is prime.

Suppose $k = 4$ (chosen such that $k + 1 = 5$ is prime and $k + 2 = 6$ is not prime). Now, both statements are satisfied as well, and here k is not prime.

Hence, we have a double case and therefore the statements together are *not* sufficient. The answer is (E).

---

[*] For math experts: We have two real solutions, one real solution, or two imaginary ones.

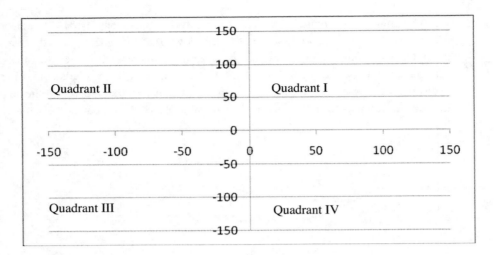

5.   In which quadrant does the point (p, q) lie?

   (1) $2p + 3q = 5$

   (2) $4p - q = 7$

Statement (1): $2p + 3q = 5$

$p = 1$ and $q = 1$ is a solution of Statement (1) since $2(1) + 3(1) = 5$, and the point $(p, q) = (1, 1)$ lies in Quadrant I (from the figure both x and y coordinates are positive in Quadrant I only).

Now, $p = -1$ and $q = 7/3$ is also a solution since $2(-1) + 3(7/3) = 5$, and the point $(p, q) = (-1, 7/3)$ lies in Quadrant II (from the figure, the x-coordinate is negative and the y-coordinate is positive in Quadrant II only).

This is a double case, so the statement is *not* sufficient.

Statement (2): $4p - q = 7$

$p = 1$ and $q = -3$ is a solution of Statement (2) since $4(1) - (-3) = 7$, and the point $(p, q) = (1, -3)$ lies in Quadrant IV (from the figure, the x-coordinate is positive and the y-coordinate negative in Quadrant IV only).

Now, $p = -1$ and $q = -11$ is a solution of Statement (2) since $4(-1) - (-11) = 7$, and the point $(p, q) = (-1, -11)$ lies in Quadrant III (from the figure, both x- and y-coordinates are negative only in Quadrant III).

This is a double case, so the statement is *not* sufficient.

With the two different linear equations, we have a single point, which lies in only one quadrant. Hence, the statements together are sufficient, and the answer is (C).

6. Is $x = 9$?

     (1) $x^2 - 7x - 18 = 0$

     (2) $x^2 - 10x + 9 = 0$

Substitute $x = 9$ to check whether either statement supports x being 9.

Statement (1): $x^2 - 7x - 18 = 9^2 - 7(9) - 18 = 81 - 63 - 18 = 0$.

Hence, Statement (1) says "yes x could be 9, but not sure x equals only 9." That is, it doesn't confirm that 9 is the only solution. The concern is that the equation $x^2 - 7x - 18 = 0$ is of degree 2 and therefore can have two different solutions (including 9) since the expression is not a perfect square trinomial. (If it were a perfect square trinomial, we would have a single solution.) We do not need to evaluate the other solution since we are sure there exists another solution other than 9. Since x could be 9 or the other solution, we have a double case. The statement is *not* sufficient.

Similarly, Statement (2) $x^2 - 10x + 9 = 9^2 - 10(9) + 9 = 81 - 90 + 9 = -9 + 9 = 0$ satisfies x being 9, but says one solution other than 9 exists as well. Hence, again, we have a double case, and therefore the statement is *not* sufficient.

Now, the statements together $x^2 - 7x - 18 = 0$ and $x^2 - 10x + 9 = 0$ indicate that each of them has exactly 2 solutions and exactly one of them is common (regardless, that is 9). Hence, with the statements together, we have a single solution, which can be compared with 9 (the solution equals 9) and answered. The answer is (C), the statements together are sufficient.

7. Is $x = 9$?

     (1) $x^2 - 7x - 18 = 0$

     (2) $x^2 - 10x + 10 = 0$

Statement (1) supports x being 9. But since it is a quadratic equation and not a perfect square trinomial, it will have one more solution as well. Hence, the statement is *not* sufficient.

Statement (2) does not support $x^2 - 10x + 10 = 0$ being 9. Hence, Statement (2) says $x = 9$ is false. The statement is sufficient.

The answer is (B).

Defined Functions

Defined functions are very common on the GMAT, and at first most students struggle with them. Yet, once you get used to them, defined functions can be some of the easiest problems on the test. In this type of problem, you will be given a symbol and a property that defines the symbol.

Before looking at some examples, let's discuss what defined functions are and what they are for. Suppose you are a businessman, and you want to offer 25% of the profit on different products as commission to a stakeholder. The calculation is (Selling Price – Cost Price) · 25/100. Reasonably, you don't want to do the entire calculation for each product each day of each month. You would prefer a facility that allows you to input the selling price and the cost price and get back the calculated commission. To reduce work is what formulae are for, frame once and use indefinitely. If something must be calculated only once, you probably would not call it a formula. Now, to have the facility on your programmable device, you would need memory elements to hold the input data—here one memory element for Selling Price and one for Cost Price. Name the memory element for the former x and for the later y. So, the formula now becomes

$$(x - y) \cdot 25/100$$

Input the formula in the calculator and use it repeatedly. Each time you only need to input the arguments, price x and cost y. This programmable advantage is the purpose of a formula.

Now, occasionally, you might need to represent the entire calculation or the formula in a short form. Hence, we need new operators (outside the basic mathematical operators: +, –, ×, and ÷). For example, suppose the tax calculated on a commission is 30%. The computation can be expanded as

Tax = Commission · 30/100 = (Value returned from commission computation) · 30/100 = $(x - y)$ · 25/100 · 30/100.

We can represent this more simply as $x * y \times 30/100$, where the computation of the commission is represented as $x * y$.

Hence, effectively, defined functions represent computations. Here, the defined function $x * y$ represents the computation $(x - y) \cdot 25/100$. Defined functions are used in traditional mathematics, such as algebra, to represent computations.

Defined functions *must* be such that even when they are nested in parentheses, the computations are always based on basic math operators such as +, –, ×, ÷, <. =, >, etc.

Why do we need to name the computations?

(1) To be able to input the computation with a value.
(2) To define the pattern of usage of the arguments.

The pattern in which arguments are put in the defined function is very important. Let's discuss what it means below.

OK. So, how do we use Defined Functions? The standard answer is plug-in by pattern.

Before studying what this means, we need to understand the difference between a generic word and a particular instance of it.

For example, coke is an instance of the generic item cool drink.

So, if "Would you prefer a cool drink or a hot drink?" is a generic question, then "Would you prefer Coke or Tea?" is an instance of the question.

Similarly, if we have a defined function like $x \dfrac{y}{z} t = \left(x^2 + y\right)/x + \dfrac{z^2/xt}{t+z}$ and are asked to evaluate $a \dfrac{b}{c} d$,

we must understand by the correspondence in the pattern (arrangement) that $a \dfrac{b}{c} d$ that a is an instance of x, y an instance of b, z an instance of c, and d an instance of t. Thus, by pattern $3 \dfrac{2}{1} 5$ we mean $\{3, 2, 1, 5\}$ is an instance of $\{x, y, z, t\}$. Thus, one-by-one we can transform the computation with corresponding instance as

3 is instance of x: $\left(3^2 + y\right)/3 + \dfrac{z^2/3t}{t+z}$

2 an instance of y: $\left(3^2 + 2\right)/3 + \dfrac{z^2/3t}{t+z}$

1 an instance of z: $\left(3^2 + 2\right)/3 + \dfrac{1^2/3t}{t+1}$

5 an instance of t: $\left(3^2 + 2\right)/3 + \dfrac{1^2/3(5)}{5+1}$

So, $3 \dfrac{2}{1} 5 = \left(3^2 + 2\right)/3 + \dfrac{1^2/3(5)}{5+1}$.

The first step is to recognize the positions.

When we say $a \dfrac{b}{c} d$ we compare this with $x \dfrac{y}{z} t$ and recognizing that a is in the position of x, b is in the position of y, c is in the position of z, and a is in the position of t.

The next step is to replace by positions.

So, replace x with a wherever it exists. We get $a \dfrac{b}{c} d$ equals $a \dfrac{y}{z} t = \left(a^2 + y\right)/a + \dfrac{z^2/at}{t+z}$

Replace y with b wherever it exists. We get $a \dfrac{b}{c} d$ equals $a \dfrac{b}{z} t = \left(a^2 + b\right)/a + \dfrac{z^2/at}{t+z}$

Replace z with c wherever it exists. We get $a \dfrac{b}{c} d$ equals $a \dfrac{b}{c} t = \left(a^2 + b\right)/a + \dfrac{c^2/at}{t+c}$

Replace t with d wherever it exists. We get $a \dfrac{b}{c} d$ equals $a \dfrac{b}{c} d = \left(a^2 + b\right)/a + \dfrac{c^2/ad}{d+c}$

Note: Functions and defined functions are effectively for the same purpose. So, they have many similarities. For example, the defined function $x \dfrac{y}{z} t = \left(x^2 + y\right)/x + \dfrac{z^2/xt}{t+z}$ can be represented as

$$f(x,y,z,t) = \left(x^2 + y\right)/x + \dfrac{z^2/xt}{t+z}$$

So, the replace-by-position method applies here as well.

$$f(a,y,z,t) = \left(a^2 + y\right)/a + \dfrac{z^2/at}{t+z}$$

$$f(a,b,z,t) = \left(a^2 + b\right)/a + \dfrac{z^2/at}{t+z}$$

$$f(a,b,c,t) = \left(a^2 + b\right)/a + \dfrac{c^2/at}{t+c}$$

$$f(a,b,c,d) = \left(a^2 + b\right)/a + \dfrac{c^2/ad}{d+c}$$

Here, a is the instance of x, b the instance of y, c the instance of z, and d the instance of t.

Example 1:   If $x * y$ represents the number of integers between x and y, then $(-2 * 8) + (2 * -8) =$

The integers between -2 and 8 are $-1, 0, 1, 2, 3, 4, 5, 6, 7$ (a total of 9). Hence, $-2 * 8 = 9$. The integers between -8 and 2 are $-7, -6, -5, -4, -3, -2, -1, 0, 1$ (a total of 9). Hence, $2 * -8 = 9$. Therefore, $(-2 * 8) + (2 * -8) = 9 + 9 = 18$.

Example 2:   For any positive integer n, $n!$ denotes the product of the integers from 1 through n. What is the value of $3!(7 - 2)!$?

$3!(7 - 2)! = 3! \cdot 5!$

As defined, $3! = 3 \cdot 2 \cdot 1 = 6$, and $5! = 5 \cdot 4 \cdot 3 \cdot 2 \cdot 1$.

Hence, $3!(7 - 2)! = 3! \cdot 5! = 6 \cdot 5 \cdot 4 \cdot 3 \cdot 2 \cdot 1 = 720$.

Example 3:   A function @ is defined on positive integers as $@(a) = @(a-1) + 1$. If the value of $@(1)$ is 1, then what is the value of $@(3)$?

The function @ is defined on positive integers by the rule $@(a) = @(a-1) + 1$.

Using the rule for $a = 2$ yields $@(2) = @(2-1) + 1 = @(1) + 1 = 1 + 1 = 2$. [Since $@(1) = 1$, given.]

Using the rule for $a = 3$ yields $@(3) = @(3-1) + 1 = @(2) + 1 = 2 + 1 = 3$. [Since $@(2) = 2$, derived.]

Hence, $@(3) = 3$.

You may be wondering how defined functions differ from the functions, $f(x)$, you studied in Intermediate Algebra and more advanced math courses. They *don't* differ. They are the same old concept you dealt with in your math classes. The function in Example 3 could just as easily be written as

$$f(a) = f(a-1) + 1$$

Defined functions can be can have more than one variable. For example, $a \xrightarrow{\dfrac{c}{d}} b = ab + bc + cd + da$ is a defined function with 4 variables. The purpose of defined functions is to see how well you can adapt to unusual structures. Once you realize that defined functions are evaluated and manipulated just as regular functions, they become much less daunting.

Since the purpose of defined functions is to simplify larger expressions, we often nest such expressions (that is, plug one expression into another) to express even bigger expressions. The GMAT will occasionally nest defined functions. Defined functions can be made more complicated only in two ways:

   1) by assigning unusual computations to the defined function

   2) by nesting a function within another function

To solve a nested defined function problem it is best to calculate the nesting level-by-level while working from the inner parentheses out. The following example will illustrate.

Example 4:   Define $x*$ by the equation $x* = \pi/x$. Then $((-\pi)*)* =$

   (A) $-1/\pi$ (B) $-1/2$ (C) $-\pi$ (D) $1/\pi$ (E) π

Calculating the nesting level-by-level while working from the inner parentheses out, we get

$$((-\pi)*)* =$$

$$(\pi/(-\pi))* =$$

$$(-1)* =$$

$$\pi/(-1) =$$

$$-\pi$$

The answer is (C).

Method II:

We can rewrite this problem using ordinary function notation. Replacing the odd symbol $x*$ with $f(x)$ gives $f(x) = \pi/x$. Now, the expression $((-\pi)*)*$ becomes the ordinary composite function

$$f(f(-\pi)) =$$

$$f(\pi/(-\pi)) =$$

$$f(-1) =$$

$$\pi/(-1) =$$

$$-\pi$$

To solve nested defined functions, work from the inner most pair of parentheses out.

Strategy

Rules can be defined in any form, in the example below, they are tabled.

Defined functions are basically simple, and complications can be added only in the way the rules are defined.

Example 5:

a	b	$a * b$	$a + b$
0	0	0	0
0	1	0	1
1	0	0	1
1	1	1	1

The operators '*' and '+' are defined on the binary numbers (binary numbers 0 and 1) x and y as shown in the table above, what is the value of $(x * y) + x$?

(1) $x + y = 1$

(2) $x * y = 1$

Statement (1): $x + y = 1$

From the table, $x + y$ equals 1 when $\{x, y\}$ is $\{0, 1\}$ or $\{1, 0\}$ or $\{1, 1\}$.

Now, collect all possible answers the statement allows for the expression $(x * y) + x$

When $\{x, y\} = \{0, 1\}$, $x * y = 0$ and $(x * y) + x = 0 + 0 = 0$.

When $\{x, y\} = \{1, 0\}$, $x * y = 0$ and $(x * y) + x = 0 + 1 = 1$.

This is a double case and therefore Statement (1) is not sufficient.

Statement (2): $x * y = 1$

From the table, $x * y$ equals 1 only when $\{x, y\}$ equals $\{1, 1\}$.

Now, collect all possible answers the statement allows for the expression $(x * y) + x$.

By substituting $\{1, 1\}$ in $(x * y) + x$, we get $(x * y) + x = (1 * 1) + 1 = 1 + 1 = 1$.

This is the only value that the statement allows for the expression. Since we have just one value, the statement is sufficient.

The answer is (B).

If the question was "Is $(x * y) + x = 1$?", then Statement (1) would yield two possible answers "Yes" and "No," while Statement (2) would yield a single answer "Yes." Hence, the answer would be (B). If it were "Is $(x * y) + x = 0$?" as well, the answer would be (B).

Example 6:

a	b	$a * b$	$a + b$
0	0	0	0
0	1	0	1
1	0	0	1
1	1	1	1

The operators '*' and '+' operate only on the numbers 0 and 1 as defined in the table. If $x * y = 1$, which one of the following does $(x * y) + x$ equal?

(A) –2   (B) –1   (C) 0   (D) 1   (E) 2

From the table, $x * y$ equals 1 only when $\{x, y\}$ equals $\{1, 1\}$.

Hence, $x * y + x = (1 * 1) + 1 = 1 + 1 = 1$. The answer is (D).

Problem Set B: Defined Functions

1. The operation denoted by the symbol ◄► is defined for all real numbers p and r as p◄►r equals the larger of p and r. For example, 5◄►$3 = 5$. Which one of the distinct numbers x, y and z is the largest?

    (1) $(x$◄►$y)$◄►$z = x$◄►z

    (2) $(x$◄►$z)$◄►$y = z$◄►y

2. The operator $a*$ is defined on a number a as equal to $(-1)^m \cdot a$, where m is an integer. If a is not equal to zero, what is $(a*)* - a$?

    (1) $a* + a = 0$

    (2) $a* \cdot a + a^2 = 0$

a	b	$a * b$	$a + b$
0	0	0	0
0	1	0	1
1	0	0	1
1	1	1	1

3. The operators '*' and '+' operate only on the numbers 0 and 1 as defined in the table. What is the value of $x * y$?

    (1) $(x * y) + y = 1$

    (2) $(x * y) + x = 1$

	P	Q	R	S
P	0	m	n	62
Q	m	0	26	75
R	n	26	0	69
S	62	75	n	0

4. An operator '' is defined on letters, and the table above shows a few results of the operation. For example, $QS = 75$ and $RQ = 26$. Is $PQ + RQ + SR$ odd?

    (1) $QP + PR + RS$ is odd.

    (2) $PQ + QR + RS$ is even.

Answers and Solutions to Problem Set B: Defined Functions

1. The operation denoted by the symbol ◄► is defined for all real numbers p and r as p◄►r equals the larger of p and r. For example, 5◄►$3 = 5$. Which one of the distinct numbers x, y and z is the largest?

   (1) $(x$◄►$y)$◄►$z = x$◄►z

   (2) $(x$◄►$z)$◄►$y = z$◄►y

Statement (1): $(x$◄►$y)$◄►$z = x$◄►z

The left-hand side of the statement can be read as "The larger of the larger of x and y, and the number z is the larger of x and y." Since the right side of the equation says this is equal to the larger of x and z, the larger of the numbers x, y, and z is either x or z and *not y*.

Hence, the statement says that the answer could be x or z, either of which is distinct from the other. Since we have more than one answer, the statement is *not* sufficient.

Statement (2): $(x$◄►$z)$◄►$y = z$◄►y

The left-hand side of the statement can be read as "The larger of the larger of x and z, and the number y is the larger of x and z." Since the right side of the equation says this is equal to the larger of z and y, the larger of the numbers x, y, and z is either z or y and *not x*.

Hence, the statement says that the answer could be y or z, either of which is distinct from the other. Since we have more than one answer, the statement is *not* sufficient.

Statement (1) eliminates y and Statement (2) eliminates x as possible answers. Hence, the only possible answer now is z. We had to use both statements to answer this and therefore the answer is (C).

2. The operator $a*$ is defined on a number a as equal to $(-1)^m \cdot a$, where m is an integer. If a is not equal to zero, what is $(a*)* - a$?

   (1) $a* + a = 0$

   (2) $a* \cdot a + a^2 = 0$

Statement (1): $a* + a = 0$.

Subtracting a from both sides of the equation $a* + a = 0$ yields

$$a* = -a$$

By definition $a* = (-1)^m \cdot a$. Hence,

$$(-1)^m \cdot a = -a$$

Dividing by a (which is not zero) yields

$$(-1)^m = -1$$

Plugging $(-1)^m = -1$ in the definition $a* = (-1)^m \cdot a$ yields $a* = (-1)^m \cdot a = -1 \cdot a = -a$.

Now, $(a*)* - a = (-a)* - a = -(-a) - a = a - a = 0$

The statement is sufficient.

The answer is (D).

Statement (2): $a* \cdot a + a^2 = 0$.

Factoring a from the terms of the equation $a* \cdot a + a^2 = 0$ yields

$$a(a* + a) = 0$$

This happens when a is zero or $a* + a = 0$. Since a is given not equal to zero, $a* + a$ must equal 0. This is what Statement (1) directly says. Therefore, Statement (2) is sufficient just as Statement (1) is.

a	b	$a * b$	$a + b$
0	0	0	0
0	1	0	1
1	0	0	1
1	1	1	1

3.   The operators '*' and '+' operate only on the numbers 0 and 1 as defined in the table. What is the value of $x * y$?

(1) $(x * y) + y = 1$

(2) $(x * y) + x = 1$

Let's extend the table for the expressions in the statements as follows:

a for x	b for y	$a * b$	$a + b$	$(x * y) + y$	$(x * y) + x$
0	0	0	0	$0 + 0 = 0$	$0 + 0 = 0$
0	1	0	1	$0 + 1 = 1$	$0 + 0 = 0$
1	0	0	1	$0 + 0 = 0$	$0 + 1 = 1$
1	1	1	1	$1 + 1 = 1$	$1 + 1 = 1$

Statement (1): $(x * y) + y = 1$

From the table, $(x * y) + y$ equals 1 when $\{x, y\}$ is $\{0, 1\}$ or $\{1, 1\}$.

When $\{x, y\} = \{0, 1\}$, $x * y = 0$.

When $\{x, y\} = \{1, 1\}$, $x * y = 1$.

This is a double case.

Hence, Statement (1) is not sufficient.

Statement (2): $(x * y) + x = 1$

From the table, $(x * y) + x$ equals 1 only when $\{x, y\}$ equals $\{1, 1\}$.

Hence, $x * y + x$ can be calculated with these values and we would have a unique value. So, the statement is sufficient. Let's calculate the value:

$$(1 * 1) + 1 = 1 + 1 = 1$$

Hence, Statement (2) alone is sufficient.

The answer is (B).

	P	Q	R	S
P	0	m	n	62
Q	m	0	26	75
R	n	26	0	69
S	62	75	n	0

4.   An operator ' ' is defined on letters, and the table above shows a few results of the operation. For example, $QS = 75$ and $RQ = 26$. Is $PQ + RQ + SR$ odd?

(1) $QP + PR + RS$ is odd.

(2) $PQ + QR + RS$ is even.

From the table, $PQ = m$, $RQ = 26$, and $SR = n$. Hence, $PQ + RQ + SR = m + 26 + n$.

From the table, $QP = m$, $PR = n$, and $RS = 69$. Hence, $QP + PR + RS = m + n + 69$.

From the table, $PQ = m$, $QR = 26$, and $RS = 69$. Hence, $PQ + QR + RS = m + 26 + 69$.

Hence, we can transform the question as

Is $m + 26 + n$ odd?

(1) $m + n + 69$ is odd.

(2) $m + 26 + 69$ is even.

Statement (1): $m + n + 69$ is odd.

$m + n + \text{odd} = \text{odd}$.

$m + n = \text{odd} - \text{odd} = \text{even}$.

Hence, $m + n + 26 = \text{even} + 26 = \text{even} + \text{even} = $ even.

The statement is sufficient.

Statement (2): $m + 26 + 69$ is even.

$m + 26 + 69 = \text{even}$

$m + \text{even} + \text{odd} = \text{even}$

$m + \text{odd} = \text{even}$ (since even + odd = odd).

$m = \text{even} - \text{odd} = \text{odd}$.

Now, $m + 26 + n$ is odd when n is even, and it is even when n is odd. For example, when $n = 1$, $m + 26 + n = \text{odd} + \text{even} + \text{odd} = \text{even}$; and when $n = 2$, $m + 26 + n = \text{odd} + \text{even} + \text{even} = \text{odd}$.

Since we have a double case, the statement is *not* sufficient.

The answer is (A).

Number Theory

This broad category is a popular source for GMAT questions. At first, students often struggle with these problems since they have forgotten many of the basic properties of arithmetic. So, before we begin solving these problems, let's review some of these basic properties.

➤ **Division: Take the ratio x/y of two numbers x and y also written as $x \div y$. Here, x is called the dividend, y is called the divisor, and x/y is called the quotient. If left unevaluated, x/y is called a fraction, where x is the numerator and y is the denominator.**

➤ *"The remainder is r when p is divided by k"* **means $p = kq + r$; the integer q is called the quotient.** For instance, *"The remainder is 1 when 7 is divided by* 3*"* means $7 = 3 \cdot 2 + 1$. Dividing both sides of $p = kq + r$ by k gives the following alternative form $p/k = q + r/k$.

➤ **A remainder can be negative as well.** For example, when dividing -3.7 by 1.1 ($-3.7 = -3 \cdot 1.1 - .4$).

➤ **If you said $7 \div 2 = 2 + 3/2$ and therefore concluded that 3 is the remainder, it is mistake. You must check that the number cannot be further divided by the quotient. $7 \div 2 = 2 + 3/2 = 3 + 1/2$. Since 1 cannot be further divided by 2, 1 is the remainder.**

Example 1:   The remainder is 57 when a number is divided by 10,000. What is the remainder when the same number is divided by 1,000?

Since the remainder is 57 when the number is divided by 10,000, the number can be expressed as $10,000n + 57$, where n is an integer. Rewriting 10,000 as 1,000(10) yields

$$1,000(10)n + 57 =$$

$$1,000(10n) + 57 =$$

Now, since n is an integer, $10n$ is an integer. Letting $10n = q$, we get

$$1,000q + 57 =$$

Hence, the remainder is still 57 (by the $p = kq + r$ form) when the number is divided by 1,000.

Method II (Alternative form)

Since the remainder is 57 when the number is divided by 10,000, the number can be expressed as $10,000n + 57$. Dividing this number by 1,000 yields

$$\frac{10,000n + 57}{1000} =$$

$$\frac{10,000n}{1,000} + \frac{57}{1,000} =$$

$$10n + \frac{57}{1,000}$$

Hence, the remainder is 57 (by the alternative form $p/k = q + r/k$).

➤ **The remainder is the same for all the multiples of the divisors and to the specific factors of the divisor that are bigger than the remainder. For example,**

The remainder of $1057 \div 1000$ is 57.

10,000 is a multiple of 1,000 and the remainder of $1057 \div 10,000$ is 57.

100 is a factor of 1,000 and the remainder of $1057 \div 100$ is 57.

10 is a factor of 1000 but the remainder of $1057 \div 10$ is not 57 because 57 is greater than 10.

➤ **A number *n* is even if the remainder is zero when *n* is divided by 2: *n* = 2*z* + 0, or *n* = 2*z*, where *z* is an integer. Hence, …, –4, –2, 0, 2, 4, … are even numbers.**

➤ **A number *n* is odd if the remainder is one when *n* is divided by 2: *n* = 2*z* + 1, where *z* is an integer. Hence, …, –3, –1, 1, 3, … are odd numbers.**

➤ **Memorize the following properties for odd and even numbers:**

$$even \times even = even$$

$$odd \times odd = odd$$

$$even \times odd = even$$

$even + even = even$	$even - even = even$
$odd + odd = even$	$odd - odd = even$
$even + odd = odd$	$even - odd = odd$

Even ÷ *even* is not necessarily *even* as we see from two results that we know

Case (1): *even* × *even* is *even*, so *even* ÷ *even* may be *even*

Case (2): *even* × *odd* is *even*, so *even* ÷ *even* may be *odd*

$4 \div 2 = 2$, even; $6 \div 2 = 3$, odd hence the double case.

odd ÷ *odd* = *odd* because *odd* × *odd* is *odd*.

even ÷ *odd* = *even* because *even* × *odd* is *even*

Example 2:   If n is a positive integer and $(n + 1)(n + 3)$ is odd, then $(n + 2)(n + 4)$ must be a multiple of which one of the following?

(A) 3   (B) 5   (C) 6   (D) 8   (E) 16

Remember *even* × *even* = *even*, *odd* × *odd* = *odd*, and *even* × *odd* = *even*.

$(n + 1)(n + 3)$ is odd only when both $(n + 1)$ and $(n + 3)$ are odd.

Now, remember *even* + *even* = *even*, *odd* + *odd* = *even*, and *even* + *odd* = *odd*. Hence, $n + 1$ is odd or $n + 3$ is *odd* is possible only when n is *even*. Hence, $n = 2m$, where m is a positive integer. Then

$(n + 2)(n + 4) =$

$(2m + 2)(2m + 4) =$

$2(m + 1)2(m + 2) =$

$4(m + 1)(m + 2) =$

4 × (product of two consecutive positive integers, one of which must be even) =

4 × (an even number), and this equals a number that is at least a multiple of 8

Hence, the answer is (D).

➤   **Consecutive integers are written as x, $x + 1$, $x + 2$, . . .**

➤   **Consecutive even or odd integers are written as x, $x + 2$, $x + 4$, . . .**

➤   **The integer zero is neither positive nor negative, but it is even: $0 = 2 \times 0$.**

➤   **A *prime number* is an integer that is divisible only by itself and 1.**

The prime numbers are 2, 3, 5, 7, 11, 13, 17, 19, 23, 29, 31, 37, 41, . . .

➤   **A number is divisible by 3 if the sum of its digits is divisible by 3.**

For example, 135 is divisible by 3 because the sum of its digits (1 + 3 + 5 = 9) is divisible by 3.

➤   **A *common multiple* is a multiple of two or more integers.**

For example, some common multiples of 4 and 10 are 20, 40, 60, and 80.

➤   **The *least common multiple* (LCM) of two integers is the smallest positive integer that is a multiple of both.**

For example, the LCM of 4 and 10 is 20. The standard method of calculating the LCM is to prime factor the numbers and then form a product by selecting each factor the greatest number of times it occurs. For 4 and 10, we get

$$4 = 2^2$$

$$10 = 2 \cdot 5$$

In this case, select 2^2 instead of 2 because it has the greater number of factors of 2, and select 5 by default since there are no other factors of 5. Hence, the LCM is $2^2 \cdot 5 = 4 \cdot 5 = 20$.

For another example, let's find the LCM of 8, 36, and 54. Prime factoring yields

$$8 = 2^3$$

$$36 = 2^2 \cdot 3^2$$

$$54 = 2 \cdot 3^3$$

In this case, select 2^3 because it has more factors of 2 than 2^2 or 2 itself, and select 3^3 because is has more factors of 3 than 3^2 does. Hence, the LCM is $2^3 \cdot 3^3 = 8 \cdot 27 = 216$.

A shortcut for finding the LCM is to just keep adding the largest number to itself until the other numbers divide into it evenly. For 4 and 10, we would add 10 to itself: $10 + 10 = 20$. Since 4 divides evenly in to 20, the LCM is 20. For 8, 36, and 54, we would add 54 to itself: $54 + 54 + 54 + 54 = 216$. Since both 8 and 36 divide evenly into 216, the LCM is 216.

➤ **The absolute value of a number, | |, is always positive. In other words, the absolute value symbol eliminates negative signs.**

For example, $\left|-7\right| = 7$ and $\left|-\pi\right| = \pi$. Caution, the absolute value symbol acts only on what is inside the symbol, $|\ |$. For example, $-\left|-(7-\pi)\right| = -(7-\pi)$. Here, only the negative sign inside the absolute value symbol but outside the parentheses is eliminated.

Example 3: The number of prime numbers divisible by 2 plus the number of prime numbers divisible by 3 is

(A) 1   (B) 2   (C) 3   (D) 4   (E) 5

A prime number is divisible by no other numbers, but itself and 1. Hence, the only prime number divisible by 2 is 2 itself; and the only prime number divisible by 3 is 3 itself. Hence, The number of prime numbers divisible by 2 is one, and the number of prime numbers divisible by 3 is one. The sum of the two is $1 + 1 = 2$. The answer is (B).

Example 4: If $15x + 16 = 0$, then $15|x|$ equals which one of the following?

(A) 15   (B) $-16x$ (C) $15x$ (D) 16   (E) $16x$

Solving the given equation $15x + 16 = 0$ for x yields $x = \dfrac{-16}{15}$.

Substituting this into the expression $15|x|$ yields

$$15|x| = 15\left|\frac{-16}{15}\right| = 15\left(\frac{16}{15}\right) = 16$$

The answer is (D).

➤ **The product (or quotient) of positive numbers is positive.**

➤ **The product (quotient) of a positive number and a negative number is negative.**

For example, $-5(3) = -15$ and $\dfrac{6}{-3} = -2$.

➤ **The product (or quotient) of an even number of negative numbers is positive.**

For example, $(-5)(-3)(-2)(-1) = 30$ is positive because there is an even number, 4, of negatives.

$\dfrac{-9}{-2} = \dfrac{9}{2}$ is positive because there is an even number, 2, of negatives.

➤ **The product (or quotient) of an odd number of negative numbers is negative.**

For example, $(-2)(-\pi)(-\sqrt{3}) = -2\pi\sqrt{3}$ is negative because there is an odd number, 3, of negatives.

$\dfrac{(-2)(-9)(-6)}{(-12)\left(-18\big/2\right)} = -1$ is negative because there is an odd number, 5, of negatives.

➤ **The sum of negative numbers is negative.**

For example, $-3 - 5 = -8$. Some students have trouble recognizing this structure as a sum because there is no plus symbol, +. But recall that subtraction is defined as negative addition. Hence, $-3 - 5 = -3 + (-5)$.

➤ **A number raised to an even exponent is greater than or equal to zero.**

For example, $(-\pi)^4 = \pi^4 \geq 0$, and $x^2 \geq 0$, and $0^2 = 0 \cdot 0 = 0 \geq 0$.

➤ **A number can be expressed in terms of its digits based on the location of the digits in the number.**

For example, 253.801 can be expressed as $2 \cdot 100 + 5 \cdot 10 + 3 \cdot 1 + 8/10 + 0/100 + 1/1000$ because 2 is in the hundred's position, 5 in ten's, 3 in unit's, 8 in tenth's, 0 in hundredth's, and 1 in thousandth's.

Note that hundred's digit has more weight than the ten's digit, which has more weight than the unit's digit, which has more weight than the digits after the decimal point. The reverse trend follows for digits after the decimal point.

Example 5:   What is the maximum possible difference between two three-digit positive integers each of which is made up of all the digits 1, 2, and 3?

(A) 156   (B) 168   (C) 176   (D) 196   (E) 198

The difference between the two positive integers is a maximum when one of the numbers takes the largest possible value and the other one takes the smallest possible value.

The largest possible three-digit number that can be formed using all three digits—1, 2, and 3—is formed by assigning bigger numbers to the higher significant digits. Hence, the number is $3 \cdot 100 + 2 \cdot 10 + 1 = 321$.

The smallest possible three-digit number that can be formed from all three digits—1, 2, and 3—is formed by assigning smaller numbers to higher significant digits. Hence, the number is $1 \cdot 100 + 2 \cdot 10 + 3 = 123$.

The difference between the two numbers is $321 - 123 = 198$. The answer is (E).

Problem Set C: Number Theory

1. Does *a* equal *b*?

    (1)   *a* and *b* are positive integers.

    (2)   *a* plus *b* equals 3.

2. What is the remainder when *m* is divided by 3?

    (1)   The remainder when *m* is divided by 6 is 2.

    (2)   The remainder when *m* is divided by 12 is 2.

3. What is the remainder when *m* is divided by 12?

    (1)   The remainder when *m* is divided by 3 is 2.

    (2)   The remainder when *m* is divided by 6 is 2.

4. What does the number *x* equal?

    (1)   The quotient when the number is divided by 7 is 52.

    (2)   The remainder when the number is divided by 7 is 2.

5. Is *m* divisible by *n*?

    (1) $m + n$ is divisible by $m - n$.

    (2) $m + n$ is divisible by *n*.

6. Is *r* a multiple of *s*?

    (1) $r + 2s$ is a multiple of *s*.

    (2) $2r + s$ is a multiple of *s*.

7. Is the integer *k* a prime number?

    (1) $k + 1$ is prime.

    (2) $k + 2$ is not prime.

8. Is the integer *k* a prime number?

    (1) $k + 1$ is prime.

    (2) $k + 2$ is a multiple of 6.

9.   Is p an odd prime integer?

   (1) p is odd

   (2) p is prime

10.   If m and n are positive integers, then is $5m + 2n$ divisible by $3m + n$?

   (1) m is divisible by n

   (2) m is divisible by 15 and n is divisible by 2

11.   Are x and y integers?

   (1) $x + y$ is an odd.

   (2) $x - y$ is an even.

12.   Is $x = y$?

   (1) xy is negative.

   (2) $x + y$ is positive.

13.   Is the sum of the digits of an integer equal to 25?

   (1)   The integer has 5 digits.

   (2)   Each digit of the integer is either 4 or 6.

14.   If m and n are positive integers, then is p equal to product of m and n?

   (1) p is a product of two prime numbers.

   (2) m and n are prime numbers.

15.   Is n an integer?

   (1) $n^3 + 3n$ is an integer.

   (2) $n^4 + 4n$ is an integer.

Answers and Solutions to Problem Set C: Number Theory

1.   Does *a* equal *b*?

   (1)   *a* and *b* are positive integers.

   (2)   *a* plus *b* equals 3.

If two positive integers sum to 3, then the numbers must be 1 and 2. Clearly, the two numbers are not equal. Hence, the statements together are sufficient. The answer is (C).

2.   What is the remainder when *m* is divided by 3?

   (1)   The remainder when *m* is divided by 6 is 2.

   (2)   The remainder when *m* is divided by 12 is 2.

Statement (1): The remainder when *m* is divided by 6 is 2.

Here, *m* can be represented as $6p + 2$, where *p* is an integer. Now, $m/3 = (6p + 2)/3 = 2p + 2/3$, 2 is the remainder

Statement (2): The remainder when *m* is divided by 12 is 2.

Here, *m* can be represented as $12q + 2$, where *q* is an integer. Now, $m/3 = (12q + 2)/3 = 4q + 2/3$, 2 is the remainder.

Hence, either statement is sufficient. The answer is (D).

3.   What is the remainder when *m* is divided by 12?

   (1)   The remainder when *m* is divided by 3 is 2.

   (2)   The remainder when *m* is divided by 6 is 2.

Statement (1): The remainder when *m* is divided by 3 is 2

Here, *m* can be represented as $3p + 2$, where *p* is an integer.

Now, $m/12 = (3p + 2)/12$, where *p* could be any integer.

If *p* is a multiple of 4 such as $4 \times 2 = 8$, then *p* can be expressed as $4q$. Then

$m/12 = [3(4q) + 2]/12$

$\qquad = [12q + 2]/12$

$\qquad = q + 2/12$, 2 is the remainder.

If *p* is a multiple of 4 plus 1 such as $4 \times 2 + 1 = 9$, then *p* can be expressed as $4q + 1$. Then

$m/12 = [3(4q + 1) + 2]/12$

$\qquad = [12q + 5]/12$

$\qquad = q + 5/12$, 5 is the remainder.

Now, if *p* is a multiple of 4 plus 2 or a multiple of 4 plus 3 or so on, we get, by calculating the remainder in the same fashion, that the remainders are respectively 8 and 11.

Since there is more than one possible solution—2, 5, 8, and 11—the statement is *not* sufficient.

Statement (2): The remainder when *m* is divided by 6 is 2

Here, *m* can be represented as $6p + 2$, where *p* is an integer.

Now, $m/12 = (6p + 2)/12$, where *p* could be any integer.

If *p* is a multiple of 2 plus 1, then *p* can be expressed as $2q + 1$. Then

$m/12 = [6(2q + 1) + 2]/12$

$\qquad = [12q + 8]/12$

$\qquad = q + 8/12$, 8 is remainder.

If *p* is a multiple of 2 plus 2 (invariably a multiple of 2), then *p* can be expressed as $2q + 2$. Then

$m/12 = [6(2q + 2) + 2]/12$

$\qquad = [12q + 14]/12$

$\qquad = 12q/12 + 14/12$

$\qquad = q + 1\ 2/12$, 2 is the remainder.

Since there is more than one possible solution, 2 and 8, the statement is *not* sufficient.

The solution set of Statement (1) is {2, 5, 8, 11}, and the solution set of Statement (2) is {2, 8}. In either set "," means "or." The solution set of the two statements together consists of elements common to the two sets {2, 5, 8, 11} and {2, 8}, which is {2, 8}. Since there is more than one possible solution (2 and 8), the statements together are not sufficient. The answer is (E).

4.   What does the number x equal?

    (1)   The quotient when the number is divided by 7 is 52.

    (2)   The remainder when the number is divided by 7 is 2.

The number equals the Quotient × 7 + the Remainder = 52 [from Statement (1)] × 7 + 2 [from Statement (2)] = 364 + 2 = 366. The statements are together sufficient. With Statement (1) alone, we do not have the remainder; and with Statement (2) alone, we do not have the quotient. Hence, neither statement is sufficient alone. The answer is (C).

5.   Is m divisible by n?

    (1) $m + n$ is divisible by $m - n$.

    (2) $m + n$ is divisible by n.

Let's write m as kn (k is not integer unless m is divisible by n). Now, rewrite the question as "Is k an integer?" And replace m in the statements with kn. Then the statements can be written as

Statement (1): $kn + n$ is divisible by $kn - n$.

This means $(kn + n)/(kn - n)$ is an integer. Let's express this as

    $(kn + n)/(kn - n)$ = integer.

    $n(k + 1)/[n(k - 1)]$ =

    $(k + 1)/(k - 1)$ =

    $(k - 1 + 1 + 1)/(k - 1)$ =

    $(k - 1)/(k - 1) + 2/(k - 1)$ =

    $1 + 2/(k - 1)$ = integer

This is integer only when $2/(k - 1)$ is an integer. Now $2/(k - 1)$ may be an integer whether k is an integer or not.

For example, if $k = 2$, $2/(k - 1) = 2$ (an integer) and if $k = 1.5$, $2/(k - 1) = 2/0.5 = 4$ (an integer).

This means that k need not be an integer to make $(kn + n)/(kn - n)$ an integer, so $(kn + n)/(kn - n)$ being an integer isn't an indicator of whether m is divisible by n or not.

The statement is *not* sufficient.

The answer is (B).

Statement (2): $kn + n$ is divisible by n.

This means $(kn + n)/n$ is an integer. Let's express this as

    $(kn + n)/n$ =

    $n(k + 1)/n$ =

    $k + 1$ = an integer (given)

    k = an integer minus 1, which is again an integer.

Hence, k is integer which means m is divisible by n.

The statement is sufficient.

6.   Is *r* a multiple of *s*?

    (1)   *r* + 2*s* is a multiple of *s*.

    (2)   2*r* + *s* is a multiple of *s*.

Any number (integer or decimal or non-terminating number) can be a multiple of the another if the ratio of the former to later is an integer other than 0. For example, 4.5 is a multiple of 1.5 by 3 (= 4.5/1.5 which happens to be an integer) times.

Statement (1): *r* + 2*s* is a multiple of *s*.

This means $(r + 2s) \div s$ is an integer. Let's express this as

    $(r + 2s) \div s = $ integer

    $r/s + 2s/s = $ integer

    $r/s + 2 = $ integer

    $r/s = $ integer − 2 = another integer.

So, *r* is a multiple of *s*. The statement is sufficient.

Statement (2): 2*r* + *s* is a multiple of *s*.

This means $(2r + s) \div s$ is an integer. Let's express this as

    $(2r + s) \div s = $ integer

    $2r/s + s/s = $ integer

    $2r/s + 1 = $ integer

    $2r/s = $ integer − 1 = another integer

    $r/s = $ another integer/2

An integer divided by 2 may or may not be an integer. For example, 2/2 = 1 is an integer, but 3/2 = 1.5 is not an integer. So, the statement is *not* sufficient.

The answer is (A).

7.   Is the integer *k* a prime number?

    (1)   *k* + 1 is prime.

    (2)   *k* + 2 is not prime.

Suppose *k* = 2. Then *k* + 1 = 3 is prime and *k* + 2 = 4 is not prime (both statements satisfied). Here, *k* is prime.

Suppose *k* = 4. Then *k* + 1 = 5 is prime and *k* + 2 = 6 is not prime (both statements satisfied). Here, *k* is not prime.

Since we have a double case, the statements together are *not* sufficient. The answer is (E).

8.   Is the integer k a prime number?

   (1) $k + 1$ is prime.

   (2) $k + 2$ is a multiple of 6.

Statement (1): $k + 1$ is prime.

Suppose $k = 2$. Then $k + 1 = 3$ is prime (the statement is satisfied). Here, k is prime.

Suppose $k = 4$. Then $k + 1 = 5$ is prime (the statement is satisfied). Here, k is *not* prime.

Hence, the statement being satisfied is not an indication of whether k is prime or not. The statement is *not* sufficient.

The answer is (B).

Statement (2): $k + 2$ is a multiple of 6.

Here, $k + 2$ must be an even number (multiples of even numbers are even).

Hence, $k =$ even number $- 2 =$ even. No even number other than 2 is prime since even numbers are multiples of 2. If k were 2, $k + 2 = 4$ would not be a multiple of 6. Hence, the statement is sufficient.

9.   Is p an odd prime integer?

   (1) p is odd

   (2) p is prime

Let's draw a Venn diagram to represent the odd numbers and the prime numbers (see figure below). Statement (1), p is odd, is represented by the region to the left in the Venn diagram. Statement (2), p is prime, is represented by the region to the right in the Venn diagram. Not all odd numbers are prime, and not all prime numbers are odd. Hence, the two regions have some exclusive space. There is at least one odd prime number. Hence, the common region of the two statements is not blank. But the common region expects a number to be both odd and prime. Hence, the statements together are sufficient because the common region equals neither of the two sets.

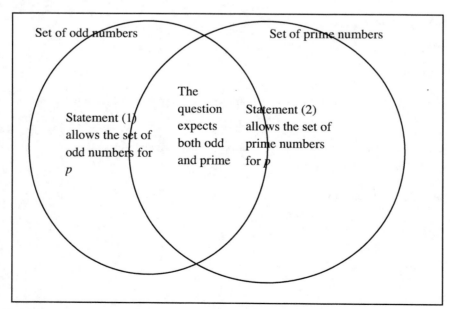

The answer is (C).

10. If m and n are positive integers, then is $5m + 2n$ divisible by $3m + n$?

    (1) m is divisible by n

    (2) m is divisible by 15 and n is divisible by 2

Statement (1): m is divisible by n

Let $m = kn$, k is some integer. Now, let's substitute as shown

$$\frac{5m + 2n}{3m + n} = \frac{5(kn) + 2n}{3(kn) + n} = \frac{5k + 2}{3k + 1}$$

Suppose $k = 1$. Then $\frac{5k + 2}{4} = \frac{7}{4}$, which is not an integer.

Here, $5m + 2n$ is not divisible by $3m + n$.

But sometimes it is divisible. For example, suppose $k = 2$. Then

$$\frac{5k + 2}{4} = \frac{5(2) + 2}{4} = \frac{12}{4} = 3$$

which is an integer. Here, $5m + 2n$ is divisible by $3m + n$.

Since we have a double case, the statement is not sufficient.

Statement (2): m is divisible by 15 and n is divisible by 2.

Let m equal $15s$ and n equal $2t$, where s and t are integers. Now, let's substitute as shown

$$\frac{5m + 2n}{3m + n} = \frac{5(15s) + 2(2t)}{3(15s) + (2t)} = \frac{75s + 4t}{45s + 2t}$$

Since both m and n are positive, s and t must be non-zero. So, the ratio $\frac{75s + 4t}{45s + 2t}$ must be positive.

Now, suppose $75s + 4t$ is divisible by $45s + 2t$. Then the ratio of the two must be a positive integer. Suppose the ratio equals 1.

$$\frac{75s + 4t}{45s + 2t} = 1$$
$$75s + 4t = 45s + 2t$$
$$30s + 2t = 0$$

Since s and t are positive (we know),

$$\frac{75s + 4t}{45s + 2t} = 2$$
$$75s + 4t = 90s + 4t$$
$$0 = 15s$$

Since s is positive (we know), this is impossible.

Suppose

$$\frac{75s + 4t}{45s + 2t} = 3$$
$$75s + 4t = 135s + 6t$$
$$0 = 60s + 2t$$

Since s and t are positive (we know), this is impossible. Similarly, no higher integer value of the ratio $\frac{75s + 4t}{45s + 2t}$ is possible, i.e.,

$$\frac{5m + 2n}{3m + n} = \frac{75s + 4t}{45s + 2t} = 1, 2, 3, 4, \ldots \text{ are all}$$

impossible. Hence, $5m + 2n$ is never divisible by $3m + n$. The statement alone answers this and therefore the statement is sufficient.

The answer is (B).

11.   Are x and y integers?

(1) $x + y$ is an odd.

(2) $x - y$ is an even.

Suppose $x - y = e$, an even integer; and suppose $x + y = o$, an odd integer. Summing the two equations yields

$$(x + y) + (x - y) = o + e$$
$$2x = o + e$$
$$x = \frac{o + e}{2} = \frac{odd}{2}$$

Since $\frac{odd}{2}$ is never an integer, x is not an integer.

Subtracting the equation $x - y = e$ from the equation $x + y = o$ yields

$$(x + y) - (x - y) = o - e$$
$$2y = o - e$$
$$y = \frac{o - e}{2} = \frac{odd}{2}$$

Since $\frac{odd}{2}$ is never an integer, y is not an integer.

The statements together answer the question, and the answer is (C).

12.   Is $x = y$?

(1) xy is negative.

(2) $x + y$ is positive.

Statement (1): xy is negative.

xy is negative indicates neither x nor y is zero. Now, suppose $x = y$. Then $xy = x(x) = x^2$, which must be positive (square of a non-zero number is always positive).

This contradicts the statement. So, our supposition, $x = y$, is wrong. Hence, $x \neq y$.

The statement is sufficient.

The answer is (A).

Statement (2): $x + y$ is positive.

Suppose $x = 1$ and $y = 1$. Here, $x + y$ is positive and $x = y$.

Now, suppose $x = 1$ and $y = 2$. Here, $x + y$ is positive, and x is not equal to y.

We have a double case and therefore the statement alone is *not* sufficient.

13.   Is the sum of the digits of an integer equal to 25?

(1)   The integer has 5 digits.

(2)   Each digit of the integer is either 4 or 6.

Statement (1): The integer has 5 digits.

Choose 5 digits which sum to 25. For example, 55555.

Choose 5 digits that do not sum to 25. For example, 55554.

This is a double case and therefore the statement is *not* sufficient.

Statement (2): Each digit of the number is either 4 or 6.

4 and 6 are even numbers while 25 is odd. The sum of a set of even numbers is even. So, the sum of the digits, which are 4 or 6, can never equal 25. The statement is sufficient.

The answer is (B).

14.   If m and n are positive integers, then is p equal to product of m and n?

(1) p is a product of two prime numbers.

(2) m and n are prime numbers.

There are many prime numbers, and m and n are just two of them. Hence, p could be the product of any two of them, not just m and n. Hence, the statements together are *not* sufficient. The answer is (E).

15.   Is n an integer?

   (1) $n^3 + 3n$ is an integer.

   (2) $n^4 + 4n$ is an integer.

Statement (1): $n^3 + 3n$ is an integer.

If n is an integer, then $n^3 + 3n$ is surely an integer. This does not mean that if $n^3 + 3n$ is an integer, n is an integer.

Let's check if n is not an integer, then $n^3 + 3n$ could be an integer. If the answer is a strict "No", the data is sufficient. If the answer is "Yes" or "Might or Might not be," we have a double case and the data is *not* sufficient.

Now, if n is *not* an integer, then it must be a decimal. A decimal will have at least one non-zero digit after decimal point.

If n has 1 non-zero digit after the decimal point, then n^3 would have at least one more digit after decimal point with at least one of the digits being non-zero.

Summing two numbers one with one digit after decimal point and one with more than one digit after decimal point will never yield an integer.

For example, if $n = 1.2$, $n^3 = 1.2^3 = 1.728$ and $3n = 3.6$, then the sum of 3.6 and 1.728 is not an integer.

Now, if n has two such digits after the decimal point, $3n$ would also have two such digits after decimal point and n^3 would have at least one more digit after decimal point.

Thus, the number of digits after the decimal point increases faster for n^3 than for $3n$. Hence, their sum would never be an integer. This means $n^3 + 3n$ is never an integer for decimal n. This also says that $n^3 + 3n$ must be an integer because n is an integer.

If $n^3 + 3n$ is an integer, n is an integer; and if not, n is not. This is what we call a one-to-one relation. Such a relationship between a statement and the question makes the statement sufficient.

The answer is (D).

Statement (2): $n^4 + 4n$ is an integer.

Similar analysis as in Statement (1) applies to $n^4 + 4n$. Hence, if $n^4 + 4n$ is an integer, n must be an integer.

For decimal values of n, n^4 would have at least one more decimal digit than $4n$. Hence, the sum would not be an integer.

The statement is sufficient.

Geometry

About one-fourth of the data sufficiency problems on the GMAT involve geometry. (There are no proofs.) Unfortunately, the figures on the GMAT are usually not drawn to scale.

Following is a discussion of the basic properties of geometry. You probably know many of these properties. Memorize any that you do not know.

Lines & Angles

➤ When two straight lines meet at a point, they form an angle. The point is called the vertex of the angle, and the lines are called the sides of the angle.

The angle to the right can be identified in three ways:

1. $\angle x$
2. $\angle B$
3. $\angle ABC$ or $\angle CBA$

➤ When two straight lines meet at a point, they form four angles. The angles opposite each other are called vertical angles, and they are congruent (equal). In the figure to the right, $a = b$, and $c = d$. Given an angle, the measure of it's vertical angle can be known (answered) since both are equal; Data Sufficient.

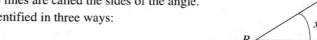

$a = b$ and $c = d$

➤ Angles are measured in degrees, °. By definition, a circle has 360°, so an angle can be measured by its fractional part of a circle. For example, an angle that is $\dfrac{1}{360}$ of the arc of a circle is 1°. And an angle that is $\dfrac{1}{4}$ of the arc of a circle is $\dfrac{1}{4} \times 360 = 90°$.

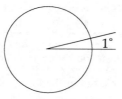

1/360 of an arc
of a circle

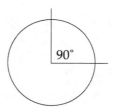

1/4 of an arc
of a circle

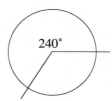

2/3 of an arc
of a circle

There are four major types of angle measures:

An **acute angle** has measure less than 90°:

A **right angle** has measure 90°:

An **obtuse angle** has measure greater than 90°:

A **straight angle** has measure 180°:

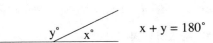

$x + y = 180°$

➢   A triangle can have at most one right angle, and a triangle can have at most one obtuse angle. Hence, in a right triangle, or in an obtuse triangle, the other two angles must be acute angles.

➢   The angle in a straight angle measures 180°. So, if there are n angles that make a straight line, the average angle is $180/n$.

➢   Usually, the equations in a geometry problem are linear. (For example, the angle sum of a triangle is 180 degrees can be depicted as $a + b + c = 180$, which is a linear equation. The sum of the remote interior angles equals the exterior angle can be depicted as, say, $x = y + z$ which is a linear equation, etc.) Note: Usually, each linear equation in n variables reduces the degree of freedom by 1.

➢   **Example:** In the figure, the three lines intersect at O.
         What is the value of a ?

(1) $y = x + 10$

(2) $x = ay$

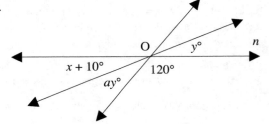

Equating vertical angles yields $y = x + 10$, which is same as Statement (1). Since this is a direct result from the figure, Statement (1) is not sufficient.

Now, Statement (2) says, $x = ay$. Solving this equation for y and plugging it into $y = x + 10$ yields $x/a = x + 10$. Solving for x yields $x = \dfrac{10a}{1-a}$. Also, $y = x + 10 = \dfrac{10a}{1-a} + 10 = \dfrac{10a + 10 - 10a}{1-a} = \dfrac{10}{1-a}$. Now, we know that the angle made by any point on a line is 180°. Hence, the angle made by point O on line n is 180°. Hence, $120 + ay + x + 10 = 180$. Simplifying yields $ay + x = 50$. Substituting the known results $x = \dfrac{10a}{1-a}$ and $y = \dfrac{10}{1-a}$ into this equation yields $\dfrac{10a}{1-a} + \dfrac{10a}{1-a} = 50$. Hence, $2\left(\dfrac{10a}{1-a}\right) = 50$. Multiplying both sides by $(1 - a)$ yields $20a = 50(1 - a)$. Distributing the 50 yields $20a = 50 - 50a$. Adding $50a$ to both sides yields $70a = 50$. Finally, dividing both sides by 70 yields $a = 5/7$. Since we have a single value for a, Statement (2) is sufficient and the answer is (B).

➤ Two angles are supplementary if their angle sum is 180°:

$$45 + 135 = 180$$

➤ Two angles are complementary if their angle sum is 90°:

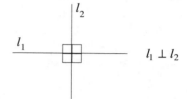

$$30 + 60 = 90$$

➤ Perpendicular lines meet at right angles:

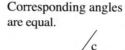

$l_1 \perp l_2$

➤ Two lines in the same plane are parallel if they never intersect. Parallel lines have the same slope.

➤ When parallel lines are cut by a transversal, three important angle relationships exist:

Alternate interior angles are equal.

Corresponding angles are equal.

Interior angles on the same side of the transversal are supplementary.

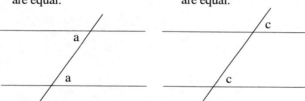

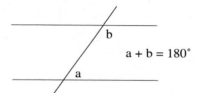

$$a + b = 180°$$

➤ The shortest distance from a point to a line is along a new line that passes through the point and is perpendicular to the original line.

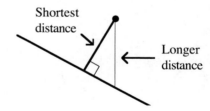

Shortest distance

Longer distance

Triangles

A triangle containing a right angle is called a *right triangle*. The right angle is denoted by a small square:

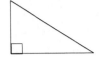

A triangle with two equal sides is called *isosceles*. The angles opposite the equal sides are called the base angles, and they are congruent (equal). A triangle with all three sides equal is called *equilateral*, and each angle is 60°. A triangle with no equal sides (and therefore no equal angles) is called *scalene*:

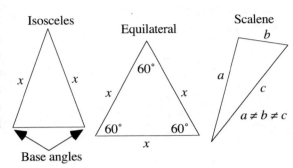

The altitude to the base of an isosceles or equilateral triangle bisects the base and bisects the vertex angle:

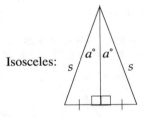

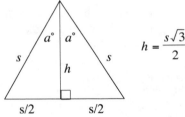

The angle sum of a triangle is 180°:

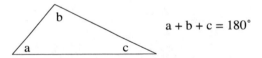

$$a + b + c = 180°$$

Example: In the figure, lines *AB* and *DE* are parallel. What is the value of *x* ?

(1) $y = 45$

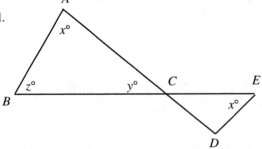

Since lines *AB* and *DE* are parallel, we can equate the alternate interior angles at *A* and *D* to get $\angle A = \angle D = x$ (from the figure). Also, equating vertical angles *ACB* and *DCE* yields $\angle ACB = \angle DCE = 45$ (from the figure). Now, we know that the angle sum of a triangle is 180°. Hence, $\angle DCE + \angle CED + \angle EDC = 180°$. Plugging the known values into this equation yields $45 + x + x = 180$. Solving this equation for *x* yields $x = 67.5$. The data is sufficient.

The area of a triangle is $\frac{1}{2}bh$, where b is the base and h is the height. Sometimes the base must be extended in order to draw the altitude, as in the third drawing directly below:

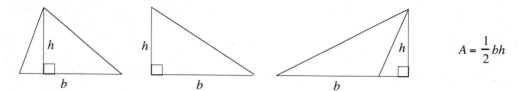

$$A = \frac{1}{2}bh$$

In a triangle, the longer side is opposite the larger angle, and vice versa:

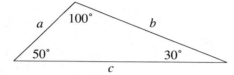

50° is larger than 30°, so side b is longer than side a.

Pythagorean Theorem (right triangles only): The square of the hypotenuse is equal to the sum of the squares of the legs.

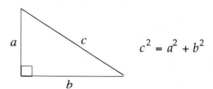

$$c^2 = a^2 + b^2$$

Pythagorean triples: The numbers 3, 4, and 5 can always represent the sides of a right triangle and they appear very often: $5^2 = 3^2 + 4^2$. Another, but less common, Pythagorean Triple is 5, 12, 13: $13^2 = 5^2 + 12^2$.

Two triangles are similar (same shape and usually different sizes) if their corresponding angles are equal. If two triangles are similar, their corresponding sides are proportional:

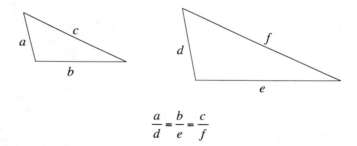

$$\frac{a}{d} = \frac{b}{e} = \frac{c}{f}$$

If two angles of a triangle are congruent to two angles of another triangle, the triangles are similar.

In the figure to the right, the large and small triangles are similar because both contain a right angle and they share $\angle A$.

Two triangles are congruent (identical) if they have the same size and shape.

In a triangle, an exterior angle is equal to the sum of its remote interior angles and is therefore greater than either of them:

$$e = a + b \text{ and } e > a \text{ and } e > b$$

In a triangle, the sum of the lengths of any two sides is greater than the length of the remaining side:

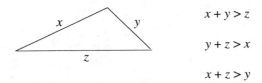

$$x + y > z$$

$$y + z > x$$

$$x + z > y$$

Example: Two sides of a triangle measure 4 and 12. Which one of the following could equal the length of the third side of a triangle: 5 or 9 or 17?

(A) 5

(B) 9

(C) 17

Each side of a triangle is shorter than the sum of the lengths of the other two sides, and, at the same time, longer than the difference of the two. Hence, the length of the third side of the triangle in the question is greater than the difference of the other two sides (12 − 4 = 8) and smaller than their sum (12 + 4 = 16). Since only choice (B) lies between the values, the answer is (B).

In a 30°–60°–90° triangle, the sides have the following relationships:

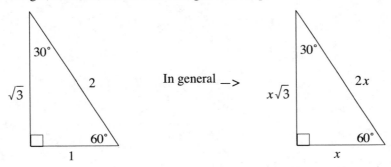

In general →

In a 45°–45°–90° triangle, the sides have the following relationships:

Quadrilaterals

A *quadrilateral* is a four-sided closed figure, where each side is a straight line.

The angle sum of a quadrilateral is 360°. You can view a quadrilateral as being composed of two 180-degree triangles:

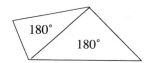

A *parallelogram* is a quadrilateral in which the opposite sides are both parallel and congruent. Its area is *base × height*:

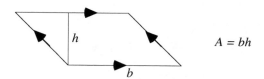

$A = bh$

The diagonals of a parallelogram bisect each other:

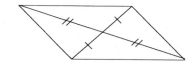

A parallelogram with four right angles is a *rectangle*. If w is the width and l is the length of a rectangle, then its area is and its perimeter is $P = 2w + 2l$.

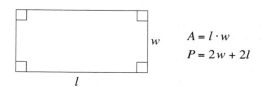

$A = l \cdot w$
$P = 2w + 2l$

Example:

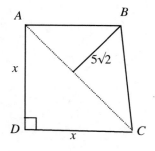

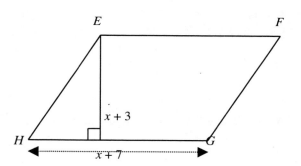

What is the area of parallelogram *EFGH* ?

(1) In the figure, the area of quadrilateral *ABCD* is 75.

(2) In the figure, the sum of the areas of *ABCD* and *EFGH* is 246.

Statement (1) alone:

In the figure, ΔACD is right angled. Hence, by The Pythagorean Theorem, $AC^2 = AD^2 + DC^2 = x^2 + x^2 = 2x^2$. Square rooting both sides yields $AC = x\sqrt{2}$.

The formula for the area of a triangle is $1/2 \times base \times height$. Hence, the area of the right-triangle ACD is $1/2 \cdot x \cdot x$, and the area of triangle ABC is $\frac{1}{2} \cdot AC \cdot$ (altitude from B on AC) $= \frac{1}{2} \cdot x\sqrt{2} \cdot 5\sqrt{2} = 5x$. Now, the area of quadrilateral $ABCD$, which is given to be 75, is the sum of areas of the two triangles: $x^2/2 + 5x$. Hence, $x^2/2 + 5x = 75$. Multiplying both sides by 2 yields $x^2 + 10x = 150$.

Now, the formula for the area of a parallelogram is *base × height*. Hence, the area of $EFGH$ is $(x + 3)(x + 7) = x^2 + 10x + 21 = (x^2 + 10x) + 21 = 150 + 21$ (since $x^2 + 10x = 150$) $= 171$.

Statement (2) alone:

$x^2 + 10x + 21 + x^2/2 + 5x = 246$

$3/2\ x^2 + 15x = 225$

$3/2\ (x^2 + 10x) = 225$

$(x^2 + 10x) = 2/3 \cdot 225 = 2/3 \cdot 225 = 150.$

Statement (2) alone is sufficient.

The answer is (D).

If the opposite sides of a rectangle are equal, it is a square and its area is $A = s^2$ and its perimeter is $P = 4s$, where s is the length of a side:

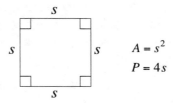

The diagonals of a square bisect each other and are perpendicular to each other:

A quadrilateral with only one pair of parallel sides is a *trapezoid*. The parallel sides are called *bases*, and the non-parallel sides are called *legs*:

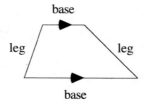

The area of a trapezoid is the average of the two bases times the height:

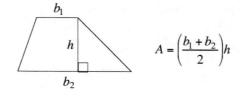

Volume

The volume of a rectangular solid (a box) is the product of the length, width, and height. The surface area is the sum of the area of the six faces:

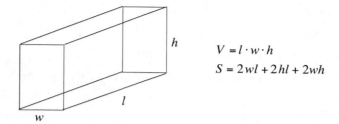

$$V = l \cdot w \cdot h$$
$$S = 2wl + 2hl + 2wh$$

If the length, width, and height of a rectangular solid (a box) are the same, it is a cube. Its volume is the cube of one of its sides, and its surface area is the sum of the areas of the six faces:

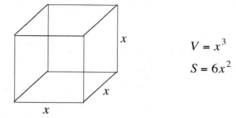

$$V = x^3$$
$$S = 6x^2$$

Example: The length, width, and depth of a rectangular tank are 6 feet, 5 feet, and 7 feet, respectively. A hose supplies water at a rate of 6 cubic feet per minute. How much time in minutes would it take to fill a conical tank whose volume is three times the volume of the rectangle tank?

The volume of a rectangular tank is *length × width × depth* = 6 feet × 5 feet × 7 feet. Hence, the volume of the conical box, which is 3 times the volume of rectangular box, is 3(6 × 5 × 7). Now, the time taken to fill a tank equals the (volume of the tank) ÷ (the rate of filling) = 3(6 × 5 × 7) feet/6 cubic feet per minute = 105 minutes.

The volume of a cylinder is $V = \pi r^2 h$, and the lateral surface (excluding the top and bottom) is $S = 2\pi rh$, where r is the radius and h is the height:

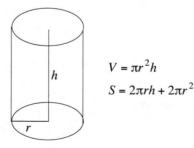

$$V = \pi r^2 h$$
$$S = 2\pi rh + 2\pi r^2$$

Circles

A circle is a set of points in a plane equidistant from a fixed point (the center of the circle). The perimeter of a circle is called the *circumference*.

A line segment from a circle to its center is a *radius*.

A line segment with both end points on a circle is a *chord*.

A chord passing though the center of a circle is a *diameter*.

A diameter can be viewed as two radii, and therefore a diameter's length is twice that of a radius.

A line passing through two points on a circle is a *secant*.

A piece of the circumference is an *arc*.

The area bounded by the circumference and an angle with vertex at the center of the circle is a *sector*.

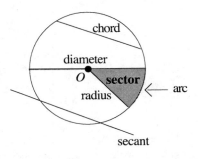

A tangent line to a circle intersects the circle at only one point. The radius of the circle is perpendicular to the tangent line at the point of tangency:

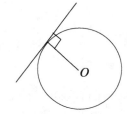

Two tangents to a circle from a common exterior point of the circle are congruent:

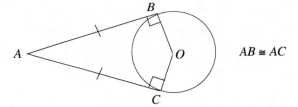

$AB \cong AC$

An angle inscribed in a semicircle is a right angle:

A central angle has by definition the same measure as its intercepted arc:

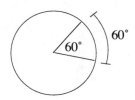

An inscribed angle has one-half the measure of its intercepted arc:

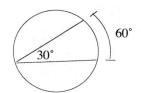

The area of a circle is πr^2, and its circumference (perimeter) is $2\pi r$, where r is the radius:

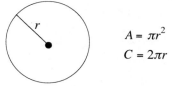

$$A = \pi r^2$$
$$C = 2\pi r$$

On the GMAT, $\pi \approx 3$ is a sufficient approximation for π. You don't need $\pi \approx 3.14$.

Example: In the circle shown in the figure, the length of the arc ACB is 3 times the length of the arc AB. What is the length of the line segment AB ?

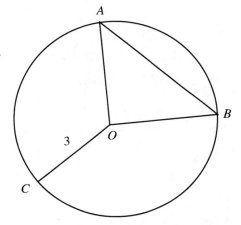

Since the length of the arc ACB is 3 times the length of the arc AB, the angle made by the arc ACB must be three times the angle made by the arc AB. Now, the two arcs together make 360° at the center of the circle. Hence, the smaller angle, the angle made by the arc AB, must equal one-quarter of the full angle, which is 360°. One-quarter of 360° is 90°. Hence, $\angle AOB = 90°$. Hence, triangle AOB is a right triangle, and applying The Pythagorean Theorem to the triangle yields

$$AB^2 = OA^2 + OB^2$$

$$= 3^2 + 3^2 = 9 + 9 = 18 \qquad OA = OB = \text{radius of circle} = OC = 3 \text{ (from the figure)}$$

$$AB = \sqrt{18} = 3\sqrt{2}$$

The answer is $3\sqrt{2}$.

Shaded Regions

To find the area of the shaded region of a figure, subtract the area of the unshaded region from the area of the entire figure.

Example: In the figure, *ABCD* is a rectangle. What is the area of the shaded region in the figure?

(A) 15

(B) 18

(C) 21

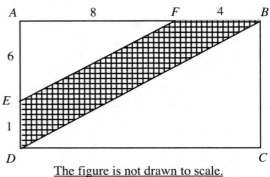

The figure is not drawn to scale.

From the figure, the area of the shaded region equals

(Area of ∆*ABD*) – (Area of ∆*AFE*)

The area of ∆*ABD*, by the formula 1/2 × *base* × *height*, equals

$$1/2 \times AB \times AD = (1/2)(AF + FB)(AE + ED) = (1/2)(8 + 4)(6 + 1) = (1/2)(12)(7) = 6 \times 7 = 42$$

And the area of ∆*AFE* equals

$$1/2 \times AF \times AE = 1/2 \times 8 \times 6 = 4 \times 6 = 24$$

Hence, the area of the shaded region equals

(Area of ∆*ABD*) – (Area of ∆*AFE*) =

42 – 24 =

18

The answer is 18.

Example: What is the area of shaded region in the figure?

(A) $10\pi + 27\sqrt{3}$

(B) $10\pi + \dfrac{27}{4}\sqrt{3}$

(C) $30\pi + 27\sqrt{3}$

(D) $30\pi + 9\sqrt{3}$

(E) $36\pi + 27\sqrt{3}$

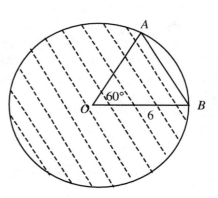

From the figure, we have

The Area of the Shaded Region = (Area of Circle) – (Area of Sector *AOB*) + (Area of ∆*AOB*)

The area of the circle in the figure is

$$\pi \times radius^2 = \pi(6)^2 = 36\pi$$

The formula for the area of a sector is

$$(\text{Angle made by sector}/360°) \times (\text{Area of the circle}) =$$

$$60/360 \times 36\pi =$$

$$1/6 \times 36\pi =$$

$$6\pi$$

Since *OA* and *OB* are radii of the circle, they are equal and therefore the angles opposite them are equal. Hence, *AOB* is an isosceles triangle with one angle ($\angle OAB$ =) 60°. An isosceles triangle with one angle measuring 60° is always an equilateral triangle.

Now, the formula for the area of an equilateral triangle is $\dfrac{\sqrt{3}}{4} \cdot side^2$. Hence, the area of $\triangle AOB$ is

$$\frac{\sqrt{3}}{4} \cdot 6^2 = \frac{\sqrt{3}}{4} \cdot 36 = 9\sqrt{3}$$

Hence, the area of the shaded region is $36\pi - 6\pi + 9\sqrt{3} = 30\pi + 9\sqrt{3}$. The answer is (D).

"Degree of Freedom" Method

Angle Facet: To find an angle of a triangle, constructing a similar triangle is sufficient.

Side Facet: To find a side of a triangle, the exact triangle is needed.

The degree of freedom is 2 for the *angle facet*. This can be explained as follows: Because we know the rule "the sum of three angles of a triangle is 180 degrees," an angle equals 180 degrees minus the other two angles of the triangle. Hence, the angle is dependent on other two angles, and the degree of freedom is 2.

The degree of freedom is 3 for the *side facet*. This is explained as follows: Unless we are given a *side and two angles* or *two sides and one angle* or *all three sides* of the triangle, the triangle cannot be fixed (constructed uniquely) and therefore the side cannot be measured. In any of the three cases, we need 3 variables, and therefore the degree of freedom is 3.

To find an angle, either an angle facet or a side facet helps. But, to find a side, a side facet is the only way.

Example: In the figure, lines *AB* and *DE* are parallel. What is the value of *x* ?

(1) $y = 45$

(2) $z = 67.5$

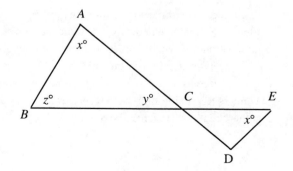

To determine the measure of angle x, we just need to draw a similar figure (angle facet), a precise figure (side facet) is not necessary. In other words, we do not need to form an exact replica (side facet) of the figure; a similar figure (angle facet) will suffice.

We have defined angle facet as the situation where we can apply the rule "The angle sum of a triangle equals 180 degrees." When we cannot apply the rule, we have a side facet.

The degree of freedom in the angle facet is 2; and in the side facet, it is 3.

The angle facet is to construct a similar triangle, and the side facet is to construct the exact triangle.

If the question asked for a side, we would need a side facet. But the question here asks for just angle x. So, we can do with either an angle facet or a side facet.

Since the lengths of none of the sides of the figure are given, we rule out using a side facet.

In the angle facet, as we know, we have the degree of freedom 2 (which means we need two rules). We have the property $\angle B = \angle E$, or $z = x$ (since AB and DE are parallel lines, we equate the alternate interior angles). This is a different linear equation from any of the equations we already have (we have angles sum to 180 degrees) and therefore it reduces the degree of freedom by 1 (degree of freedom reduces by 1 per equation or property). Hence, the degree of freedom now is $2 - 1 = 1$. Thus, we are short one angle (by angle facet). So, we still need one more rule. At this point, we stop looking at the question and start looking at the statements. This is because we know that we need to analyze a Question Setup in a Data Sufficiency problem only until we reduce the degree of freedom to 1. This is the minimum degree of freedom to which the question itself (without statements) can ever reduce.

Now, either statement $y = 45$ or $z = 67.5$ is a rule in the angle facet. Hence, either statement alone is sufficient, and the answer is (D).

Example: In the figure, lines AB and DE are parallel. What is the measure of AB ?

(1) $y = 45$

(2) $z = 67.5$

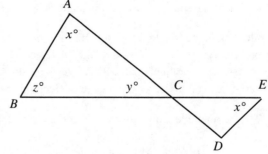

This problem is similar to the previous example, but now a side must be evaluated, whereas before only an angle had to be evaluated. So, using the side facet is inevitable. The degree of freedom for the side facet is 3 (at least one of which is reserved for a side length) for any triangle. But with the statements together, we have only two different angle rules $y = 45$ and $z = 67.5$ and no side rule. These two together reduce the degree of freedom to $3 - 2 = 1$. We sure have another rule: Angle sum = 180 degrees, or $x + y + z = 180$, but this is not a side rule. So, we neglect it. The degree of freedom did not reduce to 0. So, the statements together are not sufficient. The answer is (E).

Example: In the figure, lines *AB* and *DE* are parallel.
What is the measure of *AB* ?

(1) $BC = 10$

(2) $z = 67.5$

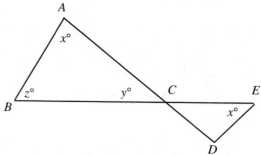

The question asks for a side. So, we need a side facet. This problem is same as the previous example, but with Statement (1) replaced with a detail of the side of the triangle. We know that the degree of freedom is 3 for the side facet.

Now, the two angle rules "Angles sum to 180 degrees," and "$x + y + z = 180$," and the rule from Statement (2) $z = 67.5$ together reduce the degree of freedom (one each) to $3 - 1 - 1 = 1$. The rule *AB* parallel to *DE* (so $x = z$) is no longer be needed. The last degree is reserved for a side that Statement (1) fills. Therefore, both statements together are sufficient, and the answer is (C).

Example: In the figure, lines *AB* and *DE* are parallel.
What is the measure of *AB* ?

(1) $CD = 10$

(2) $z = 67.5$

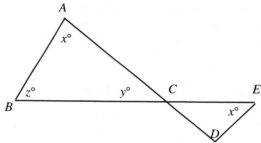

This problem is same as the previous example, but with Statement (1) replaced with a detail from the other triangle. Statement (1) does not decrease the degree of the triangle because it mentions a side outside the triangle (outside the system). Statement (2) surely reduces the degree of the problem by 1. The degree of freedom is $3 - 1 = 2$. The two rules "angle *z* equals *x* (*AB* being parallel to *DE*)" and "the angle sum being 180 degrees" could only reduce the degree of freedom of the problem to $2 - 1 = 1 \neq 0$ as discussed; it does not affect the one degree of freedom reserved for a side. Hence, the answer is (E).

Example: In the figure, lines *AB* and *DE* are parallel.
What is the measure of *AB* ?

(1) $z = 67.5$

(2) $AB + BC = 10$

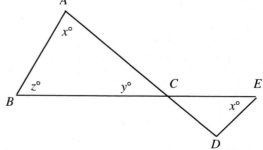

Unlike in the previous problem, we sure have a side rule [Statement (1)] on the same triangle *ABC*. But, this rule fails to nullify the degree of freedom reserved for a side because the rule does not determine any side. For example, with $z = 67.5$, $x + y + z = 180$, and $z = x$, we sure can evaluate all three angles, but with the rule $AB + BC = 10$, we can have multiple values for *AB* for multiple values of *BC*. Hence, the degree of freedom reserved for the side in the side facet is not nullified. So, the statements together are not sufficient. The answer is (E).

Example: In the figure, lines *AB* and *DE* are parallel.
What is the measure of *AB* ?

(1) $AB - BC = 5$

(2) $AB + BC = 10$

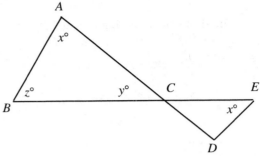

The two statements can determine the sides *AB* and *BC* as follows: $AB - BC = 5$ plus $AB + BC = 10$ is $2AB = 15$ or $AB = 15/2$ and $AB + BC = 10$ minus $AB - BC = 5$ yields $2BC = 5$ or $BC = 5/2$. To determine *AB*, we need a side facet. Knowing the sides *AB* and *BC* reduces the degree of freedom to $3 - 2 = 1$. But the angle rules $x = z$ and $x + y + z = 180$ cannot determine at least one of the angles of the triangle *ABC*. Hence, the degree of freedom is still 1 and not nullified. Hence, the statements together are not sufficient, and the answer is (E).

Most geometry problems on the GMAT require straightforward calculations. However, some problems measure your insight into the basic rules of geometry. For this type of problem, you should step back and take a "birds-eye" view of the problem. The following example will illustrate.

Example: In the figure, *O* is the center of the circle. What is
the length of diagonal *PS* ?

(1)   The radius of the circle is 2.

(2)   *O* is also a vertex of the square *OPRS*.

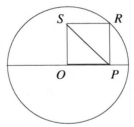

The diagonals of a square are equal. Hence, line segment *OR* (not shown) is equal to *SP*. Now, *OR* is a radius of the circle and therefore $OR = 2$. Hence, $SP = 2$ as well. Clearly, both statements were used based on the need, and the answer is (C).

Tip!

When Drawing a Geometric Figure or Checking a Given One, Be Sure to Include Drawings of Extreme Cases As Well As Ordinary Ones.

Example 1:   In the figure, what is the value of angle *x* ?

(1)   *AC* is a chord.

(2)   *B* is a point on the circle.

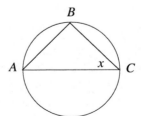

Although in the drawing AC looks to be a diameter, that cannot be assumed. All we know is that AC is a chord. Hence, numerous cases are possible, three of which are illustrated below:

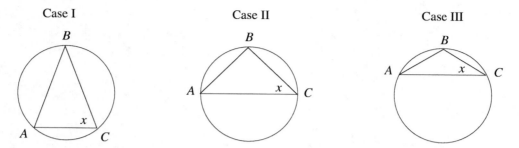

Case I   Case II   Case III

In Case I, x is greater than 45°; in Case II, x equals 45°; in Case III, x is less than 45°. Hence, the answer is (E): the statements together are not sufficient.

Example 2:   Three rays emanate from a common point and form three angles with measures p, q, r. Is $q + r > 180°$?

It is natural to make the drawing symmetric as follows:

In this case, $p = q = r = 120°$, so $q + r = 240°$. However, there are other drawings possible. For example:

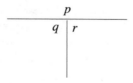

In this case, $q + r = 180°$ and therefore it cannot be determined from the information given.

Strategy

Constructability Technique.

If we can construct the system (in geometry, it will be a unique figure), we can say data sufficient for any question about the system (any side length or angle measure of the system).

This technique is best for establishing data sufficiency, but still works well for establishing data insufficiency.

Example:

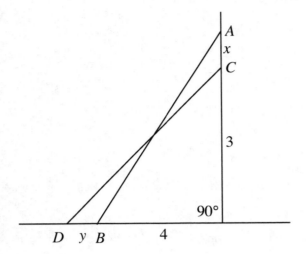

Does *AB* equal *CD* ?

    (1) $x = 2$

    (2) $y = 3$

Construct a right angle. On one arm of the angle, locate a point 4 units away from the knee (name it *B*); and on another arm, locate a point 3 units away from the knee (name it *C*). Note that the two points are not on the same triangle. Extend the arms to accommodate the points *A* and *D* still not located.

Statement (1): $x = 2$	Statement (2): $y = 3$
We do not have any information about where on the first arm the point *D* is located. Point *D* could be any point after point *B* on the first arm. So, the length *CD* is not known, and there is no question of comparing it with any other length for equality. We surely have a double case since the value of at least one of the two quantities we are comparing is not fixed.	We do not have any information about where on the second arm the point *A* must be located. Point *A* could be any point after point *C* on the second arm. So, the length *AB* is not known and there is no question of comparing it with any other length for equality. We surely have a double case since the value of at least one of the two quantities we are comparing is not fixed.
The statement is *not* sufficient.	The statement is *not* sufficient.
Point *A* is located 2 (= *x*) units after point *C* on the second arm. Join *A* and *B* and measure *AB*.	Point *D* is located 3 (= *y*) units after point *B* on the first arm. Join *C* and *D* and measure *CD*.
AB is fixed and *CD* is variable.	*CD* is fixed and *AB* is variable.

From the two statements together, we can fix both *AB* and *CD*. So, comparison of the two fixed quantities is possible. Together the statements are sufficient, and the answer is (C).

Locus Technique.

A locus is set of feasible figures for a geometric context. If in all the feasible figures (called loci), we have single value for the *question*, the data is sufficient. Otherwise, the data is insufficient.

Sometimes, we will have only one feasible figure. This means, we have single value for the *question* and therefore the data is sufficient.

Example:

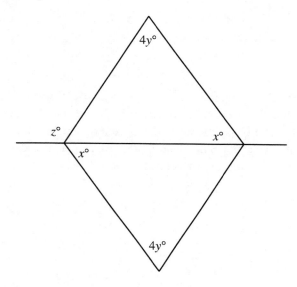

What is the value of z ?

    (1) $x = 40$

    (2) $y = 20$

Since the exterior angle of a triangle equals the sum of the remote interior angles, we have $z = x + 4y$. So, z is a one-to-one function of x and y and therefore given x and y, we can answer the question. So, the statements together will at least answer the question, which eliminates (E).

Next, test whether the statements have a one-to-one relationship between themselves. If Statement (1) implies Statement (2), the answer is (A) or (C) or (D); and if Statement (2) implies Statement (1), the answer is (B) or (C) or (D).

Statement (1): $x = 40$

With Statement (1), $x = 40$, we can draw an arbitrary line DB and from B draw a line at an angle $x°$. Now, A could be any point on this line.

Statement (2): $y = 20$

So, $4y$ equals 80, and we have the value of $\angle A = 80°$.

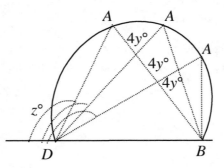

The locus of the point is the circular arc above, where BD acts as a chord. Now, $\angle A$ measures 80 degrees throughout the arc. But z has different values for different points A on the arc (as shown in the figure). Since we do not have a unique value for z, the statement is *not* sufficient.

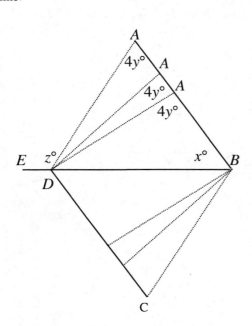

Though for each point x is fixed, we see that $\angle BAD$, which equals $4y$, is varying (precisely decreasing as A moves upwards). So, angle $\angle ADE$ (= z, from the figure), which is the exterior angle of $\triangle BAD$, equals the sum of its interior opposite angles, x and $4y$. Hence, $\angle ADE = z = x + 4y$. Recalling that though x has been fixed, since $4y$ is varying, $x + 4y$ is as well varying (precisely, decreasing as A moves upwards). Hence, z varies as well. This means, z is not fixed by the statement. In other words, z cannot be calculated by the statement and therefore the statement is *not* sufficient.

From the equation $z = x + 4y$, we know z is a function of x and y. Hence, the statements together, which collect the values of x and y, are sufficient. The answer is (C).

Equation Method

Based on the properties of the problem, collect all equations and either by the "degree of freedom" paradigm or by physically solving the problem, answer the question.

Example: In the figure, lines *AB* and *DE* are parallel. What is the value of x ?

(1) $y = 45$

(2) $z = 67.5$

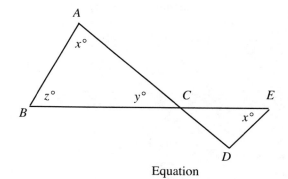

Math Property	Equation
Question:	
Angles of a triangle sum to 180 degrees	$x + y + z = 180$
Alternate interior angles are equal for parallel lines	$x = z$
Statement (1):	$y = 45$
Statement (2):	$z = 67.5$

The question setup plus Statement (1) form the system

$$x + y + z = 180$$

$$x = z$$

$$y = 45$$

Since the system of equations can be solved for x, Statement (1) alone is sufficient.

The question setup plus Statement (2) form the system

$$x + y + z = 180$$

$$x = z$$

$$z = 67.5$$

Since the system of equations can be solved for x, Statement (2) also is sufficient.

The answer is (D).

Complicated figures like quadrilaterals can be drawn and data sufficiency evaluated by consecutively applying the evaluation from one basic figure to the other using one of the given methods — degree of freedom, constructability, or locus.

For example, constructing a quadrilateral can be viewed as two adjacent triangles sharing a common side. So, analyze data sufficiency for the triangles one after the other.

Example:

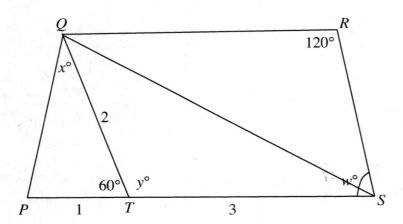

The figure is not drawn to scale.

What is the perimeter of *PQRS*?

(1) $x = 30$

(2) $w = 45$

We begin by evaluating the basic figures, the triangles in the order : ΔPQT, ΔQTS, and ΔQRS.

In ΔPQT, one angle ($\angle QTP = 60°$) and two sides ($PT = 1$ and $QT = 2$) are given. So, the triangle can be fully constructed. Hence, $\angle Q = x°$ can be measured even before we start to use Statement (1). Therefore, the statement is not required.

Since the angle in a line is 180°, $\angle PTQ + \angle QTS = 180°$, or $60° + \angle QTS = 180°$, or $\angle QTS = 180° - 60° = 120°$. Also $\angle QRS = 120°$ from the figure. We know that constructing a quadrilateral is like constructing two triangles with a common side (which acts as a diagonal of the quadrilateral). Since in ΔQTS we know the measures of one angle ($\angle T$) and two sides (ST and QT), the triangle can be fully constructed. From this triangle, side QS and the other two angles, one of which is $\angle QST$, can be measured. Now, let's collect details for ΔQRS. We have the measures of one angle $\angle R$ and one side QS. So, we need at least one angle of the triangle or at least one side of the triangle to be able to construct the triangle and measure the perimeter. One angle is given by Statement (2): $w = \angle QST + \angle QSR = 45°$. Since we already known $\angle QST$ (we can measure from the drawing), the only unknown in the equation is $\angle QSR$, which can be calculated from it. Now, we have two angles and one side in ΔQRS, so Statement (2) is sufficient.

The answer is (B), Statement (1) not required and Statement (2) is sufficient.

Problem Set D: Geometry

1. What is the sum of the equal angles of $\triangle RST$?

    (1) $\angle R = 50°$

    (2) $\angle S = 65°$

2. What is the sum of the equal angles of the isosceles triangle PQR?

    (1) $\angle P = 44°$

    (2) $\angle Q = 92°$

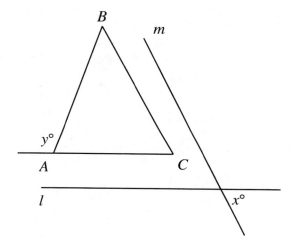

3. The sides AC and BC of $\triangle ABC$ are parallel, respectively, to the lines l and m outside the triangle. What is the value of x ?

    (1) $\angle B = 40°$

    (2) $y = 100°$

4. A ladder leans against a vertical wall. The base of the ladder is 15 feet away from the wall and the top of the ladder is 20 feet above the ground on the wall. The wall is perpendicular to the ground. The ladder is pulled farther from the wall causing the top of the ladder to fall by x feet. How far away was the base of the ladder moved?

    (1) $x = 1$.

    (2) The length of the ladder is 25 feet.

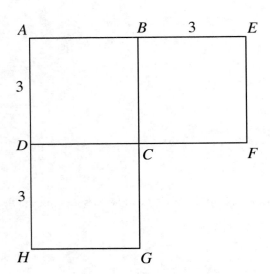

5.   In the figure, is $a < b < c$?

(1) $x = \dfrac{y + z}{2}$

(2) $y = \dfrac{z - x}{2}$

6.   In the figure, *BEFC* and *DCGH* are rectangles. Is *ABCD* a square?

(1) *BEFC* is a square.

(2) *CGHD* is not a square.

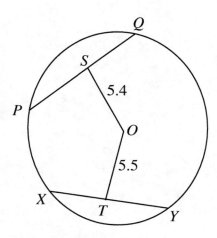

7.   The chords *PQ* and *XY* are located at a distance of 5.4 and 5.5 respectively from the center of circle. What is the length of *ST*?

  (1) $PQ = 5.5$

  (2) $XY = 5.4$

8.   *P*, *Q*, and *R* are three different points on a plane. Which one of the lines *PQ*, *QR*, and *RP* is the longest?

  (1)   *P*, *Q*, and *R* are adjacent vertices of a right triangle.

  (2)   *P*, *Q*, and *R* are adjacent vertices of a rectangle, in that order.

9.   *ABCD* is a quadrilateral. A rhombus is a quadrilateral whose sides are all congruent. *BCEF* is a rhombus and shares a common side with the quadrilateral *ABCD*. The area of which one is greater: *ABCD* or *BCEF* ?

  (1)   *ABCD* is a square.

  (2)   *BCEF* is not a square.

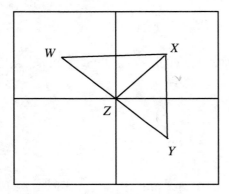

10.   Is *ABC* an equilateral triangle?

(1) $BD/AD = DC/DB$

(2) $AB^2 + CD^2 = AD^2 + BC^2$

Figure not drawn to scale

11.   The four small squares placed as shown in the figure form a big square. If $\triangle WXY$ is formed by joining the centers of three of the four small squares as shown in the figure and if *Z* is the center of the big square, then what is the perimeter of the big square?

(1) $WY = \sqrt{2}$

(2) $ZX = \dfrac{1}{\sqrt{2}}$

Answers and Solutions to Problem Set D: Geometry

1.   What is the sum of the equal angles of $\triangle RST$?

    (1) $\angle R = 50°$

    (2) $\angle S = 65°$

If all three angles were equal, each angle would be 60°. Thus, the statements together say that not all angles are equal. Such derivations can be safely applied to the question. So, the question can be restated as "Two angles of $\triangle RST$ are equal. What's their sum?"

There are two equal angles and therefore one unequal angle in the triangle. The sum of the three angles is 180° and therefore the sum of the equal angles plus the unequal angle equals 180°, which means the sum of the equal angles equals 180° minus the unequal angle.

Statement (1): $\angle R = 50°$

$\angle R$ is either the unequal angle or one of the equal angles.

In the first case, the sum of the equal angles is $180° - \angle R = 180° - 50° = 130°$; and in the second case, the sum equals $\angle R + \angle R = 2\angle R = 2(50°) = 100°$.

We have a double case and therefore the statement is not sufficient.

Statement (2): $\angle S = 65°$

$\angle S$ is either the unequal angle or it is one of the equal angles.

In the first case, the sum of the equal angles is $180° - \angle S = 180° - 65° = 115°$; and in the second case, the sum equals $\angle S + \angle S = 2\angle S = 2(65°) = 130°$.

We have a double case and therefore the statement is not sufficient.

The only common solution with the statements together is 130°. Hence, the statements together are sufficient, and the answer is (C). We also get to know that $\angle R$ is the unequal angle and $\angle S$ and $\angle T$ are the equal angles.

Method II: (Degree of Freedom Method)

Let x, y, and z be the angles of the triangle, and let y and z ($y = z$) be the equal angles. Then the question can be rephrased as "what is $y + z = 2y$?"

Rule 1: Since the angles sum to 180 degrees, we have $x + y + z = 180$. The degree of freedom reduces to $3 - 1 = 2$.

Rule 2: $y = z$. Degree of freedom reduces to $2 - 1 = 1$.

Since the degree is now 1, let's turn to the statements.

Statement (1):

Rule 3: x could equal 50, and y could equal 65.

Or

    y could equal 50 and x could equal 80. We have a double case for y here and the rule fails to reduce the degree. So, the statement is not sufficient.

Statement (2):

Rule 4:   *x* could equal 65, and *y* could equal 57.5.

Or

> *y* could equal 65 so that *x* could equal 50. We have a double case for *y* here and the rule fails to reduce the degree. So, the statement is not sufficient.

Combining all the rules including 3 and 4 could reduce to single solution: *y* to equal 65 and *x* to equal 50. Here, we do not have a double case for *y*. So, the data is sufficient. The answer is (C).

2.   What is the sum of the equal angles of the isosceles triangle *PQR*?

> (1) $\angle P = 44°$

> (2) $\angle Q = 92°$

There are two equal angles and therefore one unequal angle in the triangle. The sum of the three angles is 180° and therefore the sum of the equal angles plus the sum of the unequal angle equals 180°. Hence, the sum of the equal angles is 180° minus the unequal angle.

Statement (1): $\angle P = 44°$

There are two equal angles and one unequal angle (suppose that the third angle is unequal).

If $\angle P$ is one of the equal angles, the sum of the equal angles is $\angle P + \angle P = 44° + 44° = 88°$.

If $\angle P$ is not one of the unequal angles, the sum equals 180° minus the unequal angle = $180° - \angle P$ $= 180° - 44° = 136°$

We have a double case and therefore the statement is *not* sufficient.

Statement (2): $\angle Q = 92°$

The equal angles of an isosceles triangle are never greater than or equal to a right angle (because then the angle sum would exceed 180°.)

Let's proceed the same way as in Statement (1).

There are two equal angles and one unequal angle.

If $\angle P$ is one of the equal angles, the sum of the equal angles is $\angle P + \angle P = 92° + 92° = 184°$, which is greater than 180° (the sum of angles in a triangle) and therefore the result is impossible.

If $\angle P$ is not one of the unequal angles, the sum equals 180° minus the unequal angle = $180° - \angle P$ $= 180° - 44° = 136°$.

We have a single solution here and therefore the statement is sufficient.

The answer is (B).

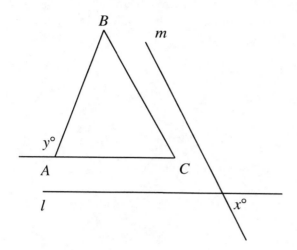

3.   The sides *AC* and *BC* of Δ*ABC* are parallel, respectively, to the lines *l* and *m* outside the triangle. What is the value of *x* ?

(1)   ∠*B* = 40°

(2)   *y* = 100°

Since the pair of lines *AC* and *BC* are parallel to the pair of lines *l* and *m*, respectively, corresponding angles between the pairs are equal. So, ∠*C* equals *x*°, and the question transforms to "What is ∠*C*?" with the parallel lines *l* and *m* now out of the picture. We do not need them anymore. So, this is now a triangle problem.

From the figure, it is clear that *y*° = ∠*B* + ∠*C* (An exterior angle equals the sum of the remote interior angles). Now, ∠*C* equals *y*° – ∠*B*. This says that both *y*° and ∠*B* are needed unless either derives the other. Now, angles *y*° and ∠*B* are independent of each other and neither derives the other. Therefore, both statements are needed and sufficient. The answer is (C).

$$∠C = y° – ∠B = 100° \text{ [from Statement (2)]} – 40° \text{ [from Statement (1)]} = 60°$$

4.   A ladder leans against a vertical wall. The base of the ladder is 15 feet away from the wall and the top of the ladder is 20 feet above the ground on the wall. The wall is perpendicular to the ground. The ladder is pulled farther from the wall causing the top of the ladder to fall by *x* feet. How far away was the base of the ladder moved?

(1)   *x* = 1.

(2)   The length of the ladder is 25 feet.

Since the wall is inclined at right angle with the ground, The Pythagorean Theorem is applicable to the triangle that the ground and the wall make with the ladder. So, *ladder²* = *ground²* + *wall²*. In the initial position, *ground* = 20, and *wall* = 15. So, *ladder²* = 20² + 15² = 25². Therefore, *ladder* = 25. Since this is a known result that can be derived from the question, which is what Statement (2) just repeats, the statement is not required. The statement is *not* sufficient.

Now since the ladder drops by x feet, the *wall* changes to $15 - x = 15 - 1$ [from Statement (1)] $= 14$. Since the length of the ladder remains the same even after movement, *ladder* $= 25$. Applying the Pythagorean Theorem yields

$$ladder^2 = ground^2 + wall^2$$

$$25^2 = ground^2 + 14^2$$

$$ground = \sqrt{25^2 - 14^2} = \sqrt{625 - 196} = \sqrt{429}$$

So, the leg of the ladder has moved by $\sqrt{429} - 20$ units. So, Statement (1) alone is sufficient.

The answer is (A).

Method II:

Let a wall incline perpendicularly with ground. Locate a point on the ground 15 units away from the wall. Locate a point on the wall 20 units above the ground. Make a ladder that exactly fits the length between the two points. Measure the length of the ladder. The length must be in accordance with Statement (2). So, Statement (2) alone is *not* sufficient. Now, move the leg of the ladder away from wall by x units [the value of x is given in Statement (1)] on the ground. Now, the top of the ladder would automatically slide down by a certain length. Measure it and this is the answer. So, Statement (1), which we used in our way, is clearly sufficient. The answer is (A).

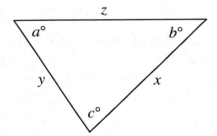

5.   In the figure, is $a < b < c$?

    (1) $x = \dfrac{y + z}{2}$

    (2) $y = \dfrac{z - x}{2}$

The inequality $a < b < c$ can be split as "Is $a < b$?" <u>and</u> "Is $b < c$?".

If you transformed the question as "Is $a < b$ and is $a < c$?", that might not be correct since the two inequalities cannot be combined again to "$a < b < c$."

Either prove both inequalities are true (to answer the question as "Yes") or prove at least one false (to answer the question as "No"). The data sufficiency test passes either way.

Statement (1): $x = \dfrac{y + z}{2}$

When x equals the average of y and z, there are two possibilities:

   1) x lies between y and z.
   2) x, y, and z are equal.

The possibilities are analyzed below:

Possibility 1):
x lies between y and z (For example, 4 is the average of 3 and 5 and lies between 3 and 5). This is an inequality relation and the angles opposite the sides x, y, and z would also follow the same relation [which means a (which is opposite x) lies between b (which is opposite y) and c (which is opposite z). This says that the inequality $a < b < c$ is false since a does not come in middle of the inequality. (In either order: increasing or decreasing. So, further analysis is not needed.)

Possibility 2):
x, y, and z are equal which means $x = y = z$. This can be considered as an inequality and the inequality relation can be applied to the angles opposite the sides. So, $a = b = c$. This says the inequality $a < b < c$ is false.

In either case, the answer is false, so the statement is sufficient.

The answer is (A).

Statement (2): $y = \dfrac{z - x}{2}$

We can have $x = 1$, $y = 1$ and $z = 3$. Here, $x = y < z$ and following the relation to opposite sides yields $a = b < c$, which says $a < b < c$ is false. We can have $x = 1$, $y = 2$ and $z = 5$. Here, $x < y < z$ and following the relation to opposite sides yields $a < b < c$. This is a double case and the therefore the statement is not sufficient.

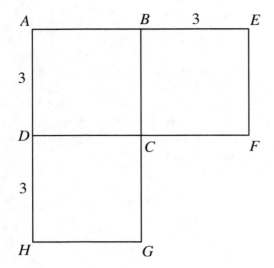

6.   In the figure, *BEFC* and *DCGH* are rectangles. Is *ABCD* a square?

(1) *BEFC* is a square.

(2) *CGHD* is not a square.

In a square, all sides are equal. So, if *ABCD* is a square, *AB* must equal *CD* must equal *AD*, which equals 3. So, the question can be transformed as "Is $AB = 3$ and $BC = 3$ and $DC = 3$?" or "Is $AB \neq 3$ or $BC \neq 3$ or $DC \neq 3$?"

Statement (1): *BEFC* is a square.

This indicates the sides *BC* and *BE* are equal in length. So, $BC = BE = 3$. But, we do not know about the other two sides *AB* and *DC* in the transformed question. So, the statement is *not* sufficient.

Statement (2): *DCGH* is not a square

Hence, $DC \neq DH$, which equals 3. Hence, $DC \neq 3$. This makes us answer the whole question "Is $AB = BC = DC = 3$" false. We are thus able to answer the question and the statement is sufficient to do that.

The answer is (B).

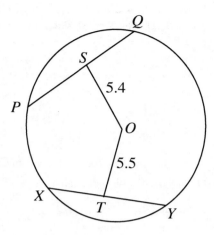

7. The chords _PQ_ and _XY_ are located at a distance of 5.4 and 5.5 respectively from the center of circle. What is the length of _ST_?

(1) $PQ = 5.5$

(2) $XY = 5.4$

We have two sides _SO_ and _OT_ in triangle _SOT_. To determine the third side, we need at least one angle or the third side (minimum requirement to construct the triangle), which even the statements together do not give. So, the statements together are _not_ sufficient. The answer is (E).

8. _P_, _Q_, and _R_ are three different points on a plane. Which one of the lines _PQ_, _QR_, and _RP_ is the longest?

(1)   _P_, _Q_, and _R_ are adjacent vertices of a right triangle.

(2)   _P_, _Q_, and _R_ are adjacent vertices of a rectangle, in that order.

Statement (1): _P_, _Q_, and _R_ are vertices of a right triangle.

This does not tell us which one of the three vertices — _P_, _Q_, and _R_ — is the right angle. So, we do not know which side is the hypotenuse and therefore the longest side. So, the statement alone is _not_ sufficient.

Statement (2): _P_, _Q_, and _R_ are adjacent vertices of the rectangle, in that order.

Following the given order of the vertices, we can draw the rectangle as shown

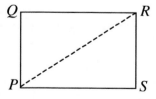

_S_ is an arbitrary fourth vertex. From, the figure, _Q_ is the right angle and the side (diagonal) _PR_ opposite the angle is the longest side. We have sufficient data with the statement.

The answer is (B).

9.   *ABCD* is a quadrilateral. A rhombus is a quadrilateral whose sides are all congruent. *BCEF* is a rhombus and shares a common side with the quadrilateral *ABCD*. The area of which one is greater: *ABCD* or *BCEF* ?

   (1)   *ABCD* is a square.

   (2)   *BCEF* is not a square.

The question is about the inequality between the areas of *ABCD* and *BCEF*.

In either statement alone, the size of the quadrilateral *BCEF* is uncontrolled and its area can range from 0 through unlimited value. So, neither statement is sufficient to do the comparison in the question.

With the statements together, we have that *ABCD* is a square and *BCEF* is *not* a square. The two quadrilaterals share a common side *BC*. Since sides of a square are equal and sides of a rhombus are equal, the sides of the square and the rhombus all equal *BC*.

Since a rhombus is inclined towards the ground (unlike a square that stands upright), the area of a rhombus increases as the inclination decreases and is a maximum when the rhombus becomes a square. But since the rhombus *BCEF* is *not* a square, the area of *BCEF* is less than the area of *ABCD*. The figure below illustrates what the area of *BCEF* is less than the area of *ABCD*.

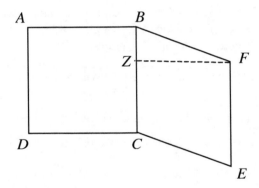

   Area equals base × altitude. The altitude *ZF* of the rhombus is less than the
   altitude *AB* of the square, and the base is the same for the rhombus and the
   square. So, area of the rhombus is smaller.

The statements together are sufficient, and the answer is (C).

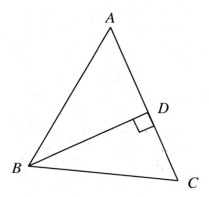

10.   Is *ABC* an equilateral triangle?

    (1)   *BD/AD = DC/DB*

    (2) $AB^2 + CD^2 = AD^2 + BC^2$

Statement (1): *BD/AD = DC/DB*

In the two triangles, *ABD* and *BCD*, a pair of corresponding angles $\angle ADB$ and $\angle CDB$ are equal (both equal 90°).

Also, the corresponding sides are in the same ratio *BD/AD = DC/DB*.

Hence, the triangles *ADB* and *BDC* are similar. So, $\angle A$ equals $\angle DBC$, which is only part of $\angle B$. Hence, $\angle A \neq \angle B$. So, not all sides of the triangle are equal and therefore the triangle is not equilateral. The statement is sufficient.

Statement (2): $AB^2 + CD^2 = AD^2 + BC^2$

Applying Pythagorean theorem to triangle *ABC* yields

$$AD^2 + BD^2 = AB^2$$

Applying Pythagorean theorem to triangle *BDC* yields

$$BC^2 = BD^2 + DC^2$$

Summing the equations yields

$$AD^2 + BC^2 = AB^2 + DC^2$$

This is a known result and we have not used the statement but derived it from the question. Such a statement is *not* sufficient.

The answer is (A).

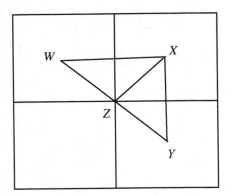

<u>Figure not drawn to scale</u>

11.   The four small squares placed as shown in the figure form a big square. If △*WXY* is formed by joining the centers of three of the four small squares as shown in the figure and if *Z* is the center of the big square, then what is the perimeter of the big square?

(1) $WY = \sqrt{2}$

(2) $ZX = \dfrac{1}{\sqrt{2}}$

The centers of the squares are bisecting points. Hence, *WZ, XZ,* and *YZ* equal half the diagonal length of the small squares. Now, *WY* equals *WZ + ZY =* 2 times the diagonal of the small squares. The diagonal of the bigger square contains two diagonals of the smaller squares. So, the diagonal length of the bigger square equals 2 times the diagonal length of smaller squares. Once we have the diagonal length of the bigger square, we can evaluate the area by either drawing the figure or applying formula for the same. Hence, the question can be transformed to "What is the diagonal length of the smaller square?" It equals 4 times *XZ* [Statement (1) sufficient] or 2 times *WY* [Statement (2) sufficient]. Either statement is sufficient, and the answer is (D).

Coordinate Geometry

On a number line, the numbers increase in size to the right and decrease to the left:

If we draw a line through the point 0 perpendicular to the number line, we will form a grid:

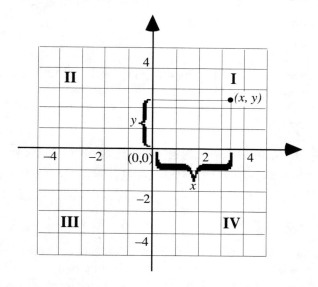

The thick horizontal line in the above diagram is called the x-axis, and the thick vertical line is called the y-axis. The point at which the axes meet, $(0, 0)$, is called the origin. On the x-axis, positive numbers are to the right of the origin and increase in size to the right; further, negative numbers are to the left of the origin and decrease in size to the left. On the y-axis, positive numbers are above the origin and ascend in size; further, negative numbers are below the origin and descend in size. As shown in the diagram, the point represented by the ordered pair (x, y) is reached by moving x units along the x-axis from the origin and then moving y units vertically. In the ordered pair (x, y), x is called the *abscissa* and y is called the *ordinate*; collectively they are called coordinates. The x and y axes divide the plane into four quadrants, numbered I, II, III, and IV counterclockwise. Note, if $x \neq y$, then (x, y) and (y, x) represent different points on the coordinate system. The points $(2, 3)$, $(-3, 1)$, $(-4, -4)$, and $(4, -2)$ are plotted in the following coordinate system:

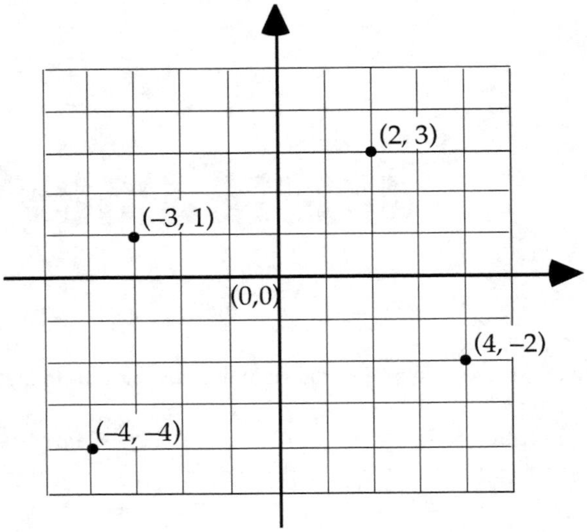

Example: Is $a + b$ positive?

  (1)   The point (a, b) is in Quadrant II.

  (2) $|a| - |b| > 0$

We are given that the point (a, b) is in Quadrant II. In Quadrant II, the x-coordinate is negative and the y-coordinate is positive. Hence, $a < 0$ and $b > 0$.

Since a is negative and b is positive, $a < b$.

Since a is negative, $|a|$ equals $-a$; and since b is positive, $|b|$ equals b. So, $a + b = -|a| + |b| = -(|a| - |b|)$. Now, since $|a| - |b|$ is given to be positive, $-(|a| - |b|)$ must be negative. So, $a + b < 0$. The answer is (C): data is sufficient only if both statements are used.

Distance Formula:

The distance formula is derived by using the Pythagorean theorem. Notice in the figure below that the distance between the points (x, y) and (a, b) is the hypotenuse of a right triangle. The difference $y - b$ is the measure of the height of the triangle, and the difference $x - a$ is the length of base of the triangle. Applying the Pythagorean theorem yields

$$d^2 = (x - a)^2 + (y - b)^2$$

Taking the square root of both sides of this equation yields

$$\boxed{d = \sqrt{(x - a)^2 + (y - b)^2}}$$

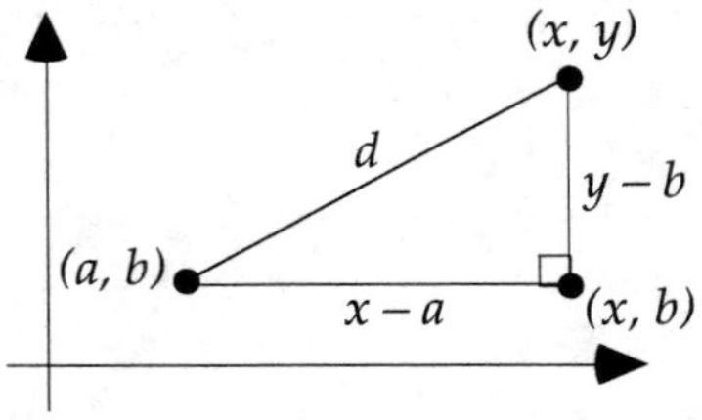

Example: If C is the midpoint of the points $A(-3, -4)$ and B, then $AC =$

    (1) $B = (-5, 6)$

    (2) $BC = \sqrt{26}$

Using the distance formula to calculate the distance between A and B yields

$$AB = \sqrt{\left(-3-(-5)\right)^2 + \left(-4-6\right)^2} = \sqrt{2^2 + (-10)^2} = \sqrt{4+100} = \sqrt{104} = 2\sqrt{26}$$

Since C is the midpoint of AB, $AC = \dfrac{AB}{2} = \dfrac{2\sqrt{26}}{2} = \sqrt{26}$. Hence, Statement (1) is sufficient.

Since the point C is the midpoint of AB, $AC = BC = \sqrt{26}$, given. Hence, Statement (2) is also sufficient.

The answer is (D).

Midpoint Formula:

The midpoint M between points (x, y) and (a, b) is given by

$$\boxed{M = \left(\frac{x+a}{2}, \frac{y+b}{2}\right)}$$

In other words, to find the midpoint, simply average the corresponding coordinates of the two points.

Example: If $(-3, -5)$ is the midpoint of the part of the line between the x and y axes, then what is the slope of the line?

We have that $(-3, -5)$ is the midpoint of the line between the x-intercept $(X, 0)$ and the y-intercept $(0, Y)$. The formula for the midpoint of two points (x_1, y_1) and (x_2, y_2) is $((x_1 + x_2)/2, (y_1 + y_2)/2)$. Hence, the midpoint of $(X, 0)$ and $(0, Y)$ is $((X + 0)/2, (0 + Y)/2) = (X/2, Y/2)$. Equating this to the given midpoint yields $(X/2, Y/2) = (-3, -5)$. Equating corresponding coordinates yields $X/2 = -3$, or $X = -6$, and $Y/2 = -5$, or $Y = -10$. Hence, the slope of the line between $(X, 0)$, which equals $(-6, 0)$, and $(0, Y)$, which equals $(0, -10)$, is

$$\frac{y_2 - y_1}{x_2 - x_1} =$$

$$\frac{-10 - 0}{0 - (-6)} =$$

$$\frac{-10}{6} =$$

$$-\frac{5}{3}$$

The slope is $-5/3$.

Slope Formula:

The slope of a line measures the inclination of the line. By definition, it is the ratio of the vertical change to the horizontal change (see figure below). The vertical change is called the *rise*, and the horizontal change is called the *run*. Thus, the slope is the *rise over the run*.

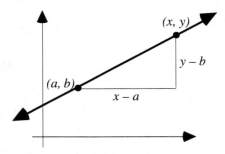

Forming the *rise over the run* in the above figure yields

$$m = \frac{y-b}{x-a}$$

Example: In the figure, what is the slope of line passing through the two points?

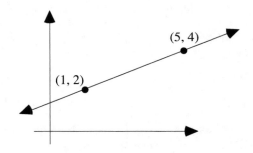

The slope formula yields $m = \dfrac{4-2}{5-1} = \dfrac{2}{4} = \dfrac{1}{2}$.

Slope-Intercept Form:

Multiplying both sides of the equation $m = \dfrac{y-b}{x-a}$ by $x - a$ yields

$$y - b = m(x - a)$$

Now, if the line passes through the y-axis at $(0, b)$, then the equation becomes

$$y - b = m(x - 0)$$

or

$$y - b = mx$$

or

$$y = mx + b$$

This is called the slope-intercept form of the equation of a line, where m is the slope and b is the y-intercept. This form is convenient because it displays the two most important bits of information about a line: its slope and its y-intercept.

Example: In the figure, the equation of the line is $y = \dfrac{9}{10}x + k$. Which one of the following ing

must be true about line segments AO and BO ?

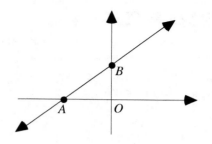

(A) $AO > BO$

(B) $AO < BO$

(C) $AO \le BO$

(D) $AO = BO$

(E) $AO = BO/2$

Since $y = \dfrac{9}{10}x + k$ is in slope-intercept form, we know the slope of the line is $\dfrac{9}{10}$. Now, the ratio of BO to AO is the slope of the line (rise over run). Hence, $\dfrac{BO}{AO} = \dfrac{9}{10}$. Multiplying both sides of this equation by AO yields $BO = \dfrac{9}{10}AO$. In other words, BO is $\dfrac{9}{10}$ the length of AO. Hence, AO is longer than BO. That is, $AO > BO$, and the answer is (A).

Intercepts:

The x-intercept is the point where the line crosses the x-axis. It is found by setting $y = 0$ and solving the resulting equation. The y-intercept is the point where the line crosses the y-axis. It is found by setting $x = 0$ and solving the resulting equation.

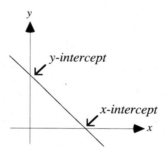

Example: Graph the equation $x - 2y = 4$.

Solution: To find the x-intercept, set $y = 0$. This yields $x - 2 \cdot 0 = 4$, or $x = 4$. So, the x-intercept is $(4, 0)$. To find the y-intercept, set $x = 0$. This yields $0 - 2y = 4$, or $y = -2$. So, the y-intercept is $(0, -2)$. Plotting these two points and connecting them with a straight line yields

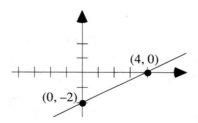

Areas and Perimeters:

Often, you will be given a geometric figure drawn on a coordinate system and will be asked to find its area or perimeter. In these problems, use the properties of the coordinate system to deduce the dimensions of the figure and then calculate the area or perimeter. For complicated figures, you may need to divide the figure into simpler forms, such as squares and triangles. A couple examples will illustrate:

Example: What is the area of the quadrilateral in the coordinate system?

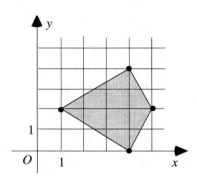

If the quadrilateral is divided horizontally through the line $y = 2$, two congruent triangles are formed. As the figure to the right shows, the top triangle has height 2 and base 4. Hence, its area is

$$A = \frac{1}{2}bh = \frac{1}{2} \cdot 4 \cdot 2 = 4$$

The area of the bottom triangle is the same, so the area of the quadrilateral is $4 + 4 = 8$.

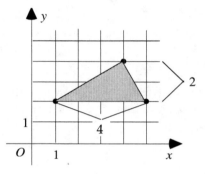

Example: What is the perimeter of Triangle *ABC* in the figure?

    (A) $5 + \sqrt{5} + \sqrt{34}$

    (B) $10 + \sqrt{34}$

    (C) $5 + \sqrt{5} + \sqrt{28}$

    (D) $2\sqrt{5} + \sqrt{34}$

    (E) $\sqrt{5} + \sqrt{28}$

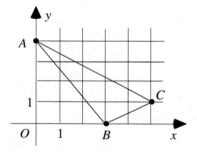

Point *A* has coordinates (0, 4), point *B* has coordinates (3, 0), and point *C* has coordinates (5, 1). Using the distance formula to calculate the distances between points *A* and *B*, *A* and *C*, and *B* and *C* yields

$$\overline{AB} = \sqrt{(0-3)^2 + (4-0)^2} = \sqrt{9+16} = \sqrt{25} = 5$$

$$\overline{AC} = \sqrt{(0-5)^2 + (4-1)^2} = \sqrt{25+9} = \sqrt{34}$$

$$\overline{BC} = \sqrt{(5-3)^2 + (1-0)^2} = \sqrt{4+1} = \sqrt{5}$$

Adding these lengths gives the perimeter of Triangle *ABC*:

$$\overline{AB} + \overline{AC} + \overline{BC} = 5 + \sqrt{34} + \sqrt{5}$$

The answer is (A).

Since coordinate geometry is part of geometry, all the strategies that apply to the geometry apply to the coordinate geometry as well.

Here are a couple properties that we already discussed in the previous chapter:

Pythagorean Theorem (right triangles only): The square of the hypotenuse is equal to the sum of the squares of the legs.

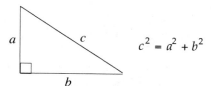

In a triangle, the sum of the lengths of any two sides is greater than the length of the remaining side:

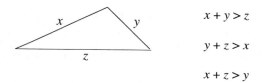

$$x + y > z$$

$$y + z > x$$

$$x + z > y$$

Shaded Regions

To find the area of the shaded region of a figure, subtract the area of the unshaded region from the area of the entire figure.

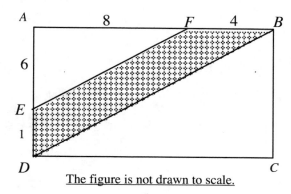

The figure is not drawn to scale.

For example, the area of the shaded region in the figure can be calculated as either

The Area of Triangle *ABD* – The area of Triangle *AFE*

or as

The Area of Triangle *ABCD* – The Area of Triangle *AFE* – The Area of Triangle *BCD*

"Degree of Freedom" Method

The degree of freedom method is a common way of solving Data Sufficiency problems and forms one of the paradigms of Data Sufficiency. Generally, in geometry, we get linear equations forming the system.

Here are a few points that are useful when solving a Data Sufficiency geometry problems:

➤ Usually, the Degree of Freedom of a triangle is 2 if only angle measures are given. Hence, given two angles, the third angle can be calculated (since the angles sum to 180 degrees).

➤ To find a side of a triangle, we need at least one other side of the triangle. Otherwise, the triangle can be indefinitely expanded or ablated and we will have different measures for the required side.

➤ To constrict the expansion, we need at least one side length. So, the degree of freedom when sides are given is 1 more than the degree of freedom only when angles are involved.

When Drawing a Geometric Figure or Checking a Given One, Be Sure to Include Drawings of Extreme Cases As Well As Ordinary Ones.

Strategy

We discussed the Locus method before. Now, let's represent the method in two steps.

- Draw the locus to determine whether we have a single value for the question.

- If yes, Data Sufficient. Otherwise, there must be more than one possible answer for the question and therefore Data Insufficient.

An example is shown below. But before that, read the following note:

The advantage of the Locus Technique over the Constructability Technique is that Constructability is better in determining Data sufficiency but the Data Insufficiency may not sometimes be reliable. For example, sometimes we do not need to construct the whole figure with exact dimensions to answer a particular question. A model of the figure should help. Especially, if we want angles, we would need just a model. Usually, if we want length related quantities, we need the exact figure. The Locus technique wins over the Constructability technique in many cases.

Example: What is the center of the parallelogram?

(1) The midpoint of two adjacent vertices on the parallelogram is (2, 4).

(2) The midpoint two opposite vertices on the parallelogram is (3, 6).

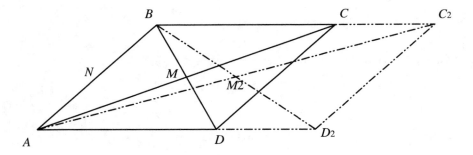

Statement (1):

Information about only two adjacent vertices is just information about the side joining the two points. The midpoint of the parallelogram depends upon the entire construct of the parallelogram. So, even by knowing a single side, we cannot construct the parallelogram and therefore the midpoint. As in the figure, if *ABCD* were the original parallelogram and *M* the original midpoint, then while we are given the midpoint of *AB* which is *N*, we can still have more than one midpoint. For example, *M*, M_2, for the parallelogram. So, the statement is *not* sufficient.

The answer is (B).

Statement (2):

In a parallelogram, the midpoint must be the midpoint of the opposite points. Hence, Statement (2) is sufficient. As in the figure, if *ABCD* is the original parallelogram, the midpoint is *M*, we are directly given *M* in Statement (2).

The Equations Approach.

Strategy

If there is a universal method to solve any math problem, it would be to collect all possible properties of the problem and solve them. Here is a small example.

Example: Does the point (p, q) lie on the line $y = mx + c$ (p, m, and c are non-zero)?

(1)   The line $y = mx - c$ passes through the point (p, q).

(2)   The line $y = -mx + c$ passes through the point (p, q).

The line $y = mx + c$ passes through the point (p, q) only if the point satisfies the equation. So, the question can be recast as "Is $q = mp + c$?" [result of substituting the point (p, q) in the line equation $y = mx + c$].

So, the question can be written as A) "Is $q - mp = c$?" (a transformation) or "Is $q - mp \neq c$?" (counter) or B) "Is $q - c = mp$?" (a transformation) or "Is $q - c \neq mp$?" (counter).

Statement (1): The line $y = mx - c$ passes through the point (p, q).

Substituting the point (p, q) in the line $y = mx - c$ yields $q = mp - c$. Subtracting mp from both sides yields $q - mp = -c$. Since $c \neq 0$ (given), c would not equal $-c$. Hence, we can say $q - mp \neq c$. So, data is sufficient with the statement.

(Note: If we were not given that $c \neq 0$, then the statement would not have been sufficient.)

The answer is (D).

Statement (2): The line $y = -mx + c$ passes through the point (p, q).

Substituting the point (p, q) in the line $y = -mx + c$ yields $q = -mp + c$. Subtracting c from both sides yields $q - c = -mp$. Now, since m and p are not zero, mp is not zero and therefore mp is not equal to $-mp$. Hence, $q - c \neq mp$, and the statement is sufficient.

(Note: If we were not given that $m \neq 0$ and $p \neq 0$, then the statement would *not* have be sufficient.)

Complicated figures like quadrilaterals can be drawn and data sufficiency evaluated by consecutively applying the evaluation from one basic figure to the other using either of the given methods—degree of freedom, constructability, or locus.

For example, constructing a quadrilateral can be considered to involve two adjacent triangles sharing one common side. So, analyze the data sufficiency for the triangles one after the other (picking analysis results from each previous one and applying to the next).

Problem Set E: Coordinate Geometry

1.   *B* is a point equidistant from points *A* and *C*. How far is *B* from either point?

   (1)   The coordinates of the points *A* and *C* are (1, 2) and (2, 1), respectively.

   (2)   The distant between *A* and *C* is $\sqrt{2}$.

2.   In the coordinate system, does the line *l* pass through the point (1, 2)?

   (1)   The slope of the line is 1/2, and the line passes through the origin (0, 0).

   (2)   The equation of the line is $y = \dfrac{1}{2}x$.

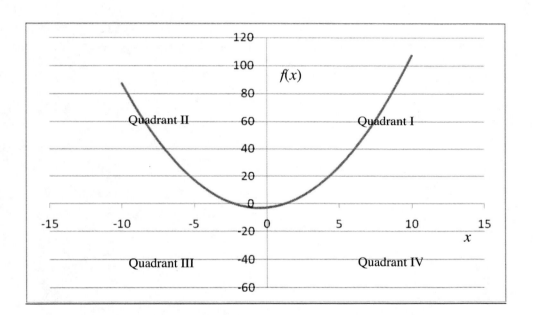

Figure not drawn to scale

3.   The equation of the curve shown in the figure is given by $af(x) = ax^2 + bx - 3b$. If (1, *t*) is a point on the curve, then in which quadrant does the point lie?

   (1)   (2, 3) is a point on the curve.

   (2)   (3, 9) is a point on the curve.

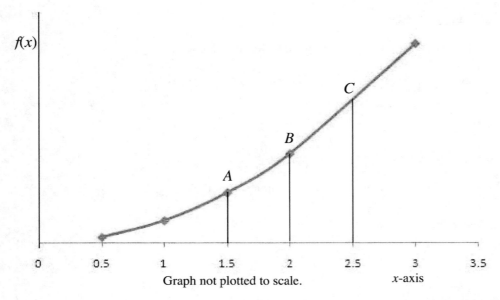

Graph not plotted to scale.

4.   The graph above shows the curve of $f(x)$. A, B, and C are three points on the graph. If the function $f(x)$ is defined as ax^2, then what are the coordinates of point C?

(1) $A = (1.5, 9)$

(2) $B = (2, 16)$

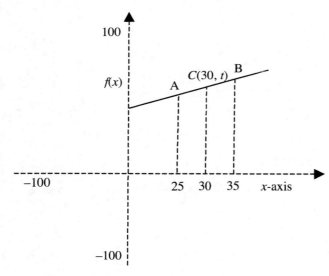

5. A, B, and C are three points on the line shown in the figure. In the figure, is t equal to 55?

(1) $A = (25, 50)$

(2) $B = (35, 60)$

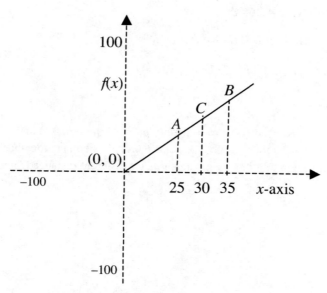

6.   What are the coordinates of point *C* ?

(1)   *A* = (4, 10)

(2)   *B* = (5, 12.5)

Answers and Solutions to Problem Set E: Coordinate Geometry

1.   *B* is a point equidistant from points *A* and *C*. How far is *B* from either point?

   (1)   The coordinates of the points *A* and *C* are (1, 2) and (2, 1), respectively.

   (2)   The distant between *A* and *C* is $\sqrt{2}$.

The answer is (E). No surprise that any point on the perpendicular from the midpoint of the points *A* and *B* is equidistant from either (means the perpendicular line is the focus of the point *B*). The statements together do not fix the point *B* on the coordinate plane. Each point on the perpendicular has a different distance from *A* and *C*.

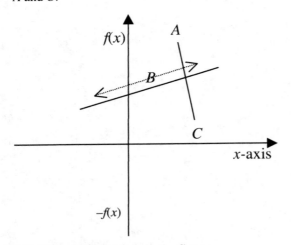

The locus of *B* is shown in the figure.

2.   In the coordinate system, does the line *l* pass through the point (1, 2)?

   (1)   The slope of the line is 1/2, and the line passes through the origin (0, 0).

   (2)   The equation of the line is $y = \dfrac{1}{2}x$.

To test whether (1, 2) lies on the line we either need to know the equation (and test whether the point (1, 2) satisfies the equation) or by constructing both the line and the point on a coordinate plane and testing if the point lies on the line. So, the question can be changed to "Can we find the equation or can we construct the line in the plane?" Statement (2) directly gives the equation and therefore is sufficient.

The general form of a linear equation is $y = mx + c$, where *m* is the slope and *c* is the *y*-intercept. *m* and *c* are the two parameters of the linear equation. To solve for the two unknowns, we need two equations. Statement (1) gives two distinct properties:

   1) The slope of the line is 1/2 ($m = 1/2$).

   2) The line passes through the origin (0, 0).

Since we have two distinct properties, the statement is sufficient. The calculations are shown below.

The answer is (D).

Placing $m = 1/2$ (the first property) in the linear equation $y = mx + c$ yields $y = (1/2)x + c$. The line passes through origin $(0, 0)$. Substituting this point in the linear equation yields $0 = (1/2)0 + c$, or $c = 0$. Substituting this value for c in the linear equation yields $y = (1/2)x + 0$, or $y = (1/2)x$. Substituting the point $(1, 2)$ in the line yields $2 = (1/2)1$, which is an invalid result. Since the point does not satisfy the line equation, it is not on the line.

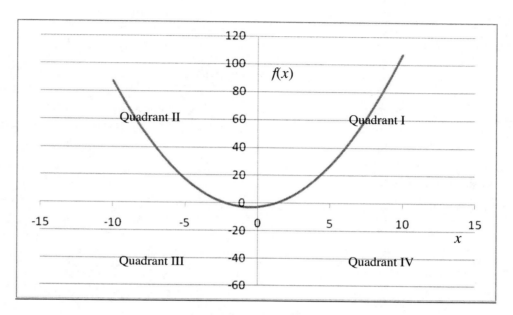

Figure not drawn to scale

3.   The equation of the curve shown in the figure is given by $af(x) = ax^2 + bx - 3b$. If $(1, t)$ is a point on the curve, then in which quadrant does the point lie?

(1) $(2, 3)$ is a point on the curve.

(2) $(3, 9)$ is a point on the curve.

While I speculate from figure that $(1, t)$ lies below the x-axis, a colleague of mine speculates that it looks like it is on the x-axis, and for someone else it might look like it is above the x-axis.

As the figure shows, x is on the horizontal line (say x-axis) and $f(x)$ is on the vertical line (say y-axis). We call the intersection point of the two lines (axes) the origin.

Now, dividing the given equation $af(x) = ax^2 + bx - 3b$ by a (a is not 0 because then the curve in the figure would not be definable) yields

$$\frac{af(x)}{a} = \frac{ax^2}{a} + \frac{bx}{a} - \frac{3b}{a}$$
$$f(x) = x^2 + (b/a)x - 3(b/a)$$

Let b/a equal a new parameter l. Then the equation becomes $f(x) = x^2 + lx - 3l$. So, we have the equation in the parameter l with degree 1 (the power of l is 1). So, just one point should probably be enough to evaluate the parameter. Let's evaluate the parameter l and therefore the point $(1, t)$: putting the point $(1, t)$ in $f(x) = x^2 + lx - 3l$ yields $t = 1^2 + l(1) - 3l = 1 - 2l$. Clearly, l must be evaluated to evaluate $(1, t)$. Let's try it out.

Statement (1): (2, 3) is a point on the curve.

Putting the point (2, 3) in the equation $f(x) = x^2 + lx - 3l$ yields

$$3 = (2)^2 + l(2) - 3l$$
$$3 = 4 + 2l - 3l$$
$$3 = 4 - l$$
$$l = 1$$

Hence, the equation is $f(x) = x^2 + x - 3$. Since the point $(1, t)$ is on the curve, it must satisfy the curve equation

$$f(x) = x^2 + x - 3$$
$$t = 1^2 + 1 - 3$$
$$t = -1$$

Hence, the answer is $(1, -1)$. This is in Quadrant IV. The statement is sufficient.

The answer is (A).

Statement (2): (3, 9) is a point on the curve.

Putting the point (3, 9) in the equation

$$f(x) = x^2 + lx - 3l$$

yields

$$9 = 3^2 + l(3) - 3l$$
$$9 = 9 + 3l - 3l$$
$$0 = 0$$

A known result. This means that irrespective of the value of l, the value of f equals x^2 for $x = 3$. Hence, at least this point does not help evaluate the parameter l. Hence, the statement is not sufficient.

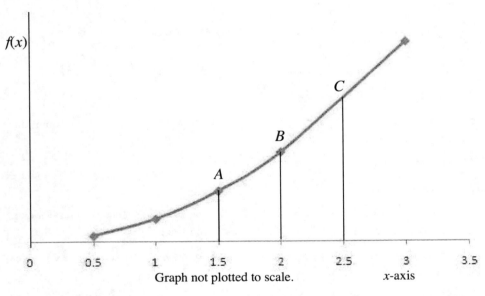

Graph not plotted to scale.   *x*-axis

4.   The graph above shows the curve of $f(x)$. A, B, and C are three points on the graph. If the function $f(x)$ is defined as ax^2, then what are the coordinates of point C?

(1) $A = (1.5, 9)$

(2) $B = (2, 16)$

The function $f(x) = ax^2$ has a single parameter (right now, we can call it a single unknown) and that is a (regardless of whether it has exponents). Hence, any point on the graph can determine the unknown (by substituting the point in the function, we get an equation in only a, which can be solved). Once we have a, the function is uniquely determined. So, the y-coordinate of point C whose x-coordinate is 2.5 can be calculated by substitution. Each statement gives one point on the curve and therefore either statement is sufficient. The answer is (D). Let's still evaluate the point C.

Statement (1): $A = (1.5, 9)$

Plugging in the function $f(x) = ax^2$ yields $9 = a(1.5)^2$ or $a = 9/(1.5)^2 = 4$. So, if $x = 2.5$, $f(x) = ax^2 = 4x^2 = 4(2.5)^2 = 25$.

So, $C = (2.5, 25)$.

Statement (2): $B = (2, 16)$

Plugging in the function $f(x) = ax^2$ yields $16 = a(2)^2$ or $a = 16/4 = 4$. So, if $x = 2.5$, $f(x) = ax^2 = 4x^2 = 4(2.5)^2 = 25$.

So, $C = (2.5, 25)$.

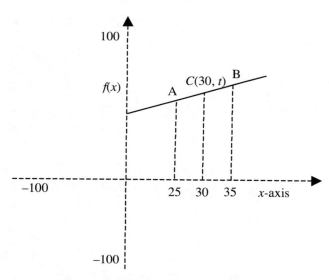

5. A, B, and C are three points on the line shown in the figure. In the figure, is t equal to 55?

   (1) $A = (25, 50)$

   (2) $B = (35, 60)$

A linear equation has the form $y = mx + c$, where m is the slope and c is the constant that's said to be the height of the line above the point $x = 0$ (equal to the y-intercept).

Thus, here we have two parameters. Hence, to determine the two parameters, we need at least two different equations in the two parameters (treating them as unknowns). So, we need at least two points which by substituting in the linear equation $y = mx + c$ we get two equations to determine the parameters. Once we determine the parameters, we can evaluate any point above a given x-coordinate. Hence, the two points in the two statements are required to evaluate the x-coordinate. So, the answer is (C), both statements required.

With the two statements, we have

   $50 = 25m + c$

   $60 = 35m + c$

Which yields $m = 1$ and $c = 25$. Hence, $t = 30m + c = 30(1) + 25 = 55$.

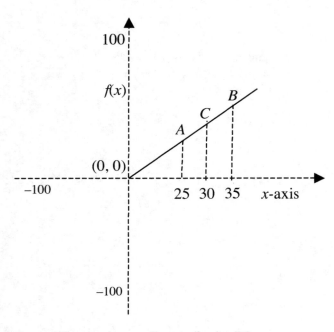

6.   What are the coordinates of point C ?

(1) $A = (4, 10)$

(2) $B = (5, 12.5)$

Analysis 1:

The equation of a line through the origin has the form $y = mx$. Here, we have only one parameter, m. Hence, we need a single point on the graph to evaluate the parameter. So, either statement is sufficient.

Analysis 2:

The equation of a line is $y = mx + c$. Here, we have two parameters, m and c. So, we need at least two points on the graph to evaluate the parameters. One of the points is the origin (from the figure). So, we need just one other point to evaluate the parameters, which either statement can provide. So, either statement is sufficient.

The answer is (D).

Inequalities

Inequalities are manipulated algebraically the same way as equations with one exception:

 Multiplying or dividing both sides of an inequality by a negative number reverses the inequality. That is, if $x > y$ and $c < 0$, then $cx < cy$.

Example: For which values of x is $4x + p > 6x - q$?

    (1) $x > -3$

    (2) $p = 3 - q$

Here, the confirmed property is $4x + p > 6x - q$. So, we start with this.

Adding q to both sides of the equation $p = 3 - q$ yields $p + q = 3$. So, the values of x for which $4x + p > 6x - q$ are $x < (-p - q)/2 = -(p + q)/2 = -3/2$. So, for any $x < -3/2$, $4x + p$ is greater than $6x - q$. Statement (2) alone is sufficient since it yields numerical bounds.

Now, if you thought that $x > -3$ is a constraint and combining it with the result $x < -3/2$ yields $-3 < x < -3/2$ and therefore the statements together are required, you are mistaken.

Also, if you thought the problem is open-ended for example because if we add a third statement like $x > -2$ x would be further limited to $-2 > x > -3$ and therefore thought data is insufficient with the statements together, you are again mistaken.

The question must be answered as "$4x \mp p > 6x - q$ for all $x < -3/2$ [found by using Statement (2)] irrespective of the range we allow for x [So, Statement (1) $x > -2$ is irrelevant.]." So, the answer is (B).

So, what you regarded as an open-ended question is actually a close-ended one. That's how the problem seeks you to analyze a question thoroughly before proceeding to statements.

Note: Questions that start with the phrases such as "For which" or "For what" are never open-ended.

Questions that start with the phrases such as "Which" or "What" can be open-ended.

Determine whether the following example is a Data Sufficiency problem or a Multiple-Choice problem.

Example: For which values of x is $p > q$ if $4x + p = 6x + q$?

    (1) $x > 0$

    (2) $x > 3$

    (3) $x > -2$

Clearly, (1), (2), and (3) are conditions, not properties. So, they are answer-choices and this is a multiple-choice problem.

Example: For which values of x is $p > q$ if $4x + p = 6y + q$ is the only constraint?

    (1) $y = 3$

    (2) $y > 2$

The question asks us to assume that $4x + p = 6y + q$ and $p > q$ are known properties. Flipping the direction of the inequality yields $q < p$. Adding this to $4x + p = 6y + q$ yields $4x + p + q < 6y + q + p$. Canceling $p + q$ from both sides yields $4x < 6y$. This is true when $x < (6/4)y = (3/2)y$.

Given, the value of y, we can evaluate the range of x. Thus, Statement (1) is sufficient.

Multiplying the inequality in Statement (2) by $3/2$ yields $(3/2)y > 3/2 \cdot 2 = 3$. Hence, we have the inequality $(3/2)y > 3$, which cannot combined with the inequality $x < 3/2\ y$ because of their direction incompatibility. Therefore, nothing can be derived from the statement. The statement is not sufficient. If we could have combined, we would have gotten the range for x and the statement would have been sufficient.

Method II: Substitute $p = 6y + q - 4x$ in the inequality $p > q$. So, the p would have been greater than true when $6y + q - 4x > q$; $6y - 4x > 0$; $6y > 4x$; $x < 3/2\ y$. Thus, we could have gotten the range for x had we known the exact value of y. The statement (1) is sufficient and Statement (2) isn't.

The answer is (A).

Positive & Negative Numbers

A number greater than 0 is positive. On the number line, positive numbers are to the right of 0. A number less than 0 is negative. On the number line, negative numbers are to the left of 0. Zero is the only number that is neither positive nor negative; it divides the two sets of numbers. On the number line, numbers increase to the right and decrease to the left.

The expression $x > y$ means that x is greater than y. In other words, x is to the right of y on the number line:

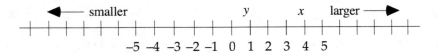

We usually have no trouble determining which of two numbers is larger when both are positive or one is positive and the other negative (e.g., $5 > 2$ and $3.1 > -2$). However, we sometimes hesitate when both numbers are negative (e.g., $-2 > -4.5$). When in doubt, think of the number line: if one number is to the right of the number, then it is larger. As the number line below illustrates, –2 is to the right of –4.5. Hence, –2 is larger than –4.5.

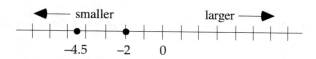

Miscellaneous Properties of Positive and Negative Numbers

1. The product (quotient) of positive numbers is positive.

2. The product (quotient) of a positive number and a negative number is negative.

3. The product (quotient) of an even number of negative numbers is positive.

4. The product (quotient) of an odd number of negative numbers is negative.

5. The sum of negative numbers is negative.

6. A number raised to an even exponent is greater than or equal to zero.

Example: Which two of the following three inequalities must be true $xz < 0$, $yz < 0$, and $yx < 0$?

    (1) $xy^2z < 0$

    (2) $x^2yz < 0$

For convenience, let's represent the inequalities $xz < 0$, $yz < 0$, and $yx < 0$ as A, B, and C, respectively.

Statement (1): Since a number raised to an even exponent is greater than or equal to zero, we know that y^2 is positive (it cannot be zero because the product xy^2z would then be zero). Hence, we can divide both sides of the inequality $xy^2z < 0$ by y^2:

$$\frac{xy^2z}{y^2} < \frac{0}{y^2}$$

Simplifying yields $xz < 0$

Therefore, A: $xz < 0$ is true. This also indicates that exactly one of x and z must be negative. Therefore, whether y is negative or positive, exactly one of xy and yz must be negative. Hence, exactly one of B: $yz < 0$ and C: $yx < 0$ must be true. So, Statement (1) says that exactly two of the three inequalities A, B, and C is true, but doesn't say which two. Since the question is not fully answered, the statement is not sufficient.

Statement (2): $x^2yz < 0$. Since a number raised to an even exponent is greater than or equal to zero, we know that x^2 is positive (it cannot be zero because the product x^2yz would then be zero). Hence, we can divide both sides of the inequality $xy^2z < 0$ by x^2:

$$\frac{x^2yz}{x^2} < \frac{0}{x^2}$$

Simplifying yields $yz < 0$

Therefore, B: $yz < 0$ is true. This also indicates that exactly one of y and z must be negative so that the product yz is negative. Hence, exactly one of A: $xz < 0$ and C: $xy < 0$ must be true. So, Statement (2) says that exactly two of the three inequalities A, B, and C are true, but again does not say which two. Since the question is not fully answered, the statement is not sufficient.

Statement (1) says exactly two of A, B, and C are true with A surely true.

Statement (2) says exactly two of A, B, and C are true with B surely true.

So, the two statements together say that exactly two of A, B, and C are true with A and B both being true. This only indicates that A and B are true and C is false.

Therefore, the statements together specifically indicate the two inequalities that are true. Hence, the statements together are sufficient.

The answer is (C).

Example: Is it true that exactly two of the three inequalities $xz < 0$, $yz < 0$ and $yx < 0$ are true?

(1) $xy^2z < 0$

(2) $x^2yz < 0$

This problem is same as the previous one, except that the question is more relaxed. It is relaxed in the sense that here we only need to find the truth that exactly one of the two inequalities A, B, and C labeled as in the problem above is true. In the previous problem, where apart from the truth, we had to determine which two inequalities are true.

We learned in Part II of the book that as we decrease the expectation of the question setup, the answer tends to move upward in the data sufficiency order:

$$\frac{\substack{\text{Question alone sufficient.} \\ A, B}}{\substack{D \\ C \\ E}}$$

. Now, let's tackle the problem.

Statement (1) says A is true and either B or C is true. Hence, exactly two of the inequalities A, B, and C are true. The question is answered and therefore the statement is sufficient.

Statement (2) says B is true and either A or C is true. Hence, exactly two of the inequalities A, B, and C are true. The question is answered and therefore the statement is sufficient.

The answer is (D).

Are you able to see that since the expectation of the question decreased the answer-choice moved up the data sufficiency order shown above?

Absolute Value

The absolute value of a number is its distance on the number line from 0. Since distance is a positive number, absolute value of a number is positive. Two vertical bars denote the absolute value of a number: $|x|$. For example, $|3| = 3$ and $|-3| = 3$. This can be illustrated on the number line:

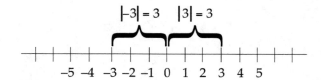

Students rarely struggle with the absolute value of numbers: if the number is negative, simply make it positive; and if it is already positive, leave it as is. For example, since –2.4 is negative, $|-24| = 2.4$ and since 5.01 is positive $|5.01| = 5.01$.

Further, students rarely struggle with the absolute value of positive variables: if the variable is positive, simply drop the absolute value symbol. For example, if $x > 0$, then $|x| = x$.

However, negative variables can cause students much consternation. If x is negative, then $|x| = -x$. This often confuses students because the absolute value is positive but the $-x$ appears to be negative. It is actually positive—it is the negative of a negative number, which is positive. To see this more clearly let $x = -k$, where k is a <u>positive</u> number. Then x is a negative number. So, $|x| = -x = -(-k) = k$. Since k is positive so is $-x$. Another way to view this is $|x| = -x = (-1) \cdot x = (-1)(\text{a negative number}) = $ a positive number.

Example: Which of the statements $x = 0$, $x < 0$, and $x > 0$ <u>could</u> be true?

(1) $x = -|x|$

(2) $x^2 = |x|$

Statement (1) is possible when either $x = 0$ or $x < 0$.

Statement (2) is possible when $x = 1$ (which means $x > 0$) or $x = 0$ or $x = -1$ (which means $x < 0$).

Together, statements (1) and (2) constrict the possibilities to $x = 0$ when $x < 0$. We certainly have the complete list of the inequalities that could be true. But still the answer is not (C), which is explained below.

The problem is open-ended, which means that there exist additional conditions, such as $x = 0$, which can turn a could-be-true statement (the statement $x < 0$) into a never-true statement. All open-ended problems end with the answer (E), which is the answer here.

Example: Which <u>one</u> of the statements $x = 0$, $x < 0$, and $x > 0$ <u>could</u> be true?

(1) $x = -|x|$

(2) $x^2 > -|x|$

Exactly one of the three statements $x = 0$, $x < 0$, and $x > 0$ can be true at a time. This means exactly two of the three inequalities are false at any time. Hence, the question can be transformed as "Which two of the statements $x = 0$, $x < 0$, and $x > 0$ must be false?"

Statement (1): $x = -|x|$

I: $x = 0$ could be true because $-|0| = -(+0) = -(0) = 0$.

II: $x < 0$ could be true because the right side of the equation is always negative $[-|x| = -(\text{a positive number})$ $=$ a negative number]. Now, if one side of an equation is always negative, then the other side must always be negative, otherwise the opposite sides of the equation would not be equal.

III: Since $x > 0$ is the opposite of Statement II ($x < 0$), it must be false. Let's show this explicitly: Suppose x were positive. Then $|x| = x$, and the equation $x = -|x|$ becomes $x = -x$. Dividing both sides of this equation by x yields $1 = -1$. This is contradiction. Hence, x cannot be positive.

Statement (1) says that I could be true or II could be true.

There are infinitely many numbers, both positive and negative, where $x^2 \neq -|x|$. So, Statement (2) alone is not sufficient.

But with Statement (2) alone, it is clear that I cannot be true: $x^2 \neq -|x|$.

I: $x = 0$ is not true because $0^2 \neq -|0|$ is false.

Hence, with the statements together, II: $x < 0$ is the only inequality that could be true for example when $x = -2$.

The answer is (C).

Higher Order Inequalities

These inequalities have variables whose exponents are greater than 1. For example, $x^2 + 4 < 2$ and $x^3 - 9 > 0$. The number line is often helpful in solving these types of inequalities.

Example: Is $x^2 > -6x - 5$?

      (1) $-5 < x < -1$

      (2) $-4 < x < -2$

First, let's determine for which values of x is $x^2 > -6x - 5$?

First, replace the inequality symbol with an equal symbol:	$x^2 = -6x - 5$
Adding $6x$ and 5 to both sides yields	$x^2 + 6x + 5 = 0$
Factoring yields (see General Trinomials in the chapter Factoring)	$(x + 5)(x + 1) = 0$
Setting each factor to 0 yields	$x + 5 = 0$ and $x + 1 = 0$
Or	$x = -5$ and $x = -1$

Now, the only numbers at which the expression can change sign are −5 and −1. So, −5 and −1 divide the number line into three intervals. Let's set up a number line and choose test points in each interval:

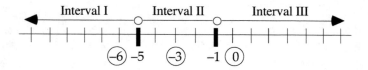

When $x = -6$, $x^2 > -6x - 5$ becomes $36 > 31$. This is true. Hence, all numbers in Interval I satisfy the inequality. That is, $x < -5$. When $x = -3$, $x^2 > -6x - 5$ becomes $9 > 13$. This is false. Hence, no numbers in Interval II satisfy the inequality. When $x = 0$, $x^2 > -6x - 5$ becomes $0 > -5$. This is true. Hence, all numbers in Interval III satisfy the inequality. That is, $x > -1$. The graph of the solution follows:

Note, if the original inequality had included the greater-than-or-equal symbol, $\geq$, the solution set would have included both –5 and –1. On the graph, this would have been indicated by filling in the circles above –5 and –1. The open circles indicate that –5 and –1 are not part of the solution.

Summary of steps for solving higher order inequalities:

1. Replace the inequality symbol with an equal symbol.

2. Move all terms to one side of the equation (usually the left side).

3. Factor the equation.

4. Set the factors equal to 0 to find zeros.

5. Choose test points on either side of the zeros.

6. If a test point satisfies the original inequality, then all numbers in that interval satisfy the inequality. Similarly, if a test point does not satisfy the inequality, then no numbers in that interval satisfy the inequality.

Now, let's get back to the problem. The inequality $x^2 > -6x - 5$ is false in the region $-5 < x < -1$. This statement is bigger than and contains the statement $-4 < x < -2$. So, even this later statement is also sufficient. The answer is (D).

Transitive Property

$$\boxed{\text{If } x < y \text{ and } y < z, \text{ then } x < z}$$

Example: Is $1 > Q^2$?

(1) $\dfrac{1}{Q} > 1$

(2) $1 < Q^2$

Since $\dfrac{1}{Q} > 1$ and $1 > 0$, we know from the transitive property that $\dfrac{1}{Q}$ is positive. Hence, Q is positive.

Therefore, we can multiply both sides of $\dfrac{1}{Q} > 1$ by Q without reversing the inequality:

$$Q \cdot \dfrac{1}{Q} > 1 \cdot Q$$

Reducing yields $1 > Q$

Multiplying both sides again by Q yields $Q > Q^2$

Using the transitive property to combine the last two inequalities yields $1 > Q^2$

Statement (1) is sufficient.

Reversing the inequality $1 < Q^2$ yields $1 > Q^2$. Statement (2) is also sufficient. The answer is (D).

Like Inequalities Can Be Added

> **If $x < y$ and $w < z$, then $x + w < y + z$**

Example: Is $-3 < x - y < 2$?

(1) $2 < x < 5$

(2) $3 < y < 5$

Multiplying both sides of $3 < y < 5$ by -1 yields $-3 > -y > -5$. Now, we usually write the smaller number on the left side of the inequality. So, $-3 > -y > -5$ becomes $-5 < -y < -3$. Add this inequality to the like inequality $2 < x < 5$:

$$
\begin{array}{r}
2 < x < 5 \\
(+) \quad -5 < -y < -3 \\
\hline
-3 < x - y < 2
\end{array}
$$

The answer is (C), the statements together are sufficient.

Suppose the question were "Is $-4 < x - y < 2$?" or "Is $x - y < 2$?", then we would have our bound -3 through -2 inside the bounds that the question asks in either case. Hence, the data is sufficient together. Since we have the bound for $x - y$ as -3 through -2, any further statements or other constrains have to split a pie in this region only. So, finally, in spite of any number of constrains, the region sure is within "-4 through 2" or "< 2" or "> -3." Therefore, the answer is (C).

Example: Adam, Bob, Carl, David, Eric, Frank, George, and Hank are basketball players.

>   Frank is the same height as Hank.

>   George is taller than Frank.

>   Eric is taller than Adam.

Is Carl taller than David?

(1)   Adam is taller than David and Carl.

(2)   Bob is shorter than Carl.

Suppose $a, b, c, d, e, f, g,$ and h are the heights of the respective players. Then the problem can be converted to

If $f = h$, $g > f$, $e > a$, then is $c > d$?

(1) $a > d$ and $a > c$

(2) $b < c$

Recalling the given inequalities (which are known properties of the problem only: $f = h$, $g > f$, $e > a$, then is $c > d$) yields

$$g > f = h$$

$$e > a$$

We need an inequality between c and d, that is, "if $c > d$?"

Statement (1): $a > d$ and $a > c$

Combining Statement (1), $a > d$ and $a > c$, alone with the known inequalities yields

$$g > f = h$$

$e > a > d$ and $e > a > c$ (and the last two inequalities cannot be combined since we would not know whether d comes first in the order or c comes first.)

We still do not have an inequality directly between c and d. So, Statement (1) alone is not sufficient.

Statement (2): $b < c$

Combining Statement (2), $b < c$, alone with the known inequalities yields

$$g > f = h$$

$$e > a$$

$b < c$ (nowhere to combine this)

We still do not have an inequality directly between c and d. So, Statement (2) alone is not sufficient.

Combining the inequality in Statement (2) $b < c$ at the right place from the inequalities known from the first column (the column for Statement (1) yields

$$g > f = h$$

$$e > a > d \text{ and } e > a > c > b$$

Now, still we do not have the inequality between c and d. Hence, the statements together are not sufficient. The answer is (E).

Suppose only the question (the unknown property) is changed to (without changing the problem setup) say

Is Bob taller than Eric?

(1) Adam is taller than David and Carl

(2) Bob is shorter than Carl

The overall problem converts to (the statements have not changed, nor did the problem setup):

If $f = h$, $g > f$, $e > a$, then is $b > e$?

(1) $a > d$ and $a > c$

(2) $b < c$

So far, we have the inequalities

$$g > f = h$$

$$e > a$$

which do not help determine the inequality between b and e.

Statement (1):

From the statement, which has not changed, we earlier had the inequalities

$$g > f = h$$

$$e > a > d \text{ and } e > a > c$$

from which we do not have the inequality between b and e. So, Statement (1) alone is not sufficient.

Statement (2):

From the statement, which has not changed, we earlier had the inequalities

$$g > f = h$$

$$e > a$$

$$b < c$$

Still do not have an inequality between b and e. So, Statement (2) alone is not sufficient.

From the statements together, we had the inequalities

$$g > f = h$$

$$e > a > d \text{ and } e > a > c > b$$

which is sure to let us know that $b > e$ is false. Hence, the statements together are sufficient, and the answer is (C).

Problem Set F: Inequalities

1.   *x* units of Product A costs *y* dollars.
      y units of Product B costs *x* dollars.

   Which product A or B costs more?

   (1) $x^2 + 1 > y^2$

   (2) $x^2 > y^2 + 1$

2.   Is $x + y > 6$?

   (1) $x + 2y > 8$

   (2) $2x + y > 8$

3.   If *r*, *s* and *t* are not zero, is $r > s > t$?

   (1) $rs/s > rs/r$

   (2) $st/s > ts/t$

4.   Is *p* greater than 0.3 ?

   (1) $p \geq 3/10$

   (2) $3 - 2p < 2.4$

5.   Is $(ab)^2 > ab$?

   (1) $a + 3 = b + 6 = 0$

   (2) $0 > a > b$

6.   Is $a^2b > ab^2$?

   (1) $a > b > ab$

   (2) $0 > a > b$

7.   If square roots of numbers are considered positive and $\sqrt{a} + \sqrt{b} = \sqrt{c} + \sqrt{d} + \sqrt{e}$, then is $a < c$?

   (1) $c = d$

   (2) $\sqrt{b} + \sqrt{d} < \sqrt{e}$

8.   Is $y = 0$ or $y > 0$?

    (1) $x + y \geq 5$

    (2) $x - y \leq 5$

9.   Is $x + y$ equal to 3.6 ?

    (1) $x \geq 1.7$

    (2) $y > 1.9$

10.   Is $z > 10 - z$?

    (1)   Arnold scored z points more than Jessie.

    (2)   Together Arnold and Jessie scored 10 points.

Answers and Solutions to Problem Set F: Inequalities

1.

> x units of Product A costs y dollars.
>
> y units of Product B costs x dollars.

Which product A or B costs more?

(1) $x^2 + 1 > y^2$

(2) $x^2 > y^2 + 1$

Since x units of Product A costs y dollars, the cost per unit is y dollars/x units = y/x. Since y units of Product B costs x dollars, the cost per unit is x dollars/y units = x/y.

Hence, the question becomes "Which one is greater y/x or x/y?"

Multiplying each fraction by xy (which is positive, being the product of two costs, which are positive), changes the question to "Which one is greater y^2 or x^2?"

Letting $a = x^2$ and $b = y^2$, we can transform the problem as

Which one is greater a or b given a and b are positive?

(1) $a + 1 > b$

(2) $a > b + 1$

Statement (1): $a + 1 > b$

If $a = 1$ and $b = 1.5$, then $a + 1 > b$ and b is greater than a.

If $a = 1$ and $b = 0.5$, then $a + 1 > b$ and a is greater than b.

We have a double case here and therefore the statement is *not* sufficient.

Statement (2): $a > b + 1$

Assume, a equals b. This violates the inequality $a > b + 1$, so a cannot equal b.

Next, assume $b > a$. Then $b + 1 > a + 1$. Now, $a + 1$ is always greater than a. Combining the two inequalities yields $b + 1 > a + 1 > a$, or simply $b + 1 > a$, which is a direct violation of the statement. So, b cannot be greater than a.

Hence, by elimination, $a > b$ must be true.

The statement is sufficient.

The answer is (B).

2.   Is $x + y > 6$?

    (1) $x + 2y > 8$

    (2) $2x + y > 8$

Statement (1): $x + 2y > 8$

$$x + 2y > 8$$

$$x + y > 8 - y$$

This is greater than 6 only when

$$8 - y > 6$$

$$y < 2$$

We do not have any such restriction so far, so the statement alone is *not* sufficient.

Statement (2): $2x + y > 8$

$$2x + y > 8$$

$$x + y > 8 - x$$

This is greater than 6 whenever

$$8 - x > 6 \text{ or}$$

$$x < 2$$

We do not have any such restriction again, so the statement alone is *not* sufficient.

From the two statements together, we have $x + 2y > 8$ and $2x + y > 8$. Summing the two yields $(x + 2y) + (2x + y) > 8 + 8$, or $3x + 3y > 16$, or $3(x + y) > 16$, or $x + y > 16/3 \approx 5.33$. So, $x + y$ might still be greater than 6 or less than 6. This is a double case. Since the statements together do not constrain the problem to a single case, the answer is (E).

3.   If r, s and t are not zero, is $r > s > t$?

    (1) $rs/s > rs/r$

    (2) $st/s > ts/t$

Here, we effectively have two questions: "Is $r > s$?" and is "$s > t$?"

The inequality $r > s > t$ is true when both inequalities $r > s$ and $s > t$ are true and false when at least one of the inequalities $r > s$ and $s > t$ is false.

If we can show that one of the above two cases is true, then the data is sufficient.

Statement (1): $rs/s > rs/r$

Canceling s from both the numerator and the denominator of the left side and canceling r from both the numerator and the denominator of the right side yields

$$r > s$$

Here, we do not have any clue whether $s > t$ or not. If it is, the answer to the question is "Yes;" and if not, the answer is "No." Hence, with the statement alone "We can't say." Hence, the statement is not sufficient.

Statement (2): $st/s > ts/t$

Canceling s from both the numerator and the denominator of the left side and canceling t from both the numerator and the denominator of the right side yields

$$t > s$$

Hence, $s > t$ is false, and therefore at least one of the two inequalities $r > s$ and $s > t$ is false. Hence, the complete inequality is false. Certainly, we do not have a clue whether the inequality $r > s$ is true here. But whether it is true or not, the answer to the question is "No." Hence, it is irrelevant. The statement is sufficient to answer the question. Often, to determine "No" is easier than to determine "Yes."

So, the answer is (B), Statement (2) alone is sufficient and Statement (1) alone is not.

4.   Is p greater than 0.3 ?

(1) $p \geq 3/10$

(2) $3 - 2p < 2.4$

Statement (1): $p \geq 3/10$

The statement says $p \geq 3/10$. Hence, p could equal $3/10$ (here p is not greater than 0.3) or p could be greater than $3/10$. This is a double case and therefore the statement is *not* sufficient.

Statement (2): $3 - 2p < 2.4$

Subtracting 3 from both sides of the inequality $3 - 2p < 2.4$ yields $-2p < -0.6$. Dividing both sides by -2 and flipping the direction of the inequality yields

$$-2p/-2 > -0.6/-2$$
$$p > 0.3$$

This statement is sufficient to say "Yes, p is greater than 0.3."

The answer is (B).

5.   Is $(ab)^2 > ab$?

(1) $a + 3 = b + 6 = 0$

(2) $0 > a > b$

Statement (1): $a + 3 = b + 6 = 0$

Splitting the equation $a + 3 = b + 6 = 0$, we have $a + 3 = 0$ and $b + 6 = 0$.

Solving the equations yields $a = -3$ and $b = -6$.

Hence, $ab = (-3)(-6) = 18$ and $(ab)^2 = 18^2 = 324$. So, $(ab)^2 > ab$, and the statement is sufficient.

Statement (2): $0 > a > b$

The inequality $0 > a > b$ indicates that a and b are negative.

So, ab = negative × negative = positive.

$(ab)^2$ is also positive, but need not be greater than ab.

For example,

If ab equals 0.5, $(ab)^2$ equals 0.25 and here $ab > (ab)^2$.

If ab equals 1, $(ab)^2$ equals 1. Here $ab = (ab)^2$.

Thus, we have a double case and therefore the statement alone is *not* sufficient.

The answer is (A).

6.   Is $a^2b > ab^2$?

   (1) $a > b > ab$

   (2) $0 > a > b$

Statement (1): $a > b > ab$

Suppose $a = 0.3$ and $b = 0.2$. Then $ab = 0.06$. This satisfies Statement (1) and here

$$ab^2 = (0.3)(0.2)^2 = 0.012$$

and

$$a^2b = (0.3)^2(0.2) = 0.018$$

Here, $a^2b > ab^2$.

Now, if $a = 3$ and $b = -0.2$, then $ab = -0.6$.

This satisfies Statement (1) and here

$$ab^2 = (3)(-0.2)^2 = \text{a positive value}$$

and

$$a^2b = (3)^2(-0.2) = \text{a negative value}$$

Here, a^2b is not greater than b^2a. This is a double case and therefore the statement is *not* sufficient.

The answer is (B).

Statement (2): $0 > a > b$

From the inequality $0 > a > b$, we have that a and b are negative. Hence, ab is positive. Multiplying the inequality by the positive value ab yields

$$0 > a(ab) > b(ab)$$
$$0 > a^2b > ab^2$$

Hence, the statement is sufficient.

7.   If square roots of numbers are considered positive and $\sqrt{a} + \sqrt{b} = \sqrt{c} + \sqrt{d} + \sqrt{e}$, then is $a < c$?

(1) $c = d$

(2) $\sqrt{b} + \sqrt{d} < \sqrt{e}$

Statement (1): $c = d$

Square rooting both sides of the equation $c = d$ yields $\sqrt{c} = \sqrt{d}$.

Substituting in the equation $\sqrt{a} + \sqrt{b} = \sqrt{c} + \sqrt{d} + \sqrt{e}$ yields

$$\sqrt{a} + \sqrt{b} = \sqrt{c} + \sqrt{c} + \sqrt{e}$$

$$\sqrt{a} + \sqrt{b} = 2\sqrt{c} + \sqrt{e} \qquad \ldots (1)$$

Suppose $a = 1$ and $c = 2$. Substituting in equation **(1)** yields

$$\sqrt{1} + \sqrt{b} = 2\sqrt{2} + \sqrt{e}$$

So, choose b and e such that the equation is satisfied. Here, $a < c$ is true.

Similarly, suppose $a = c = 1$. Then substituting in equation **(1)** yields

$$\sqrt{1} + \sqrt{b} = 2\sqrt{1} + \sqrt{e}$$

So, choose b and e such that the equation is satisfied. Here $a < c$ is false.

Thus, we have a double case and the statement is *not* sufficient.

The answer is (**B**).

Statement (2): $\sqrt{b} + \sqrt{d} < \sqrt{e}$

Multiplying the inequality given in the question $\sqrt{a} + \sqrt{b} = \sqrt{c} + \sqrt{d} + \sqrt{e}$ by -1 yields

$$-\sqrt{a} - \sqrt{b} = -\sqrt{c} - \sqrt{d} - \sqrt{e}$$

Adding this equation to the inequality $\sqrt{b} + \sqrt{d} < \sqrt{e}$ yields

$$-\sqrt{a} - \sqrt{b} + \sqrt{b} + \sqrt{d} < -\sqrt{c} - \sqrt{d} - \sqrt{e} + \sqrt{e}$$

$$-\sqrt{a} + \sqrt{d} < -\sqrt{c} - \sqrt{d}$$

$$-\sqrt{a} < -\sqrt{c} - 2\sqrt{d}$$

$$\sqrt{a} > \sqrt{c} + 2\sqrt{d}$$

Now, since square roots are considered positive, $\sqrt{a}$, $\sqrt{c}$, and $2\sqrt{d}$ are positive. The inequality can be simplified to $A > C + D$, where $A = \sqrt{a}$, $C = \sqrt{c}$, $D = 2\sqrt{d}$, and A, C, and D are positive. Now, if the sum of two positive numbers is smaller than a third number, the third number must be greater than each of them. For example, $4 > 2 + 1$ and $4 > 2$ and $4 > 1$.

Hence, $A > C$ or $\sqrt{a} > \sqrt{c}$. Since $\sqrt{a}$ and $\sqrt{c}$ are positive, we can safely square both sides of the inequality without flipping the direction of the inequality. Hence, we have $a > c$. The statement is sufficient

210 GMAT Data Sufficiency Prep Course

8.   Is $y = 0$ or $y > 0$?

    (1) $x + y \geq 5$

    (2) $x - y \leq 5$

Statement (1): $x + y \geq 5$

If $x = 0$ and $y = 6$, then $x + y = 6 \geq 5$.

If $x = 10$ and $y = -4$, then $x + y = 6 \geq 5$.

We have a double case: Answer could be "Yes, y could be 0 or greater" or "No, y could be negative—not 0 or greater." Hence, the data is insufficient.

Statement (2): $x - y \leq 5$

The contexts of statements (1) and (2) are similar, so we have two similar cases as we had with Statement (1). Hence, the data is insufficient.

Multiplying the inequality $x - y \leq 5$ by -1 and flipping the direction of inequality yields $y - x \geq -5$. Adding this inequality to the inequality $x + y \geq 5$ yields $(y - x) + (x + y) \geq -5 + 5$, or $2y \geq 0$, or $y \geq 0$. This means that the answer is "Yes, $y = 0$ or $y > 0$." Hence, the answer is (C).

9.   Is $x + y$ equal to 3.6 ?

    (1) $x \geq 1.7$

    (2) $y > 1.9$

Summing the inequalities $x \geq 1.7$ and $y > 1.9$ yields $x + y > 1.7 + 1.9 = 3.6$ (Note it is not $\geq$). Hence, the statements say that $x + y$ doesn't equal 3.6. The answer is (C), both statements required.

10.   Is $z > 10 - z$?

    (1)   Arnold scored z points more than Jessie.

    (2)   Together Arnold and Jessie scored 10 points.

If Arnold scored a points and Jessie scored j points, then from statements (1) and (2) we have the equations $a = j + z$ and $a + j = 10$, respectively. Plugging the first equation in the second one yields $(j + z) + j = 10$, or $z = 10 - 2j$.

Replacing z with $10 - 2j$ in the inequality in the question setup $z > 10 - z$ yields

$$(10 - 2j) > 10 - (10 - 2j)$$
$$10 - 2j > 10 - 10 + 2j$$
$$10 - 2j > 2j$$
$$10 > 4j$$
$$10/4 > j$$
$$2.5 > j$$

The inequality $z > 10 - z$ is true when $j < 2.5$, but j ranges between 0 and 10. So, j could be in the range 0 through 2.5 or out of this range. When in the range, the inequality $z > 10 - z$ is true; and when out of the range, $z > 10 - z$ is not true.

This is a double case, and the answer is (E).

Fractions & Decimals

A fraction consists of two parts: a numerator and a denominator.

$$\frac{numerator}{denominator}$$

If the numerator is smaller than the denominator, the fraction is called *proper* and is less than one. For example: $\frac{1}{2}$, $\frac{4}{5}$, and $\frac{3}{\pi}$ are all proper fractions and therefore less than 1.

If the numerator is larger than the denominator, the fraction is called *improper* and is greater than 1. For example: $\frac{3}{2}$, $\frac{5}{4}$, and $\frac{\pi}{3}$ are all improper fractions and therefore greater than 1.

An improper fraction can be converted into a *mixed fraction* by dividing its denominator into its numerator. For example, since 2 divides into 7 three times with a remainder of 1, we get

$$\frac{7}{2} = 3\frac{1}{2}$$

To convert a mixed fraction into an improper fraction, multiply the denominator and the integer and then add the numerator.   write the result over the denominator. For example, $5\frac{2}{3} = \frac{3 \cdot 5 + 2}{3} = \frac{17}{3}$.
        Then

In a negative fraction, the negative symbol can be written on the top, in the middle, or on the bottom; however, when a negative symbol appears on the bottom, it is usually moved to the top or the middle: $\frac{5}{-3} = \frac{-5}{3} = -\frac{5}{3}$. If both terms in the denominator of a fraction are negative, the negative symbol is often factored out and moved to the top or middle of the fraction: $\frac{1}{-x-2} = \frac{1}{-(x+2)} = -\frac{1}{x+2}$ or $\frac{-1}{x+2}$.

Strategy

To compare two fractions, cross-multiply. The larger number will be on the same side as the larger fraction.

Example: Which of the following fractions is larger?

$$\frac{9}{10} \qquad\qquad \frac{10}{11}$$

Cross-multiplying gives $9 \cdot 11$ versus $10 \cdot 10$, which reduces to 99 versus 100. Now, 100 is greater than 99. Hence, $\dfrac{10}{11}$ is greater than $\dfrac{9}{10}$.

 Strategy

Always reduce a fraction to its lowest terms.

Example: If $x \neq -1$, then $\dfrac{2cx^2 + 4cx + cy}{c(x+1)^2} =$

(1) $y = 2$

(2) $c = 3$

Factor out the c in the expression:

$$\frac{c\left(2x^2 + 4x + y\right)}{c(x+1)^2} =$$

$$\frac{\left(2x^2 + 4x + y\right)}{(x+1)^2}$$

Since c is no longer in the expression, we have no way to determine the value of y in terms of c, or c in terms of y. Hence, Statement (2), which indicates the value of c, is not required.

Statement (1): $y = 2$. Plugging this in the expression $\dfrac{\left(2x^2 + 4x + y\right)}{(x+1)^2}$ yields

$$\frac{\left(2x^2 + 4x + 2\right)}{(x+1)^2}$$

Factoring the quadratic expressions yields

$$\frac{2(x+1)(x+1)}{(x+1)(x+1)}$$

Finally, canceling the $(x + 1)$'s gives 2. The statement is sufficient.

The answer is (A).

 Strategy

To solve a fractional equation, multiply both sides by the LCD (lowest common denominator) to clear fractions.

Example: If $\dfrac{x+3}{x-3} = y$, what is the value of x?

    (1) $\sqrt{y+10} = 4$

    (2) $\dfrac{-3y-3}{1-y} = 6$

First, multiply both sides of the equation by $x-3$:

$$(x-3)\frac{x+3}{x-3} = (x-3)y$$

Cancel the $(x-3)$'s on the left side of the equation:

$$x+3 = (x-3)y$$

Distribute the y:

$$x+3 = xy - 3y$$

Subtract xy and 3 from both sides:

$$x - xy = -3y - 3$$

Factor out the x on the left side of the equation:

$$x(1-y) = -3y - 3$$

Finally, divide both sides of the equation by $1-y$:

$$x = \frac{-3y-3}{1-y}$$

So, Statement (2) alone, which gives the value of $\dfrac{-3y-3}{1-y}$, is sufficient.

The expression $\dfrac{-3y-3}{1-y}$ can be calculated given the value of y. The value of y can be calculated by the equation $\sqrt{y+10} = 4$. Squaring yields $y + 10 = 16$, or $y = 16 - 10 = 6$. Hence, Statement (1) is also sufficient.

The answer is (D).

Example: Is $x = 3$?

    (1) $x = \dfrac{-3y-3}{1-y}$

    (2) $\dfrac{|x|}{x} + x|x| > 0$

Statement (1): Suppose $x = 3$. Then $3 = \dfrac{-3y-3}{1-y}$, or $3(1-y) = -3y-3$, or $3 - 3y = -3y - 3$, or $3 = -3$. But this is impossible. Hence, Statement (1) alone is sufficient and says that "No, x is not 3."

Statement (2): $\dfrac{|x|}{x} + x|x| > 0$. Suppose $x = 3$. Then $\dfrac{|3|}{3} + 3|3| > 0$, or $1 + 9 = 10 > 0$. This doesn't prevent x being equal to 3, nor does it support it. So, Statement (2) alone is not sufficient.

The answer is (A).

Complex Fractions: When dividing a fraction by a whole number (or vice versa), you must keep track of the main division bar:

$$\frac{a}{b/c} = a \cdot \frac{c}{b} = \frac{ac}{b}. \text{ But } \frac{a/b}{c} = \frac{a}{b} \cdot \frac{1}{c} = \frac{a}{bc}.$$

Example: $\dfrac{1 - \dfrac{1}{2}}{3} =$

(A) 6   (B) 3   (C) 1/3   (D) 1/6   (E) 1/8

Solution: $\dfrac{1 - \dfrac{1}{2}}{3} = \dfrac{\dfrac{2}{2} - \dfrac{1}{2}}{3} = \dfrac{\dfrac{2-1}{2}}{3} = \dfrac{\dfrac{1}{2}}{3} = \dfrac{1}{2} \cdot \dfrac{1}{3} = \dfrac{1}{6}.$ The answer is (D).

Example: If $z \neq 0$ and $yz \neq 1$, then $\dfrac{1}{y - \dfrac{1}{z}} =$

(A) $\dfrac{yz}{zy-1}$ (B) $\dfrac{y-z}{z}$ (C) $\dfrac{yz-z}{z-1}$ (D) $\dfrac{z}{zy-1}$ (E) $\dfrac{y-z}{zy-1}$

Solution: $\dfrac{1}{y - \dfrac{1}{z}} = \dfrac{1}{\dfrac{z}{z} y - \dfrac{1}{z}} = \dfrac{1}{\dfrac{zy-1}{z}} = 1 \cdot \dfrac{z}{zy-1} = \dfrac{z}{zy-1}.$ The answer is (D).

 Multiplying fractions is routine: merely multiply the numerators and multiply the denominators: $\dfrac{a}{b} \cdot \dfrac{c}{d} = \dfrac{ac}{bd}.$ For example, $\dfrac{1}{2} \cdot \dfrac{3}{4} = \dfrac{1 \cdot 3}{2 \cdot 4} = \dfrac{3}{8}.$

 Two fractions can be added quickly by cross-multiplying: $\dfrac{a}{b} \pm \dfrac{c}{d} = \dfrac{ad \pm bc}{bd}$

Example: $\dfrac{1}{2} - \dfrac{3}{4} =$

(A) –5/4   (B) –2/3   (C) –1/4   (D) –1/2   (E) –2/3

Cross-multiplying the expression $\dfrac{1}{2} - \dfrac{3}{4}$ yields $\dfrac{1 \cdot 4 - 2 \cdot 3}{2 \cdot 4} = \dfrac{4 - 6}{8} = \dfrac{-2}{8} = -\dfrac{1}{4}.$ Hence, the answer is (C).

Example: Which of the following equals the average of x and $\dfrac{1}{x}$?

(A) $\dfrac{x+2}{x}$ (B) $\dfrac{x^2+1}{2x}$ (C) $\dfrac{x+1}{x^2}$ (D) $\dfrac{2x^2+1}{x}$ (E) $\dfrac{x+1}{x}$

The average of x and $\dfrac{1}{x}$ is $\dfrac{x+\dfrac{1}{x}}{2} = \dfrac{\dfrac{x^2+1}{x}}{2} = \dfrac{x^2+1}{x} \cdot \dfrac{1}{2} = \dfrac{x^2+1}{2x}$. Thus, the answer is (B).

Example: Does $x = y$?

(1) The average of x and $\dfrac{1}{x}$ equals the average of y and $\dfrac{1}{y}$.

(2) $xy = 1$

The average of x and $\dfrac{1}{x}$ is $\dfrac{x+\dfrac{1}{x}}{2} = \dfrac{\dfrac{x^2+1}{x}}{2} = \dfrac{x^2+1}{x} \cdot \dfrac{1}{2} = \dfrac{x^2+1}{2x}$. Similarly, suppose the average of y and

$1/y$ is a. Then $\dfrac{x^2+1}{2x} = a$, or $x^2 + 1 = 2ax$. The equation is of degree 2, so we should expect two solutions

for x in terms of a.

Now, we know that "The average of x and $\dfrac{1}{x}$ equals the average of y and $\dfrac{1}{y}$" which means $\dfrac{x+\dfrac{1}{x}}{2} = \dfrac{y+\dfrac{1}{y}}{2}$.

This happens when $x = y$ or when $x = \dfrac{1}{y}$. Clearly, we have the two solutions, which we could get. Now, if

$x = \dfrac{1}{y}$ were the solution, then x can still equal y if both equal 1 or –1 or x may not equal y at all. We have a

double case and therefore Statement (1) alone is not sufficient.

Now, Statement (2), $xy = 1$, says $x = y$ isn't the solution but the solution is $x = \dfrac{1}{y}$ (so the answer could be

"No, x isn't equal to y.") But even with this, $x = \dfrac{1}{y} = 1$ is possible which can say "Yes, $x = y$."

Thus, the answer is (E).

 To add three or more fractions with different denominators, you need to form a common denominator of all the fractions.

For example, to add the fractions in the expression $\dfrac{1}{3} + \dfrac{1}{4} + \dfrac{1}{18}$, we have to change the denominator of each fraction into the common denominator 36 (note, 36 is a common denominator because 3, 4, and 18 all divide into it evenly). This is done by multiply the top and bottom of each fraction by an appropriate number (this does not change the value of the expression because any number divided by itself equals 1):

$$\dfrac{1}{3}\left(\dfrac{12}{12}\right) + \dfrac{1}{4}\left(\dfrac{9}{9}\right) + \dfrac{1}{18}\left(\dfrac{2}{2}\right) = \dfrac{12}{36} + \dfrac{9}{36} + \dfrac{2}{36} = \dfrac{12+9+2}{36} = \dfrac{23}{36}$$

You may remember from algebra that to find a common denominator of a set of fractions, you prime factor the denominators and then select each factor the greatest number of times it occurs in any of the factorizations. That is too cumbersome, however. A better way is to simply add the largest denominator to itself until all the other denominators divide into it evenly. In the above example, we just add 18 to itself to get the common denominator 36.

 To find a common denominator of a set of fractions, simply add the largest denominator to itself until all the other denominators divide into it evenly.

 Fractions often behave in unusual ways: Squaring a fraction makes it smaller, and taking the square root of a fraction makes it larger. (**Caution:** This is true only for proper fractions, that is, fractions between 0 and 1.)

Example: $\left(\dfrac{1}{3}\right)^2 = \dfrac{1}{9}$ and $\dfrac{1}{9}$ is less than $\dfrac{1}{3}$. Also $\sqrt{\dfrac{1}{4}} = \dfrac{1}{2}$ and $\dfrac{1}{2}$ is greater than $\dfrac{1}{4}$.

 You can cancel only over multiplication, not over addition or subtraction.

For example, the c's in the expression $\dfrac{c+x}{c}$ cannot be canceled. However, the c's in the expression $\dfrac{cx+c}{c}$ can be canceled as follows: $\dfrac{cx+c}{c} = \dfrac{\cancel{c}(x+1)}{\cancel{c}} = x+1$.

Decimals

If a fraction's denominator is a power of 10, it can be written in a special form called a *decimal fraction*. Some common decimals are $\dfrac{1}{10} = .1, \dfrac{2}{100} = .02, \dfrac{3}{1000} = .003$. Notice that the number of decimal places corresponds to the number of zeros in the denominator of the fraction. Also, note that the value of the decimal place decreases to the right of the decimal point:

```
                 tenths
              |
              |      hundredths
              |   |
              |   |   thousandths
              |   |   |
              |   |   |   ten-thousandths
              |   |   |   |
             .1   2   3   4
```

This decimal can be written in expanded form as follows:

$$.1234 = \frac{1}{10} + \frac{2}{100} + \frac{3}{1000} + \frac{4}{10000}$$

Sometimes a zero is placed before the decimal point to prevent misreading the decimal as a whole number. The zero has no affect on the value of the decimal. For example, $.2 = 0.2$.

Fractions can be converted to decimals by dividing the denominator into the numerator. For example, to convert $\frac{5}{8}$ to a decimal, divide 8 into 5 (note, a decimal point and as many zeros as necessary are added after the 5):

$$
\begin{array}{r}
.625 \\
8\overline{)5.000} \\
\underline{48} \\
20 \\
\underline{16} \\
40 \\
\underline{40} \\
0
\end{array}
$$

The procedures for adding, subtracting, multiplying, and dividing decimals are the same as for whole numbers, except for a few small adjustments.

➤ **Adding and Subtracting Decimals:** To add or subtract decimals, merely align the decimal points and then add or subtract as you would with whole numbers.

$$
\begin{array}{r}
1.369 \\
+\ \ 9.7 \\
\hline
11.069
\end{array}
\qquad
\begin{array}{r}
12.45 \\
-\ \ 6.367 \\
\hline
6.083
\end{array}
$$

➤ **Multiplying Decimals:** Multiply decimals as you would with whole numbers. The answer will have as many decimal places as the sum of the number of decimal places in the numbers being multiplied.

$$
\begin{array}{rl}
1.23 & \text{2 decimal places} \\
\times\ \ 2.4 & \text{1 decimal place} \\
\hline
492 & \\
246 & \\
\hline
2.952 & \text{3 decimal places}
\end{array}
$$

➤ **Dividing Decimals:** Before dividing decimals, move the decimal point of the divisor all the way to the right and move the decimal point of the dividend the same number of spaces to the right (adding zeros if necessary). Then divide as you would with whole numbers.

$$
.24\overline{)\,.6} = 24\overline{)60.0}
\begin{array}{r}
2.5 \\
\end{array}
$$

$$
\begin{array}{r}
2.5 \\
24\overline{)60.0} \\
\underline{48} \\
120 \\
\underline{120} \\
0
\end{array}
$$

Example: $\dfrac{1}{5}$ of .1 percent equals:

    (A) 2   (B) .2   (C) .02   (D) .002   (E) .0002

Recall that percent means to divide by 100. So, .1 percent equals $\dfrac{.1}{100} = .001$. To convert $\dfrac{1}{5}$ to a decimal, divide 5 into 1:

$$
\begin{array}{r}
.2 \\
5\overline{)1.0} \\
\underline{10} \\
0
\end{array}
$$

In percent problems, "of" means multiplication. So, multiplying .2 and .001 yields

$$
\begin{array}{r}
.001 \\
\times\quad .2 \\
\hline
.0002
\end{array}
$$

Hence, the answer is (E). Note, you may be surprised to learn that the GMAT would consider this to be a hard problem.

Example: The decimal .1 is how many times greater than the decimal $(.001)^3$?

    (A)   10

    (B) 10^2

    (C) 10^5

    (D) 10^8

    (E) 10^{10}

Converting .001 to a fraction gives $\dfrac{1}{1000}$. This fraction, in turn, can be written as $\dfrac{1}{10^3}$, or 10^{-3}. Cubing this expression yields $(.001)^3 = \left(10^{-3}\right)^3 = 10^{-9}$. Now, dividing the larger number, .1, by the smaller number, $(.001)^3$, yields

$$\frac{.1}{(.001)^3} = \frac{10^{-1}}{10^{-9}} = 10^{-1-(-9)} = 10^{-1+9} = 10^8$$

Hence, .1 is 10^8 times as large as $(.001)^3$. The answer is (D).

Example: Let $x = .99$, $y = \sqrt{.99}$, and $z = (.99)^2$. Then which of the following is true?

    (A) $x < z < y$

    (B) $z < y < x$

    (C) $z < x < y$

    (D) $y < x < z$

    (E) $y < z < x$

Converting .99 into a fraction gives $\dfrac{99}{100}$. Since $\dfrac{99}{100}$ is between 0 and 1, squaring it will make it smaller and taking its square root will make it larger. Hence, $(.99)^2 < .99 < \sqrt{.99}$. The answer is (C). Note, this property holds for all proper decimals (decimals between 0 and 1) just as it does for all proper fractions.

Problem Set G: Fractions & Decimals

1.   If $2x + 3 = y + 1/y$, then $x + y =$

    (1) $x = -1/4$

    (2) $y = 2$

2.   What percent of the positive value of p is the positive value of q?

    (1) $\dfrac{p+q}{p-q} = 7$

    (2) $\dfrac{p+q}{p-q} + \dfrac{p-q}{p+q} = 7\dfrac{1}{7}$

3.   What is p/q?

    (1) $\dfrac{p+q}{p-q} + \dfrac{p-q}{p+q} = 5\dfrac{1}{5}$

    (2) $\dfrac{p-q}{p+q} - \dfrac{p-q}{p+q} = 4\dfrac{4}{5}$

4.   Is $\dfrac{(a-b)+(c-b)}{d} > 0$?

    (1) $a + c < 2b$

    (2) $d < 0$

5.   What fraction of the students in a class have blue eyes?

    (1)   10% of the girls have blue eyes.

    (2)   20% of the boys have blue eyes.

6.   If s and t are positive integers, then what is the remainder when s is divided by t ?

    (1) $s/t = 39.13$

    (2) $s = 17,731$ and $t = 429$

7.   In a country, 65% of male citizen and 68% of female citizen are eligible to vote. What fraction of the citizens voted during the election?

    (1)   68% of male citizens eligible to vote voted.

    (2)   65% of female citizens eligible to vote voted.

Answers and Solutions to Problem Set G: Fractions & Decimals

1.   If $2x + 3 = y + 1/y$, then $x + y =$

   (1) $x = -1/4$

   (2) $y = 2$

Statement (1): $x = -1/4$

Substituting $x = -1/4$ in the equation $2x + 3 = y + 1/y$ yields

$$2\left(-\frac{1}{4}\right) + 3 = y + \frac{1}{y}$$

$$-\frac{1}{2} + 3 = y + \frac{1}{y}$$

$$2\frac{1}{2} = y + \frac{1}{y}$$

$$2 + \frac{1}{2} = y + \frac{1}{y}$$

By comparing the left and right sides of the equation, we can say that y could be 2 or 1/2.

Hence, $x + y$ could be $-\frac{1}{4} + 2 = 1\frac{3}{4}$.

Or $x + y$ could be $-\frac{1}{4} + \frac{1}{2} = \frac{1}{4}$.

Since we have two different solutions (which means no unique answer), the statement is *not* sufficient.

The answer is (B).

Statement (2): $y = 2$

Substituting $y = 2$ in the equation $2x + 3 = y + 1/y$ yields

$$2x + 3 = 2 + \frac{1}{2}$$

$$2x = -3 + 2\frac{1}{2}$$

$$2x = -\frac{1}{2}$$

$$x = -\frac{1}{4}$$

Hence, $x + y = -\frac{1}{4} + 2 = 1\frac{3}{4}$, and the statement is sufficient.

2.   What percent of the positive value of p is the positive value of q?

   (1) $\dfrac{p+q}{p-q} = 7$

   (2) $\dfrac{p+q}{p-q} + \dfrac{p-q}{p+q} = 7\dfrac{1}{7}$

The equation in Statement (2) can be expressed as $\dfrac{p+q}{p-q} + \dfrac{1}{\dfrac{p+q}{p-q}} = 7 + \dfrac{1}{7}$, or $\dfrac{1}{7} + \dfrac{1}{\dfrac{1}{7}}$. Both sides are in the

form $a + 1/a$ where a is $\dfrac{p+q}{p-q}$ on the left side and a could be 7 or 1/7 on the right side. So, $\dfrac{p+q}{p-q}$ could

equal 7 or 1/7. Statement (1) is just one of these possibilities $\dfrac{p+q}{p-q} = 7$. Hence, if Statement (2) is

sufficient, then Statement (1) will be sufficient. Now, we have

$$\frac{p+q}{p-q} = 7 \qquad \text{and} \qquad \frac{p+q}{p-q} = \frac{1}{7}$$

Cross-multiplying the equation $\frac{p+q}{p-q} = 7$ yields

Cross-multiplying the equation $\frac{p+q}{p-q} = \frac{1}{7}$ yields

$$p+q = 7(p-q)$$
$$p+q = 7p-7q$$
$$8q = 6p$$
$$4q = 3p$$
$$\frac{q}{p} = \frac{3}{4}$$

$$7p+7q = p-q$$
$$6p = -8q$$
$$\frac{q}{p} = \frac{6}{-8} = \frac{3}{4}$$

Now, q is $\frac{q}{p} \cdot 100$ percent of p, which equals

Hence, the positive value of q is

$$\frac{|q|}{|p|} \cdot 100 = \left|\frac{q}{p}\right| \cdot 100 \text{ percent of the positive value}$$

$$\frac{3}{4} \cdot 100 = 75\%.$$

of p, which equals $\frac{6}{8} \cdot 100 = 75\%.$

Either way, the positive ratio of q/p is constant. Hence, Statement (2) alone and therefore Statement (1) alone is sufficient. The answer is (D).

3.   What is p/q?

(1) $\dfrac{p+q}{p-q} + \dfrac{p-q}{p+q} = 5\dfrac{1}{5}$

(2) $\dfrac{p-q}{p+q} - \dfrac{p-q}{p+q} = 4\dfrac{4}{5}$

Let's suppose $\dfrac{p+q}{p-q} = t$. Then $\dfrac{1}{t} = \dfrac{p-q}{p+q}$ and the two statements become (1) $t + \dfrac{1}{t} = 5\dfrac{1}{5}$ and (2) $t - \dfrac{1}{t} = 4\dfrac{4}{5}$. Cross-multiplying the equation $\dfrac{p+q}{p-q} = t$ yields

$$p + q = tp - tq$$

$$(1 - t)p = q(-1 - t)$$

$$\frac{p}{q} = \frac{-1-t}{1-t} = \frac{-(1+t)}{1-t} = \frac{(1+t)}{-(1-t)} = \frac{(1+t)}{(t-1)}$$

So, if we know t, we can evaluate the ratio p/q. The question can now be modified as

What is t?

(1) $t + \dfrac{1}{t} = \dfrac{26}{5} = 5\dfrac{1}{5}$

(2) $t - \dfrac{1}{t} = \dfrac{24}{5} = 4\dfrac{4}{5}$

Statement (1): $t + \dfrac{1}{t} = 5\dfrac{1}{5}$

The equation is satisfied for both $t = 5$ and $t = 1/5$. (The equation can have only two solutions because multiplying the equation by t yields a quadratic equation, and a quadratic equation can have at most two roots. Here, they must be 5 and 1/5.)

If $t = 5$,

$$\frac{p}{q} = \frac{t+1}{t-1} = \frac{5+1}{5-1} = \frac{6}{4} = \frac{3}{2}$$

If $t = 1/5$,

$$\frac{p}{q} = \frac{t+1}{t-1} = \frac{1/5+1}{1/5-1} = \frac{6}{-4} = \frac{-3}{2}$$

This is a double case, and therefore the statement is *not* sufficient.

Statement (2): $t - \dfrac{1}{t} = 4\dfrac{4}{5}$

$$t - \frac{1}{t} = 4\frac{4}{5} = \frac{4\cdot5+4}{5} = \frac{24}{5}$$

$$\left(= \frac{24}{5} = \frac{25-1}{5} = 5 - \frac{1}{5} \right)$$

Multiplying the equation by t yields

$$t^2 - 1 = \frac{24}{5}t$$

$$t^2 - \frac{24}{5}t - 1 = 0$$

$$t^2 - 5t + \frac{t}{5} - 1 = 0$$

$$t(t-5) + \frac{1}{5}(t-5) = 0$$

$$(t+1/5)(t-5) = 0$$

$$t = -1/5 \text{ or } t = 5$$

Hence,

$$\frac{p}{q} = \frac{t+1}{t-1} = \frac{-1/5+1}{-1/5-1} = \frac{4}{-6} = \frac{-2}{3}$$

or

$$\frac{p}{q} = \frac{t+1}{t-1} = \frac{5+1}{5-1} = \frac{6}{4} = \frac{3}{2}$$

This is a double case, and therefore the statement is *not* sufficient.

From the statements together, $t = 5$ (or $p/q = 3/2$) is the only common solution. Hence, the statements together are sufficient, and the answer is (C).

4.   Is $\dfrac{(a-b)+(c-b)}{d} > 0$?

(1) $a + c < 2b$

(2) $d < 0$

The question is about the fraction $\dfrac{(a-b)+(c-b)}{d}$. The numerator of the fraction is $(a-b)+(c-b)$ and the denominator is d.

From Statement (1), we do not have any information about d. So, if $(a-b)+(c-b)$ is negative and d is positive, the fraction is negative; and if $(a-b)+(c-b)$ is negative and d is negative, the fraction is positive. Hence, Statement (1) alone is *not* sufficient.

From Statement (2), we do not have information about the numerator $(a - b) + (c - b)$. So, if the numerator is negative and the denominator d is negative, the fraction is positive; and if the numerator is positive and the denominator d is negative, the fraction is negative. Hence, we have a double case and Statement (2) alone is *not* sufficient.

Now, the numerator is $(a - b) + (c - b) = a + c - 2b$ and according to Statement (1) alone, we have the expression is negative (< 0). Now, from statement (2) alone, we have the denominator d is negative. So, the fraction Numerator/Denominator = (a Negative Number) ÷ (a Negative Number) = a Positive Number. So, the answer is "Yes. $\dfrac{(a - b) + (c - b)}{d} > 0$". Hence, the answer is (C), the statements together are sufficient.

5.   What fraction of the students in a class have blue eyes?

(1)   10% of the girls have blue eyes.

(2)   20% of the boys have blue eyes.

Let the number of girls be g, and the number of boys be b. Hence, the number of students is $b + g$. From the statements together, we have

10% of girls are blue eyed. 10% of g is $\dfrac{10}{100}g = \dfrac{g}{10}$.

20% of boys are blue eyed. 20% of b is $\dfrac{20}{100}b = \dfrac{b}{5}$.

Hence, the total number of blue-eyed students is $\dfrac{g}{10} + \dfrac{b}{5}$.

Hence, the required fraction is $\dfrac{\dfrac{g}{10} + \dfrac{b}{5}}{b + g}$.

Dividing both the numerator and the denominator of the fraction by b yields $\dfrac{\dfrac{g}{10b} + \dfrac{1}{5}}{1 + \dfrac{g}{b}}$. Hence, to find the value of the required fraction, we need at least the ratio b/g. Since we do not have the means to evaluate the ratio, the statements together are not sufficient to answer the question. The answer is (E).

6.   If s and t are positive integers, then what is the remainder when s is divided by t ?

(1) $s/t = 39.13$

(2) $s = 17,731$ and $t = 429$

From Statement (1) alone, we have that $s/t = 39.13$. But, 39.13 is the result of one of the ratios: $\dfrac{3913}{100}$, $\dfrac{2 \times 3913}{2 \times 100}$, $\dfrac{3 \times 3913}{3 \times 100}$, ..., and so on.

The first fraction $\dfrac{3913}{100}$ equals $\dfrac{3900}{100} + \dfrac{13}{100}$, so 13 is the remainder.

The second fraction $\dfrac{7826}{200}$ equals $\dfrac{7800}{200} + \dfrac{26}{200}$, so the remainder is 26.

Hence, we do not have a unique value for the remainder. Hence, Statement (1) alone is not sufficient.

From Statement (2) alone, we have that $s = 17{,}731$ and $t = 429$. Since we have the values of the dividend and the divisor, we can find the quotient and the remainder. Hence, Statement (2) alone is sufficient. Calculating the remainder is not necessary.

The answer is (B).

7.   In a country, 65% of male citizen and 68% of female citizen are eligible to vote. What fraction of the citizens voted during the election?

   (1)   68% of male citizens eligible to vote voted.

   (2)   65% of female citizens eligible to vote voted.

Let the number of male and female citizens in the country be m and f, respectively.

Now, 65% of the male citizens are eligible to vote, and 65% of m is $\dfrac{65m}{100}$.

68% of female citizens are eligible to vote, and 68% of f is $\dfrac{68f}{100}$.

From statements (1) and (2) together, we have

68% of male citizens eligible to vote voted, and 68% of $\dfrac{65m}{100}$ is $\dfrac{68}{100} \cdot \dfrac{65m}{100} = \dfrac{65 \cdot 68m}{10{,}000}$.

65% of female citizens eligible to vote voted, and 65% of $\dfrac{68f}{100}$ is $\dfrac{65}{100} \cdot \dfrac{68f}{100} = \dfrac{65 \cdot 68f}{10{,}000}$.

So, out of the total $m + f$ citizens, the total number of voters who voted is

$$\frac{65 \cdot 68m}{10{,}000} + \frac{65 \cdot 68f}{10{,}000} = \frac{(65 \cdot 68)(m + f)}{10{,}000}$$

Hence, the required fraction is

$$\frac{\dfrac{(65 \cdot 68)(m + f)}{10{,}000}}{m + f} = \frac{65 \cdot 68}{10{,}000}$$

Hence, the statements together answer the question; and from the lack of the crucial details, the statements individually are not sufficient. Hence, the answer is (C).

Equations

When simplifying algebraic expressions, we perform operations within parentheses first and then exponents and then multiplication and then division and then addition and lastly subtraction. This can be remembered by the mnemonic:

PEMDAS

Please **E**xcuse **M**y **D**ear **A**unt **S**ally

When solving equations, however, we apply the mnemonic in reverse order: **SADMEP**. This is often expressed as follows: inverse operations in inverse order. The goal in solving an equation is to isolate the variable on one side of the equal sign (usually the left side). This is done by identifying the main operation—addition, multiplication, etc.—and then performing the opposite operation.

Example: Solve the following equation for x: $2x + y = 5$

Solution: The main operation is addition (remember addition now comes before multiplication, SADMEP), so subtracting y from both sides yields

$$2x + y - y = 5 - y$$

Simplifying yields $\qquad 2x = 5 - y$

The only operation remaining on the left side is multiplication. Undoing the multiplication by dividing both sides by 2 yields

$$\frac{2x}{2} = \frac{5-y}{2}$$

Canceling the 2 on the left side yields $\qquad x = \dfrac{5-y}{2}$

Example: Solve the following equation for x: $3x - 4 = 2(x - 5)$

Solution: Here x appears on both sides of the equal sign, so let's move the x on the right side to the left side. But the x is trapped inside the parentheses. To release it, distribute the 2:

$$3x - 4 = 2x - 10$$

Now, subtracting $2x$ from both sides yields[*]

$$x - 4 = -10$$

---

[*] Note, students often mistakenly add $2x$ to both sides of this equation because of the minus symbol between $2x$ and 10. But $2x$ is positive, so we subtract it. This can be seen more clearly by rewriting the right side of the equation as $-10 + 2x$.

Finally, adding 4 to both sides yields

$$x = -6$$

We often manipulate equations without thinking about what the equations actually say. The GMAT likes to test this oversight. Equations are packed with information. Take for example the simple equation $3x + 2 = 5$. Since 5 is positive, the expression $3x + 2$ must be positive as well. An equation means that the terms on either side of the equal sign are equal in every way. Hence, any property one side of an equation has the other side will have as well. Following are some immediate deductions that can be made from simple equations.

Equation	Deduction
$y - x = 1$	$y > x$
$y^2 = x^2$	$y = \pm x$, or $\lvert y \rvert = \lvert x \rvert$. That is, x and y can differ only in sign.
$y^3 = x^3$	$y = x$
$y = x^2$	$y \geq 0$
$\dfrac{y}{x^2} = 1$	$y > 0$
$\dfrac{y}{x^3} = 2$	Both x and y are positive or both x and y are negative.
$x^2 + y^2 = 0$	$y = x = 0$
$3y = 4x$ and $x > 0$	$y > x$ and y is positive.
$3y = 4x$ and $x < 0$	$y < x$ and y is negative.
$y = \sqrt{x + 2}$	$y \geq 0$ and $x \geq -2$
$y = 2x$	y is even
$y = 2x + 1$	y is odd
$yx = 0$	$y = 0$ or $x = 0$, or both

 In Algebra, you solve an equation for, say, y by isolating y on one side of the equality symbol. On the GMAT, however, you are often asked to solve for an entire term, say, $3 - y$ by isolating it on one side.

Example 1: $a - b =$

(1) $a + 3a$ is 4 less than $b + 3b$.

(2) $a + 3b$ is two times more than $b + 3a$.

Statement (1): $a + 3a$ is 4 less than $b + 3b$.

Translating the sentence into an equation gives	$a + 3a = b + 3b - 4$
Combining like terms gives	$4a = 4b - 4$
Subtracting $4b$ from both sides gives	$4a - 4b = -4$
Finally, dividing by 4 gives	$a - b = -1$

Statement (1) is sufficient.

Statement (2): $a + 3b$ is two times more than $b + 3a$.

Translating the sentence into an equation gives	$a + 3b = 2(b + 3a)$
Distributing the right hand side yields	$a + 3b = 2b + 6a$
Subtracting $2b$ from both sides yields	$a + b = 6a$
Subtracting a from both sides yields	$b = 5a$
Finally,	$a - b = a - 5a = -4a$

Since we do not know the value of a, the value of $-4a$ cannot be determined. So, Statement (2) is not sufficient.

The answer is (A).

 Sometimes, a system of 3 equations will be written as one long "triple" equation. For example, the three equations $x = y$, $y = z$, $x = z$, can be written more compactly as $x = y = z$.

Example 2:   If $w \neq 0$ and $w = 2x = \sqrt{2}y$, what is the value of $w - x$?

(1) $\dfrac{2}{\sqrt{2}}y = 2\sqrt{2}$

(2) $\sqrt{2y} = 2\sqrt{2}$

The equation $w = 2x = \sqrt{2}y$ stands for only two equations: $w = 2x$, $2x = \sqrt{2}y$, and the equation $w = \sqrt{2}y$ is automatically assumed. From the last equation, we get $w = \sqrt{2}y$; and from the second equation, we get $x = \dfrac{\sqrt{2}}{2}y$. Hence, $w - x = \sqrt{2}y - \dfrac{\sqrt{2}}{2}y = \dfrac{2}{2}\sqrt{2}y - \dfrac{\sqrt{2}}{2}y = \dfrac{2\sqrt{2}y - \sqrt{2}y}{2} = \dfrac{\sqrt{2}y}{2}$. So, given y, the value of the expression $\dfrac{\sqrt{2}y}{2}$ can be evaluated.

Either statement alone gives the value of y. Hence, either statement is sufficient, and the answer is (D).

 Often on the GMAT, you can solve a system of two equations in two unknowns by merely adding or subtracting the equations—instead of solving for one of the variables and then substituting it into the other equation.

Example 3:   If p and q are positive, $p^2 + q^2 = 16$, and $p^2 - q^2 = 8$, then $q =$

Subtract the second equation from the first:	$p^2 + q^2 = 16$
	$(-) \quad p^2 - q^2 = 8$
	$2q^2 = 8$
Dividing both sides of the equation by 2 gives	$q^2 = 4$
Finally, taking the square root of both sides gives	$q = \pm 2$

Eliminating The Unknowns One at a Time (Four-Step Method)

Although on the GMAT you can usually solve a system of two equations in two unknowns by merely adding or subtracting the equations, you still need to know a standard method for solving these types of systems.

The "eliminating the unknowns one at a time" method will be illustrated with the following system:

$$2x + y = 10$$

$$5x - 2y = 7$$

1) *Solve one of the equations for one of the variables*:

   Solving the top equation for y yields $y = 10 - 2x$.

2) *Substitute the result from Step 1 into the other equation*:

   Substituting $y = 10 - 2x$ into the bottom equation yields $5x - 2(10 - 2x) = 7$.

3) *Solve the resulting equation*:

$$5x - 2(10 - 2x) = 7$$

$$5x - 20 + 4x = 7$$

$$9x - 20 = 7$$

$$9x = 27$$

$$x = 3$$

4) *Substitute the result from Step 3 into the equation derived in Step 1*:

   Substituting $x = 3$ into $y = 10 - 2x$ yields $y = 10 - 2(3) = 10 - 6 = 4$.

Hence, the solution of the system of equations is the ordered pair (3, 4).

Example 4:   Is x equal to 1?

   (1) $(3x - 2) + (3x + 2) = 6$

   (2) $x^2 + 2x = 3$

Both statements satisfy $x = 1$.

Statement (1): $(3x - 2) + (3x + 2) = 6$; Here, x yields a single value. The single value yields a single result whether it equals 1 (Yes) or does not equal 1 (No). Either way, the statement is sufficient. In other words, substituting x with 1 yields $(3x - 2) + (3x + 2) = 6$; $(3 \cdot 1 - 2) + (3 \cdot 1 + 2) = 6$; $(3 - 2) + (3 + 2) = 6$; $1 + 5 = 6$. Now, don't ask for another solution, the equation being linear has a single solution, so 6 must be it. Statement (1) is sufficient.

Statement (2): $x^2 + 2x = 3$: Take the clue $x = 1$ from Statement (1). Since this is the only possible value for x according to Statement (1) (we discussed there), this must satisfy Statement (2). Anyway, we still prove that $x = 1$ is feasible for Statement (2) by separately substituting it in Statement (2). Here, we go: Substituting $x = 1$ yields $x^2 + 2x = 3$; $1^2 + 2 \cdot 1 = 3$; $1 + 2 = 3$; $3 = 3$; Valid result. So, $x = 1$ is one solution.

You can ask for another solution here, because the equation is quadratic. So, we could have one more solution. Moreover, the equation $x^2 + 2x = 3$ is not a perfect square trinomial. So, we will have two different solutions, not two equal solutions. We already know one solution is 1. We even know that there exists another solution not equal to 1. The question "Is $x = 1$?" equals Yes for former solution and equals No for the later solution. We have a double case and therefore the statement is not sufficient.

The answer is (A).

Strategy

Degree of Freedom method for linear equations and other equations.

If you have n unknowns in a system, there are n degrees of freedom.

Each different linear rule (such as a linear equation) decreases the degree of freedom by one. See Example 5 below.

Ratio rules & Non-ratio rules: Ratio rules are the rules that do not have a constant term (precisely, they do not have a non-zero constant term) in them. For example, $x = 3y$, $x/2 + z = 0$, etc. Such ratio rules only help determine the ratio solutions such as x is 3 times y or x is -2 times z, etc. And it does not help evaluate non-ratio solutions such as $x = 3$ or $y = 1$ or $z = -3/2$.

To evaluate at least one non-ratio solution, we need at least one non-ratio rule. For example, to evaluate specific values for x, y, and z above, we need a non-ratio rule (if we are given $y = 1$, we evaluate x as $x = 3y = 3(1) = 3$, and then $z = x/-2 = 3/-2 = -3/2$ or a rule like $x + z = 12$). See Example 6 below.

Example 5:   Suppose we have the system

$$2x + 5y - 13z = 1000$$

$$3x - 9y + 3z = 0$$

$$-5x + 6y + 8z = -600$$

This is a system of three different equations in three unknowns. Eliminating the unknowns one at a time, yields

$$x = 1200 \qquad y = 500 \qquad x = 300$$

This can be summarized as we have 3 unknowns in the system and three different non-ratio rules reduce the system to degree of freedom $3 - 3 = 0$, and we have the 3 non-ratio rules: [$2x + 5y - 13z = 1000$ or $3x - 9y + 3z = 0$ or $-5x + 6y + 8z = -600$] or [$x = 1200$ or $y = 500$ or $x = 300$]. This also means the system is fixed.

The following three "rules of thumb" help us to classify systems of equations in several unknowns.

(A) If a system contains more equations (rules) than unknowns (initial degree of freedom), then we have a single solution if the equations depict a single realistic system. Otherwise, we may have no solution at all (more precisely, conflicting solutions for each set of equations taken.). Anyway, the GMAT wouldn't give a system of conflicting results. So, don't worry about the later type. The degree of freedom = Unknowns – Equations = Negative. A negative Degree of freedom is equivalent to a zero degree of freedom. Systems with negative degree of freedom can be considered "over-determined" systems. To repeat, the GMAT gives only systems with at least one solution, and will not give one with no solution. Here are two examples of over-determined systems.

System 1	System 2
$x + y = 3$	$x + y = 3$
$x - y = 1$	$x - y = 1$
$x + 2y = 4$	$x + 2y = 5$

The GMAT would not give a system like System 2, because the top two equations in the system yield a solution (for x and y) that is different from the one yielded by the bottom two equations. In other words, the solution of the top two equations does not satisfy the bottom two equations.

The GMAT will only give a system like System 1 where any two equations yield a solution compatible with the other two.

(B)   If a system contains fewer equations (rules) than unknowns, then it often has infinitely many solutions (since Degree of freedom = Unknowns minus Rules is not reduced to zero or negative). If $m < n$, then a system of m equations in n unknowns will often leave $n - m$ degrees of freedom. So, the entire system is subject to change by $n - m$ variables. So, we will have multiple solutions. This might mean data insufficiency.

(C)   When a system has the same number of equations (all different) as unknowns, then it usually has just one solution. This generally means data sufficiency.

Example 6:

	A	B	C	D
A	0	x	$x + y$	$x + y + z$
B	$y/2$	0	$2x$	$2y$
C	$x + 2y - z$	$y/2 + z/2$	0	$2x$
D	$5z/2$	$2x - y + 2z$	z	0

A, B, C, and D are points on a line, in that order. The table above shows the distance between any 2 of the 4 points. For example, the distance, BD, between points B and D is $2y$ or $2x - y + 2z$, from the table. What is the distance between A and D?

(1) BC is twice AB.

(2) AC is 1.5 times CD.

Since A, B, C and D are points on a line in that order, AD equals $AB + BC + CD$.

The distance between two points is the same regardless of the direction it is measured. For example, whether the distance is measured from A to B or measured from B to A, the result is the same. Hence, $AB = BA$. If AB is read as Row 1-Column2 and BA is read as Row 2-Column 1, they are equal. So, from the table, $x = y/2$.

Similarly, Row n-Column m equals Row m-Column n. Thus, equating the corresponding blocks we get

1st row 2nd column against corresponding block: $x = y/2$

1st row 3rd column against corresponding block: $x + y = x + 2y - z$

1st row 4th column against corresponding block: $x + y + z = 5z/2$

2nd row 3rd column against corresponding block: $2x = y/2 + z/2$

2nd row 4th column against corresponding block: $2y = 2x - y + 2z$

3rd row 4th column against corresponding block: $2x = z$

Clearly, all the above rules are ratio rules (we do not have non-zero constant terms in them). We have 3 unknowns and 6 rules. However, if you thought the degree of freedom is $3 - 6 = -3$ and therefore the solution is sufficient with question alone, you are mistaken.

We need at least one non-ratio rule, but neither Statement (1) nor Statement (2) are non-ratio rules. Here is a proof:

From Row 1-Column 2, $AB = x$.
So, Row 1-Column 3 = $AC = x + y$. So, $BC = AC - AB = (x + y) - x = y$.
Row 1-Column 4 = $AD = x + y + z$.
So, $CD = AD - AB - BC = (x + y + z) - x - y = z$.
So, $AB = x$, $BC = y$, $CD = z$.

So, as an example:

Statement (1), BC is twice AB, means y is 2 times x; and Statement (2), AC is 1.5 times CD, means $(x + y)$ is 1.5 times z. So, $y = 2x$, and $z = 1.5(x + y)$ are what we have from the statements and neither of these is a non-ratio rule.

So, a solution is possible only in ratios form and not in non-ratio form (specific values form). So, AD is $x + y + z$ [which is the sum specific values (of x, y, and z)] cannot be evaluated since the specific values of the variables x, y, and z are not known. So, even with the statements together, we do not have a single non-zero constant rule. Hence, a specific solution is not possible and therefore AD cannot be evaluated. We have data insufficiency, and the answer is (E).

Strategy

Rules need not always be simultaneous linear equations.

Other rules can also constrain.

Following is the example.

Example: $m = ?$

(1) $7m + 5n = 29$

(2) m and n are positive integers.

With the statements together, we have only one equation in two variables, so it is tempting to mistakenly conclude that there is no solution for m. But the statement "m and n are positive integers" also constrains by preventing m and n from equaling any numbers other than positive integers. So, we have to check for sufficiency.

Statement (1) is just one constrain in 2 unknowns, and Statement (2) is also just one constrain in 2 unknowns. To solve for the two unknowns, m and n, we need at least 2 constraints. So, each statement alone is not sufficient.

Using both statements, we have $7m + 5n = 29$ and m and n are positive integers. Suppose $p = 7m$ and $q = 5n$. Then $p + q = 29$ and $q = 29 - p$ [(a positive multiple of 5) equals 29 − (a positive multiple of 7)]. Since m and n are positive integers, p is a multiple of 7 and q is a multiple of 5. Now,

If $p = 7$, $q = 29 - 7 = 22$, not a multiple of 5. Reject.

If $p = 14$, $q = 29 - 14 = 15$, a multiple of 5. Accept.

If $p = 21$, $q = 29 - 21 = 8$, not a multiple of 5. Reject.

If $p = 28$, $q = 29 - 28 = 1$, not a multiple of 5. Reject.

If $p \geq 35$, $q \leq 29 - 35 = -6$, not positive. Reject.

So, we have a unique solution $m = p/7 = 14/7 = 2$ and $n = q/5 = 15/5 = 3$. Hence, the answer is (C).

Strategy
Reducing equations.

Example 7: $(r - s)^6 =$

(1) $r^2 - 2rs + s^2 = 4$

(2) $(r - s)^3 = 8$

$$r^2 - 2rs + s^2 = 4$$

$$(r - s)^2 = 4 \qquad \text{by the formula } x^2 - 2xy + y^2 = (x - y)^2$$

$$\left[(r - s)^2\right]^3 = 4^3 \qquad \text{by cubing both sides of the equation, Statement (1) is sufficient.}$$

$$\left[(r - s)^3\right]^2 = 8^2 \qquad \text{by exchanging 2 and 3 in the powers, Statement (2) is sufficient.}$$

$$(r - s)^6 = 64 \qquad \text{by the rule } \left(x^a\right)^b = x^{ab}$$

The answer is (E).

Problem Set H: Equations

1. What is $4x$?

    (1) $|2x - 2| + |2x + 2| = 4$

    (2) $|3x - 1| + |3x + 1| = 6$

2. What is x ?

    (1) $x = y + 3$

    (2) $(x + y - 2)(x + 2y) = 0$

3. What is the value of $|x|$?

    (1) $|x| = 2x + 3$

    (2) $x^2 + |x| - 2 = 0$

4. What is $4n^2 + 1$?

    (1) $(4n + 1)(4n - 1) = 63$

    (2) $4|n|^2 + 4|n| + 1 = 25$

5.
$$ax + by = 10$$
$$ay + bx = 12$$

    Which one of x and y is greater in the system?

    (1) $a > b$

    (2) $\dfrac{a}{b} > 1$

6. If $x^2 - 5x + 6 = 0$, then $x =$

    (1) $x \neq 1$

    (2) $x \neq 2$

7. If a, b, c, d, and e are positive numbers and if $\sqrt{a} + \sqrt{b} = \sqrt{c} + \sqrt{d} + \sqrt{e}$ then is $b = d + e$?

    (1) $a = c$

    (2) $a = d + e$

8. $$(x - a)(x - b)(x - c)(x - d) = 0$$

$$(|y| - a)(|y| - b)(|y| - c)(|y| - d) = 0$$

A is a set holding only all possible solutions of *x*, and *B* is a set holding only all possible solutions of *y*. If *a*, *b*, *c*, and *d* are four unequal numbers, then is the number of elements in set *A* equal to the number of elements in set *B*?

(1)   *a* and *b* are positive.

(2)   *c* and *d* are negative.

9. $$x - 3 = z$$

$$y - x = 6$$

$$6 - z = t$$

A system of equations is given above, what is the value of $x + y + z + t$?

(1) $x = 4$

(2) $t = 5$

10.   A ball was thrown from the origin at an angle with the ground (horizontal) at time $t = 0$. The horizontal and the vertical position of the ball with respect to time *t* are given by the equations below:

Horizontal position $= at$

Vertical position $= st^2 + ut$

At what time does the ball touch the ground again?

(1) $a = 3$

(2) $s = 2$ and $u = 4$

11.   Is $xz = 3$?

(1) $z/4 = 3/x$

(2) $x^2 yz = 3xy$

12.   If $xyz = tyz$, is $x = t$?

(1) $x = 0$

(2) $y \neq 0$

13.   Is $b > a$?

(1) $a^4 + b^4 + c^4 = 0$

(2) $a^3 + b^3 + c^3 = 0$

14. Is $rt + ts = 1$?

    (1) $rs = 1$

    (2) $st = 1$

15.
$$3x + 4y = C$$
$$Kx + 12y = 36$$

What are the values of x and y ?

    (1) $C = 12$

    (2) $K = 9$

16.
$$(K/3)x + Ty = C$$
$$Kx + 12y = 21$$
$$Px + 15y = R$$

$(x, y) = (1, 1)$ is a solution of the system shown above. Is there any other solution?

    (1) $C = 7$

    (2) $R = 24$

17.
$$(K/3)s + Tq = C$$
$$Ks + 12q = 21$$
$$Ps + 15q = R$$

In the system above, is $s = 1$ and $q = 1$?

    (1) $C = 7$

    (2) $R = 24$

18. Is $x = 3$?

    (1) $\dfrac{(x-3)(x-4)}{(x-3)} = 0$

    (2) $(x-4)(x+4) = 0$

19. If $ab \neq 0$ and $(|x| - a)(|x| - b) = 0$, then how many possible solutions does x have?

    (1) $a = 3$

    (2) $b = -2$

20. If a and b are two numbers and $(|y| - a)(|y| - b) = 0$, then how many possible solutions does y have?

(1) a is negative.

(2) b is not negative.

21. The gravitational force with which an object of mass m is pulled by the earth of mass M is given by the expression $6.67 \cdot 10^{-11}\dfrac{mM}{d^2}$ where d is the diameter of the earth. The acceleration that an object of mass m will experience when pulled by a force F is given by $\dfrac{F}{m}$. Considering no other forces are acting on the body, what will the acceleration of the object be due to the earth's gravitational force?

(1) $m = 3$ kgs

(2) $M = 6 \cdot 10^{24}$ kgs and $d = 630,000$ meters

22. Is $x = y$?

(1) $x/y = 3$

(2) $x = 3y$

Answers and Solutions to Problem Set H: Equations

1. What is $4x$?

    (1) $|2x - 2| + |2x + 2| = 4$

    (2) $|3x - 1| + |3x + 1| = 6$

Statement (1): $|2x - 2| + |2x + 2| = 4$

We have two cases:

Case 1): $2x - 2$ is negative. Then $2x + 2$ could be negative, zero or positive. Therefore, $|2x - 2|$ equals $-(2x - 2)$ and $|2x + 2|$ could be plus or minus $(2x + 2)$. Therefore, $|2x - 2| + |2x + 2|$ (which is given equal to 4) equals $-(2x - 2) \pm (2x + 2)$ and therefore $-(2x - 2) \pm (2x + 2) = 4$.

Case 2): $2x - 2$ is zero or positive. Then $2x + 2$, which is 4 more than $2x - 2$, must be zero + 4 or positive + 4, either of which is also surely positive and $|2x - 2| = 2x - 2$. Also, $|2x + 2| = 2x + 2$.

Therefore, $|2x - 2| + |2x + 2|$ (which is given equal to 4) equals $2x - 2 + 2x + 2$ and therefore $2x - 2 + 2x + 2 = 4$.

Recalling, Case 1) $-(2x - 2) \pm (2x + 2) = 4$, we have derived two equations, shown in the columns below:

$-(2x - 2) + (2x + 2) = 4$	$-(2x - 2) - (2x + 2) = 4$
$-2x + 2 + 2x + 2 = 4$	$-2x + 2 - 2x - 2 = 4$
$2 + 2 = 4$	$-2x - 2x = 4$
Does not solve for x.	$-4x = 4$
	$x = 4/-4 = -1$

Check: The equation $|2x - 2| + |2x + 2| = 4$ is satisfied for $x = -1$.

Case 2): $2x - 2 + 2x + 2 = 4$

$4x = 4$

$x = 1$

Check: The equation $|2x - 2| + |2x + 2| = 4$ is satisfied for $x = 1$.

So, x could be -1 or 1, and $4x$ could be -4 or 4. Since we do not have a single solution, the statement is *not* sufficient.

Statement (2): $|3x - 1| + |3x + 1| = 6$

We have two cases:

Case 1) $3x - 1$ is negative. Then $3x + 1$ could be negative, zero or positive. Therefore, $|3x - 1|$ equals $-(3x - 1)$ and $|3x + 1|$ could be plus or minus $(3x + 1)$. Therefore, $|3x - 1| + |3x + 1|$ (which is given to equal 6) equals $-(3x - 1) \pm (3x + 1)$ and therefore $-(3x - 1) \pm (3x + 1) = 6$.

Case 2) $3x - 1$ is zero or positive. Then $3x + 1$, which is 2 more than $3x - 1$, must be correspondingly zero + 2 or positive + 4, either of which is also surely positive and $|3x - 1| = 3x - 1$. Also, $|3x + 1| = 3x + 1$.

Therefore, $|3x - 1| + |3x + 1|$ (which is given equal to 6) equals $3x - 1 + 3x + 1$ and therefore $3x - 1 + 3x + 1 = 6$.

Recalling, Case 1: $-(3x - 1) \pm (3x + 1) = 6$, we have derived two equations, shown in the columns below:

$-(3x - 1) + (3x + 1) = 6$	$-3x + 1 - (3x + 1) = 6$
$-3x + 1 + 3x + 1 = 6$	$-3x + 1 - 3x - 1 = 6$
$2 = 6$	$-3x - 3x = 6$
Does not solve for x and is needless at this point since it is an absurd result.	$-6x = 6$
	$x = 6/-6 = -1$

Check: The equation $|3x - 1| + |3x + 1| = 6$ is satisfied for $x = -1$.

Case 2): $3x - 1 + 3x + 1 = 6$

$6x = 6$

$x = 1$

So, x could be -1 or 1, and $4x$ could be -4 or 4. We have a double case and therefore the statement is not sufficient.

With the statements together, we still have more than one solution: $x = -1$ and 1. So, the answer is (E).

2.   What is x ?

    (1) $x = y + 3$

    (2) $(x + y - 2)(x + 2y) = 0$

Statement (1): $x = y + 3$

Here, x depends on y (x varies with y). For example, if $y = 2$, x equals 5; and if $y = 3$, x equals 6.

Since we do not know y, we cannot determine x. The statement is not sufficient.

Statement (2): $(x + y - 2)(x + 2y) = 0$

We have the equation $(x + y - 2)(x + 2y) = 0$.

The equation equals zero when either $x + y - 2 = 0$ or $x + 2y = 0$. Either way, x depends on y, and therefore the statement is *not* sufficient.

From the statements together, we have two different possible systems:

$x = y + 3$

$x + y - 2 = 0$

Adding the two equations yields

$x + x + y - 2 = y + 3$

$2x = 5$

$x = 5/2$

$x = y + 3$

$x + 2y = 0$

Subtracting 3 from both sides of the first equation yields

$y = x - 3$

Substituting this into the second equation yields

$x + 2(x - 3) = 0$

$3x - 6 = 0$

$3x = 6$

$x = 6/3 = 2$

Since the statements together still yield two solutions (not a unique solution), the statements together are not sufficient. The answer is (E).

3.   What is the value of $|x|$?

    (1) $|x| = 2x + 3$

    (2) $x^2 + |x| - 2 = 0$

Statement (1): $|x| = 2x + 3$

Assume x is positive. Then $|x| = x$, and Statement (1) becomes

$x = 2x + 3$
$0 = x + 3$
$x = -3$

This violates the assumption that x is positive. Clearly, $x = -3$ is not positive.

Now, assume x is negative. Then $|x| = -x$, and the statement becomes

$-x = 2x + 3$
$3x = -3$
$x = -1$

So, $|x| = |-1| = 1$.

Hence, Statement (1) alone is sufficient.

The answer is (D).

Statement (2): $x^2 + |x| - 2 = 0$

Whether x is positive or negative, x^2 and $|x|^2$ are the same (both are positive and have the same value). Hence, let's replace x^2 with $|x|^2$.

This yields

$|x|^2 + |x| - 2 = 0$
$|x|^2 + 2|x| - |x| - 2 = 0$
$|x|(|x| + 2) - (|x| + 2) = 0$
$(|x| - 1)(|x| + 2) = 0$
$|x| - 1 = 0$ or $|x| + 2 = 0$

Hence, $|x| = 1$ or $|x| = -2$.

The equation $|x| = -2$ is impossible since $|x|$ is the positive value of x (or zero) while -2 is negative.

Hence, $|x| = 1$ is the only possible solution.

Hence, Statement (2) alone is sufficient.

4.   What is $4n^2 + 1$?

    (1) $(4n + 1)(4n - 1) = 63$

    (2) $4|n|^2 + 4|n| + 1 = 25$

Statement (1): $(4n + 1)(4n - 1) = 63$

   $(4n + 1)(4n - 1) = 63$

   $(4n)^2 - 1^2 = 63$

   $16n^2 = 63 + 1 = 64$

   $n^2 = 64/16 = 4$

Hence, $4n^2 + 1 = 4(4) + 1 = 16 + 1 = 17$. The statement is sufficient.

Statement (2): $4|n|^2 + 4|n| + 1 = 25$

   $4|n|^2 + 4|n| + 1 = 25$

   $[2|n|]^2 + 2 \cdot 2|n| + 1 = 25$

   $(2|n| + 1)^2 = 5^2$ [by the perfect square trinomial formula $(a + b)^2 = a^2 + 2ab + b^2$]

   $2|n| + 1 = 5$ or -5

   $2|n| = 5 - 1$ or $-5 - 1$

   $2|n| = 4$ or -6

$2|n|$ must be positive and therefore cannot equal -6.

Hence, $2|n| = 4$ only, not -6.

Therefore, $|n| = 4/2 = 2$.

So, n could be -2 or 2. In either case $4n^2 + 1 = 4(2)^2 + 1$ or $4(-2)^2 + 1 = 17$.

Or, $4n^2 + 1$ always equals $4(|n|)^2 + 1 = 4(2)^2 + 1 = 17$.

The statement is sufficient.

The answer is (D).

5. $ax + by = 10$

                $ay + bx = 12$

    Which one of x and y is greater in the system?

    (1) $a > b$

    (2) $\dfrac{a}{b} > 1$

Let's transform the question as "Is $x \le y$?" If x and y are equal, the expressions in the system $ax + by$ and $ay + bx$ would be equal, and this would force 10 to equal 12. Hence, x and y are not equal. Therefore, the question reduces to "Is $x < y$?" or "Is $y - x > 0$?"

Assume, $t = y - x$ or $y = t + x$. Substituting this in the top equation in the system yields

$$ax + by = 10$$
$$ax + b(t + x) = 10$$
$$ax + bt + bx = 10$$
$$ax + bx = 10 - bt$$
$$(a + b)x = 10 - bt$$

Note: If $a + b$ equals 0, then $a = -b$. Hence, the system of equations becomes $ax - ay = 10$ and $ay - ax = 12$, which is absurd because if $ax - ay = 10$, then $ay - ax = -(ax - ay)$ must equal -10, not 12. Hence, $a + b$ is not 0 and therefore dividing by $a + b$ is safe. So, dividing both sides of the equation $(a + b)x = 10 - bt$ by $a + b$ yields

$$x = \frac{10 - bt}{a + b}$$

Substituting $t = y - x$ or $y = t + x$ in the equation $ay + bx = 12$ yields

$$ay + bx = 12$$
$$a(t + x) + bx = 12$$
$$at + ax + bx = 12$$
$$ax + bx = 12 - at$$
$$(a + b)x = 12 - at$$
$$x = \frac{12 - at}{a + b}$$

Setting the equations equal to each other yields

$$\frac{10 - bt}{a + b} = \frac{12 - at}{a + b}$$
$$\frac{10}{a + b} - \frac{bt}{a + b} = \frac{12}{a + b} - \frac{at}{a + b}$$
$$\frac{at}{a + b} - \frac{bt}{a + b} = \frac{2}{a + b}$$
$$\frac{(a - b)t}{a + b} = \frac{2}{a + b}$$

If $a - b$ equals 0, then $(a - b)t$ equals 0, not 2. So, $a - b$ is not equal to 0. Dividing the equation $\frac{(a - b)t}{a + b} = \frac{2}{a + b}$ by $a - b$ and multiplying by $a + b$ yields $t = \frac{2}{a - b}$. This is negative if $a - b$ is negative, and positive if $a - b$ is positive. Hence, the question can be transformed to "Is $a - b$ negative?"

Statement (1): $a > b$

Statement (2): $\frac{a}{b} > 1$

Statement (1) says $a > b$. So, $a - b$ must be positive. Hence, t must be positive. The statement is sufficient.

Statement (2) says $\frac{a}{b} > 1$.

Suppose b is positive. Then multiplying the inequality by b yields $a > b$. Hence, $a - b > 0$. Here, t must be positive.

Suppose b is negative. Then multiplying the inequality by b and flipping the direction yields $a < b$. Hence, $a - b < 0$. Here, t must be negative. We have a double case and therefore the statement is *not* sufficient.

The answer is (A).

6.   If $x^2 - 5x + 6 = 0$, then $x =$

(1) $x \neq 1$

(2) $x \neq 2$

$$x^2 - 5x + 6 = 0$$

$$x^2 - 2x - 3x + 6 = 0$$

$$x(x - 2) - 3(x - 2) = 0 \qquad \text{by factoring}$$

$$(x - 2)(x - 3) = 0$$

$$x - 2 = 0 \text{ or } x - 3 = 0$$

$$x = 2 \text{ or } 3$$

We have two solutions. The statement that constrains the number of solutions to just one will be the sufficient statement.

Statement (1) says $x \neq 1$, but we already know this since x equals only 2 or 3. The statement could not constrain number of solutions to one. Therefore, the statement is *not* sufficient.

Statement (2) says $x \neq 2$, which eliminates the solution $x = 2$. We now have only one possible solution, $x = 3$. The statement is sufficient.

The answer is (B).

7.   If a, b, c, d, and e are positive numbers and if $\sqrt{a} + \sqrt{b} = \sqrt{c} + \sqrt{d} + \sqrt{e}$, then is $b = d + e$?

(1) $a = c$

(2) $a = d + e$

Statement (1): $a = c$

Substituting a for c in the equation $\sqrt{a} + \sqrt{b} = \sqrt{c} + \sqrt{d} + \sqrt{e}$ yields

$$\sqrt{a} + \sqrt{b} = \sqrt{a} + \sqrt{d} + \sqrt{e}$$

$$\sqrt{b} = \sqrt{d} + \sqrt{e}$$

Squaring both sides yields

$$b = d + e + 2\sqrt{de}$$

Assume $b = d + e$ (from the question). Substituting b for $d + e$ in the equation yields

$$b = b + 2\sqrt{de}$$

$$0 = 2\sqrt{de}$$

Since d, and e are non-zero, $de \neq 0$ and therefore $2\sqrt{de} \neq 0$. Hence, our assumption is wrong. So, we can answer the question as "No. $b = d + e$ is false." The statement is sufficient.

The answer is (A).

Statement (2): $a = d + e$

Suppose $c = d = e = 1$ (keep at least two variables [here, a and b] unassigned). Then $a = d + e = 1 + 1 = 2$. Substituting in the equation $\sqrt{a} + \sqrt{b} = \sqrt{c} + \sqrt{d} + \sqrt{e}$ yields $\sqrt{2} + \sqrt{b} = \sqrt{1} + \sqrt{1} + \sqrt{1} = 3$. Here, $\sqrt{b}$ equals $3 - \sqrt{2}$, or by squaring both sides $b = (3 - \sqrt{2})^2$. Let's present this as a case where $\sqrt{a} + \sqrt{b} = \sqrt{c} + \sqrt{d} + \sqrt{e}$ is true while $a = d + e$.

Now, suppose $b = $ some number that is not equal to $(3 - \sqrt{2})^2$. This becomes a case when $\sqrt{a} + \sqrt{b} = \sqrt{c} + \sqrt{d} + \sqrt{e}$ is false while $a = d + e$. (Say, $b = 2$. $\sqrt{2} + \sqrt{2} = \sqrt{1} + \sqrt{1} + \sqrt{1}$.)

So, the statement is not a complete lead to confirm either that "$\sqrt{a} + \sqrt{b} = \sqrt{c} + \sqrt{d} + \sqrt{e}$" is true or that it is false. Hence, the statement is *not* sufficient.

8. $(x - a)(x - b)(x - c)(x - d) = 0$

                    $(|y| - a)(|y| - b)(|y| - c)(|y| - d) = 0$

   A is a set holding only all possible solutions of x, and B is a set holding only all possible solutions of y. If a, b, c, and d are four unequal numbers, then is the number of elements in set A equal to the number of elements in set B?

   (1) a and b are positive.

   (2) c and d are negative.

From the equation $(x - a)(x - b)(x - c)(x - d) = 0$, the possible solutions of x are a, b, c, and d. So, $A = \{a, b, c, d\}$. We have 4 solutions here.

Suppose k is one of the numbers a, b, c, and d.

$|y| - k$ could equal 0 only if $k = |y|$. Since $|y|$ is zero or positive, k must also be zero or positive. So, k is not a possible solution of y if k is negative. If k is 0, $y = 0$ is the only solution. If k is positive, $y = +k$ and $y = -k$ are the possible solutions (we have two solutions here).

So, unless we have data sufficient to know how many of the four numbers a, b, c, and d are zero, if any, and how many are positive, if any, we cannot count the number of solutions. It is only with the statements together that we know how many positive numbers exist. We have exactly two positive numbers (a and b. Total of 4 solutions $+a$, $-a$, $+b$, $-b$), no zeroes at all, and exactly two negative numbers (c and d. As discussed, negative numbers do not yield $|y| - k = 0$). So, we have 4 solutions listed in set B: $\{+a, -a, +b, -b\}$. So, both sets have an equal number of elements and therefore the statements together are sufficient.

The answer is (C).

9. $x - 3 = z$

                    $y - x = 6$

                    $6 - z = t$

   A system of equations is given above, what is the value of $x + y + z + t$?

   (1) $x = 4$

   (2) $t = 5$

The given system is

            $x - 3 = z$ ...(A)

            $y - x = 6$ ...(B)

            $6 - z = t$ ...(C)

Statement (1): $x = 4$

Substituting $x = 4$ in the system above yields

$$4 - 3 = z \qquad \dots(A)$$

$$y - 4 = 6 \qquad \dots(B)$$

$$6 - z = t \qquad \dots(C)$$

The value of z is unleashed from the first equation ($z = 1$). The second equation unveils the value of y as $y = 10$, and the third equation says the value of t is $t = 6 - z = 6 - 1 = 5$.

So, $x + y + z + t$ can be evaluated since the value of each term involved in the expression is known. Hence, the statement is sufficient.

Statement (2): $t = 5$

Given $t = 5$, equation (C) evaluates z as $6 - z = 5$; $6 - 5 = z$; $z = 1$. Once we have z, $x + y + z + t$ can be evaluated as in Statement (1).

Otherwise, equation (A) evaluates x as $x - 3 = z$, or $x = z + 3 = 1 + 3 = 4$. The rest of the solution may follow just as Statement (1), and the expression $x + y + z + t$ can be evaluated.

Either way, the statement is sufficient.

The answer is (D).

10. A ball was thrown from the origin at an angle with the ground (horizontal) at time $t = 0$. The horizontal and the vertical positions of the ball with respect to time t are given by the following equations:

Horizontal position $= at$

Vertical position $= st^2 + ut$

At what time does the ball touch the ground again?

(1) $a = 3$

(2) $s = 2$ and $u = 4$

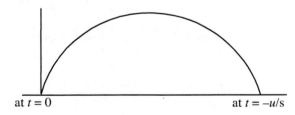

at $t = 0$ at $t = -u/s$

When the ball falls on the ground (horizontal) again, the vertical position is 0 again. Hence, equating the vertical position to 0 gives us the time t when the ball is on the ground. Doing this yields

$$st^2 + ut = 0$$

$$t(st + u) = 0$$

$$t = 0 \text{ and } st + u = 0$$

$$t = 0 \text{ and } t = -u/s$$

When $t = 0$, the ball is thrown from the ground. At time $t = -u/s$, the ball falls on the ground. So, if we know u and s [from Statement (2)], we can answer the question. We have no means to calculate u and s or to answer the question from Statement (1), so the statement is *not* sufficient.

The answer is (B).

11. Is $xz = 3$?

    (1) $z/4 = 3/x$

    (2) $x^2yz = 3xy$

Statement (1): $z/4 = 3/x$

Since the numerator of the fraction on the right-hand side, which is 3, is not 0, $z/4$ is not zero and therefore z is *not* zero.

Also, x does not equal 0 because according to the equation $z/4 = 3/x$, z wouldn't yield a finite value.

So, multiplying the equation $z/4 = 3/x$ by $4x$ is valid.

The multiplication yields $xz = 12$.

The statement is sufficient.

If x and z change, they adjust such that the product of the two remains the same 12.

The answer is (A).

Statement (2): $x^2yz = 3xy$

Subtracting $3xy$ from both sides yields

$$x^2yz - 3xy = 0$$
$$xy(xz - 3) = 0$$

The expression equals 0 when $xy = 0$ or when $xz = 3$. So, $xy = 0$ and $xz = 3$ are the solutions. So, xy may equal 0 or it may not (when $xy = 3$). Therefore, the answer to the question could be Yes or No. Hence, the statement is *not* sufficient.

12. If $xyz = tyz$, is $x = t$?

    (1) $x = 0$

    (2) $y \neq 0$

Subtracting tyz from both sides of the equation yields $xyz - tyz = 0$, or $yz(x - t) = 0$. The expression $yz(x - t)$ equals 0 when A) $z = 0$ or B) $y = 0$ or C) $x = t$.

There are three possibilities. Not all may be true. Again, the three possibilities are:

A) $z = 0$ or B) $y = 0$ or C) $x = t$.

Statement (1): $x = 0$

The statement does not eliminate any possibility. The possibility $x = t$ may or may not be simultaneously true along with $x = 0$. We have a double case and therefore the statement is *not* sufficient.

Statement (2): $y \neq 0$

The statement eliminates the second possibility but we still have two possibilities open: A) and C). The possibilities may not be simultaneously true or they might. We have a double case and therefore the statement is *not* sufficient.

With the statements together, we could eliminate the possibility B) and affirm the possibility A) $z = 0$. But the possibility C) may be false or simultaneously true along with A) in case $t = 0$. The statements together are *not* sufficient. The answer is (E).

13. Is $b > a$?

    (1) $a^4 + b^4 + c^4 = 0$

    (2) $a^3 + b^3 + c^3 = 0$

Statement (1): $a^4 + b^4 + c^4 = 0$

Unless $a = b = c = 0$, $a^4 + b^4 + c^4$ cannot equal 0. Hence, $a = b = c = 0$ must be true.

For example, if $a = -1$, $b = 0$, and $c = 1$. Then $a^4 = 1$ (becomes positive), $b^4 = 0$, and $c^4 = 1$ and the three sum to 2.

Hence, $b > a$ is false. The statement is sufficient.

Statement (2): $a^3 + b^3 + c^3 = 0$

Suppose $a = -1$, $b = 0$, and $c = 1$. Then $a^3 + b^3 + c^3 = (-1)^3 + 0^3 + 1^3 = -1 + 0 + 1 = 0$. Here, $b > a$ is true.

Suppose $a = 1$, $b = 0$, and $c = -1$. Then $a^3 + b^3 + c^3 = 1^3 + 0^3 + (-1)^3 = 1 + 0 + -1 = 0$. Here, $b > a$ is false.

We have a double case and therefore the statement is *not* sufficient.

The answer is (A).

14. Is $rt + ts = 1$?

    (1) $rs = 1$

    (2) $st = 1$

Let's convert the expression $rt + ts$ into a single variable in t, r or s.

Statement (1): $rs = 1$

Since $rs = 1$, r and s are not equal to 0. Dividing the equation by s yields $r = 1/s$; or instead, dividing by r yields $s = 1/r$.

Now, substituting either into the expression $rt + ts$ yields

    $rt + ts =$
    $rt + t(1/r) =$
    $rt + t/r =$
    $t(r + 1/r)$ (in terms of t and r)

or

    $rt + ts =$
    $(1/s)t + ts =$
    $t/s + ts =$
    $t(s + 1/s)$ (in terms of t and s)

So, far, we do not have any constrains on the value of t: it could either equal $1/(r + 1/r)$ such that $t(r + 1/r) = 1$ or it may not equal $1/(r + 1/r)$ such that $t(r + 1/r) \neq 1$. So, we have a double case and therefore the statement is *not* sufficient.

A similar analysis applies to the expression $t/(s + 1/s)$.

Statement (2): $st = 1$

Since $st = 1$, s equals $1/t$ or t equals $1/s$.

Now, substituting either into the expression $rt + ts$ yields

    $rt + ts =$
    $rt + t(1/t) =$
    $rt + 1$

or

    $rt + ts =$
    $rt + (1/s)s =$
    $rt + 1$

Either way, $rt + 1$ equals 1 only when rt equals 0. Now, rt equals 0 only when either r or t equals 0. Since st equals 1, neither s nor t is 0. So, the question is "Is r equal to 0?"

Since we do not have any leads to answer, the statement is *not* sufficient.

From the statements together we have the question "Is r equal to 0?" from Statement (2) to which Statement (1) provides the lead saying rs equal to 1 so r is not zero (Lest rs would have been 0). Hence, both statements are required and are together sufficient. The answer is (C).

15. $3x + 4y = C$

               $Kx + 12y = 36$

What are the values of x and y ?

(1) $C = 12$

(2) $K = 9$

To determine the system completely, we need both parameters C and K. Clearly, we need the statements together (neither statement alone is sufficient).

Substituting the values given in both statements into the system yields

               $3x + 4y = 12$

               $9x + 12y = 36$

Dividing the bottom equation by 3 yields the top equation. Hence, we effectively have a single equation and therefore any point (hence, there is more than one solution) on the line must be a solution. We do not have fixed solution for x and y. Hence, the statements together are not sufficient. The answer is (E).

   Language of the questions and the statements is important.

Strategy

16. $(K/3)x + Ty = C$

               $Kx + 12y = 21$

               $Px + 15y = R$

$(x, y) = (1, 1)$ is a solution of the system shown above. Is there any other solution?

(1) $C = 7$

(2) $R = 24$

Effectively, the question asks if there are even more solutions to the system than $(1, 1)$ alone. The equations in the system can be compared to lines on a coordinate plane with x- and y-axes (the loci of the equations are lines in coordinate plane). A system of two or more linear equations will have either a single common solution [when at least two of the lines in the system are different] or infinitely many solutions [when all the equations effectively are a same line (same equation)]. So, the question is "Are any two of the equations (lines) different?"

We are given that $(1, 1)$ is a solution of the system. Hence, the point satisfies all the equations and the substitution yields

               $(K/3)(1) + T(1) = C$, or $K/3 + T = C$

               $K(1) + 12(1) = 21$, or $K + 12 = 21$

               $P(1) + 15(1) = R$, or $P + 15 = R$

Solving the second equation $K + 12 = 21$ for K yields $K = 9$.

Statement (1): $C = 7$

Plugging the result $K = 9$ (we know) and $C = 7$ (from current statement) in the equation $K/3 + T = C$ yields $9/3 + T = 7$; $3 + T = 7$; $T = 4$.

Substituting known results in the given system now yields

$$\frac{9}{3}x + 4y = 7 \quad \ldots(1)$$

$$9x + 12y = 21 \quad \ldots(2)$$

$$Px + 15y = R \quad \ldots(3)$$

Dividing the second equation above by 3 yields $\frac{9}{3}x + \frac{12}{3}y = \frac{21}{3}$, which reduces to $\frac{9}{3}x + 4y = 7$. This is same as Equation (1).

If it were different, we would have answered the question as

"Yes. At least two equations are different. So, (1, 1) is the only solution."

But since they are not different, we must check whether Equation (3), $Px + 15y = R$, is different from Equation (1) or Equation (2). But to check this, we need to know P and R, which we do not know. So, we cannot answer the question with the statement alone.

If the third equation is also the same, we would answer the question as "No. No two equations are different and there are more than one solutions to (1, 1)." If we can say this either data would be sufficient.

The answer is (B).

Statement (2): $R = 24$

Plugging $R = 24$ into the known equation $P + 15 = R$ yields $P + 15 = 24$; $P = 24 - 15 = 9$.

Substituting known results in the given system yields

$$\frac{9}{3}x + Ty = C \quad \ldots(1)$$

$$9x + 12y = 21 \quad \ldots(2)$$

$$9x + 15y = 24 \quad \ldots(3)$$

We know only equations (2) and (3) completely. We can express them as

$$y = -\frac{9}{12}x + \frac{21}{2} \quad \ldots(2)$$

$$y = -\frac{9}{15}x + \frac{24}{15} \quad \ldots(3)$$

Since the slopes of the lines are unequal ($-\frac{9}{12}$ for Equation (2) and $-\frac{9}{15}$ for Equation (3)], they represent different lines. Hence, the answer to the question is "Yes. At least two equations are different. So, (1, 1) is the only solution."

The statement is sufficient.

17. $(K/3)s + Tq = C$

$Ks + 12q = 21$

$Ps + 15q = R$

In the system above, is $s = 1$ and $q = 1$?

(1) $C = 7$

(2) $R = 24$

Suppose $x = p$ and $y = q$. Thus, we could transform a system in (p, q) to a system in (x, y).

Now, in asking whether $s = 1$ (or $x = 1$) and $q = 1$ (or $y = 1$), we are effectively asking whether $(1, 1)$ is the only solution of the system below

$(K/3)x + Ty = C$

$Kx + 12y = 21$

$Px + 15y = R$

The solution now follows the solution to the previous problem. The answer is (C) again.

Or

The equations in the system can be compared to lines on a coordinate plane with x- and y-axes (the loci of the equations are lines on the coordinate plane). A system of more than one linear simultaneous equation would have either a single common solution [when at least two of the lines in the system are different] or infinitely many solutions [when all the equations effectively are a same line (same equation)]. So, effectively, the question is "Are any two of the equations (lines) different?"

We are given that $(1, 1)$ is a solution of the system (which means a common solution of the lines). Hence, the point satisfies all the equations and the substitution yields

$(K/3)(1) + T(1) = C$, or $K/3 + T = C$

$K(1) + 12(1) = 21$, or $K + 12 = 21$

$P(1) + 15(1) = R$, or $P + 15 = R$

Solving the second equation $K + 12 = 21$ for K yields $K = 9$.

Statement (1): $C = 7$

Plugging the result $K = 9$ (we know) and $C = 7$ (from current statement) in the equation: $K/3 + T = C$ yields $9/3 + T = 7$; $3 + T = 7$; $T = 4$.

Substituting known results in the given system now yields

$$\frac{9}{3}x + 4y = 7 \quad \dots(1)$$

$$9x + 12y = 21 \quad \dots(2)$$

$$Px + 15y = R \quad \dots(3)$$

Dividing the second equation above by 3 yields $\frac{9}{3}x + \frac{12}{3}y = \frac{21}{3}$, which reduces to $\frac{9}{3}x + 4y = 7$. This is same as the Equation (1).

If it were different, we would have answered the question as

"Yes. At least two equations are different. So, (1, 1) is the only solution".

But since they are not different, we must check whether Equation (3): $Px + 15y = R$ is different from Equation (1) or Equation (2) (we know either are same). But to check this, we need to know P and R, which we do not know. So, we cannot answer the question with the statement alone.

If the third equation is also the same, we would answer the question as "No. No two equations are different and there are more than one solutions to (1, 1)." If we can say this either, data would be sufficient.

The answer is (B).

Statement (2): $R = 24$

Plugging $R = 24$ into the known equation $P + 15 = R$ yields $P + 15 = 24$; $P = 24 - 15 = 9$.

Substituting known results in the given system yields

$$\frac{9}{3}x + Ty = C \quad \dots(1)$$

$$9x + 12y = 21 \quad \dots(2)$$

$$9x + 15y = 24 \quad \dots(3)$$

We know only equations (2) and (3) completely. We can express them as

$$y = -\frac{9}{12}x + \frac{21}{2} \quad \dots(2)$$

$$y = -\frac{9}{15}x + \frac{24}{15} \quad \dots(3)$$

Since the slopes of the lines are unequal ($-\frac{9}{12}$ for the Equation (2) and $-\frac{9}{15}$ for the Equation (3)], they represent different lines. Hence, the answer to the question is "Yes. At least two equations are different. So, (1, 1) is the only solution."

The statement is sufficient.

18.   Is $x = 3$?

(1) $\dfrac{(x-3)(x-4)}{(x-3)} = 0$

(2) $(x-4)(x+4) = 0$

Statement (1): $\dfrac{(x-3)(x-4)}{(x-3)} = 0$

A fraction can equal 0 only when the numerator is 0 and the denominator is not zero. So, the numerator of equation above says x equals 3 or 4 while the denominator says x is not 3. The only solution left is $x = 4$. We can answer the question as "No. $x \neq 3$."

Statement (2): $(x-4)(x+4) = 0$

The expression $(x-4)(x+4)$ equals 0 when x equals 4 or x equals –4.

This is double case and therefore the statement is *not* sufficient.

The answer is (A).

19.   If $ab \neq 0$ and $(|x| - a)(|x| - b) = 0$, then how many possible solutions does x have?

(1) $a = 3$

(2) $b = -2$

A GMAT data sufficiency question will always be assertive (close-ended).

For example, here, it will never ask "How many possible solutions could x have?" unlike in multiple-choice questions. Because then even without using any statement we can give out the current unconstrained set and say this is the answer. So, there is no way data sufficiency is being checked.

In a scenario like this, it will ask "How many possible solutions *does* x have?"

Now, since $|x|$ is never negative (it can be zero if x equals zero or it can be positive if x is negative or positive), the possible solutions of $|x|$ in the equation $(|x| - a)(|x| - b) = 0$ are the ones among a and b which are *not* negative. Now, to list possible solutions we need to know whether a and b are negative, zero or positive. We need both statements to tell us this. So, both statements are required, and the answer is (C).

Since a is positive, $|x|$ can equal a and $|x| - a$ can equal zero and therefore $(|x| - a)(|x| - b)$ can equal 0. So, $|x| = a$ is a possible.

Since b is negative, $|x|$ cannot equal b and $|x| - b$ cannot equal zero. So, $|x|$ cannot equal b. Therefore, we do not have any possible solution from here.

The possible solution of $|x|$ is a and the possible solutions of x are $+a$ and $-a$ (since a is positive, not zero both are not equal and same). So, we have in total two solutions.

Method II:

Statement (1): $a = 3$

If b is negative, we have two solutions -3 and 3.

If b is zero, we have three solutions $-3, 0,$ and 3.

If b is positive, we have four solutions $-3, -b, b$ and 3.

Since we have more than one answer possible, the statement is *not* sufficient.

Statement (2): $b = -2$

So, there is no contribution of solutions from the statement.

If a is negative, we have zero solutions.

If a is zero, we have a single solution, 0.

If a is positive, we have two solutions, $-a$ and a.

Since we have more than one answer possible, the statement is *not* sufficient.

The common answer from the statements together is only 2, meaning we have only one solution. Hence, the statements together are sufficient.

20.   If a and b are two numbers and $(|y| - a)(|y| - b) = 0$, then how many possible solutions does y have?

   (1) a is negative.

   (2) b is not negative.

Now, since $|y|$ is never negative (It can be zero if y equals zero, or it can be positive if y is negative or positive), the possible solutions of $|y|$ in the equation $(|y| - a)(|y| - b) = 0$ are the ones among a, b, c and b which are not negative. Now, to list possible solutions we need to know if a and b are negative, zero, or positive. With both statements we only know that a is negative and b is not. But they do not tell us if b is zero or positive. Hence, the statements together are *not* sufficient. The answer is (E).

Since a is negative, $|x|$ cannot equal a and $|x| - a$ cannot equal zero. So, $|x|$ cannot equal a. Therefore, we do not have any possible solution from here.

If b is not negative, $|x|$ can equal b and $|x| - b$ can equal zero and therefore $(|x| - a)(|x| - b)$ can equal 0. So, $|x| = b$ is a possible solution. But then x could be $-b$ or b. Either way, $|x| = b$.

Now, if $b = 0$, $x = -b = -0 = 0$, or $b = 0$. Here, we have one solution instead of two.

If b is positive, $x = -b$ and b are the two solutions.

Thus, we have a double case and therefore the statements together are *not* sufficient.

21.   The gravitational force with which an object of mass m is pulled by the earth of mass M is given by the expression $6.67 \cdot 10^{-11} \dfrac{mM}{d^2}$ where d is the diameter of the earth. The acceleration that an object of mass m will experience when pulled by a force F is given by $\dfrac{F}{m}$. Considering no other forces are acting on the body, what will the acceleration of the object be due to the earth's gravitational force?

   (1) $m = 3$ kgs

   (2) $M = 6 \cdot 10^{24}$ kgs and $d = 630{,}000$ meters

Suppose F is the force on the object. Then the acceleration on the object will be $\dfrac{F}{m}$. Now, if this force is the gravitational force, then the force F would equal $6.67 \cdot 10^{-11} \dfrac{mM}{d^2}$. So, the acceleration equals

$\dfrac{F}{m} = \dfrac{6.67 \cdot 10^{-11} \dfrac{mM}{d^2}}{m} = 6.67 \cdot 10^{-11} \dfrac{M}{d^2}$. From the final reduced expression, given M and r [Statement (2)], we can calculate the acceleration of the object and since m is not available in the reduced expression, m [which Statement (1) gives] is not needed. Hence, Statement (2) is sufficient while Statement (1) is *not* necessary. Hence, the answer is (B). Moreover, in the whole process, the units didn't matter. So, we might be given in the original units in pounds, miles, or some other units.

22.   Is $x = y$?

   (1) $x/y = 3$

   (2) $x = 3y$

Statement (1): $x/y = 3$

x/y equals 3 indicates the following two points:

   1) x is not equal to 0, because then x/y would equal 0, not 3

and

   2) y is not equal to 0, because then x/y would be an undefined infinite value and not 0.

So, cross-multiplying the equation (valid because we know the denominator $y \neq 0$) yields $x = 3y$. Subtracting y from both sides yields $x - y = 2y$. Since y is not equal to 0, $2y$ is not equal to zero. Hence, $x - y \neq 0$ or $x \neq y$. The statement is sufficient.

The answer is (A).

Statement (2): $x = 3y$

If $x = y = 0$, $x = 3y$ and still $x = y$ is true.

But if $x \neq 0$, since $x = 3y$, x would not equal y just as in Statement (1).

We have a double case, and therefore the statement is *not* sufficient.

Averages & Statistics

AVERAGES

Problems involving averages are very common on the GMAT. They can be classified into four major categories as follows.

Weighted average

Weighted average is an average in which each quantity is assigned a weight. These weights indicate the relative importance of each quantity in finding the average.

Example 1: If on a test three people answered 90% of the questions correctly and two people answered 80% correctly, then the average for the group is not 85% but rather $\dfrac{3\cdot 90 + 2\cdot 80}{5} = \dfrac{430}{5} = 86$. Here, 90 has a weight of 3—it occurs 3 times. Whereas 80 has a weight of 2—it occurs 2 times. So, the average is closer to 90 than to 80, as we have just calculated.

You will not be told whether you need to calculate a weighted average or a plain average. Only the context of the problem will indicate which average needs to be calculated.

Plain Average:

The plain arithmetic mean is actually a special case of the weighted mean in which all the weights are equal to 1 unit.

The average of N numbers is their sum divided by N, that is _average_ $= \dfrac{sum}{N}$**.**

➤ Average of x, $2x$, and 6—By the definition of an average, we get $\dfrac{x + 2x + 6}{3} = \dfrac{3x + 6}{3} = \dfrac{3(x + 2)}{3} = x + 2$. According to the context, this is a plain Average.

➤ The average of three observations 9.3, 9.5, 9.7 is $\dfrac{9.3 + 9.5 + 9.7}{3} = \dfrac{28.5}{3} = 9.5$. This is a Plain Average.

➤ But in case, we are sure that particular observations are more accurate than the others, we might assign bigger weights (more importance) to observations that are more likely to be accurate. For example, if 1 of 6 scientists say 9.3 is the accurate reading (this means 9.3 has 1 of 6 odds to be true), the second reading 9.5 is asserted by 3 of 6 scientists (odds is 3 of 6), while the reading 9.7 is asserted by 2 of 6 scientists (odds is 2 of 6), then we assign the weights 1/6 to first reading, 3/6 to reading 9.5, 2/6 to reading 9.7 and calculate the weighted mean as $\dfrac{9.3 \cdot \frac{1}{6} + 9.5 \cdot \frac{3}{6} + 9.7 \cdot \frac{2}{6}}{\frac{1}{6} + \frac{3}{6} + \frac{2}{6}} = 9.53$. The weights 1/6, 3/6, and 2/6 can be referred to as

the probabilities of the respective readings being true.

  We have seen how to find an average from the members.

Now, we will see how to find a member from an average.

Sometimes you will be asked to find a member by using a given average. An example will illustrate.

Example 2:   If the average of five numbers is –10, and the sum of three of the numbers is 16, then what is the average of the other two numbers?

Let the five numbers be a, b, c, d and e. Then their average is $\dfrac{a+b+c+d+e}{5} = -10$. Now, three of the numbers have a sum of 16, say, $a + b + c = 16$. So, substitute 16 for $a + b + c$ in the average above: $\dfrac{16 + d + e}{5} = -10$. Solving this equation for $d + e$ gives $d + e = -66$. Finally, dividing by 2 (to form the average) gives $\dfrac{d+e}{2} = -33$. Hence, the answer is –33.

   Average Speed = $\dfrac{\textit{Total Distance}}{\textit{Total Time}}$

Although the formula for average speed is simple, few people solve these problems correctly because most fail to find both the <u>total distance</u> and the <u>total time</u>.

Example 3:   In traveling from City A to City B, John drove for 1 hour at 50 mph and for 3 hours at 60 mph. What was his average speed for the whole trip?

The total distance is $1 \cdot 50 + 3 \cdot 60 = 230$. And the total time is 4 hours. Hence,

$$\textit{Average Speed} = \frac{\textit{Total Distance}}{\textit{Total Time}} = \frac{230}{4} = 57\,\tfrac{1}{2}$$

The answer is $57\,\tfrac{1}{2}$. Note, the answer is not the mere average of 50 and 60. Rather the average is closer to 60 because he traveled longer at 60 mph (3 hrs) than at 50 mph (1 hr).

   What is an Arithmetic Mean?

In mathematics and statistics, the **arithmetic mean** (or simply the **mean**) of a list of numbers is the sum of all of the numbers in the list divided by the number of items in the list.

You may have observed that this is merely a plain average.

The term "mean" or "arithmetic mean" is preferred in mathematics and statistics to distinguish it from other averages such as the **median** and the **mode**.

STATISTICS

Statistics is the study of the patterns and relationships of numbers and data. There are four main concepts that may appear on the test:

Median

When a set of numbers is arranged in order of size, the *median* is the middle number. For example, the median of the set {8, 9, 10, 11, 12} is 10 because it is the middle number. In this case, the median is also the mean (average). But this is usually not the case. For example, the median of the set {8, 9, 10, 11, 17} is 10 because it is the middle number, but the mean is $11 = \dfrac{8+9+10+11+17}{5}$. If a set contains an even number of elements, then the median is the average of the two middle elements. For example, the median of the set {1, 5, 8, 20} is $6.5\left(= \dfrac{5+8}{2}\right)$.

Example: What is the median of 0, –2, 256 , 18, $\sqrt{2}$?

Arranging the numbers from smallest to largest (we could also arrange the numbers from the largest to smallest; the answer would be the same), we get –2, 0, $\sqrt{2}$, 18, 256. The median is the middle number, $\sqrt{2}$.

Mode

The *mode* is the number or numbers that appear most frequently in a set. Note that this definition allows a set of numbers to have more than one mode.

Example: What is the mode of 3, –4, 3 , 7, 9, 7.5 ?

The number 3 is the mode because it is the only number that is listed more than once.

Example: What is the mode of 2, π, 2 , –9, π, 5 ?

Both 2 and π are modes because each occurs twice, which is the greatest number of occurrences for any number in the list.

Range

The *range* is the distance between the smallest and largest numbers in a set. To calculate the range, merely subtract the smallest number from the largest number.

Example: What is the range of 2, 8, 1 , –6, π, 1/2 ?

The largest number in this set is 8, and the smallest number is –6. Hence, the range is 8 – (–6) = 8 + 6 = 14.

Standard Deviation

On the test, you are not expected to know the definition of standard deviation. However, you may be presented with the definition of standard deviation and then be asked a question based on the definition. To make sure we cover all possible bases, we'll briefly discuss this concept.

Standard deviation measures how far the numbers in a set vary from the set's mean. If the numbers are scattered far from the set's mean, then the standard deviation is large. If the numbers are bunched up near the set's mean, then the standard deviation is small.

Example: Which of the following sets has the larger standard deviation?

$$A = \{1, 2, 3, 4, 5\}$$

$$B = \{1, 4, 15, 21, 27\}$$

All the numbers in Set A are within 2 units of the mean, 3. All the numbers in Set B are greater than 5 units from the mean, 15. Hence, the standard deviation of Set B is greater.

Problem Set I: Averages & Statistics

1. What is the average of the consecutive integers m through n, inclusive?

    (1)   The average of m and n is 23.5.

    (2)   The average of the integers between m and n not including either is 23.5.

2. Are all the integers arranged in order in Sequence A consecutive integers?

    (1)   The average of the sequence is not equal to the median of the sequence.

    (2)   There are an odd number of integers in the set.

Class	Class size	Mean Score
A	20	89
B	m	p
C	40	90

3. Is the average score of the students in the 3 classes together equal to 89?

    (1) $m = 40$

    (2) $p = 89$

Class	Class size	Mean Score
A	20	57
B	m	p
C	40	60

4. Is the overall average score of the 3 classes A, B, and C together is 59?

    (1) $m = 40$

    (2) $p = 59$

5. A class consists of boys and girls only. On a final exam in History, the average score of the girls is 72 and the average score of the boys is 70. Is the average score of the class 71?

    (1)   Smith is one of the classmates and Smith has the same number of boy classmates as girl classmates.

    (2)   The number of students in the class is 101.

Answers and Solutions to Problem Set I: Averages & Statistics

1.   What is the average of the consecutive integers *m* through *n*, inclusive?

   (1)   The average of *m* and *n* is 23.5.

   (2)   The average of the integers between *m* and *n* not including either is 23.5.

Statement (1): The average of *m* and *n* is 23.5.

The average of the consecutive integers *m* through *n* always equals the average of just the integers *m* and *n* since the elements in the sum are consecutive. Hence, Statement (1) alone answers the question.

For example, the average of the numbers 1 through 5 is 3, which equals (1 + 5)/2 = 6/2 = 3.

For example, the average of the numbers 1 through 6 is 3.5, which equals (1 + 6)/2 = 7/2 = 3.5.

The statement is sufficient.

Statement (2): The average of the integers between *m* and *n* not including either is 23.5.

The average of the consecutive integers between *m* and *n* not including either is the same as the average including them since the elements in the sum are consecutive. Hence, Statement (2) alone also answers the question.

For example, the average of the numbers 1, 2, 3, 4, 5 is 3, which equals (2 + 3 + 4)/2 = 3.

The average of the numbers 1, 2, 3, 4, 5, and 6 is 3.5, which equals (2 + 3 + 4 + 5)/4 = 3.5.

The statement is sufficient.

The answer is (D), either statement alone is sufficient.

2.   Are all the integers arranged in order in Sequence A consecutive integers?

   (1)   The average of the sequence is not equal to the median of the sequence.

   (2)   There is an odd number of integers in the set.

If all the integers in Sequence *A* are consecutive, then the average of the sequence must equal the median of the sequence.

For example, the average of the sequence 1, 2, 3 is 2, which is also the median.

And the average of the sequence 1, 2, 4 is 2.33, which does not equal the median (2).

Statement (1): The average of the sequence is not equal to the median of the sequence.

Statement (1) says that the median of sequence *A* is not the average of the sequence, and therefore sequence *A* is not a set of consecutive integers. So, Statement (1) is sufficient.

Statement (2): There is an odd number of integers in the set.

Not all sequences containing an odd number of elements are consecutive or vice versa. So, the statement does not help in any way.

For example, both series mentioned above 1, 2, 3 and 1, 2, 4 have an odd number of integers. But one consists of only consecutive integers and the other does not. This is a double case and therefore Statement (2) alone does not answer the question.

The answer is (A).

Class	Class size	Mean Score
A	20	89
B	m	p
C	40	90

3.   Is the average score of the students in the 3 classes together equal to 89?

   (1) $m = 40$

   (2) $p = 89$

Classes A and C together contain $20 + 40$ people. And their net score equals $20 \cdot 89$ for Class A plus $40 \cdot 90$ for Class C ($= 20 \cdot 89 + 40 \cdot 90$). Consider the collection of the two classes as a single class, say, AC. The average score of Class AC is $\dfrac{20 \cdot 89 + 40 \cdot 90}{20 + 40}$. You can calculate this value and find that the number lies between 89 and 90 (We can do without the exact value. We only need to know that the average lies between 89 and 90) or you can do some arithmetic juggling shown below to get the same.

$$\frac{20 \cdot 89 + 40 \cdot 90}{20 + 40} = \frac{20 \cdot 89 + 40 \cdot (89 + 1)}{20 + 40} = \frac{20 \cdot 89 + 40 \cdot 89 + 40 \cdot 1}{60} = \frac{60 \cdot 89 + 40 \cdot 1}{60} = 89 + \frac{40}{60} \cdot 1 > 89,$$

which says the average of *AC* is greater than 89.

$$\frac{20 \cdot 89 + 40 \cdot 90}{20 + 40} = \frac{20 \cdot (90 - 1) + 40 \cdot 90}{20 + 40} = \frac{20 \cdot 90 - 20 + 40 \cdot 90}{60} = \frac{20 \cdot 90 - 20 \cdot 1 + 40 \cdot 90}{60} = \frac{60 \cdot 90 - 20 \cdot 1}{60} = 90 - \frac{20 \cdot 1}{60} < 90,$$

which says the average of *AC* is less than 90. The average lies between the scores *A* and *C*.

We have seen that the average score of classes *A* and *C* together lies between the mean scores of the two classes.

Statement (1): $m = 40$

Let the class size and the mean score of Class B be 40 and 88 ($m = 40$ and $p = 88$). The selection is done such that the average of B and C is 89, which the average of A also equals. So, the average of the three classes A, B, and C—which is merely the weighted averages of A and the weighted average of B and C—must lie between the average of A (which is 89) and the average of B and C (which is 89). Clearly, the average of A, B and C here is 89. Or you might use the following calculation:

$$\frac{20 \cdot 89 + 40 \cdot 88 + 40 \cdot 90}{20 + 40 + 40} =$$
$$\frac{1780 + 3520 + 3600}{20 + 40 + 40} =$$
$$\frac{8900}{100} =$$
$$89$$

This is the only arrangement where the net average equals 89, and the answer to question is "Yes. The net average is 89."

Consider another arrangement, suppose $m = 40$ and $p = 89$. Then the net mean is

$$\frac{89 \cdot 20 + 89 \cdot 40 + 90 \cdot 40}{20 + 40 + 40} = 89.4 \neq 89$$

Thus, we have a double case and therefore the statement is *not* sufficient.

The answer is (B).

Statement (2): $p = 89$

Statement (2) says that p, the mean of Class B, is 89.

Now, let's discuss using the averages of Class B and the classes A and C (the unit AC).

The mean of B is 89 ($p = 89$), and the mean of the classes A and C together is greater than 89.

So, the mean of the two units (B, A and C) must be greater than 89, not 89.

The statement is sufficient to say the net mean is *not* 89.

Class	Class size	Mean Score
A	20	57
B	m	p
C	40	60

4. Is the overall average score of the 3 classes A, B, and C together is 59?

    (1) $m = 40$

    (2) $p = 59$

The class size of A is 20, and the class size of C is 40. The weight of A is $\dfrac{20}{20+40}$, which equals one-third, and the weight of Class C is the rest $\dfrac{40}{20+40}$, which equals two-thirds. So, the average of classes A and C together is equal to one-third the weight of the mean score of Class A plus two-thirds the weight of the mean score of Class C:

$$\frac{1}{3} \cdot 57 + \frac{2}{3} \cdot 60 = 59$$

So, now we can assume to have only two classes: Class AC (which is Class A plus Class C), with mean score 59 and class size $20 + 40 = 60$, and Class B, with mean score p and class size 40.

Statement (1): $m = 40$

Suppose $m = 40$ and $p = 59$. This is an arrangement where the mean is 59 in the question:

$$\frac{57 \cdot 20 + 59 \cdot 40 + 60 \cdot 40}{20 + 40 + 40} = 59$$

Suppose $m = 40$ and $p = 57$. This is an arrangement where the mean is not 59:

$$\frac{57 \cdot 20 + 57 \cdot 40 + 60 \cdot 40}{20 + 40 + 40} = 58.2$$

We have a double case and therefore the statement is *not* sufficient.

Statement (2): $p = 59$

The mean of A and C is 59, and the mean of B is also 59. So, the mean of Class AC and Class B is the same. So, irrespective of their weights (which can be calculated only if we have m), the average of each of the three classes is the same.

The statement is sufficient.

Hence, Statement (2) alone is sufficient, while Statement (1) alone is *not*. The answer is (B).

5.   A class consists of boys and girls only. On a final exam in History, the average score of the girls is 72 and the average score of the boys is 70. Is the average score of the class 71?

(1)   Smith is one of the classmates and Smith has the same number of boy classmates as girl classmates.

(2)   The number of students in the class is 101.

The average score of the class will be exactly in the middle between 70 and 72 (at 71) only if the weight of the number of boys equals the weight of the number of girls. The weight of the boys equals the weight of the girls only if the number of boys equals the number of girls.

So, the question can be transformed to "In the class, is the number of girls *equal to* the number of boys?"

Statement (1): Smith is one of the classmates and Smith has the same number of boy classmates as girl classmates.

Statement (1) says Smith has as many boy classmates as girl classmates. If Smith is a girl, the class will have one girl more; and if Smith is a boy, the class will have one boy more. So, whether Smith is a girl or a boy is irrelevant. The average is *not* in the middle. The statement answers the question as "No."

Statement (2): The number of students in the class is 101.

Suppose we have an equal number of boys and girls, and suppose the number is n. Then the class size is $n + n = 2n$, which must be even. But we are given that the class size is 101, which is odd. Hence, our assumption that we have an equal number of boys and girls is false. Hence, there is an unequal weight of boys and girls, and the average is *not* in the middle. The statement is sufficient to answer the question as "No."

The answer is (D).

Ratio & Proportion

RATIO

A ratio is simply a fraction. The following notations all express the ratio of x to y: $x:y$, $x \div y$, or $\dfrac{x}{y}$.

Writing two numbers as a ratio provides a convenient way to compare their sizes. For example, since $\dfrac{3}{\pi} < 1$, we know that 3 is less than π. A ratio compares two numbers. Just as you cannot compare apples and oranges, so to must the numbers you are comparing have the same units. For example, you cannot form the ratio of 2 feet to 4 yards because the two numbers are expressed in different units—feet vs. yards. It is quite common for the GMAT to ask for the ratio of two numbers with different units. Before you form any ratio, make sure the two numbers are expressed in the same units.

Example 1: What is the ratio of 2 feet to 4 yards?

The ratio cannot be formed until the numbers are expressed in the same units. Let's turn the yards into feet. Since there are 3 feet in a yard, 4 yards = 4 × 3 feet = 12 feet. Forming the ratio yields

$$\frac{2 \; feet}{12 \; feet} = \frac{1}{6} \; or \; 1:6$$

Note, taking the reciprocal of a fraction usually changes its size. For example, $\dfrac{3}{4} \neq \dfrac{4}{3}$. So, order is important in a ratio: $3:4 \neq 4:3$.

PROPORTION

A proportion is simply an equality between two ratios (fractions). For example, the ratio of x to y is equal to the ratio of 3 to 2 is translated as

$$\frac{x}{y} = \frac{3}{2}$$

or in ratio notation,

$$x:y::3:2$$

Two variables are *directly proportional* if one is a constant multiple of the other:

$$y = kx$$

where k is a constant.

The above equation shows that as x increases (or decreases) so does y. This simple concept has numerous applications in mathematics. For example, in constant velocity problems, distance is directly proportional to time: $d = vt$, where v is a constant. Note, sometimes the word *directly* is suppressed.

Example 2:   What is the value of y?

      (1)   The ratio of y to x is 3.

      (2)   The sum of y and x is 80.

Statement (1):

Translating *"the ratio of y to x is 3"* into an equation yields

$$\frac{y}{x} = 3$$

Since there is no way to determine y, Statement (1) alone is not sufficient.

Statement (2):

Translating *"the sum of y and x is 80"* into an equation yields

$$y + x = 80$$

Since there is no way to determine y, Statement (2) alone is not sufficient.

Statement (1) and Statement (2) together:

Solving the equation $\frac{y}{x} = 3$ for y gives $y = 3x$. Substituting this into the equation $y + x = 80$ yields

$$3x + x = 80$$

$$4x = 80$$

$$x = 20$$

Hence, $y = 3x = 3 \cdot 20 = 60$ and therefore the statements together are sufficient. The answer is (C).

In many word problems, as one quantity increases (decreases), another quantity also increases (decreases). This type of problem can be solved by setting up a *direct* proportion.

Example 3:   If Biff can shape 3 surfboards in 50 minutes, how many surfboards can he shape in 5 hours?

As time increases so does the number of shaped surfboards. Hence, we set up a direct proportion. First, convert 5 hours into minutes: 5 hours = 5 × 60 minutes = 300 minutes. Next, let x be the number of surfboards shaped in 5 hours. Finally, forming the proportion yields

$$\frac{3}{50} = \frac{x}{300}$$

$$\frac{3 \cdot 300}{50} = x$$

$$18 = x$$

The answer is 18.

Example 4:   On a map, 1 inch represents 150 miles. What is the actual distance between two cities if they are $3\frac{1}{2}$ inches apart on the map?

As the distance on the map increases, so does the actual distance. Hence, we set up a direct proportion. Let x be the actual distance between the cities. Forming the proportion yields

$$\frac{1\,in}{150\,mi} = \frac{3\frac{1}{2}\,in}{x\,mi}$$

$$x = 3\frac{1}{2} \times 150$$

$$x = 525$$

The answer is 525.

Note, you need not worry about how you form the direct proportion so long as the order is the same on both sides of the equal sign. The proportion in Example 4 could have been written as $\dfrac{1\,in}{3\frac{1}{2}\,in} = \dfrac{150\,mi}{x\,mi}$. In this case, the order is inches to inches and miles to miles. However, the following is not a direct proportion because the order is not the same on both sides of the equal sign: $\dfrac{1\,in}{150\,mi} = \dfrac{x\,mi}{3\frac{1}{2}\,in}$. In this case, the order is inches to miles on the left side of the equal sign but miles to inches on the right side.

If one quantity increases (or decreases) while another quantity decreases (or increases), the quantities are said to be *inversely* proportional. The statement "y is inversely proportional to x" is written as

$$y = \frac{k}{x}$$

where k is a constant.

Multiplying both sides of $y = \dfrac{k}{x}$ by x yields

$$yx = k$$

Hence, in an inverse proportion, the product of the two quantities is constant. Therefore, instead of setting ratios equal, we set products equal.

In many word problems, as one quantity increases (decreases), another quantity decreases (increases). This type of problem can be solved by setting up a product of terms.

Example 5:   If 7 workers can assemble a car in 8 hours, how long would it take 12 workers to assemble the same car?

As the number of workers increases, the amount time required to assemble the car decreases. Hence, we set the products of the terms equal. Let x be the time it takes the 12 workers to assemble the car. Forming the equation yields

$$7 \cdot 8 = 12 \cdot x$$

$$\frac{56}{12} = x$$

$$4\frac{2}{3} = x$$

The answer is $4\frac{2}{3}$.

To **summarize**: if one quantity increases (decreases) as another quantity also increases (decreases), set ratios equal. If one quantity increases (decreases) as another quantity decreases (increases), set products equal.

The concept of proportion can be generalized to three or more ratios. A, B, and C are in the ratio 3:4:5 means $\dfrac{A}{B} = \dfrac{3}{4}$, $\dfrac{A}{C} = \dfrac{3}{5}$, and $\dfrac{B}{C} = \dfrac{4}{5}$.

Tip: If certain quantities are in a particular ratio, and the size of one of them, or two of them, ... , or all of them, or their sum is constricted, then the size of each quantity can be determined.

Example 6:   In the figure, what is the measure of angle A?

(1)   The ratio of the three angles is 5:12:13.

(2)   The sum of the three angles is 180 degrees.

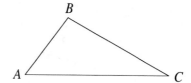

Since the angle sum of a triangle is 180°, $A + B + C = 180$. We have used a common property, not Statement (2). Such statements, already known before the statement is given, are insufficient. Forming two of the ratios yields

$$\frac{A}{B} = \frac{5}{12} \qquad \frac{A}{C} = \frac{5}{13}$$

Solving the first equation for B yields $B = \dfrac{12}{5} A$

Solving the second equation for C yields $C = \dfrac{13}{5} A$

Hence, $180 = A + B + C = A + \dfrac{12}{5} A + \dfrac{13}{5} A = 6A$. Therefore, $180 = 6A$, or $A = 30$. The answer is not (C); it is (A).

Problem Set J: Ratio & Proportion

1. If r and s are two positive numbers, what is the value of the ratio r/s ?

    (1) r is 25% greater than s.

    (2) r is 25 units greater than s.

2. Is $\dfrac{j}{m} + \dfrac{k}{n} = 2$?

    (1) $\dfrac{jk}{mn} = 1$

    (2) $\dfrac{jn}{mk} = 1$

3. The savings from a person's income is the difference between his or her income and expenditure. What is the ratio of Mr. Kelvin's savings in the year 1998 to the year 1999?

    (1) The ratio of his income in the years 1998 to 1999 is 3 : 4.

    (2) The ratio of his expenditure in the years 1998 to 1999 is 5 : 6.

4. What is the sum of the two numbers x and y?

    (1) The ratio of the sum of the reciprocals of x and y to the product of the reciprocals of x and y is 1 : 3.

    (2) The product of x and y is 11/36 units greater than the sum of x and y.

5. Which one is greater on Richard's farm: the total number of pigs and horses, or the number of chickens?

    (1) The ratio of the number of chickens to the number of pigs to the number of horses on his farm is 33 : 17 : 21.

    (2) The total number of chickens, pigs, and horses on his farm is 142.

6. What is the value of $\dfrac{x + 3y - 10z}{a + 3b - 10c}$?

    (1) $x/a = y/b = z/c$

    (2) $x = 2y = 3z$

Answers and Solutions to Problem Set J: Ratio & Proportion

1. If *r* and *s* are two positive numbers, what is the value of the ratio *r/s* ?

    (1) *r* is 25% greater than *s*.

    (2) *r* is 25 units greater than *s*.

From Statement (1) alone, we have that *r* is 25% greater than *s*. Hence, $r = (1 + 25/100)s$. Hence, $r/s = 1 + 25/100 = 1.25$. Hence, Statement (1) alone is sufficient.

From Statement (2) alone, we have that *r* is 25 units greater than *s*. Hence, we have the equation $r = s + 25$. Dividing the equation by *s* yields $r/s = s/s + 25/s = 1 + 25/s$. Since *s* is unknown, $1 + 25/s$ cannot be calculated. Hence, Statement (2) alone is not sufficient.

The answer is (A).

2. Is $\dfrac{j}{m} + \dfrac{k}{n} = 2$?

    (1) $\dfrac{jk}{mn} = 1$

    (2) $\dfrac{jn}{mk} = 1$

From Statement (1) alone, $jk/mn = 1$. Solving for *j* yields $j = mn/k$. Hence, the expression $\dfrac{j}{m} + \dfrac{k}{n}$ equals $\dfrac{mn/k}{m} + \dfrac{k}{n} = \dfrac{n}{k} + \dfrac{k}{n}$. Since we still do not have the ratio *k/n*, Statement (1) alone is not sufficient.

From Statement (2) alone, $jn/mk = 1$. Solving for *j* yields $j = mk/n$. Hence, the expression $\dfrac{j}{m} + \dfrac{k}{n}$ equals $\dfrac{mk/n}{m} + \dfrac{k}{n} = \dfrac{k}{n} + \dfrac{k}{n} = \dfrac{2k}{n}$. Since we still do not have the ratio *k/n*, Statement (2) alone is also not sufficient.

Now, equating the expressions from the two statements yields $\dfrac{n}{k} + \dfrac{k}{n} = \dfrac{2k}{n}$. Subtracting $\dfrac{k}{n}$ from both sides yields $\dfrac{n}{k} = \dfrac{k}{n}$. Multiplying both sides by $\dfrac{k}{n}$ yields $\left(\dfrac{k}{n}\right)^2 = 1$, so $\dfrac{k}{n} = +1$ or -1. Hence, $\dfrac{2k}{n}$ equals $2(-1) = -2$ or $2(1) = 2$. Hence, we have a double case, and even the statements together do not answer the question. The answer is (E).

3. The savings from a person's income is the difference between his or her income and expenditure. What is the ratio of Mr. Kelvin's savings in the year 1998 to the year 1999?

    (1) The ratio of his income in the years 1998 to 1999 is 3 : 4.

    (2) The ratio of his expenditure in the years 1998 to 1999 is 5 : 6.

Savings (in the current context) equals Income – Expenditure.

Statement (1) has information only about income, and Statement (2) has information only about expenditure. Hence, neither statement alone is sufficient to answer the question.

From the statements together, suppose Kelvin's income is $9 in 1998 and $12 in 1999 [the incomes are in accordance with the ratio in Statement (1)]. Also suppose his expenditure is $5 in 1998 and $6 in 1999 [the expenditures are in accordance with the ratio in Statement (2)]. Then the ratio of his savings in the year 1998 to 1999 would be ($9 – $5) : ($12 – $6) = $4 : $6 = 2 : 3.

In another case, suppose Kelvin's income is $12 in 1998 and $16 in 1999 [the incomes are in accordance with the ratio in Statement (1)]. Also suppose his expenditure is $10 in 1998 and $12 in 1999 [the expenditures are in accordance with the ratio in Statement (2)]. Then the ratio of his savings in 1998 to 1999 would be ($12 – $10) : ($16 – $12) = $2 : $4 = 1 : 2. We have a different savings ratio here. Hence, we already have a double case and therefore the two statements together do not determine a unique ratio for savings.

Hence, the answer is (E).

4.   What is the sum of the two numbers x and y?

    (1)   The ratio of the sum of the reciprocals of x and y to the product of the reciprocals of x and y is 1 : 3.

    (2)   The product of x and y is 11/36 units greater than the sum of x and y.

From Statement (1) alone, we have that the ratio of the sum of the reciprocals of x and y to the product of the reciprocals of x and y is 1 : 3. Writing this as an equation yields

$$\frac{\dfrac{1}{x}+\dfrac{1}{y}}{\dfrac{1}{x}\cdot\dfrac{1}{y}}=\frac{1}{3}$$

$$\frac{\dfrac{x+y}{xy}}{\dfrac{1}{xy}}=\frac{1}{3}$$

$$\frac{x+y}{xy}\cdot\frac{xy}{1}=\frac{1}{3}$$

$$x+y=\frac{1}{3}\qquad\text{by canceling } xy \text{ from the numerator and denominator}$$

Hence, Statement (1) alone is sufficient.

From Statement (2) alone, we have that the product of x and y is 11/36 units greater than the sum of x and y. Writing this as an equation yields

$$xy-(x+y)=11/36$$

$$x+y=xy-11/36\qquad\text{by solving for } x+y$$

Since we do not know the value of xy, we cannot determine the value of $x + y$. Hence, Statement (2) alone is not sufficient.

The answer is (A).

5.   Which one is greater on Richard's farm: the total number of pigs and horses, or the number of chickens?

(1)   The ratio of the number of chickens to the number of pigs to the number of horses on his farm is $33 : 17 : 21$.

(2)   The total number of chickens, pigs, and horses on his farm is 142.

Let the number of chickens, pigs and horses on Richard's farm be c, p, and h. From Statement (1), we have that the ratio of the three is $c : p : h = 33 : 17 : 21$. So, let c equal $33k$, p equal $17k$, and h equal $21k$, where k is some positive integer (such that $c : p : h = 33 : 17 : 21$). Then the total number of pigs and horses is $17k + 21k = 38k$; and since this is greater than $33k$, the number of chickens, the answer to the question is "The total number of pigs and horses is greater than the number of chickens." Hence, Statement (1) alone is sufficient to answer the question.

Next, Statement (2) alone gives the total number of the three species available, which is of no use. Hence, Statement (2) alone is not sufficient.

The answer is (A).

6.   What is the value of $\dfrac{x + 3y - 10z}{a + 3b - 10c}$?

(1) $x/a = y/b = z/c$

(2) $x = 2y = 3z$

From Statement (1) alone, we have $x/a = y/b = z/c$. Now, let $a = b = c = 1$, and let $x = y = z = 1$. Then

$$\frac{x + 3y - 10z}{a + 3b - 10c} = \frac{1 + 3 \cdot 1 - 10 \cdot 1}{1 + 3 \cdot 1 - 10 \cdot 1} = \frac{1 + 3 - 10}{1 + 3 - 10} = \frac{-6}{-6} = 1$$

Now, let $x = 1$, $y = 2$, and $z = 3$; and let $a = 2$, $b = 4$, and $c = 6$. Then

$$\frac{x + 3y - 10z}{a + 3b - 10c} = \frac{1 + 3 \cdot 2 - 10 \cdot 3}{2 + 3 \cdot 4 - 10 \cdot 6} = \frac{1 + 6 - 30}{2 + 12 - 60} = \frac{-23}{-46} = \frac{1}{2}$$

We have a double case, and therefore Statement (1) alone is not sufficient.

Now, with Statement (2) alone, we have $x = 2y = 3z$. Since there is no mention of the variables a, b, and c here, the variables are free to take any value independently and therefore $\dfrac{x + 3y - 10z}{a + 3b - 10c}$ may take any ratio. Hence, Statement (2) alone is not sufficient.

From the statements together, we have $x/a = y/b = z/c$ and $x = 2y = 3z$. Now, let $x = 6$, $y = 3$, and $z = 2$, and let $a = 6$, $b = 3$, and $c = 2$. Then

$$\frac{x + 3y - 10z}{a + 3b - 10c} = \frac{6 + 3 \cdot 3 - 10 \cdot 2}{6 + 3 \cdot 3 - 10 \cdot 2} = \frac{6 + 9 - 20}{6 + 9 - 20} = \frac{-5}{-5} = 1$$

Now, let $a = 12$, $b = 6$, and $c = 4$ and let $x = 6$, $y = 3$, and $z = 2$. Then

$$\frac{x + 3y - 10z}{a + 3b - 10c} = \frac{6 + 3 \cdot 3 - 10 \cdot 2}{12 + 3 \cdot 6 - 10 \cdot 4} = \frac{6 + 9 - 20}{12 + 18 - 40} = \frac{-5}{-10} = \frac{1}{2}$$

We have a double case, and therefore the statements together are not sufficient. The answer is (E).

Exponents & Roots

EXPONENTS

Exponents afford a convenient way of expressing long products of the same number. The expression b^n is called a power and it stands for $b \times b \times b \times \cdots \times b$, where there are n factors of b. b is called the base, and n is called the exponent. By definition, $b^0 = 1$.*

There are six rules that govern the behavior of exponents:

Rule 1: $x^a \cdot x^b = x^{a+b}$ Example, $2^3 \cdot 2^2 = 2^{3+2} = 2^5 = 32$. Caution, $x^a + x^b \neq x^{a+b}$

Rule 2: $\left(x^a\right)^b = x^{ab}$ Example, $\left(2^3\right)^2 = 2^{3 \cdot 2} = 2^6 = 64$

Rule 3: $(xy)^a = x^a \cdot y^a$ Example, $(2y)^3 = 2^3 \cdot y^3 = 8y^3$

Rule 4: $\left(\dfrac{x}{y}\right)^a = \dfrac{x^a}{y^a}$ Example, $\left(\dfrac{x}{3}\right)^2 = \dfrac{x^2}{3^2} = \dfrac{x^2}{9}$

Rule 5: $\dfrac{x^a}{x^b} = x^{a-b}$, if $a > b$.   Example, $\dfrac{2^6}{2^3} = 2^{6-3} = 2^3 = 8$

       $\dfrac{x^a}{x^b} = \dfrac{1}{x^{b-a}}$, if $b > a$.   Example, $\dfrac{2^3}{2^6} = \dfrac{1}{2^{6-3}} = \dfrac{1}{2^3} = \dfrac{1}{8}$

Rule 6: $x^{-a} = \dfrac{1}{x^a}$ Example, $z^{-3} = \dfrac{1}{z^3}$. Caution, a negative exponent does not make the number negative; it merely indicates that the base should be reciprocated. For example, $3^{-2} \neq -\dfrac{1}{3^2}$ or $-\dfrac{1}{9}$.

Problems involving these six rules are common on the GMAT, and they are often listed as hard problems. However, the process of solving these problems is quite mechanical: simply apply the six rules until they can no longer be applied.

---

* Any term raised to the zero power equals 1, no matter how complex the term is. For example, $\left(\dfrac{x + 5\pi}{y}\right)^0 = 1$.

Example: If $x \neq 0$, what is x ?

(1) $\dfrac{x\left(x^5\right)^2}{x^4} = 128$

(2) $\dfrac{x\left(x^2\right)^5}{x^3} = 256$

Statement (1): $\dfrac{x\left(x^5\right)^2}{x^4} = 128$

First, apply the rule $\left(x^a\right)^b = x^{ab}$ to the expression $\dfrac{x\left(x^5\right)^2}{x^4}$:

$$\frac{x \cdot x^{5 \cdot 2}}{x^4} = \frac{x \cdot x^{10}}{x^4}$$

Next, apply the rule $x^a \cdot x^b = x^{a+b}$:

$$\frac{x \cdot x^{10}}{x^4} = \frac{x^{11}}{x^4}$$

Finally, apply the rule $\dfrac{x^a}{x^b} = x^{a-b}$:

$$\frac{x^{11}}{x^4} = x^{11-4} = x^7$$

This says Statement (1) is true.

Statement (2): $\dfrac{x\left(x^2\right)^5}{x^3} = 256$

By steps similar to the analysis of Statement (1), we reduce Statement (2) to $x^8 = 256$. We can take the clue from Statement (1) that $x = 2$. Since this is the only solution possible according to Statement (1), we do not need to realize that $x = 2$ is one of the feasible solutions of Statement (2). But we still realize it for you by saying, substituting x with 2 in the equation $\dfrac{x\left(x^2\right)^5}{x^3} = 256$, or $\dfrac{2\left(2^2\right)^5}{2^3} = 256$, yields a valid result. Hence $x = 2$ is feasible. Now, as we discussed, our job in Statement (2) reduces to determining whether there could be any other solution for x apart from 2. If yes, we wrap up saying we have a double case and Statement (2) alone is *data insufficient*. If no, we wrap up saying Statement (2) alone is *data sufficient*. Did we use the clue to save time. Luckily, even when $x = -2$, x^8 is even and therefore it has two roots (two solutions). Since 2 is one solution and x^8 equals 256 when x is either 2 or -2, we do not have a single answer and therefore the statement is not sufficient.

The answer is (A).

If instead, Statement (2) was analyzed first, we would have gotten $x = -2$ or $+2$. Statement (1) can take this as a clue. We can be sure that at least one of the clues is feasible here. This can be checked by substituting both $x = 2$ and $x = -2$ and selecting the feasible ones. Note that at least one would be feasible, lest the system wouldn't be realistic. Apart from this, Statement (1) must as well check whether any other solution also exists in Statement (1). Here, no other solution is possible. So, Statement (1) is sufficient. The answer is (A). Now, do we need to find more solutions if both -2 and $+2$ satisfy? No, because whether we have more solutions or not, the answer is the same, data insufficient (because we already have 2 solutions).

Note: Typically, there are many ways of evaluating these types of problems. For this example, we could have begun with Rule 5, $\dfrac{x^a}{x^b} = \dfrac{1}{x^{b-a}}$:

$$\frac{x\left(x^5\right)^2}{x^4} = \frac{\left(x^5\right)^2}{x^{4-1}} = \frac{\left(x^5\right)^2}{x^3}$$

Then apply Rule 2, $\left(x^a\right)^b = x^{ab}$:

$$\frac{\left(x^5\right)^2}{x^3} = \frac{x^{10}}{x^3}$$

Finally, apply the other version of Rule 5, $\dfrac{x^a}{x^b} = x^{a-b}$:

$$\frac{x^{10}}{x^3} = x^7$$

ROOTS

The symbol $\sqrt[n]{b}$ is read the *n*th root of *b*, where *n* is called the index, *b* is called the base, and $\sqrt{}$ is called the radical. $\sqrt[n]{b}$ denotes that number which raised to the *n*th power yields *b*. In other words, *a* is the *n*th root of *b* if $a^n = b$. For example, $\sqrt{9} = 3^*$ because $3^2 = 9$, and $\sqrt[3]{-8} = -2$ because $(-2)^3 = -8$. Even roots occur in pairs: both a positive root and a negative root. For example, $\sqrt[4]{16} = 2$ since $2^4 = 16$, and $\sqrt[4]{16} = -2$ since $(-2)^4 = 16$. Odd roots occur alone and have the same sign as the base: $\sqrt[3]{-27} = -3$ since $(-3)^3 = -27$. If given an even root, you are to assume it is the positive root. However, if you introduce even roots by solving an equation, then you <u>must</u> consider both the positive and negative roots:

$$x^2 = 9$$
$$\sqrt{x^2} = \pm\sqrt{9}$$
$$x = \pm 3$$

Square roots and cube roots can be simplified by removing perfect squares and perfect cubes, respectively. For example,

$$\sqrt{8} = \sqrt{4 \cdot 2} = \sqrt{4}\sqrt{2} = 2\sqrt{2}$$
$$\sqrt[3]{54} = \sqrt[3]{27 \cdot 2} = \sqrt[3]{27}\sqrt[3]{2} = 3\sqrt[3]{2}$$

Radicals are often written with fractional exponents. The expression $\sqrt[n]{b}$ can be written as $b^{1/n}$. This can be generalized as follows:

$$b^{m/n} = \left(\sqrt[n]{b}\right)^m = \sqrt[n]{b^m}$$

Usually, the form $\left(\sqrt[n]{b}\right)^m$ is better when calculating because the part under the radical is smaller in this case. For example, $27^{2/3} = \left(\sqrt[3]{27}\right)^2 = 3^2 = 9$. Using the form $\sqrt[n]{b^m}$ would be much harder in this case: $27^{2/3} = \sqrt[3]{27^2} = \sqrt[3]{729} = 9$. Most students know the value of $\sqrt[3]{27}$, but few know the value of $\sqrt[3]{729}$.

If *n* is even, then

$$\sqrt[n]{x^n} = |x|$$

For example, $\sqrt[4]{(-2)^4} = |-2| = 2$. With odd roots, the absolute value symbol is not needed. For example, $\sqrt[3]{(-2)^3} = \sqrt[3]{-8} = -2$.

To solve radical equations, just apply the rules of exponents to undo the radicals. For example, to solve the radical equation $x^{2/3} = 4$, we cube both sides to eliminate the cube root:

$$\left(x^{2/3}\right)^3 = 4^3$$
$$x^2 = 64$$
$$\sqrt{x^2} = \sqrt{64}$$
$$|x| = 8$$
$$x = \pm 8$$

---

* With square roots, the index is not written, $\sqrt[2]{9} = \sqrt{9}$.

Even roots of negative numbers do not appear on the GMAT. For example, you will not see expressions of the form $\sqrt{-4}$; expressions of this type are called complex numbers.

The following rules are useful for manipulating roots:

$$\sqrt[n]{xy} = \sqrt[n]{x}\sqrt[n]{y}$$ For example, $\sqrt{3x} = \sqrt{3}\sqrt{x}$.

$$\sqrt[n]{\frac{x}{y}} = \frac{\sqrt[n]{x}}{\sqrt[n]{y}}$$ For example, $\sqrt[3]{\frac{x}{8}} = \frac{\sqrt[3]{x}}{\sqrt[3]{8}} = \frac{\sqrt[3]{x}}{2}$.

Caution: $\sqrt[n]{x+y} \neq \sqrt[n]{x}+\sqrt[n]{y}$. For example, $\sqrt{x+5} \neq \sqrt{x}+\sqrt{5}$. Also, $\sqrt{x^2+y^2} \neq x+y$. This common mistake occurs because it is similar to the following valid property: $\sqrt{(x+y)^2} = x+y$ (If $x+y$ can be negative, then it must be written with the absolute value symbol: $|x+y|$). Note, in the valid formula, it's the whole term, $x+y$, that is squared, not the individual x and y.

To add two roots, both the index and the base must be the same. For example, $\sqrt[3]{2} + \sqrt[4]{2}$ cannot be added because the indices are different, nor can $\sqrt{2}+\sqrt{3}$ be added because the bases are different. However, $\sqrt[3]{2} + \sqrt[3]{2} = 2\sqrt[3]{2}$. In this case, the roots can be added because both the indices and bases are the same. Sometimes radicals with different bases can actually be added once they have been simplified to look alike. For example, $\sqrt{28} + \sqrt{7} = \sqrt{4\cdot 7} + \sqrt{7} = \sqrt{4}\sqrt{7} + \sqrt{7} = 2\sqrt{7} + \sqrt{7} = 3\sqrt{7}$.

You need to know the approximations of the following roots: $\sqrt{2} \approx 1.4$ $\sqrt{3} \approx 1.7$ $\sqrt{5} \approx 2.2$

Example 4:   Is $x > y$?

   (1) $x^2 = 4$

   (2) $y^3 = -8$

$y^3 = -8$ yields one cube root, $y = -2$. However, $x^2 = 4$ yields two square roots, $x = \pm 2$. Now, if $x = 2$, then $x > y$; but if $x = -2$, then $x = y$. Hence, $x > y$ is not necessarily true. The answer is (E).

Example 5:   What is x if y is 9?

   (1) y is 5 more than the square of x.

   (2) $x < 0$

In this type of problem, we must express x solely in terms of y. At the same time, the resultant expression in y must be one-to-one with x.

Statement (1): Translating the expression *"y is 5 more than the square of x"* into an equation yields:

$$y = x^2 + 5$$

$$y - 5 = x^2$$

$$\pm\sqrt{y-5} = x$$

We have two expressions possible for x (one with + and the other one with −). So, y is not one-to-one with x. Hence, given the value of y alone, Statement (1) won't determine a unique x. The statement is not sufficient.

Statement (2): $x < 0$ is clearly not sufficient.

With both statements together, we have that $x < 0$. Hence, we take the negative root, $-\sqrt{y-5} = x$.

The answer is (C), both statements required.

RATIONALIZING

A fraction is not considered simplified until all the radicals have been removed from the denominator. If a denominator contains a single term with a square root, it can be rationalized by multiplying both the numerator and denominator by that square root. If the denominator contains square roots separated by a plus or minus sign, then multiply both the numerator and denominator by the conjugate, which is formed by merely changing the sign between the roots.

Example: Rationalize the fraction $\dfrac{2}{3\sqrt{5}}$.

Multiply top and bottom of the fraction by $\sqrt{5}$: $\qquad \dfrac{2}{3\sqrt{5}} \cdot \dfrac{\sqrt{5}}{\sqrt{5}} = \dfrac{2\sqrt{5}}{3\cdot\sqrt{25}} = \dfrac{2\sqrt{5}}{3\cdot 5} = \dfrac{2\sqrt{5}}{15}$

Example: Rationalize the fraction $\dfrac{2}{3-\sqrt{5}}$.

Multiply top and bottom of the fraction by the conjugate $3+\sqrt{5}$:

$$\dfrac{2}{3-\sqrt{5}} \cdot \dfrac{3+\sqrt{5}}{3+\sqrt{5}} = \dfrac{2\left(3+\sqrt{5}\right)}{3^2 + 3\sqrt{5} - 3\sqrt{5} - \left(\sqrt{5}\right)^2} = \dfrac{2\left(3+\sqrt{5}\right)}{9-5} = \dfrac{2\left(3+\sqrt{5}\right)}{4} = \dfrac{3+\sqrt{5}}{2}$$

Problem Set K: Exponents & Roots

1. m is negative, and n is an integer. Is m^n positive?

    (1) m is odd.

    (2) n is odd.

2. If p is a positive integer, and $x = m^{1/3}$, $y = n^{1/2}$, and $z = 2p$, then which one of x, y, and z is the greatest?

    (1) $4p^3 = 5m$

    (2) $5n = 3p^2$

3. Which is greater: $\sqrt[m]{4^{m+n}}$ or $\sqrt[n]{3^{m+n}}$?

    (1) $3m = 4n$

    (2) $m = -4$

4. Is a^x equal to 4?

    (1) $a^{x+1} = 4$

    (2) $(a+1)^x = 4$

5. If m and n are integers, then what is the value of $(-1)^m + (-1)^n + (-1)^m \cdot (-1)^n$?

    (1) $m = 23522101$

    (2) $n = 63522251$

6. If m and n are integers and $x*y$ is defined as $(-1)^x + (-1)^y + (-1)^x \cdot (-1)^y$, then what is the value of $m*n$?

    (1) $m*n = 2 + [(-1)^m \cdot (-1)^n]$

    (2) $(-1)^m \cdot (-1)^n = 1$

Answers and Solutions to Problem Set K: Exponents & Roots

1. m is negative, and n is an integer. Is m^n positive?

    (1) m is odd.

    (2) n is odd.

Note that even numbers and odd numbers are as likely to be negative as positive.

Statement (1): m is odd.

Statement (1) is irrelevant because m^n could be negative or positive whether m is odd or even. m^n is negative only if m is negative, and m^n is positive only if m is positive or n is even or 0. So, we have the double case, and the statement alone is not sufficient.

Statement (2): n is odd.

A negative number raised to an odd power (positive or negative) is always negative. So, the statement says that m^n is negative (not positive). For example, $(-3)^3 = -27$ is negative, and $(-3)^{-3} = 1/(-3)^3 = 1/(-27)$ is negative. So, the statement alone is sufficient.

The answer is (B).

2. If p is a positive integer, and $x = m^{1/3}$, $y = n^{1/2}$, and $z = 2p$, then which one of x, y, and z is the greatest?

    (1) $4p^3 = 5m$

    (2) $5n = 3p^2$

Using Statement (1), we get $m = 4p^3/5$. Using Statement (2), we get $n = 3p^2/5$.

Statement (1): $m = 4p^3/5$

We have the system: $x = m^{1/3}$, $y = n^{1/2}$, and $z = 2p$.

Substituting $m = 4p^3/5$ in the system yields

$x = m^{1/3} = (4p^3/5)^{1/3}$

$y = n^{1/2}$

$z = 2p$

So, the question asks for the greater number of $(4p^3/5)^{1/3}$, $n^{1/2}$, and $2p$.

To answer the question, we need to convert n into p or p into n. Since we do not have a relationship between n and p, we cannot compare. The statement is *not* sufficient.

Statement (2): $n = 3p^2/5$

We have the system: $x = m^{1/3}$, $y = n^{1/2}$, and $z = 2p$.

Substituting $n = 3p^2/5$ in the system yields

$x = m^{1/3}$

$y = n^{1/2} = (3p^2/5)^{1/2}$

$z = 2p$

So, the question asks for the greater number of $m^{1/3}$, $(3p^2/5)^{1/2}$, and $2p$.

Since we do not know the relationship between m and p, we cannot answer the question. The statement is *not* sufficient.

With the statements together, we need to compare the terms $(4/5)^{1/3}p$, $(3/5)^{1/2}p$, and $2p$. Since p is positive, we can divide and thus cancel p from each term. The corresponding terms become $(4/5)^{1/3}$, $(3/5)^{1/2}$, and 2. We can calculate, compare, and answer the question, which is just a numerical calculation. We do not need to do the calculation; we just need to know whether we can.

Hence, the statements are together sufficient, and the answer is (C).

3. Which is greater: $\sqrt[m]{4^{m+n}}$ or $\sqrt[n]{3^{m+n}}$?

    (1) $3m = 4n$

    (2) $m = -4$

Statement (1): $3m = 4n$

Using Statement (1) alone gives

$$\sqrt[m]{4^{m+n}} =$$
$$4^{\frac{m+n}{m}} =$$
$$4^{\frac{m}{m}+\frac{n}{m}} =$$
$$4^{1+\frac{n}{m}} =$$
$$4^{1+\frac{3}{4}}$$

$$\sqrt[n]{3^{m+n}} =$$
$$3^{\frac{m+n}{n}} =$$
$$3^{\frac{m}{n}+\frac{n}{n}} =$$
$$3^{\frac{m}{n}+1} =$$
$$3^{\frac{4}{3}+1}$$

These are numeric values, and they can be compared and question answered. The statement is sufficient.

Statement (2): $m = -4$

Using Statement (2) alone gives

$$\sqrt[m]{4^{m+n}} =$$
$$4^{\frac{m+n}{m}} =$$
$$4^{\frac{m}{m}+\frac{n}{m}} =$$
$$4^{1+\frac{n}{m}} =$$
$$4^{1+\frac{n}{-4}}$$

$$\sqrt[n]{3^{m+n}} =$$
$$3^{\frac{m+n}{n}} =$$
$$3^{\frac{m}{n}+\frac{n}{n}} =$$
$$3^{\frac{m}{n}+1} =$$
$$3^{\frac{-4}{n}+1}$$

For $n > 4$, $1 + n/{-4}$ is negative and $1 + -4/n$ is positive. Here, $4^{1 + n/-4}$ is less than 1 and $3^{-4/n + 1}$ is greater than 1. So, $3^{-4/n + 1} > 4^{1 + n/-4}$.

For $0 < n < 4$, $1 + n/{-4}$ is positive and $-4/n + 1$ is negative. Here, $4^{1 + n/-4}$ is greater than 1, and $3^{-4/n + 1}$ is less than 1. So, $3^{-4/n + 1} < 4^{1 + n/-4}$.

We have a double case and therefore the statement is *not* sufficient.

The answer is (A).

4.   Is a^x equal to 4?

    (1) $a^{x+1} = 4$

    (2) $(a + 1)^x = 4$

Statement (1): $a^{x+1} = 4$

Common sense solution: A function like a^x either increases continuously with x or decreases continuously with x depending on the value of a.

Exceptions:
$a = 0$ when a^x becomes $0 \neq 4$,
$a = 1$ when a^x becomes $1 \neq 4$,

and

a is negative when a^x, a^{x+1}, a^{x+2}, ... ,
and so on would alternatively be to either side of number line. Here since a^{x+1} is positive, a^x which equals a^{x+1}/a = positive/negative = negative. So, if $a^{x+1} = 4$ (positive) $a^x =$ is negative (not equal to 4).

Alternate solution: If a^x is to equal 4 even as a^{x+1} equals the 4 as stated by the statement, then we have $a^{x+1} = a^x$ (= 4), which dividing by a^x yields $a^{x+1}/ a^x = a^x/a^x$; $a = 1$; and when a equals 1, neither a^{x+1} nor a^x equals 2 (they equal 1 only). This makes Statement (1) absurd. Hence, $a^x \neq 4$, or in other words, if a were 1, then a^{x+1} anyway equals 1 and does not equal 4. The answer to the question is No. The statement is sufficient.

The answer is (A).

Statement (2): $(a + 1)^x = 4$

Unlike in Statement (1), the function a^x need not continuously increase or continuously decrease with x and a.

Assume a^x equals 4 even as we know the statement: $(a + 1)^x$ equals 4. Then, $a^x = (a + 1)^x$ which is possible for example when bases are equated (exponents being the same). This yields $a = a + 1$; $0 = 1$, absurd. So, a^x may not equal 4. The answer could be No.

Or if x is even, then a^x equals $(-a)^x$ which means $(a + 1)^x = (-a)^x = 2$. Equating bases as exponents are there, we can get one feasible solution. This says $a + 1 = -a$, or $2a = -1$ or $a = -1/2$.

So, $a = -1/2$ and x even (say 2) could be one possibility where a^x equals 4 as a^{x+1} equals 4. Here, the answer is Yes.

Thus, we have a double case and therefore the statement is *not* sufficient.

5.   If m and n are integers, then what is the value of $(-1)^m + (-1)^n + (-1)^m \cdot (-1)^n$?

(1) $m = 23522101$

(2) $n = 63522251$

Now, m and n could be odd or even. Form a table:

$(-1)^m + (-1)^n + (-1)^m \cdot (-1)^n$ equals what when m is what and n is what?	n as odd	n as even
m as odd	$(-1)^m + (-1)^n + (-1)^m \cdot (-1)^n =$ $(-1)^{odd} + (-1)^{odd} + (-1)^{odd} \cdot (-1)^{odd} =$ $-1 + (-1) + (-1) \cdot (-1) =$ $-1 - 1 + 1 =$ -1	$(-1)^m + (-1)^n + (-1)^m \cdot (-1)^n =$ $(-1)^{odd} + (-1)^{even} + (-1)^{odd} \cdot (-1)^{even} =$ $-1 + 1 + (-1) \cdot (1) =$ $-1 + 1 - 1 =$ -1
m as even	$(-1)^m + (-1)^n + (-1)^m \cdot (-1)^n =$ $(-1)^{even} + (-1)^{odd} + (-1)^{even} \cdot (-1)^{odd} =$ $1 + (-1) + (1) \cdot (-1) =$ $1 - 1 - 1 =$ -1	$(-1)^m + (-1)^n + (-1)^m \cdot (-1)^n =$ $(-1)^{even} + (-1)^{even} + (-1)^{even} \cdot (-1)^{even} =$ $1 + 1 + (1) \cdot (1) =$ $1 + 1 + 1 =$ 3

So, $(-1)^m + (-1)^n + (-1)^m \cdot (-1)^n$ has only two results. One of which is the value when n is even (which is -1) and the other one is the value when n is odd (which is 3). Hence, we only need to know if n is odd or even. So, we are interested in n only. Statement (2) alone is sufficient. Note that knowing Statement (1), if m is odd or even, will not help determine whether n is odd or even. Hence, Statement (1) is not sufficient. The answer is (B).

6.   If m and n are integers and $x*y$ is defined as $(-1)^x + (-1)^y + (-1)^x \cdot (-1)^y$, then what is the value of $m*n$?

(1) $m*n = 2 + [(-1)^m \cdot (-1)^n]$

(2) $(-1)^m \cdot (-1)^n = 1$

According to definition, $m*n$ is defined as $(-1)^m + (-1)^n + (-1)^m \cdot (-1)^n$

Let's reduce the problem as

What is $m*n$?

(1) $m*n = 2 + [(-1)^m \cdot (-1)^n]$; $(-1)^m + (-1)^n + \cancel{(-1)^m \cdot (-1)^n} = 2 + \cancel{[(-1)^m \cdot (-1)^n]}$; $(-1)^m + (-1)^n = 2$

(2) $(-1)^m \cdot (-1)^n = 1$

The max values of $(-1)^m$ and $(-1)^n$ are each 1 and they sum to 2 only when they are at their max values. So, $(-1)^m$ and $(-1)^n$ both must equal 1 then. So, $m*n = (-1)^m + (-1)^n + (-1)^m \cdot (-1)^n = 1 + 1 + 1 = 3$. Statement (1) is sufficient.

$(-1)^m \cdot (-1)^n$ equals 1 when either both m and n are odd or when both are even. When both are odd, $m*n = (-1)^m + (-1)^n + (-1)^m \cdot (-1)^n = -1 - 1 + 1 = -1$; and when both are odd, we already saw that $m*n = (-1)^m + (-1)^n = 1 + 1 + 1 = 3$. We have a double case and therefore the statement is not sufficient.

The answer is (A).

Factoring

To factor an algebraic expression is to rewrite it as a product of two or more expressions, called factors. In general, any expression on the GMAT that can be factored should be factored, and any expression that can be un-factored (multiplied out) should be un-factored.

DISTRIBUTIVE RULE

The most basic type of factoring involves the distributive rule:

$$ax + ay = a(x + y)$$

When this rule is applied from left to right, it is called factoring. When the rule is applied from right to left, it is called distributing.

For example, $3h + 3k = 3(h + k)$, and $5xy + 45x = 5xy + 9 \cdot 5x = 5x(y + 9)$. The distributive rule can be generalized to any number of terms. For three terms, it looks like $ax + ay + az = a(x + y + z)$. For example, $2x + 4y + 8 = 2x + 2 \cdot 2y + 2 \cdot 4 = 2(x + 2y + 4)$. For another example, $x^2 y^2 + xy^3 + y^5 = y^2(x^2 + xy + y^3)$.

Example: Is $\left(x - \dfrac{y}{3} \right) - \left(y - \dfrac{x}{3} \right) = 11$?

(1) $x - y = 9$

(2) $x + y = 11$

$$\left(x - \frac{y}{3} \right) - \left(y - \frac{x}{3} \right) =$$

$x - \dfrac{y}{3} - y + \dfrac{x}{3} =$ by distributing the negative sign

$\dfrac{4}{3}x - \dfrac{4}{3}y =$ by combining the fractions

$\dfrac{4}{3}(x - y) =$ by factoring out the common factor $\dfrac{4}{3}$

$\dfrac{4}{3}(9) =$ since $x - y = 9$

12

The answer is (A), Statement (2) is not sufficient since we cannot reduce the expression to $x + y$.

DIFFERENCE OF SQUARES

One of the most important formulas on the GMAT is the difference of squares:

$$x^2 - y^2 = (x + y)(x - y)$$

Caution: a sum of squares, $x^2 + y^2$, does not factor.

Example: If $x \neq -2$, then what is $\dfrac{3x^2 + 6}{3x + 4}$ equal to?

(1) $\dfrac{8x^2 - 32}{4x + 8} = 2$

(2) $\dfrac{x^2 + 2}{3x + 4} = \dfrac{11}{13}$

In most algebraic expressions involving multiplication or division, you won't actually multiply or divide, rather you will factor and cancel, as in this problem. Turning to Statement (1), we have

$$\dfrac{8x^2 - 32}{4x + 8} = 2$$

$$\dfrac{8(x^2 - 4)}{4(x + 2)} = 2 \qquad \text{by the distributive property } ax + ay = a(x + y)$$

$$\dfrac{8(x + 2)(x - 2)}{4(x + 2)} = 2 \qquad \text{by the difference of squares } x^2 - y^2 = (x + y)(x - y)$$

$$2(x - 2) = 2 \qquad \text{by canceling common factors}$$

$$x - 2 = 1$$

$$x = 2 + 1 = 3$$

Therefore, $\dfrac{3x^2 + 6}{3x + 4}$ can be evaluated by substituting the known value of x. Statement (1) is sufficient.

Multiplying Statement (2) $\dfrac{x^2 + 2}{3x + 4} = \dfrac{11}{13}$ by 3 yields $\dfrac{3x^2 + 6}{3x + 4} = \dfrac{33}{13}$. Statement (2) as well is sufficient.

The answer is (D).

PERFECT SQUARE TRINOMIALS

Like the difference of squares formula, perfect square trinomial formulas are very common on the GMAT.

$$x^2 + 2xy + y^2 = (x + y)^2$$
$$x^2 - 2xy + y^2 = (x - y)^2$$

For example, $x^2 + 6x + 9 = x^2 + 2(3x) + 3^2 = (x + 3)^2$. Note, in a perfect square trinomial, the middle term is twice the product of the square roots of the outer terms.

GENERAL TRINOMIALS

$$x^2 + (a+b)x + ab = (x+a)(x+b)$$

The expression $x^2 + (a+b)x + ab$ tells us that we need two numbers whose product is the last term and whose sum is the coefficient of the middle term. Consider the trinomial $x^2 + 5x + 6$. Now, two factors of 6 are 1 and 6, but $1 + 6 \neq 5$. However, 2 and 3 are also factors of 6, and $2 + 3 = 5$. Hence, $x^2 + 5x + 6 = (x + 2)(x + 3)$.

Example: Is $x = 9$?

(1) $x^2 - 7x - 18 = 0$

(2) $x^2 - 10x + 9 = 0$

Let's see what we can do with Statement (1).

Both 2 and –9 are factors of –18, and $2 + (-9) = -7$. Hence, $x^2 - 7x - 18 = (x + 2)(x - 9) = 0$. Setting each factor equal to zero yields $x + 2 = 0$ and $x - 9 = 0$. Solving these equations yields $x = -2$ and 9.

Now, let's see what we can do with Statement (2).

Both –1 and –9 are factors of 9, and $-1 + (-9) = -10$. Hence, $x^2 - 10x + 9 = (x - 1)(x - 9) = 0$. Solving these equations yields $x = 1$ and 9.

The statements individually yield two solutions. So, neither alone is sufficient. But together they yield a single solution, 9. The answer is (C).

COMPLETE FACTORING

When factoring an expression, first check for a common factor, then check for a difference of squares, then for a perfect square trinomial, and then for a general trinomial.

Example: Factor the expression $2x^3 - 2x^2 - 12x$ completely.

Solution: First check for a common factor: $2x$ is common to each term. Factoring $2x$ out of each term yields $2x\left(x^2 - x - 6\right)$. Next, there is no difference of squares, and $x^2 - x - 6$ is not a perfect square trinomial since x does not equal twice the product of the square roots of x^2 and 6. Now, –3 and 2 are factors of –6 whose sum is –1. Hence, $2x\left(x^2 - x - 6\right)$ factors into $2x(x - 3)(x + 2)$.

Problem Set L: Factoring

1. If r and s are two positive numbers, what is the value of the ratio r/s ?

   (1) r is 25% greater than s.

   (2) r is 25 units greater than s.

2. Is $2p - 3q$ not equal to 0?

   (1) $4p$ is not equal to $6q$.

   (2) p is not equal to q.

3. If m and n are positive integers, then is $m + 2n$ an even integer?

   (1) $m = 3n + 1$

   (2) Exactly one of the two numbers m and n is even.

4. Is x divisible by 14?

   (1) $x/4$ is a positive integer.

   (2) $x/6$ is a positive integer.

5. If $x^2 - y^2 = 15$, is $x + y > x - y$?

   (1) $x - y = 5$

   (2) $x + y = 3$

6. Is $(x - 2)(x - 3) > 0$?

   (1) $x < 2$

   (2) $x < 3$

7. Is $\dfrac{(a - b) + (c - b)}{d} > 0$?

   (1) $a + c < 2b$

   (2) $d < 0$

8. Does the integer m have at least 4 positive prime factors?

   (1) $m/14$ is a positive integer.

   (2) $m/15$ is a positive integer.

9.   Does the positive integer n have at least 3 positive prime factors?

(1) $n/10$ is an integer.

(2) $n/30$ is an integer.

10.   If x is not equal to 1, then is y equal to zero?

(1) $y = \dfrac{1}{x-1}$

(2) $y = \dfrac{x}{6}$

11.   If n is a positive integer, then is $(n + 1)(n + 3)$ a multiple of 4?

(1) $(n + 2)(n + 4)$ is odd.

(2) $(n + 3)(n + 6)$ is even.

12.   If $m = k \cdot p$, where k and m are different positive integers, then does m have more than 5 prime factors?

(1) k has 5 different prime factors.

(2) p has 5 different prime factors.

13.   Is $\dfrac{50 + 5n}{n^2}$ an integer?

(1) $n/5$ is a positive integer.

(2) $n/10$ is a positive integer.

Answers and Solutions to Problem Set L: Factoring

1.   If r and s are two positive numbers, what is the value of the ratio r/s ?

   (1) r is 25% greater than s.

   (2) r is 25 units greater than s.

From Statement (1) alone, we have that r is 25% greater than s. Hence, $r = (1 + 25/100)s$. Hence, $r/s = 1 + 25/100 = 1.25$. Hence, Statement (1) alone is sufficient.

From Statement (2) alone, we have that r is 25 units greater than s. Hence, we have the equation $r = s + 25$. Dividing the equation by s yields $r/s = s/s + 25/s = 1 + 25/s$. Since s is unknown, $1 + 25/s$ cannot be calculated. Hence, Statement (2) alone is not sufficient.

The answer is (A).

2.   Is $2p - 3q$ not equal to 0?

   (1) $4p$ is not equal to $6q$.

   (2) p is not equal to q.

From Statement (1) alone, we have that $4p \neq 6q$. Dividing both sides by 2 yields $2p \neq 3q$. Subtracting $3q$ from both sides yields $2p - 3q \neq 0$. Hence, Statement (1) alone is sufficient to answer the question.

From Statement (2) alone, we have $p \neq q$. Multiplying both sides by 2 yields $2p \neq 2q$. Subtracting $3q$ from both sides yields $2p - 3q \neq -q$. Now, if q equals 0, then $2p - 3q$ does not equal 0. But if q does not equal 0, then $2p - 3q$ may equal 0 [For example, when $p = 3$ and $q = 2$, then $2p - 3q = 2(3) - 3(2) = 0$]. Hence, we have a double case, and Statement (2) alone is not sufficient.

Since Statement (1) alone is sufficient, the answer is (A).

3.   If m and n are positive integers, then is $m + 2n$ an even integer?

   (1) $m = 3n + 1$

   (2)   Exactly one of the two numbers m and n is even.

From Statement (1) alone, we have $m = 3n + 1$. Hence, $m + 2n = (3n + 1) + 2n = 5n + 1$.

If n is even, then $5n$ is even and $5n + 1$ is odd.

If n is odd, then $5n$ is odd and $5n + 1$ is even.

Thus, we have a double case, and Statement (1) alone is not sufficient. Also, in either case, only one of the two numbers m and n is even. Hence, Statement (2) is a derivation of Statement (1). Hence, we can use the same two cases in Statement (1) to determine that Statement (2) alone is not sufficient. The answer is (E).

4.   Is x divisible by 14?

   (1) $x/4$ is a positive integer.

   (2) $x/6$ is a positive integer.

Statement (1): $x/4$ is a positive integer when x is a multiple of 4. Now, not every multiple of 4 is divisible by 14. For example, 28 is a multiple of 4 and divisible by 14, but 32 is a multiple of 4 and not divisible by 14. Hence, Statement (1) alone is not sufficient.

Statement (2): $x/6$ is a positive integer when x is a multiple of 6. Now, not every multiple of 6 is divisible by 14. For example, 42 is a multiple of 6 and divisible by 14, but 48 is a multiple of 6 and not divisible by 14. Hence, Statement (2) alone is not sufficient.

With statements (1) and (2) together, we have that x is a multiple of both 4 and 6. Hence, x must be a multiple of the least common multiple of 4 and 6, which is 12. Hence, x is a multiple of 12. Now, not every multiple of 12 is divisible by 14. For example, 84 is a multiple of 12 and divisible by 14, but 24 is a multiple of 12 and not divisible by 14. Hence, even statements (1) and (2) together do not answer the question. The answer is (E).

5.   If $x^2 - y^2 = 15$, is $x + y > x - y$?

   (1) $x - y = 5$

   (2) $x + y = 3$

We are given the expression $x^2 - y^2 = 15$. Applying the Difference of Squares formula $(a + b)(a - b) = a^2 - b^2$ to the left-hand side yields $(x + y)(x - y) = 15$.

From Statement (1) alone, we have $x - y = 5$. Plugging this in the equation $(x + y)(x - y) = 15$ yields $(x + y)(5) = 15$. Dividing both sides by 5 yields $x + y = 3$. Hence, $x + y < x - y$ because $3 < 5$. Hence, Statement (1) alone is sufficient. The answer is "No. $x + y > x - y$ is false."

From Statement (2) alone, we have $x + y = 3$. Plugging this in the equation $(x + y)(x - y) = 15$ yields $3(x - y) = 15$. Dividing both sides by 3 yields $x - y = 5$. Hence, $x + y < x - y$ because $3 < 5$ Hence, Statement (2) alone is sufficient. The answer is "No. $x + y$ is not greater than $x - y$."

The answer is (D).

6.   Is $(x - 2)(x - 3) > 0$?

   (1) $x < 2$

   (2) $x < 3$

From Statement (1) alone, we have the inequality $x < 2$. So, $x - 2$ is negative. So, $x - 3 = x - 2 - 1 =$ a Negative Number $- 1 =$ a Negative Number. So, $(x - 2)(x - 3) =$ a Negative Number $\times$ a Negative Number $=$ a Positive Number. Hence, Statement (1) alone is sufficient.

From Statement (2) alone, we have the inequality $x < 3$.

Now, suppose $x = 2.5$. Then $x - 2 = 2.5 - 2 = 0.5$ and $x - 3$ equals $2.5 - 3 = -0.5$. Hence, $(x - 2)(x - 3) = (0.5)(-0.5) = -0.25$. So, $(x - 2)(x - 3)$ is negative.

Now, suppose $x = 1$. Then $x - 2 = 1 - 2 = -1$, and $x - 3 = 1 - 3 = -2$. Hence, $(x - 2)(x - 3) = (-1)(-2) = 2$. So, $(x - 2)(x - 3)$ is positive.

Hence, we have a double case, and Statement (2) alone is *not* sufficient.

The answer is (A), Statement (1) alone sufficient and Statement (2) alone *not* sufficient.

7.   Is $\dfrac{(a - b) + (c - b)}{d} > 0$?

    (1) $a + c < 2b$

    (2) $d < 0$

The question is about the fraction $\dfrac{(a - b) + (c - b)}{d}$. The numerator of the fraction is $(a - b) + (c - b)$ and the denominator is d.

From Statement (1), we do not have any information about d. So, if $(a - b) + (c - b)$ is negative and d is positive, the fraction is negative; and if $(a - b) + (c - b)$ is negative and d is negative, the fraction is positive. Hence, Statement (1) alone is *not* sufficient.

From Statement (2), we do not have any information about the numerator $(a - b) + (c - b)$. So, if the numerator is negative and the denominator d is negative, the fraction is positive; and if the numerator is positive and the denominator d is negative, the fraction is negative. Hence, we have a double case and Statement (2) alone is *not* sufficient.

Now, the numerator is $(a - b) + (c - b) = a + c - 2b$ and according to Statement (1) alone, we have the expression is negative (< 0). Now, from statement (2) alone, we have the denominator d is negative. So, the fraction Numerator/Denominator = a Negative Number ÷ a Negative Number = a Positive Number. So, the answer is "Yes. $\dfrac{(a - b) + (c - b)}{d} > 0$". Hence, the answer is (C), the statements together are sufficient.

8.   Does the integer m have at least 4 positive prime factors?

    (1) $m/14$ is a positive integer.

    (2) $m/15$ is a positive integer.

From Statement (1) alone, we have that $m/14$ is an integer. Now, suppose $m = 42$. Then $m/14 = 3$, a positive integer.

Now, $m = 42 = 2 \cdot 3 \cdot 7$. The prime factors of m are 2, 3, and 7. Hence, the number of prime factors of m is 3. Here, the answer is "No. m does not have even 4 prime factors."

Now, suppose $m = 210 = 2 \cdot 3 \cdot 5 \cdot 7$. Here, $m/14 = 3 \cdot 5$, a positive integer, and m has 4 prime factors: 2, 3, 5, and 7.

Here, the answer is "Yes. m has exactly 4 prime factors." Hence, we have a double case, and Statement (1) alone is not sufficient.

From Statement (2) alone, we have that $m/15$ is an integer.

Now, suppose $m = 30$. Then $m/15 = 2$, a positive integer. Now, $m = 30 = 2 \cdot 3 \cdot 5$, so the prime factors of m are 2, 3, and 5. Hence, the number of prime factors of m is 3. Here, the answer is "No. m does not have even 4 prime factors."

Now, suppose $m = 2 \cdot 3 \cdot 5 \cdot 7 = 210$. Here, $m/15 = 2 \cdot 7$, a positive integer, and m has 4 prime factors: 2, 3, 5, and 7. Here, the answer is "Yes. m has exactly 4 prime factors." Hence, we have a double case, and Statement (2) alone is not sufficient.

Now, with statements (1) and (2) together, we have that m is divisible by both 14 and 15. Hence, m is a multiple of both 14 and 15. Hence, m must equal the least common multiple of 14 and 15 or its multiple. Let's assume that m is only equal to the LCM. The LCM of 14 ($= 2 \cdot 7$) and 15 ($= 3 \cdot 5$) is $2 \cdot 7 \cdot 3 \cdot 5$ ($= 210$). The LCM itself has 4 prime factors 2, 7, 3, and 5. Hence, its multiples might have more prime factors. Hence, both statements are required to answer that m has at least 4 prime factors. Hence, the statements together answer the question. The answer is (C).

9.   Does the positive integer n have at least 3 positive prime factors?

   (1) $n/10$ is an integer.

   (2) $n/30$ is an integer.

From Statement (1) alone, we have that $n/10$ is an integer. Hence, n is either equal to 10 or a multiple of 10.

Suppose $n = 10$. Then $n/10 = 10/10 = 1$, an integer. The number 10 factors into the primes $2 \cdot 5$. Hence, n has exactly 2 (not at least 3) prime factors. Here, n does not even have 3 prime factors.

Now, suppose $n = 30$. Then $n/10$ equals 3 an integer. Now, n factors into the primes $2 \cdot 3 \cdot 5$ and has exactly 3 prime factors.

Hence, we have a double case, and therefore Statement (1) alone is not sufficient to answer the question.

From Statement (2) alone, we have that $n/30$ is an integer. Hence, n is equal to either 30 or a multiple of 30. The number 30 factors into the primes $2 \cdot 3 \cdot 5$, and multiples of 30 may have even more prime factors. Hence, n has at least 3 prime factors 2, 3, and 5. So, Statement (2) alone is sufficient to answer the question.

The answer is (B).

10.   If x is not equal to 1, then is y equal to zero?

   (1) $y = \dfrac{1}{x-1}$

   (2) $y = \dfrac{x}{6}$

From Statement (1) alone, we have that $y = \dfrac{1}{x-1}$. For any value of x, $\dfrac{1}{x-1}$ cannot equal 0. For example, suppose $\dfrac{1}{x-1} = 0$. Then multiplying the equation by $x-1$ yields a false result $1 = 0$. Hence, the assumption that $y = \dfrac{1}{x-1} = 0$ is false. Hence, Statement (1) alone is sufficient to answer the question. The answer is "No. y is not equal to 0."

From Statement (2) alone, we have that $y = x/6$. Now, suppose $x = 0$. Then $y = x/6 = 0/6 = 0$. But if x is not zero, say $x = 2$, then $y = x/6 = 2/6 \neq 0$. Hence, we have a double case, and therefore Statement (2) alone is not sufficient to answer the question.

The answer is (A).

11.   If n is a positive integer, then is $(n + 1)(n + 3)$ a multiple of 4?

    (1) $(n + 2)(n + 4)$ is odd.

    (2) $(n + 3)(n + 6)$ is even.

If n is odd, then both $n + 1$ and $n + 3$ are even and their product $(n + 1)(n + 3)$ is a multiple of 4 (For example, $6 \times 8 = 48$, a multiple of 4).

If n is even, then both $n + 1$ and $n + 3$ are odd and their product $(n + 1)(n + 3)$ is odd, which is not a multiple of 4.

These are the only two significant cases.

Hence, $(n + 1)(n + 3)$ is a multiple of 4 only when n is odd. Hence, the question can be reduced to "Is n odd?"

Now, from Statement (1) alone, we have that $(n + 2)(n + 4)$ is odd. Hence, we have

$$(n + 2)(n + 4) = \text{Odd}$$
$$n^2 + 6n + 8 = \text{Odd}$$
$$n^2 + 2(3n + 4) = \text{Odd}$$
$$n^2 + \text{Even Number} = \text{Odd}$$
$$n^2 = \text{An Odd Number} - \text{An Even Number} = \text{An Odd Number}$$
$$n = \text{Square Root of an Odd Number} = \text{Odd Number}$$

Hence, Statement (1) alone is sufficient to answer the question: "Is n odd?" The answer is "Yes."

From Statement (2) alone, we have that $(n + 3)(n + 6)$ is even.

Now, suppose n is even. Then $n + 3$ must be odd and $n + 6$ must be even and the product $(n + 3)(n + 6)$ must be even. Now, suppose n is odd. Then $n + 3$ must be even and $n + 6$ must be odd and the product $(n + 3)(n + 6)$ is even, again.

Hence, $(n + 3)(n + 6)$ is even, whether n is odd or even. Hence, Statement (2) alone is *not* sufficient to answer the question.

The answer is (A).

12.   If $m = k \cdot p$, where k and m are different positive integers, then does m have more than 5 prime factors?

   (1) k has 5 different prime factors.

   (2) p has 5 different prime factors.

Certainly, both k and p may have five different prime factors, but there is a possibility that the prime factors may be the same for the two or that k and p may have at least one different factor.

In the first case, m, which equals $k \cdot p$, will have exactly 5 different prime factors.

In the second case, m, which equals $k \cdot p$, may have more than 5 prime factors.

Hence, we have a double case, and statements (1) and (2) together do not answer the question.

The answer is (E).

For example, $k = 2 \cdot 2 \cdot 3 \cdot 5 \cdot 7 \cdot 11$ and $p = 2 \cdot 3 \cdot 5 \cdot 7 \cdot 11$. Hence,

$$m = k \cdot p = (2 \cdot 2 \cdot 3 \cdot 5 \cdot 7 \cdot 11) \cdot (2 \cdot 3 \cdot 5 \cdot 7 \cdot 11)$$

Here, the prime factors of m are the five numbers: 2, 3, 5, 7, and 11.

Now, take another example, $k = 2 \cdot 2 \cdot 3 \cdot 5 \cdot 7 \cdot 11$ and $p = 2 \cdot 3 \cdot 5 \cdot 7 \cdot 13$. Hence,

$$m = k \cdot p = (2 \cdot 2 \cdot 3 \cdot 5 \cdot 7 \cdot 11) \cdot (2 \cdot 3 \cdot 5 \cdot 7 \cdot 13)$$

Here, the prime factors of m are the six numbers: 2, 3, 5, 7, 11, and 13. Hence, we have a double case.

13.   Is $\dfrac{50 + 5n}{n^2}$ an integer?

   (1) $n/5$ is a positive integer.

   (2) $n/10$ is a positive integer.

From Statement (2) alone, we have that $n/10$ is a positive integer. Hence, n must be a multiple of 10.

Suppose $n = 10$, a multiple of 10. Then the expression $\dfrac{50 + 5n}{n^2}$ equals $\dfrac{50 + 5 \times 10}{10^2} = \dfrac{50 + 50}{100} = \dfrac{100}{100} = 1$, an integer.

Now, suppose $n = 20$, a multiple of 10. Then the expression $\dfrac{50 + 5n}{n^2}$ equals $\dfrac{50 + 5 \times 20}{20^2} = \dfrac{50 + 100}{400} = \dfrac{150}{400}$, not an integer.

This is a double case, and therefore Statement (2) alone is not sufficient.

Now, if n is a multiple of 10, it is a multiple of 5. Hence, the same two case studies in the above explanation ($n = 10$ and $n = 20$) also indicate that Statement (1) alone is *not* sufficient. Additionally, the same two cases also indicate that statements (1) and (2) together are *not* sufficient.

Hence, the answer is (E).

Algebraic Expressions

A mathematical expression that contains a variable is called an algebraic expression. Some examples of algebraic expressions are x^2, $3x - 2y$, $2z(y^3 - \frac{1}{z^2})$. Two algebraic expressions are called like terms if both the variable parts and the exponents are identical. That is, the only parts of the expressions that can differ are the coefficients. For example, $5y^3$ and $\frac{3}{2}y^3$ are like terms, as are $x + y^2$ and $-7(x + y^2)$. However, x^3 and y^3 are not like terms, nor are $x - y$ and $2 - y$.

ADDING & SUBTRACTING ALGEBRAIC EXPRESSIONS

Only like terms may be added or subtracted. To add or subtract like terms, merely add or subtract their coefficients:

$$x^2 + 3x^2 = (1 + 3)x^2 = 4x^2$$

$$2\sqrt{x} - 5\sqrt{x} = (2 - 5)\sqrt{x} = -3\sqrt{x}$$

$$.5\left(x + \frac{1}{y}\right)^2 + .2\left(x + \frac{1}{y}\right)^2 = (.5 + .2)\left(x + \frac{1}{y}\right)^2 = .7\left(x + \frac{1}{y}\right)^2$$

$$\left(3x^3 + 7x^2 + 2x + 4\right) + \left(2x^2 - 2x - 6\right) = 3x^3 + (7 + 2)x^2 + (2 - 2)x + (4 - 6) = 3x^3 + 9x^2 - 2$$

You may add or multiply algebraic expressions in any order. This is called the commutative property:

$$\boxed{x + y = y + x}$$

$$\boxed{xy = yx}$$

For example, $-2x + 5x = 5x + (-2x) = (5 - 2)x = 3x$ and $(x - y)(-3) = (-3)(x - y) = (-3)x - (-3)y = -3x + 3y$.

Caution: the commutative property does not apply to division or subtraction: $2 = 6 \div 3 \neq 3 \div 6 = \frac{1}{2}$ and $-1 = 2 - 3 \neq 3 - 2 = 1$.

When adding or multiplying algebraic expressions, you may regroup the terms. This is called the associative property:

$$\boxed{x + (y + z) = (x + y) + z}$$

$$\boxed{x(yz) = (xy)z}$$

Notice in these formulas that the variables have not been moved, only the way they are grouped has changed: on the left side of the formulas the last two variables are grouped together, and on the right side of the formulas the first two variables are grouped together.

For example, $(x - 2x) + 5x = (x + [-2x]) + 5x = x + (-2x + 5x) = x + 3x = 4x$

and

$2(12x) = (2 \cdot 12)x = 24x$

The associative property doesn't apply to division or subtraction: $4 = 8 \div 2 = 8 \div (4 \div 2) \neq (8 \div 4) \div 2 = 2 \div 2 = 1$

and

$-6 = -3 - 3 = (-1 - 2) - 3 \neq -1 - (2 - 3) = -1 - (-1) = -1 + 1 = 0.$

Notice in the first example that we changed the subtraction into negative addition: $(x - 2x) = (x + [-2x])$. This allowed us to apply the associative property over addition.

PARENTHESES

When simplifying expressions with nested parentheses, work from the inner most parentheses out:

$$5x + (y - (2x - 3x)) = 5x + (y - (-x)) = 5x + (y + x) = 6x + y$$

Sometimes when an expression involves several pairs of parentheses, one or more pairs are written as brackets. This makes the expression easier to read:

$$2x(x - [y + 2(x - y)]) =$$
$$2x(x - [y + 2x - 2y]) =$$
$$2x(x - [2x - y]) =$$
$$2x(x - 2x + y) =$$
$$2x(-x + y) =$$
$$-2x^2 + 2xy$$

ORDER OF OPERATIONS: (PEMDAS)

When simplifying algebraic expressions, perform operations within parentheses first and then exponents and then multiplication and then division and then addition and lastly subtraction. This can be remembered by the mnemonic:

PEMDAS

Please **E**xcuse **M**y **D**ear **A**unt **S**ally

This mnemonic isn't quite precise enough. Multiplication and division are actually tied in order of operation, as is the pair addition and subtraction. When multiplication and division, or addition and subtraction, appear at the same level in an expression, perform the operations from left to right. For example, $6 \div 2 \times 4 = (6 \div 2) \times 4 = 3 \times 4 = 12$. To emphasize this left-to-right order, we can use parentheses in the mnemonic: **PE(MD)(AS)**.

Example 1: $2 - \left(5 - 3^3\left[4 \div 2 + 1\right]\right) =$

(A) –21   (B) 32   (C) 45   (D) 60   (E) 78

$2 - \left(5 - 3^3\left[4 \div 2 + 1\right]\right) =$

$2 - \left(5 - 3^3\left[2 + 1\right]\right) =$ By performing the division within the innermost parentheses

$2 - \left(5 - 3^3\left[3\right]\right) =$ By performing the addition within the innermost parentheses

$2 - (5 - 27[3]) =$ By performing the exponentiation

$2 - (5 - 81) =$ By performing the multiplication within the parentheses

$2 - (-76) =$ By performing the subtraction within the parentheses

$2 + 76 =$ By multiplying the two negatives

78

The answer is (E).

FOIL MULTIPLICATION

You may recall from algebra that when multiplying two expressions you use the FOIL method: **F**irst, **O**uter, **I**nner, **L**ast:

$$(x + y)(x + y) = xx + xy + xy + yy$$

Simplifying the right side yields $(x + y)(x + y) = x^2 + 2xy + y^2$. For the product $(x - y)(x - y)$, we get $(x - y)(x - y) = x^2 - 2xy + y^2$. These types of products occur often, so it is worthwhile to memorize the formulas. Nevertheless, you should still learn the FOIL method of multiplying because the formulas do not apply in all cases.

Examples (FOIL):

$$\left(2 - y\right)\left(x - y^2\right) = 2x - 2y^2 - xy + yy^2 = 2x - 2y^2 - xy + y^3$$

$$\left(\frac{1}{x} - y\right)\left(x - \frac{1}{y}\right) = \frac{1}{x}x - \frac{1}{x}\frac{1}{y} - xy + y\frac{1}{y} = 1 - \frac{1}{xy} - xy + 1 = 2 - \frac{1}{xy} - xy$$

$$\left(\frac{1}{2} - y\right)^2 = \left(\frac{1}{2} - y\right)\left(\frac{1}{2} - y\right) = \left(\frac{1}{2}\right)^2 - 2\left(\frac{1}{2}\right)y + y^2 = \frac{1}{4} - y + y^2$$

DIVISION OF ALGEBRAIC EXPRESSIONS

When dividing algebraic expressions, the following formula is useful:

$$\frac{x+y}{z} = \frac{x}{z} + \frac{y}{z}$$

This formula generalizes to any number of terms.

Examples:

$$\frac{x^2 + y}{x} = \frac{x^2}{x} + \frac{y}{x} = x^{2-1} + \frac{y}{x} = x + \frac{y}{x}$$

$$\frac{x^2 + 2y - x^3}{x^2} = \frac{x^2}{x^2} + \frac{2y}{x^2} - \frac{x^3}{x^2} = x^{2-2} + \frac{2y}{x^2} - x^{3-2} = x^0 + \frac{2y}{x^2} - x = 1 + \frac{2y}{x^2} - x$$

When there is more than a single variable in the denomination, we usually factor the expression and then cancel, instead of using the above formula.

Example 2: $\dfrac{x^2 - 2x + 1}{x - 1} =$

        (A) $x + 1$ (B) $-x - 1$ (C) $-x + 1$ (D) $x - 1$ (E) $x - 2$

$\dfrac{x^2 - 2x + 1}{x - 1} = \dfrac{(x-1)(x-1)}{x-1} = x - 1$. The answer is (D).

Problem Set M: Algebraic Expressions

1. x is how many times y if $y \neq 0$?

    (1) $\dfrac{x}{y} + \dfrac{y}{x - 2y} = 0$

    (2) $x = \dfrac{2y}{x + y}$

2. Is $p + q = 0$?

    (1) $p = \dfrac{1}{1 + q}$

    (2) $2q = \dfrac{1}{1 - p}$

3. Is $a + b = 0$?

    (1) $a/b > 1$

    (2) $ab > 1$

4. Does the sum $p + q + r + s$ equal 1?

    (1) $(p + q)/(r + s) = 1$

    (2) $p = q$ and $r = s$

5. Is $\dfrac{p + q}{q + s}$ equal to 1?

    (1) $\dfrac{p + q}{r + s} = 1$

    (2) $\dfrac{p + s}{r + q} = 1$

6. Is $\dfrac{ps + qr}{pq + rs} = 1$?

    (1) $\dfrac{p + q}{r + s} = 1$

    (2) $\dfrac{p + s}{r + q} = 1$

7. Is $2y = 20 - p$?

    (1) $x = y + p$

    (2) $x + y = 10$

8.   What is the value of $x + y$?

    (1) $a = 3x$ and $b = 4y$

    (2) $d = x + y/2$

9.   Is $x = 1$, $y = 2$, and $z = 3$?

    (1) $5x + 2z = 3x + 4y = y + 3z$

    (2) $5x + 2z = 3x + 4y$ and $3x + 4y = y + 3z$

10.   Is $x = 1$, $y = 2$, and $z = 3$?

    (1) $5x + 2z + 3 = 3x + 4y = y + 2z + 3$

    (2) $5x + z + 3 = 3x + 4y$ and $3x + 4y = y + 2z + 3$

11.   What is 50% of x plus 25% of y ?

    (1)   25% of x plus 50% of y equals 20.

    (2) x% of 25 plus y% of 50 equals 20.

12.   Is $2m - 3n$ equal to 0 ?

    (1) $2|m| - 3|n| = 0$

    (2) m/n is positive.

Answers and Solutions to Problem Set M: Algebraic Expressions

1. x is how many times y if $y \neq 0$?

   (1) $\dfrac{x}{y} + \dfrac{y}{x - 2y} = 0$

   (2) $x = \dfrac{2y}{x + y}$

Effectively, the question is "What is x/y?" (also, since y is not zero the transformation is valid). Assign a new variable t to the expression x/y. So, the question is "What is t?" Often, in this book, we do this to reduce a problem in two variable, here x and y, to just one variable, t, if possible. If it is not possible, then t clearly depends on x or y or both, which are not given. So, we would have data insufficiency.

Now, with the assignment, we can write x equals t times y, or $x = ty$. Let's use it in the statements.

Statement (1): $\dfrac{x}{y} + \dfrac{y}{x - 2y} = 0$

   $\dfrac{ty}{y} + \dfrac{y}{ty - 2y} = 0$

   $t + \dfrac{y}{(t - 2)y} = 0$

   $t + \dfrac{1}{t - 2} = 0$

(Canceling y is valid because $y \neq 0$.)

Multiplying each side by $t - 2$ yields

$$t^2 - 2t + 1 = 0$$

Multiplying by $t - 2$ is valid since $t - 2$ is not 0. If it were 0, then t would equal 2, which $-\dfrac{1}{t - 2}$ cannot equal.

The equation $t^2 - 2t + 1 = 0$ is quadratic (degree 2). So, we must have two different solutions or a single solution that occurs twice (for perfect square trinomial equations).

The above equation is a perfect square trinomial. So,

   $t^2 - 2(1)(t) + 1^2 = 0$

   $(t - 1)^2 = 0$

   $t = 1$

So, $t = 1$ is the only solution. The statement is sufficient.

Statement (2): $x = \dfrac{2y}{x + y}$

   $ty = \dfrac{2y}{ty + y}$

   $ty = \dfrac{2y}{y(t + 1)}$

   $ty = \dfrac{2}{(t + 1)}$

   $t = \dfrac{2}{y(t + 1)}$

Clearly, t depends on y, which we do not know. So, the statement is not sufficient.

The answer is (A), Statement (1) alone is sufficient, and Statement (2) alone is not sufficient.

2.   Is $p + q = 0$?

   (1) $p = \dfrac{1}{1 + q}$

   (2) $2q = \dfrac{1}{1 - p}$

Statement (1): $p = \dfrac{1}{1 + q}$

p equals $\dfrac{1}{1 + q}$. So, $p + q$ equals

$$p + q = \dfrac{1}{1 + q} + q$$

$$= \dfrac{1 + q(1 + q)}{1 + q} = \dfrac{1 + q + q^2}{1 + q}$$

This equals zero when the numerator $1 + q + q^2$ is 0 and the denominator $1 + q$ is not zero. But $1 + q + q^2$ would never be zero because $q + q^2$ would never equal -1. This is explained below.

If q is 0 or positive, q^2 would be zero or positive and both would sum to 0 or positive (positive plus positive). So, $q + q^2$ is not -1.

If q lies in the region $-1 < q < 0$, then q is negative. Multiplying the inequality by q and flipping the direction yields $-q > q^2 > 0$. Adding q to each part yields $q - q > q + q^2 > q$. So, $q + q^2 > q$, while q is greater than -1. So, $q + q^2$ is not equal to -1.

If q lies in the region $q \leq -1$, q is negative and multiplying the inequality by q and flipping direction yields $q^2 \geq -q$. Adding q to both sides yields $q^2 + q \geq 0$. This inequality says $q^2 + q$ is not negative and therefore not equal to -1.

All regions have been studied and in none did $q^2 + q$ equal -1. So, Statement (1) is sufficient.

Statement (2): $2q = \dfrac{1}{1 - p}$

$$2q = \dfrac{1}{1 - p}$$

$$q = \dfrac{1}{2(1 - p)}$$

Hence,

$$p + q = p + \dfrac{1}{2(1 - p)}$$

$$= p + \dfrac{1}{2 - 2p} =$$

$$\dfrac{2p - 2p^2 + 1}{2 - 2p}$$

This equals 0 when the numerator $-2p^2 + 2p + 1$ equals 0 and the denominator $2 - 2p$ doesn't equal 0. So, the equation under test for trueness is

$$2p - 2p^2 + 1 = 0$$

$$p + \dfrac{1}{2} = p^2$$

When $p = 1$,

$$p^2 = 1 \text{ and } p + \dfrac{1}{2} = 1\dfrac{1}{2}$$

Here, $p + \dfrac{1}{2}$ is greater than p^2 (Here, $p + \dfrac{1}{2} \neq p^2$)

When $p = 2$,

$$p^2 = 4 \text{ and } p + \dfrac{1}{2} = 2\dfrac{1}{2}$$

Here, $p + \dfrac{1}{2}$ is less than p^2. (Here, $p + \dfrac{1}{2} \neq p^2$)

So, there must be some point between $p = 1$ and $p = 2$ when $p + \dfrac{1}{2}$ would have equaled p^2 (Here, $p + \dfrac{1}{2} = p^2$). Thus, the statement is *not* sufficient.

The answer is (A).

3.   Is $a + b = 0$?

    (1) $a/b > 1$

    (2) $ab > 1$

Subtracting b from both sides, we get $a + b$ equals 0 only when $a = -b$.

Statement (1): $a/b > 1$

Dividing both sides of the equation $a = -b$ by b yields $a/b = -1$. However, Statement (1) says $a/b > 1$ and therefore prevents the possibility of a/b equaling -1. So, the statement is sufficient.

Statement (2): $ab > 1$

Multiplying both sides of the equation $a = -b$ by b yields $ab = -b^2$, which is zero or negative. However, Statement (2) says $ab > 1$ and therefore prevents the possibility of a equaling $-b$. So, the statement is sufficient.

The answer is (D).

Method II:

Subtracting b from both sides yields $a + b$ equals 0 only when $a = -b$. This means, $a + b$ equals 0 only when a and b are both equal numerically but are on opposite sides of 0 on the number line (are at equal distance to either side of 0 on the number line). Both statements individually prevent a and b from being zero. So, each statement is sufficient. The answer is (D).

4.   Does the sum $p + q + r + s$ equal 1?

    (1) $(p + q)/(r + s) = 1$

    (2) $p = q$ and $r = s$

Substituting $p = q$ and $r = s$ from Statement (2) in Statement (1) yields

$$\frac{q + q}{s + s} = 1$$
$$\frac{2q}{2s} = 1$$
$$q = s$$

Combining this equation with the known equations $p = q$ and $r = s$ yields $p = q = s = r$. Clearly, p, q, r and s are equal, but we do not know what they are equal to. Hence, we cannot evaluate the required expression. Suppose they all equal 1. Then $p + q + r + s = 1 + 1 + 1 + 1 = 4$. Now, suppose all equal 2, then $p + q + r + s = 2 + 2 + 2 + 2 = 8$. The statements together are *not* sufficient. The answer is (E).

5.   Is $\dfrac{p+q}{q+s}$ equal to 1?

   (1) $\dfrac{p+q}{r+s} = 1$

   (2) $\dfrac{p+s}{r+q} = 1$

Cross-multiplying the equation in Statement (1) yields

$$p + q = r + s \qquad \ldots(A)$$

Cross-multiplying the equation in Statement (2) yields

$$p + s = r + q \qquad \ldots(B)$$

Adding equations (A) and (B) yields

$$p + q + p + s = r + s + r + q$$
$$2p + q + s = 2r + s + q$$
$$2p = 2r$$
$$p = r$$

Subtracting equation (A) from equation (B) yields

$$p + q - (p + s) = r + s - (r + q)$$
$$p + q - p - s = r + s - r - q$$
$$q - s = s - q$$
$$2q = 2s$$
$$q = s$$

We have extracted all the information from both statements. Now,

$$\frac{p+r}{q+s} = \frac{p+p}{q+q} \qquad \text{(since } p = r \text{ and } q = s\text{)}$$

$$\frac{2p}{2q} =$$

$$\frac{p}{q}$$

Since we do not know the ratio $\dfrac{p}{q}$, we cannot evaluate the ratio $\dfrac{p+r}{q+s}$. Hence, the statements together are *not* sufficient and the answer is (E).

Method II:

Suppose $p = r = 1$ and $q = s = 2$.

Then Statement (1) $\dfrac{p+q}{r+s} = \dfrac{1+2}{1+2} = \dfrac{3}{3} = 1$ is satisfied and Statement (2) $\dfrac{p+s}{r+q} = \dfrac{1+2}{1+2} = \dfrac{3}{3} = 1$ is satisfied.

But $\dfrac{p+q}{r+s} = \dfrac{1+1}{2+2} = \dfrac{2}{4} = \dfrac{1}{2} \neq 1$. But in case, $p = r = q = s$, then $\dfrac{p+r}{q+s} = \dfrac{p+p}{p+p} = \dfrac{2p}{2p} = 1$.

Thus, we have a double case and therefore the statement alone is *not* sufficient.

6.   Is $\dfrac{ps+qr}{pq+rs} = 1$?

   (1) $\dfrac{p+q}{r+s} = 1$

   (2) $\dfrac{p+s}{r+q} = 1$

Cross-multiplying the equation in Statement (1) yields

   $p + q = r + s$ …(A)

Cross-multiplying the equation in Statement (2) yields

   $p + s = r + q$ …(B)

Adding equations (A) and (B) yields

   $p + q + p + s = r + s + r + q$
   $2p + q + s = 2r + s + q$
   $2p = 2r$
   $p = r$

Subtracting equation (A) from equation (B) yields

   $p + q - (p + s) = r + s - (r + q)$
   $p + q - p - s = r + s - r - q$
   $q - s = s - q$
   $2q = 2s$
   $q = s$

Thus, we have sufficiently used both statements.

$\dfrac{ps+qr}{pq+rs} = \dfrac{pq+qr}{pq+rq}$ [Since $s = q$] $\dfrac{pq+qp}{pq+qp}$ [Since $r = p$] $= \dfrac{2pq}{2pq} = 1$.

Hence, the statements together answer the question, and the answer is (C).

7.   Is $2y = 20 - p$?

(1) $x = y + p$

(2) $x + y = 10$

Adding p to both sides of the question "$2y = 20 - p$?" yields "Is $2y + p = 20$?" Let the expression to be checked "$2y + p$" be t. Then $p = t - 2y$.

Statement (1): $x = y + p$ Statement (2): $x + y = 10$

We have $x = y + p$. Putting $t - 2y$ for p yields

$$x = y + t - 2y = t - y$$

$$t = x + y$$

Since $x + y$ is unknown, the statement alone is *not* sufficient.

We have $x + y = 10$. Since there is no p in the statement, the statement does not constrain the value of t (which is a function of p as $2y + p$) from being a particular value. Hence, the statement is not sufficient alone.

With the statements together, we have $t = x + y$ [from Statement (1)] $= 10$ [from Statement (2)]. Hence, the statements together answer the question. The answer is (C).

8.   What is the value of $x + y$?

(1) $a = 3x$ and $b = 4y$

(2) $d = x + y/2$

Statement (1): $a = 3x$ and $b = 4y$ Statement (2): $d = x + y/2$

Solving $a = 3x$ for x yields $x = a/3$. And solving $b = 4y$ for y yields $y = b/4$. Hence,

$$x + y = a/3 + b/4$$

Since d is a new variable used in Statement (1) constraining x and y, the statement is new and irrelevant information.

Since we do not know a and b, which are new and have been constraining x and y, the statements are irrelevant and the statement is not sufficient.

Since each statement has irrelevant information, the statements together cannot solve. The answer is (E).

9.   Is $x = 1$, $y = 2$, and $z = 3$?

(1) $5x + 2z = 3x + 4y = y + 3z$

(2) $5x + 2z = 3x + 4y$ and $3x + 4y = y + 3z$

Suppose $x = 1$, $y = 2$, and $z = 3$, which satisfy both statements. Next, suppose $x = 2$, $y = 4$, and $z = 6$, which also satisfy both statements. Both statements reveal the same and therefore together are not sufficient. The answer is (E).

10. Is $x = 1$, $y = 2$, and $z = 3$?

    (1) $5x + 2z + 3 = 3x + 4y = y + 2z + 3$

    (2) $5x + z + 3 = 3x + 4y$ and $3x + 4y = y + 2z + 3$

Statement (1): $5x + 2z + 3 = 3x + 4y = y + 2z + 3$

There are 3 sides in the equation in the statement. So, if you thought side 1 = side 2, side 2 = side 3, and side 1 = side 3 are the three equations in the three variables x, y, and z and therefore thought that the solution might exist for all the three unknowns, rethink.

Actually, the third equation side 3 = side 1 is a derivation from the first two equations [side 1 = side 2 and side 2 = side 3 so side 1 = side 3]. So, the third equation cannot be considered different from the first two equations. So, the statement effectively means the two equations side 1 = side 2 and side 2 = side 3. So, even if the first two equations are different, we have only 2 equations in 3 unknowns and therefore not all three variables x, y, and z can be determine. Hence, the statement is *not* sufficient.

Statement (2): $5x + z + 3 = 3x + 4y = y + 2z + 3$

The statement is the same as the three equations in Statement (1) minus the third equation (which is not different from the first two). So, effectively the statement reduces to side 1 = side 2 and the side 2 = side 3; and just as with Statement (1), the statement is not sufficient.

The statements mean the same and together are not sufficient since they are individually not sufficient. The answer is (E).

11. What is 50% of x plus 25% of y ?

    (1)   25% of x plus 50% of y equals 20.

    (2) x% of 25 plus y% of 50 equals 20.

50% of x plus 25% of y equals $\dfrac{50}{100} \cdot x + \dfrac{25}{100} \cdot y = \dfrac{x}{2} + \dfrac{y}{4}$.

Statement (1): 25% of x plus 50% of y is 20.

So,
$$\frac{25}{100} \cdot x + \frac{50}{100} \cdot y = 20$$
$$\frac{x}{4} + \frac{y}{2} = 20$$

Statement (2): x% of 25 plus y% of 50 is 20.

So,
$$\frac{x}{100} \cdot 25 + \frac{y}{100} \cdot 50 = 20$$
$$\frac{x}{4} + \frac{y}{2} = 20$$

So, both statements mean the same thing. So, either statement is sufficient or neither statement is sufficient. Given $\dfrac{x}{4} + \dfrac{y}{2} = 20$, $\dfrac{x}{2} + \dfrac{y}{4}$ cannot be calculated (double case as shown below). So, either statement is not sufficient and therefore neither statement is sufficient. The answer is (E).

If $x = 40$ and $y = 20$, $\dfrac{x}{4} + \dfrac{y}{2} = 20$ (the statements satisfied) and here $\dfrac{x}{2} + \dfrac{y}{4} = 25$.

If $x = 32$ and $y = 24$, $\dfrac{x}{4} + \dfrac{y}{2} = 20$ (the statements satisfied) and here $\dfrac{x}{2} + \dfrac{y}{4} = 28$.

We have a double case.

12.   Is $2m - 3n$ equal to 0 ?

    (1) $2|m| - 3|n| = 0$

    (2) m/n is positive.

Statement (1): $2|m| - 3|n| = 0$

    $2|m| - 3|n| = 0$

    $2|m| = 3|n|$

    $2(\pm m) = 3(\pm n)$

Statement (2): m/n is positive.

The statement is clearly irrelevant.

Four possibilities:

    $2m = 3n$

    $2m = -3n$

    $-2m = 3n$

    $-2m = -3n$

In the first and last cases,

    $2m - 3n = 0$

And in the middle two cases,

    $2m + 3n = 0$

Hence, we have a double case and therefore the statement is not sufficient alone.

Let's recollect the four possibilities:

$$2m = 3n$$
$$2m = -3n$$
$$-2m = 3n$$
$$-2m = -3n$$

In the middle two cases m/n is negative (not positive) as against Statement (2). Hence, eliminate them. In the left out first and the last cases, $2m - 3n$ sure is 0. So, the answer is (C), both statements are required.

Percents

Problems involving percent are common on the GMAT. The word *percent* means "divided by one hundred." When you see the word "percent," or the symbol %, remember it means $\dfrac{1}{100}$. For example,

25 percent

↓   ↓

$$25 \times \frac{1}{100} = \frac{1}{4}$$

To convert a decimal into a percent, move the decimal point two places to the right. For example,

$$0.25 = 25\%$$

$$0.023 = 2.3\%$$

$$1.3 = 130\%$$

Conversely, to convert a percent into a decimal, move the decimal point two places to the left. For example,

$$47\% = .47$$

$$3.4\% = .034$$

$$175\% = 1.75$$

To convert a fraction into a percent, first change it into a decimal (by dividing the denominator [bottom] into the numerator [top]) and then move the decimal point two places to the right. For example,

$$\frac{7}{8} = 0.875 = 87.5\%$$

Conversely, to convert a percent into a fraction, first change it into a decimal and then change the decimal into a fraction. For example,

$$80\% = .80 = \frac{80}{100} = \frac{4}{5}$$

Following are the most common fractional equivalents of percents:

$$33\frac{1}{3}\% = \frac{1}{3} \qquad\qquad 20\% = \frac{1}{5}$$

$$66\frac{1}{3}\% = \frac{2}{3} \qquad\qquad 40\% = \frac{2}{5}$$

$$25\% = \frac{1}{4} \qquad\qquad 60\% = \frac{3}{5}$$

$$50\% = \frac{1}{2} \qquad\qquad 80\% = \frac{4}{5}$$

 Percent problems often require you to translate a sentence into a mathematical equation.

Example 1:   What percent of 25 is 5?

        (A) 10%   (B) 20%   (C) 30%   (D) 35%   (E) 40%

Translate the sentence into a mathematical equation as follows:

What	percent	of	25	is	5
↓	↓	↓	↓	↓	↓
x	$\frac{1}{100}$	·	25	=	5

$$\frac{25}{100}x = 5$$

$$\frac{1}{4}x = 5$$

$$x = 20$$

The answer is (B).

Example 2:   2 is 10% of what number

        (A) 10   (B) 12   (C) 20   (D) 24   (E) 32

Translate the sentence into a mathematical equation as follows:

2	is	10	%	of	what number
↓	↓	↓	↓	↓	↓
2	=	10	$\frac{1}{100}$	·	x

$$2 = \frac{10}{100}x$$

$$2 = \frac{1}{10}x$$

$$20 = x$$

The answer is (C).

Example 3:   What percent of a is $3a$?
   (A) 100%   (B) 150%   (C) 200%   (D) 300%   (E) 350%

Translate the sentence into a mathematical equation as follows:

What	percent	of	a	is	$3a$
↓	↓	↓	↓	↓	↓
x	$\dfrac{1}{100}$	·	a	=	$3a$

$$\frac{x}{100} \cdot a = 3a$$

$$\frac{x}{100} = 3 \quad \text{(by canceling the } a\text{'s)}$$

$$x = 300$$

The answer is (D).

Example 4:   If there are 15 boys and 25 girls in a class, what percent of the class is boys?

   (A)   10%

   (B)   15%

   (C)   18%

   (D)   25%

   (E)   37.5%

The total number of students in the class is $15 + 25 = 40$. Now, translate the main part of the sentence into a mathematical equation:

what	percent	of	the class	is	boys
↓	↓	↓	↓	↓	↓
x	$\dfrac{1}{100}$	·	40	=	15

$$\frac{40}{100}x = 15$$

$$\frac{2}{5}x = 15$$

$$2x = 75$$

$$x = 37.5$$

The answer is (E).

Often you will need to find the percent of increase (or decrease). To find it, calculate the increase (or decrease) and divide it by the original amount:

$$\text{Percent of change: } \frac{Amount\ of\ change}{Original\ amount} \times 100\%$$

Example 5: The population of a town was 12,000 in 1980 and 16,000 in 1990. What was the percent increase in the population of the town during this period?

(A) $33\frac{1}{3}\%$

(B) 50%

(C) 75%

(D) 80%

(E) 120%

The population increased from 12,000 to 16,000. Hence, the change in population was 4,000. Now, translate the main part of the sentence into a mathematical equation:

Percent of change:

$$\frac{Amount\ of\ change}{Original\ amount} \times 100\% =$$

$$\frac{4000}{12000} \times 100\% =$$

$$\frac{1}{3} \times 100\% = \quad \text{(by canceling 4000)}$$

$$33\frac{1}{3}\%$$

The answer is (A).

Problem Set N: Percents

1. By what percent did the company's earnings increase this year in terms of US dollars?

    (1) The company earned 18% more Canadian dollars this year.

    (2) The company earned 100,000 Canadian dollars this year.

2. If each customer purchases exactly one copy of the book, did the book sell at least 500 copies overall on the online book selling portal *XYZ* ?

    (1) The portal *XYZ* found that after selling 5 copies on a particular day, the percentage of customers who ultimately buy the book after viewing it increased from 46% to 47%.

    (2) On a particular day, the portal *XYZ* found that 10 consecutive customers who viewed the item purchase some other book and the percentage dipped from 47% to 46%.

3. How much is 20 percent of a certain number *a* ?

    (1) 20 is 20 percent of the number *a*.

    (2) 80 percent of the number *a* is 80.

4. If *r* and *s* are two positive numbers, what is the value of the ratio *r*/*s* ?

    (1) *r* is 25% greater than *s*.

    (2) *r* is 25 units greater than *s*.

5. What number is 25 percent of *x* ?

    (1) 50 percent of *x* is 50.

    (2) 9/100 of *x* is 9.

6. What is the value of $x - y$?

    (1) *x* is 50% more than *y*.

    (2) *x* is the sum of *y* and 20.

Answers and Solutions to Problem Set N: Percents

1. By what percent did the company's earnings increase this year in terms of US dollars?

    (1) The company earned 18% more Canadian dollars this year.

    (2) The company earned 100,000 Canadian dollars this year.

The statements are entirely in Canadian dollars, while the question setup expects the answer in US dollars. Even with the two statements together, we are not told whether the exchange rate changed this year from last year. Hence, we cannot answer the question. The answer is (E).

2. If each customer purchases exactly one copy of the book, did the book sell at least 500 copies overall on the online book selling portal *XYZ* ?

    (1) The portal *XYZ* found that after selling 5 copies on a particular day, the percentage of customers who ultimately buy the book after viewing it increased from 46% to 47%.

    (2) On a particular day, the portal *XYZ* found that 10 consecutive customers who viewed the item purchase some other book and the percentage dipped from 47% to 46%.

Suppose x is the number of sales so far. Then the question can be reworded as "Is $x \geq 500$?"

Statement (1): **Tip:** If x books account for 46% of the visits, then test whether $x + 5$ books can account for 47% of visits in future after, say, v additional visits.

Now, 46% of the visits converting to x book sales implies the equation $46\%(visits) = x$, or $visits = \dfrac{x}{0.46}$.

On the day, if an additional v visits, which means net $\dfrac{x}{0.46} + v$ visits, converts to 47% of book sales, which is $x + 5$, we have the equation

$$47\%\left(\frac{x}{0.46} + v\right) = x + 5;$$

$$\frac{x}{0.46} + v = \frac{x+5}{47\%} = \frac{x+5}{0.47};$$

$$v = \frac{x+5}{0.47} - \frac{x}{0.46} = \frac{x}{0.47} + \frac{5}{0.47} - \frac{x}{0.46} =$$

$$\frac{x}{0.47} - \frac{x}{0.46} + \frac{5}{0.47} = \frac{0.46x - 0.47x}{0.47} + \frac{5}{0.47} =$$

$$\frac{-0.01x}{0.47} + \frac{5}{0.47} = 10.6 - \frac{x}{47}$$

Since each customer can purchase only one book and the book has sold an additional 5 copies, v is greater than or equal to 5. Hence,

$$10.6 - \frac{x}{47} \geq 5, \text{ or } 10.6 \geq 5 + \frac{x}{47}, \text{ or } 10.6 - 5 \geq \frac{x}{47}, \text{ or } 5.6 \geq \frac{x}{47}, \text{ or } 47 \cdot 5.6 \geq x, \text{ or } 263.2 \geq x$$

This inequality says that the net sales of the book so far hasn't been at least 500. The statement is sufficient.

Statement (2): If x sales converts to 47% of visitors, then $x = (47\%)v$, or $v = x/0.47$. The sales are still x when the visitors increased by 10 (that is, to $v + 10 = x/0.47 + 10$), so the percentage of visitors who bought the book is reduced to 46%. Hence, we have

$$\frac{x}{\dfrac{x}{0.47}+10} = 46\% = 0.46, \text{ or } x = 0.46\left(\frac{x}{0.47}+10\right) = \frac{0.46x}{0.47}+4.6, \text{ or } x - \frac{0.46x}{0.47} = 4.6, \text{ or } x\left(\frac{0.47-0.46}{0.47}\right) = 4.6, \text{ or}$$

$$x\frac{0.01}{0.47} = 4.6, \text{ or } x = 4.6 \cdot \frac{0.47}{0.01} = 460 \cdot 0.47$$

This is less than 500. Hence, Statement (2) is also sufficient.

The answer is (D).

3.   How much is 20 percent of a certain number a ?

   (1)   20 is 20 percent of the number a.

   (2)   80 percent of the number a is 80.

From Statement (1) alone, we have that 20 is 20 percent of a. Hence, we have 20% × a = 20. Hence, Statement (1) alone is sufficient.

Now, from Statement (2) alone, we have that 80 is 80 percent of a. Now, 80 percent of a is 80/100 × a. Equating this to 80 yields 80/100 × a = 80. Solving this equation for a yields a = 100/80 × 80 = 100. Hence, Statement (2) alone is sufficient.

The answer is (D).

4.   If r and s are two positive numbers, what is the value of the ratio r/s ?

   (1) r is 25% greater than s.

   (2) r is 25 units greater than s.

From Statement (1) alone, we have that r is 25% greater than s. Hence, $r = (1 + 25/100)s$. Hence, $r/s = 1 + 25/100 = 1.25$. Hence, Statement (1) alone is sufficient.

From Statement (2) alone, we have that r is 25 units greater than s. Hence, we have the equation $r = s + 25$. Dividing the equation by s yields $r/s = s/s + 25/s = 1 + 25/s$. Since s is unknown, $1 + 25/s$ cannot be calculated. Hence, Statement (2) alone is not sufficient.

The answer is (A).

5.   What number is 25 percent of x ?

   (1)   50 percent of x is 50.

   (2)   9/100 of x is 9.

25 percent of x is $25/100 \cdot x$. We can evaluate this if we have the value of x. Hence, the question effectively is "What is the value of x ?"

From Statement (1) alone, we have that 50 percent of x is 50. Hence, we have the equation $\dfrac{50}{100}x = 50$, or $\dfrac{x}{2} = 50$, or $x = 100$. Hence, Statement (1) alone is sufficient to answer the question.

From Statement (2) alone, we have that 9/100 of x is 9. Hence, we have the equation $\dfrac{9}{100}x = 9$, or $x = \dfrac{100}{9} \times 9 = 100$. Hence, Statement (2) alone is sufficient to answer the question.

Hence, the answer is (D).

6.   What is the value of $x - y$?

   (1) x is 50% more than y.

   (2) x is the sum of y and 20.

From Statement (1) alone, we have that x is 50% more than y. Now, 50% of y is $\dfrac{50}{100}y = \dfrac{y}{2}$. Hence, $x = y + \dfrac{y}{2} = \dfrac{3y}{2}$. Subtracting y from both sides yields $x - y = \dfrac{y}{2}$. Hence, the value of $x - y$ depends on the value of y, which is unknown. Hence, Statement (1) alone is not sufficient.

From Statement (2) alone, we have that x is the sum of y and 20. Hence, we have the equation $x = y + 20$. Subtracting y from both sides yields $x - y = 20$. Hence, Statement (2) alone is sufficient to answer the question.

The answer is (B).

Graphs

Questions involving graphs are more common on the new GMAT. Rarely do these questions involve any significant calculating. Usually, the solution is merely a matter of interpreting the graph.

Problem Set O: Graphs

Chart A:

Distribution of usage of state tax for Education & Health Services for every 1 million dollars.

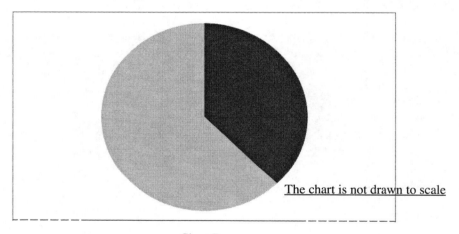

The chart is not drawn to scale

Chart B:

Distribution of usage of central tax for Education & Health Services for every 1 million dollars.

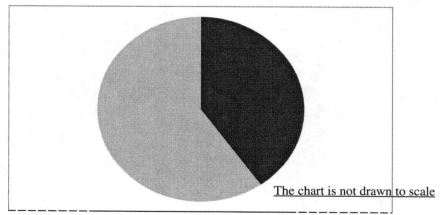

The chart is not drawn to scale

1. How much funding did the Education & Health Services get through state and central funding in the year?

    (1) The thick shaded region in Chart A represents 3,54,300 dollars.

    (2) The thick shaded region in Chart B represents 2,32,482 dollars.

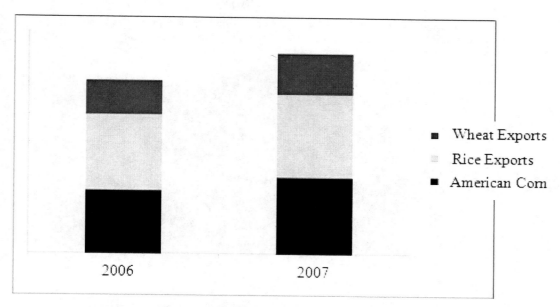

Graph not plotted to scale.

2. The graph shows the exports by the state of Ohio in 2006 and 2007. By how many times <u>in dollars</u> did the American corn export increase over Wheat export from 2006 to 2007?

    (1) The exports of Rice and American Corn together in the two years are $2 million and $3 million, respectively.

    (2) The exports of Wheat and Rice together in the two years are $4 million and $7 million, respectively.

Chain Account usage: Distribution of usage of every 1 million dollars profit from chain market this fiscal year to Research & Development by Robert's shoe making company.

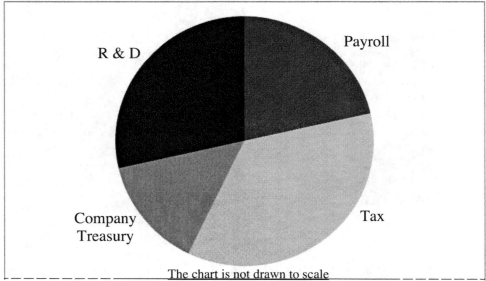

The chart is not drawn to scale

Non-Chain Account usage: Distribution of usage of every 1 million dollars profit from non-chain market this fiscal year to Research & Development by Robert's shoe making company.

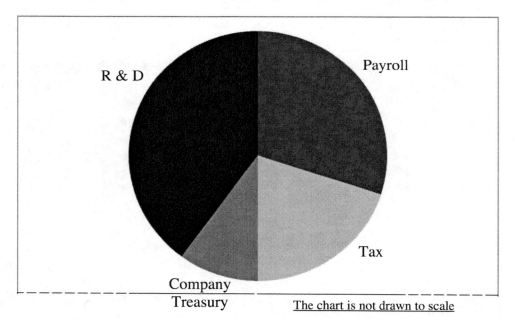

The chart is not drawn to scale

3. An expense reduction consulting company needs to analyze tips to cut cost in a company. To help in doing this, they need the fraction of R & D expenditure that's funded through the non-chain market. The charts above show the distribution of the profits to different categories of expenses of Robert's shoe making company. What's the fraction as calculated by the consulting company, assuming the calculations it did are correct?

    (1)   Dossier has the true information: R & D in the chain account chart represents 4,22,051 dollars.

    (2)   Dossier has the true information: R & D in the non-chain account chart represents 3,33,235 dollars.

Answers and Solutions to Problem Set O: Graphs

Chart A:

Distribution of usage of state tax for Education & Health Services for every 1 million dollars.

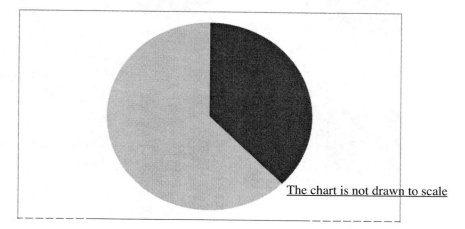

The chart is not drawn to scale

Chart B:

Distribution of usage of central tax for Education & Health Services for every 1 million dollars.

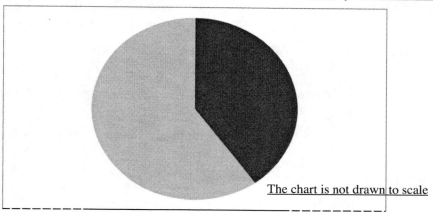

The chart is not drawn to scale

1. How much funding did the Education & Health Services get through state and central funding in the year?

    (1) The thick shaded region in Chart A represents 3,54,300 dollars.

    (2) The thick shaded region in Chart B represents 2,32,482 dollars.

From the distribution in the two charts and the two statements, we have that the 3,54,300 dollars of <u>every</u> 1 million dollars of state tax is the funding from the part of the state tax that Education & Health services get. But we do not know how many millions of dollars is the state tax. Similarly, 2,32,482 dollars of <u>every</u> 1 million dollars of central tax is the funding from the part of the central tax to Educational & Health services. But we do not know how many millions of dollars is the central tax. Hence, we cannot determine the net contribution to the services. The answer is (E).

The net contribution would be 3,54,300/10,00,000 × State tax + 2,32,482/10,00,000 × Central tax.

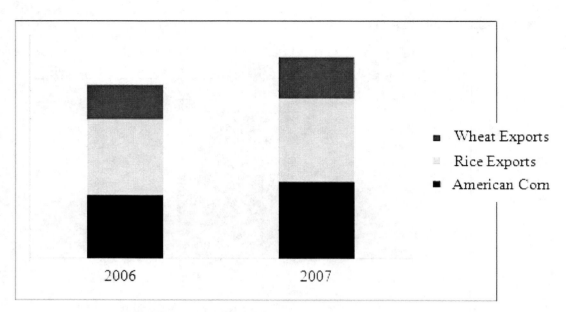

Graph not plotted to scale.

2.   The graph shows the exports by the state of Ohio in 2006 and 2007. By how many times in dollars did the American corn export increase over Wheat export from 2006 to 2007?

(1)   The exports of Rice and American Corn together in the two years are $2 million and $3 million, respectively.

(2)   The exports of Wheat and Rice together in the two years are $4 million and $7 million, respectively.

Suppose Rice exports is r, the American Corn exports is a, and the Wheat exports is w, all in million dollars.

Then in 2006, $r + a = 2$ [from Statement (1)]; and in 2007, $w + r = 4$ [from Statement (2)].

And in 2007, $r + a = 4$ [from statement (1)]; and in 2007, $w + r = 7$ [from Statement (2)].

Subtracting the equation for 2006 $r + a = 2$ from the equation $w + r = 4$ yields $(w + r = 4) - (r + a = 2)$, or $w + r - (r + a) = 4 - 2$, or $w - a = 2$.

Subtracting the equation for 2007 $r + a = 4$ from the equation $w + r = 7$ yields $(w + r = 7) - (r + a = 4)$, or $w + r - (r + a) = 7 - 4$, or $w + r - r - a = 7 - 4$, or $w - a = 3$.

The answer is the ratio $w - a$ in 2007 to $w - a$ in 2006, which equals $3 : 2$. The two statements are required to answer the question. The answer is (C).

Chain Account usage: Distribution of usage of every 1 million dollars profit from chain market this fiscal year to Research & Development by Robert's shoe making company.

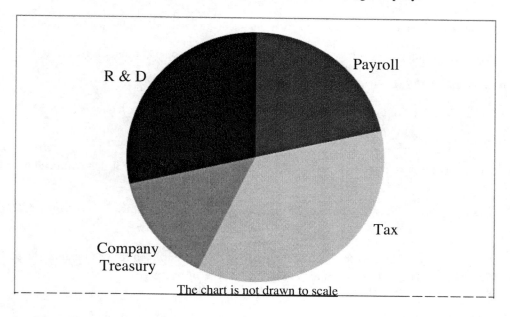

The chart is not drawn to scale

Non-Chain Account usage: Distribution of usage of every 1 million dollars profit from non-chain market this fiscal year to Research & Development by Robert's shoe making company.

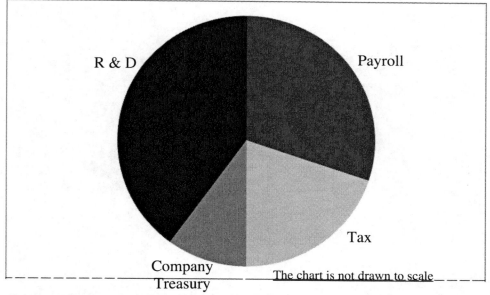

The chart is not drawn to scale

3. An expense reduction consulting company needs to analyze tips to cut cost in a company. To help in doing this, they need the fraction of R & D expenditure that's funded through the non-chain market. The charts above show the distribution of the profits to different categories of expenses of Robert's shoe making company. What's the fraction as calculated by the consulting company, assuming the calculations it did are correct?

    (1) Dossier has the true information: R & D in the chain account chart represents 4,22,051 dollars.

    (2) Dossier has the true information: R & D in the non-chain account chart represents 3,33,235 dollars.

If you thought we are not given the profit routes other than the chain and the non-chain profit routes, you are mistaken. If a chain is a particular profit route, a non-chain represents all other profit routes. So, you actually have all the needed profit routes to analyze.

From the distribution in the two charts and the two statements, we have the following two points:

The 4,22,051 dollars of <u>every</u> 1 million dollars of profit from chain account is funded to R & D.

Let's formulate it as 4,22,051/1 million × Profit from chain in dollars.

The 3,33,235 dollars of <u>every</u> 1 million dollars of profit from non-chain account is funded to R & D.

Let's formulate it as 3,33,235/1 million × Profit from non-chain in dollars.

The total of the two funds is the fund received by R & D. Hence, the part of it that is funded by non-chain equals

[3,33,235/1 million × Profit from non-chain]/[3,33,235/1 million × Profit from non-chain + 4,22,051/1 million × Profit from chain]

To calculate this we need at least the ratio of the profit of the chain to the profit of the non-chain. Since we do not have that, the statements together are *not* sufficient. The answer is (E).

Word Problems

Before we begin solving word problems, we need to be very comfortable with translating words into mathematical symbols. Following is a partial list of words and their mathematical equivalents.

Concept	Symbol	Words	Example	Translation
equality	=	Is	2 plus 2 is 4	$2 + 2 = 4$
		equals	x minus 5 equals 2	$x - 5 = 2$
		is the same as	multiplying x by 2 is the same as dividing x by 7	$2x = x/7$
addition	+	Sum	the sum of y and π is 20	$y + \pi = 20$
		plus	x plus y equals 5	$x + y = 5$
		Add	how many marbles must John add to collection P so that he has 13 marbles	$x + P = 13$
		increase	a number is increased by 10%	$x + 10\%x$
		more	the perimeter of the square is 3 more than the area	$P = 3 + A$
subtraction	–	minus	x minus y	$x - y$
		difference	the difference of x and y is 8	$\lvert x - y \rvert = 8$
		subtracted	x subtracted from y	$y - x$ *
		less than	the circumference is 5 less than the area	$C = A - 5$
Multiplication	× or ·	times	the acceleration is 5 times the velocity	$a = 5v$
		product	the product of two consecutive integers	$x(x + 1)$
		Of	x is 125% of y	$x = 125\%y$
division	÷	quotient	the quotient of x and y is 9	$x \div y = 9$
		divided	if x is divided by y, the result is 4	$x \div y = 4$

---

* Notice that with "minus" and "difference" the terms are subtracted in the same order as they are written, from left to right (x minus $y \longrightarrow x - y$). However, with "subtracted" and "less than," the order of subtraction is reversed (x subtracted from $y \longrightarrow y - x$). Many students translate "subtracted from" in the wrong order.

Although exact steps for solving word problems cannot be given, the following guidelines will help:

(1) First, choose a variable to stand for the least unknown quantity, and then try to write the other unknown quantities in terms of that variable.

> For example, suppose we are given that Sue's age is 5 years less than twice Jane's and the sum of their ages is 16. Then Jane's age would be the least unknown, and we let $x = Jane's\ age$. Expressing Sue's age in terms of x gives $Sue's\ age = 2x - 5$.

(2) Second, write an equation that involves the expressions in Step 1. Most (though not all) word problems pivot on the fact that two quantities in the problem are equal. Deciding which two quantities should be set equal is usually the hardest part in solving a word problem since it can require considerable ingenuity to discover which expressions are equal.

> For the example above, we would get $(2x - 5) + x = 16$.

(3) Third, solve the equation in Step 2 and interpret the result.

> For the example above, we would get by adding the x's: $3x - 5 = 16$
>
> Then adding 5 to both sides gives $3x = 21$
>
> Finally, dividing by 3 gives $x = 7$
>
> Hence, Jane is 7 years old and Sue is $2x - 5 = 2 \cdot 7 - 5 = 9$ years old.

MOTION PROBLEMS

Virtually, all motion problems involve the formula *Distance = Rate × Time*, or

$$D = R \times T$$

Overtake: In this type of problem, one person catches up with or overtakes another person. The key to these problems is that at the moment one person overtakes the other they have traveled the same distance.

Example: Scott starts jogging from point X to point Y. A half-hour later, his friend Garrett who jogs 1 mile per hour slower than twice Scott's rate starts from the same point and follows the same path. If Garrett overtakes Scott in 2 hours, how many miles will Garrett have covered?

(A) $2\frac{1}{5}$ (B) $3\frac{1}{3}$ (C) 4   (D) 6   (E) $6\frac{2}{3}$

Following Guideline 1, we let $r = Scott's\ rate$. Then $2r - 1 = Garrett's\ rate$. Turning to Guideline 2, we look for two quantities that are equal to each other. When Garrett overtakes Scott, they will have traveled the same distance. Now, from the formula $D = R \times T$, Scott's distance is $D = r \times 2\frac{1}{2}$

and Garrett's distance is $D = (2r - 1)2 = 4r - 2$

Setting these expressions equal to each other gives $4r - 2 = r \times 2\frac{1}{2}$

Solving this equation for r gives $r = \frac{4}{3}$

Hence, Garrett will have traveled $D = 4r - 2 = 4\left(\frac{4}{3}\right) - 2 = 3\frac{1}{3}$ miles. The answer is (B).

Opposite Directions: In this type of problem, two people start at the same point and travel in opposite directions. The key to these problems is that the total distance traveled is the sum of the individual distances traveled.

Example: Two people start jogging at the same point and time but in opposite directions. What is the rate of the faster jogger?

(1) The rate of one jogger is 2 mph faster than the other.

(2) After 3 hours, they are 30 miles apart.

Let r be the rate of the slower jogger. Then the rate of the faster jogger is $r + 2$. Since they are jogging for 3 hours, the distance traveled by the slower jogger is $D = rt = 3r$, and the distance traveled by the faster jogger is $3(r + 2)$. Since they are 30 miles apart, adding the distances traveled gives

$$3r + 3(r + 2) = 30$$

$$3r + 3r + 6 = 30$$

$$6r + 6 = 30$$

$$6r = 24$$

$$r = 4$$

Hence, the rate of the faster jogger is $r + 2 = 4 + 2 = 6$. Both statements are needed and therefore the answer is (C).

Round Trip: The key to these problems is that the distance going is the same as the distance returning.

Example: A cyclist travels 20 miles at a speed of 15 miles per hour. If he returns along the same path, at what speed did he return?

(1) The cyclist took 2 hrs for the entire trip.

(2) The average speed for the round trip is 20 miles per hour.

The average speed for the round trip (which spans 20 miles to plus 20 miles back for a total of 40 miles) is 20 miles per hour. So, the time taken is

The Distance/Average Speed = 40 mi/20 mph = 2 hrs

This is precisely what Statement (1) says. So, we can consider Statement (1) equivalent to Statement (2). Now, let's use either statement to determine data sufficiency [in which case the answer is (D)] or data insufficiency [in which case the answer is (E).]

Solving the formula $D = R \times T$ for T yields $T = \dfrac{D}{R}$. For the first half of the trip, this yields $T = \dfrac{20}{15} = \dfrac{4}{3}$ hours. Since the entire trip takes 2 hours, the return trip takes $2 - \dfrac{4}{3}$ hours, or $\dfrac{2}{3}$ hours. Now, the return trip is also 20 miles, so solving the formula $D = R \times T$ for R yields $R = \dfrac{D}{T} = \dfrac{20}{2/3} = 20 \cdot \dfrac{3}{2} = 30$. So, either statement alone is sufficient. The answer is (D).

Compass Headings: In this type of problem, typically two people are traveling in perpendicular directions. The key to these problems is often the Pythagorean Theorem.

Example: At 1 PM, Ship A leaves port heading due west at x miles per hour. Two hours later, Ship B is 100 miles due south of the same port and heading due north at y miles per hour. At 5 PM, how far apart are the ships?

(A) $\sqrt{(4x)^2 + (100 + 2y)^2}$

(B) $x + y$

(C) $\sqrt{x^2 + y^2}$

(D) $\sqrt{(4x)^2 + (2y)^2}$

(E) $\sqrt{(4x)^2 + (100 - 2y)^2}$

Since Ship A is traveling at x miles per hour, its distance traveled at 5 PM is $D = rt = 4x$. The distance traveled by Ship B is $D = rt = 2y$. This can be represented by the following diagram:

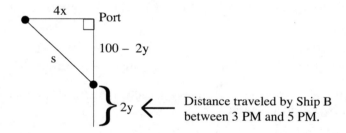

Applying the Pythagorean Theorem yields $s^2 = (4x)^2 + (100 - 2y)^2$. Taking the square root of this equation gives $s = \sqrt{(4x)^2 + (100 - 2y)^2}$. The answer is (E).

Circular Motion: In this type of problem, the key is often the arc length formula $S = R\theta$, where S is the arc length (or distance traveled), R is the radius of the circle, and θ is the angle.

Example: The figure shows the path of a circular racetrack. What is the length of the circular arc AB?

(1) The perimeter of the sector in miles is $\frac{\pi}{6} + 1$.

(2) The combined length of the two arms (straight lines) of the sector is 1.

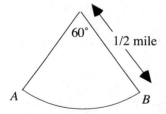

If you thought arc AB equals the perimeter of the sector minus the arms and concluded both statements are required, you are mistaken.

The arms (radii) of the sector are equal in length. The combined length of the two is 1, so the length of each is 1/2.

When calculating distance, degree measure must be converted to radian measure. To convert degree measure to radian measure, multiply by the conversion factor $\frac{\pi}{180}$. Multiplying 60° by $\frac{\pi}{180}$ yields $60 \cdot \frac{\pi}{180} = \frac{\pi}{3}$. Now, the length of arc traveled by the car in moving from point A to point B is S. Plugging this information into the formula $S = R\theta$ yields $S = \frac{1}{2} \cdot \frac{\pi}{3} = \frac{\pi}{6}$. Now, π is a numeric constant, approximately equal to 3.14. Therefore, Statement (2) alone is sufficient.

Statement (1) gives $\frac{\pi}{6} + 1$ for the perimeter of the sector. Suppose the length of each arm is r. Then the length of the two arms is $2r$, and the length of the circular arc is the central angle $\frac{\pi}{3}$ times the arm length r: $\frac{\pi}{3}r$. So, the combined length of the two is $\frac{\pi}{3}r + 2r = r\left(\frac{\pi}{3} + 2\right)$. Statement (1) gives that this equals $\frac{\pi}{6} + 1$.

Therefore, we have $r\left(\frac{\pi}{3} + 2\right) = \frac{\pi}{6} + 1$, or $r = \frac{\frac{\pi}{6} + 1}{\frac{\pi}{3} + 2} = \frac{1}{2}$. The length of the arc AB equals $\frac{\pi}{3}$ times the arm length, which is 1/2, and this equals $\frac{\pi}{6}$. Therefore, the statement is sufficient.

The answer is (D), either statement alone is sufficient.

Example: If a wheel is spinning at 1200 revolutions per minute, how many revolutions will it make in t seconds?

(A) $2t$ (B) $10t$ (C) $20t$ (D) $48t$ (E) $72t$

Since the question asks for the number of revolutions in t seconds, we need to find the number of revolutions per second and multiply that number by t. Since the wheel is spinning at 1200 revolutions per minute and there are 60 seconds in a minute, we get $\frac{1200 \text{ revolutions}}{60 \text{ seconds}} = 20 \text{ rev/sec}$. Hence, in t seconds, the wheel will make $20t$ revolutions. The answer is (C).

WORK PROBLEMS

The formula for work problems is _Work = Rate × Time_, or $W = R \times T$. The amount of work done is usually 1 unit. Hence, the formula becomes $1 = R \times T$. Solving this for R gives $R = \frac{1}{T}$.

Example: How long would it take Bobby working alone to mow the lawn?

(1) Johnny can mow the lawn in 30 minutes.

(2) Johnny and Bobby together can mow the lawn in 20 minutes.

Let $r = 1/t$ be Bobby's rate. Now, the rate at which they work together is merely the sum of their rates:

$$Total\ Rate = Johnny's\ Rate + Bobby's\ Rate$$

$$\frac{1}{20} = \frac{1}{30} + \frac{1}{t}$$
$$\frac{1}{20} - \frac{1}{30} = \frac{1}{t}$$

$$\frac{30-20}{30 \cdot 20} = \frac{1}{t}$$

$$\frac{1}{60} = \frac{1}{t}$$

$$t = 60$$

Hence, working alone, Bobby can do the job in 1 hour. The answer is (C), data is sufficient with the statements together.

Example: A tank is being drained at a constant rate. If it takes 3 hours to drain $\frac{6}{7}$ of its capacity, how much longer will it take to drain the tank completely?

    (A) 1/2 hour   (B) 3/4 hour   (C) 1 hour   (D) 3/2 hours   (E) 2 hours

Since 6/7 of the tank's capacity was drained in 3 hours, the formula $W = R \times T$ becomes $\frac{6}{7} = R \times 3$. Solving for R gives $R = 2/7$. Now, since 6/7 of the work has been completed, 1/7 of the work remains. Plugging this information into the formula $W = R \times T$ gives $\frac{1}{7} = \frac{2}{7} \times T$. Solving for T gives $T = 1/2$. The answer is (A).

MIXTURE PROBLEMS

The key to these problems is that the combined total of the concentrations in the two parts must be the same as the whole mixture.

Example: How many ounces of a solution that is 30 percent salt must be added to a 50-ounce solution that is 10 percent salt so that the resulting solution is 20 percent salt?

    (A) 20   (B) 30   (C) 40   (D) 50   (E) 60

Let x be the ounces of the 30 percent solution. Then $30\%x$ is the amount of salt in that solution. The final solution will be $50 + x$ ounces, and its concentration of salt will be $20\%(50 + x)$. The original amount of salt in the solution is $10\% \cdot 50$. Now, the concentration of salt in the original solution plus the concentration of salt in the added solution must equal the concentration of salt in the resulting solution:

$$10\% \cdot 50 + 30\%x = 20\%(50 + x)$$

Multiply this equation by 100 to clear the percent symbol and then solving for x yields $x = 50$. The answer is (D).

COIN PROBLEMS

The key to these problems is to keep the quantity of coins distinct from the value of the coins. An example will illustrate.

Example: Laura has 20 coins consisting of quarters and dimes. If she has a total of $3.05, how many dimes does she have?

    (A) 3   (B) 7   (C) 10   (D) 13   (E) 16

Let D stand for the number of dimes, and let Q stand for the number of quarters. Since the total number of coins in 20, we get $D + Q = 20$, or $Q = 20 - D$. Now, each dime is worth 10¢, so the value of the dimes is

10*D*. Similarly, the value of the quarters is 25*Q* = 25(20 – *D*). Summarizing this information in a table yields

	Dimes	Quarters	Total
Number	*D*	20 – *D*	20
Value	10*D*	25(20 – *D*)	305

Notice that the total value entry in the table was converted from $3.05 to 305¢. Adding up the value of the dimes and the quarters yields the following equation:

$$10D + 25(20 - D) = 305$$

$$10D + 500 - 25D = 305$$

$$-15D = -195$$

$$D = 13$$

Hence, there are 13 dimes, and the answer is (D).

Example: If Ana and Mathew are children of Mrs. Smith, how many brothers and sisters are there in Mrs. Smith's family?

(1)   Ana has the same number of brothers as sisters.

(2)   Mathew has twice as many sisters as brothers.

From Statement (1) alone, we have that Anna has the same number of brothers as sisters. If *m* is the number of male children Mrs. Smith has (so Anna has this many brothers), then she must have *m* sisters also. Hence, including Anna, Mrs. Smith has *m* + 1 female children. Now, the number of children Mrs. Smith has equals $m + (m + 1) = 2m + 1$. But, we still do not know the value of *m*. Hence, Statement (1) alone is not sufficient.

From Statement (2) alone, we have that Mathew has twice as many sisters as brothers. Hence, if Mathew has, say, *m* – 1 brothers, then he must have 2(*m* – 1) sisters. Hence, the total number of children of Mrs. Smith equals

$$m - 1 \text{ brothers of Mathew} + 1 \text{ (Mathew himself)} + 2(m - 1) \text{ sisters} =$$

$$3m - 2$$

But, since we do not know the value *m*, Statement (2) alone is not sufficient.

Equating the number of children from both statements yields $2m + 1 = 3m - 2$. Solving this equation for *m* yields *m* = 3. Hence, the number of children of Mrs. Smith is $2m + 1 = 2 \cdot 3 + 1 = 7$. Hence, the statements together answer the question.

The answer is (C).

AGE PROBLEMS

Typically, in these problems, we start by letting x be a person's current age and then the person's age a years ago will be $x - a$ and the person's age a years in future will be $x + a$. An example will illustrate.

Example: What is Steve's age?

(1) John is 20 years older than Steve.

(2) In 10 years, Steve's age will be half that of John's.

Steve's age is the most unknown quantity. So, we let x = Steve's age and then $x + 20$ is John's age. Ten years from now, Steve and John's ages will be $x + 10$ and $x + 30$, respectively. Summarizing this information in a table yields

	Age now	**Age in 10 years**
Steve	x	$x + 10$
John	$x + 20$	$x + 30$

Since "in 10 years, Steve's age will be half that of John's," we get

$$\frac{1}{2}(x + 30) = x + 10$$

$$x + 30 = 2(x + 10)$$

$$x + 30 = 2x + 20$$

$$x = 10$$

Hence, Steve is 10 years old, and the answer is (C), the statements together answer the question.

INTEREST PROBLEMS

These problems are based on the formula

$$\text{INTEREST} = \text{AMOUNT} \times \text{TIME} \times \text{RATE}$$

Often, the key to these problems is that the interest earned from one account plus the interest earned from another account equals the total interest earned:

Total Interest = (Interest from first account) + (Interest from second account)

An example will illustrate.

Example: A total of $1200 is deposited in two savings accounts for one year, part at 5% and the remainder at 7%. If $72 was earned in interest, how much was deposited at 5%?

(A) 410
(B) 520
(C) 600
(D) 650
(E) 760

Let x be the amount deposited at 5%. Then $1200 - x$ is the amount deposited at 7%. The interest on these investments is $.05x$ and $.07(1200 - x)$. Since the total interest is $72, we get

$$.05x + .07(1200 - x) = 72$$

$$.05x + 84 - .07x = 72$$

$$-.02x + 84 = 72$$

$$-.02x = -12$$

$$x = 600$$

The answer is (C).

Problem Set P: Word Problems

1. Does the population of rats in a zoo double every day?

    (1) The population increased by 12 on a particular day.

    (2) The population increased by 18 on a particular day.

2. Steve deposited $100 to open a savings account. If there are no other transactions in the account, what amount of money would the account accrue in 6 months after opening the account?

    (1) The interest rate is 4%.

    (2) Interest is compounded quarterly.

3. Waugh jogged to a restaurant at x miles per hour, and jogged back home along the same route at y miles per hour. He took 30 minutes for the whole trip. What is the average speed at which he jogged for the whole trip?

    (1) The restaurant is 2 miles from home.

    (2) $x = 12$ and $y = 6$.

4. The savings from a person's income is the difference between his or her income and expenditure. What is the ratio of Mr. Kelvin's savings in the year 1998 to the year 1999?

    (1) The ratio of his income in the years 1998 to 1999 is 3 : 4.

    (2) The ratio of his expenditure in the years 1998 to 1999 is 5 : 6.

5. What is the average temperature from Monday through Saturday of a week?

    (1) The average temperature from Monday through Wednesday of the week is 36°C.

    (2) The minimum and maximum temperatures between Thursday and Saturday of the week are 25°C and 38°C, respectively.

6. In a factory, there are workers, executives, and clerks. How many employees are there in the factory?

    (1) 41% of the employees are workers, 460 are executives, and the remaining 720 employees are clerks.

    (2) 460 of the employees are executives and account for 23% of the employees in the factory.

7. How many families in the town of Windsor have exactly one car?

    (1) 250 families have at least one car.

    (2) 60 families have at least two cars.

8. The population of the town of Paxton continuously increased in the two decades 1960 through 1969 and 1970 through 1979. Was the percentage increase greater in the first decade than in the second decade?

    (1) The population increase in the first decade was 10,082.

    (2) The population increased by the same amount in both decades.

9. What is the average speed of the car during its entire trip?

    (1) The car traveled at 75 mph for the first half (by time) of the trip and at 40 mph for the second half of the trip.

    (2) The car would have taken 5 hrs to complete the trip if it traveled at 75 mph for the entire trip.

10. The cost of production of a certain instrument increases with the number of units produced. What is the cost of production for 270 units?

    (1) The cost of production for 300 units is $300.

    (2) The cost of production is directly proportional to the number of units produced.

11. A worker is hired for 7 days. Each day, he is paid 11 dollars more than what he is paid for the preceding day of work. How much was he paid in total for the 7 days of work?

    (1) The total amount he was paid in the first 4 days of work equaled the total amount he was paid in the last 3 days.

    (2) The total amount he was paid in the last 3 days of work equaled $132 more than the total amount he was paid in the first 3 days of work.

12. Which one is greater on Richard's farm: the total number of pigs and horses, or the number of chickens?

    (1) The ratio of the number of chickens to the number of pigs to the number of horses on his farm is $33 : 17 : 21$.

    (2) The total number of chickens, pigs, and horses on his farm is 142.

13. Train X leaves Los Angeles at 10:00AM and travels East at a constant speed of x miles per hour. If another Train Y leaves Los Angeles at 11:30AM and travels East along the same tracks at speed y, then at what time will Train Y catch Train X?

    (1) $y = 4x/3$

    (2) $x = 60$ miles per hour

14. If Ms. Ana and Mr. Mathew are children of Mrs. Smith, how many brothers and sisters are there in Mrs. Smith's family?

   (1) Ms. Ana has the same number of brothers and sisters.

   (2) Mr. Mathew has twice as many sisters as brothers.

15. An off-season discount of x percent is being offered at a store for any purchase with list price above $500. No other discounts are offered at the store. John purchased a computer from the store. Did he get the discount offer?

   (1) John paid $459 for the computer.

   (2) $x = 10\%$

16. The profit earned by selling a commodity is generally given by the selling price of the commodity minus the cost of the commodity. Each year, both the price and the cost increase for commodity A. By what percentage will the profit on commodity A grow next year?

   (1) Next year, the cost of the commodity to retailers will increase by 9%.

   (2) Next year, the selling price of the commodity by retailers will increase by 10%.

17. An old man distributed his estate worth x dollars to his three sons Allen, Tommy, and Peter. Who received the smallest part of the estate?

   (1) Allen got 4/5 of what Tommy got and 3/5 of what Peter got.

   (2) Peter got 5/4 of what Tommy got and Tommy got 100 dollars more than what Allen got.

18. A bank compounds interest for its customers annually. How much interest is earned in one year on $300?

   (1) Interest rate per annum is 20%.

   (2) Interest earned in two years on $300 is $132.

19. Brand *A* bike costs twice as much as the Brand *B* bike. The monthly maintenance cost of the Brand B bike is twice the monthly maintenance cost of Brand A. John purchased a Brand A bike, and Peter purchased a Brand B bike. If at any time the total expenditure on a bike is calculated as the purchase cost plus the maintenance cost up to that time, then after how many months would John and Peter have spent equal amounts on their bikes?

   (1) The monthly maintenance cost of the Brand A bike is 5% of the cost of the bike.

   (2) John and Peter purchased their bikes on the same day.

20. A father distributed his total wealth to his two sons. How much wealth did the father have?

   (1) The elder son received 3/5 of the wealth.

   (2) The younger son received $30,000.

21. Chelsea traveled from point A to point B and then from point B to point C. If she took 1 hour to complete the trip, what is the total distance she traveled?

   (1) From A to B, her average speed was 40 mph, and from B to C her average speed was 60 mph.

   (2) Her average speed for the complete trip was 50 mph.

22. The total income of Mr. Teng in the years 2003, 2004, and 2005 was $36,400. What was his income in 2005?

   (1) His income increased by 20% each year.

   (2) His income in 2004 was $2000 more than in 2003.

23. In a country, 65% of male citizen and 68% of female citizen are eligible to vote. What fraction of the citizens voted during the election?

   (1) 68% of male citizens eligible to vote voted.

   (2) 65% of female citizens eligible to vote voted.

24. In a country, 65% of male citizen and 68% of female citizen are eligible to vote. What percentage of the voters voted during the election?

   (1) 65% of eligible male citizens voted.

   (2) 68% of eligible female citizens voted.

25. The price of a car was m dollars. It then depreciated by $x\%$. Later, it appreciated by $y\%$ to n dollars. If there are no other changes in the price, is $m > n$?

   (1) $y = \dfrac{x}{1 - \dfrac{x}{100}}$

   (2) $y = \dfrac{3x}{4}$

26. The costs of equities of type A and type B (in dollars) are two different positive integers. What is the total cost of 2 equities of type A and 3 equities of type B?

    (1)   4 type A equities and 5 type B equities together cost 27 dollars.

    (2)   Cost of a type A equity plus the Cost of a type B equity is 6 dollars.

27. Station B is to the East of Station A. A train starts from Station A at 12 noon, traveling at a constant speed of x miles per hour toward Station B. At 12:30 PM, a train starts from Station B at a constant speed of y miles per hour toward Station A. When will they meet each other?

    (1) $y = 4x/3$

    (2) $x = 60$ miles per hour

28. How much time does Mr. Richards take to reach his office from home?

    (1)   One day, he started 30 minutes late from home and reached his office 50 minutes late, while driving 25% slower than his regular speed.

    (2)   He needs to drive at a constant speed of 25 miles per hour to reach his office just in time if he is 30 minutes late from home.

29. Mr. David usually starts at 9:00AM and reaches his office just in time, driving at his regular speed. Last Wednesday, he started at 9:30AM and drove 25% faster than his regular speed. Did he reach the office in time?

    (1)   Last Monday, he started to his office 20 minutes early, drove 20% slower than his regular speed, and reached his office just in time.

    (2)   Last Tuesday, he started to his office 10 minutes early, and reached the office 10 minutes early driving at his regular speed.

30. Did the seller earn a profit?

    (1)   The selling price of 20 items equals the cost of 15 items.

    (2)   The cost of 10 items is $55 greater than the selling price of 8 items.

Answers and Solutions to Problem Set P: Word Problems

Remember: You need not always do the calculations in a Data Sufficiency problem. Usually, you just need to determine whether you can calculate. Still there are exceptions.

1.   Does the population of rats in a zoo double every day?

   (1)   The population increased by 12 on a particular day.

   (2)   The population increased by 18 on a particular day.

Assume the population doubles every day, and suppose on a particular day the population is n.

Then the population in the successive days, in order, is $2n$, $4n$, $8n$, …. So, the successive increases are multiples of 2, 4, 8, …. We will use this fact in Statement (1).

So, the population increase in the 2nd, 3rd, and 4th days, … is $4n - 2n = 2n$, $8n - 4n = 4n$, $16n - 8n = 8n$, ….

Note that even the population increase each day has been increasing successively with the same trend as the population itself. Also note that the above analysis applies only if the population is doubling every day.

If a statement contradicts the above point, it means that the population doesn't double each day. Then the answer would be "No" and therefore data is sufficient.

No contradiction does not mean the population doubles. It just keeps the option open for further analysis.

Statement (1): The population increased by 12 on a particular day.

A population increase of 12 is only a multiple of 2 and 4, not of 8 or other larger numbers.

So, we have two possibilities: the increase of 12 equals $2n$ or it equals $4n$. If it equals $2n$, n equals $12/2 = 6$; and if it equals $4n$, n equals $12/4 = 3$.

If the population is not doubling each day and if 3 is the population on a given day and the next day it is 15 (did not double), then the increase is still 12.

We have a double case here and therefore the statement alone is *not* sufficient.

Statement (2): The population increased by 18 on a particular day.

A population increase of 18 is possible when $2n = 18$.

If the population is not doubling each day and if 3 is the population on a given day and the next day it is 21 (did not double), then the increase is still 18.

We have a double case here and therefore the statement alone is *not* sufficient.

We already noted that the population is increasing continuously. So, the increase of 12 in Statement (1) must be pertaining to some day before the day the increase was 18, as in Statement (2).

Now, if the population is doubling each day and if the population increase on a particular day is 12, then the next day it must be $2 \times 12 = 24$, and the day after that, it must be $2 \times 24 = 48$, and so on. The mentioned population increase of 18 does not appear in the series. Hence, our assumption that the population is doubling each day must be wrong. So, we can answer the question as "No, the population is not doubling each day." We have data sufficiency with the statements together, and the answer is (C).

2.   Steve deposited $100 to open a savings account. If there are no other transactions in the account, what amount of money would the account accrue in 6 months after opening the account?

(1)   The interest rate is 4%.

(2)   Interest is compounded quarterly.

Compound interest is the concept of adding accumulated interest to the principal so that interest is earned on the new principal from that moment onward. The act of declaring interest to be principal is called compounding (i.e., interest is compounded).

To calculate the interest earned or the balance at any point, apart from the interest earned, we also need the frequency of compounding of the interest. Hence, both statements are required to answer the question. The answer is (C).

3.   Waugh jogged to a restaurant at x miles per hour, and jogged back home along the same route at y miles per hour. He took 30 minutes for the whole trip. What is the average speed at which he jogged for the whole trip?

(1)   The restaurant is 2 miles from home.

(2) $x = 12$ and $y = 6$.

Remember that *Average Speed = Net Distance ÷ Time Taken*. We are given that the time taken for the full trip is 30 minutes. Hence, we need only the distance traveled.

From Statement (1) alone, we have that the restaurant is 2 miles from home. Since Waugh jogs back along the same route, the net distance he traveled is 2 miles + 2 miles = 4 miles. Hence, his average speed is 4 miles ÷ 30 minutes, which can be calculated. Hence, Statement (1) alone is sufficient.

From Statement (2) alone, we have that $x = 12$ and $y = 6$. Let d be the distance to the restaurant. Then the time taken to jog to the restaurant, by the formula *Time = Distance ÷ Speed*, equals $d ÷ x = d/12$; and to return home from restaurant, the time taken equals $d ÷ y = d ÷ 6$. Hence, the total time taken equals $d/12 + d/6$, which is given to be 30 minutes (1/2 hour). Hence, d can be calculated from this formula, and therefore the average speed can be calculated using *Distance ÷ Time* $= \dfrac{2d}{\dfrac{1}{2} \text{ hours}} = 4\,d$. Hence, Statement (2) alone is also sufficient.

The answer is (D).

4.   The savings from a person's income is the difference between his or her income and expenditure. What is the ratio of Mr. Kelvin's savings in the year 1998 to the year 1999?

   (1)   The ratio of his income in the years 1998 to 1999 is 3 : 4.

   (2)   The ratio of his expenditure in the years 1998 to 1999 is 5 : 6.

Savings (in the current context) equals Income − Expenditure.

Statement (1) has information only about income, and Statement (2) has information only about expenditure. Hence, neither statement alone is sufficient to answer the question.

From the statements together, suppose Kelvin's income is $9 in 1998 and $12 in 1999 [the incomes are in accordance with the ratio in Statement (1)]. Also suppose his expenditure is $5 in 1998 and $6 in 1999 [the expenditures are in accordance with the ratio in Statement (2)]. Then the ratio of his savings in the year 1998 to 1999 would be ($9 − $5) : ($12 − $6) = $4 : $6 = 2 : 3.

In another case, suppose Kelvin's income is $12 in 1998 and $16 in 1999 [the incomes are in accordance with the ratio in Statement (1)]. Also suppose his expenditure is $10 in 1998 and $12 in 1999 [the expenditures are in accordance with the ratio in Statement (2)]. Then the ratio of his savings in 1998 to 1999 would be ($12 − $10) : ($16 − $12) = $2 : $4 = 1 : 2. We have a different savings ratio here. Hence, we already have a double case and therefore the two statements together do not determine a unique ratio for savings.

Hence, the answer is (E).

5.   What is the average temperature from Monday through Saturday of a week?

   (1)   The average temperature from Monday through Wednesday of the week is 36°C.

   (2)   The minimum and maximum temperatures between Thursday and Saturday of the week are 25°C and 38°C, respectively.

From Statement (1), we have information about the average temperature only for the period Monday through Wednesday. Since there is no relevant information for the rest of the week, Statement (1) alone is not sufficient.

Statement (2) has information about the minimum and the maximum temperatures for the period Thursday through Saturday. It does not help us evaluate the average temperature for the period.

With the two statements together, we do not have information about average temperatures for the complete week. Hence, the statements together are not sufficient to answer the question.

The answer is (E).

6.   In a factory, there are workers, executives, and clerks. How many employees are there in the factory?

   (1)   41% of the employees are workers, 460 are executives, and the remaining 720 employees are clerks.

   (2)   460 of the employees are executives and account for 23% of the employees in the factory.

Let E represent the total number of employees. Let w represent the number of workers, x the number of executives, and c the number of clerks. Then we have

$$E = w + x + c \qquad (1)$$

From Statement (1) alone, we have that 41% of the employees E are workers (w), 460 are executives (x), and the remaining 720 employees are clerks (c). Hence, we have the equations

$$w = 41/100 \times E \qquad (2)$$

$$x = 460 \qquad (3)$$

$$c = 720 \qquad (4)$$

With equations (1), (2), (3), and (4), we have four different linear equations in four unknowns E, w, x, and c. Hence, a unique solution must be possible and can be determined. Hence, Statement (1) alone is sufficient. The answer to the question is $E = 2000$.

From Statement (2) alone, we have that the number of executives (x) is 460, and this is 23% of the total number of employees (E). Hence, we have

$$23\% \text{ of } E = x = 460$$

$$(23/100)E = 460$$

$$E = 460/23 \times 100 = 2000$$

Hence, Statement (2) alone is sufficient.

Since either statement (1) or (2) is sufficient, the answer is (D).

7.   How many families in the town of Windsor have exactly one car?

   (1)   250 families have at least one car.

   (2)   60 families have at least two cars.

Let A be the set of families having exactly one car. Then the question is how many families are there in set A.

Next, let B be the set of families having exactly two cars, and let C be the set of families having more than two cars.

Then the set of families having at least one car is the collection of the three sets A, B, and C. Since Statement (1) gives only the total number of families in the three sets, the statement is not sufficient.

Next, the set of families having at least two cars is the collection of the two sets *B* and *C*. Since Statement (2) does not have any information about set *A*, Statement (2) alone is not sufficient.

Now, from the statements together we have that

The number of families in all the three sets *A*, *B*, and *C* together = 250 [from Statement (1)]

and

The number of families in the two sets *B* and *C* together = 60 [from Statement (2)]

Since set *A* is the difference between a set containing the three families of *A*, *B*, and *C* and a set of families of *B* and *C* only, The number of families in set *A* =

(The number of families in sets *A*, *B*, and *C* together) – (the number of families in sets *B* and *C*) =

250 – 60 =

190

Hence, both statements are required to answer the question, and the answer is (C).

8.   The population of the town of Paxton continuously increased in the two decades 1960 through 1969 and 1970 through 1979. Was the percentage increase greater in the first decade than in the second decade?

(1)   The population increase in the first decade was 10,082.

(2)   The population increased by the same amount in both decades.

Let *p* be the population of Paxton in 1960.

Then from Statement (1) alone, the population increased by 10,082 in the first decade. So, the new population is $p + 10{,}082$. Hence, the percentage increase in the population is $10{,}082/p \times 100$. Since we do not know the population increase in the second decade, we cannot calculate the percentage increase and therefore Statement (1) alone is not sufficient.

From Statement (2) alone, we have that the population increase was the same (say, *i*) in each decade. Hence, the population should be $p + i$ at the end of the year 1969 and $(p + i) + i = p + 2i$ at the end of the second decade. So, the percentage increase in population in the first decade equals

$$\frac{\text{Increase in population in the first decade}}{\text{The population in 1960}} \times 100 = \frac{i}{p} \times 100$$

Also, the percentage increase in population in the second decade equals

$$\frac{\text{Increase in population in the second decade}}{\text{The population in 1970}} \times 100 = \frac{i}{p+i} \times 100$$

Now, since both p and i are positive, $\dfrac{i}{p}$ is greater than $\dfrac{i}{p+i}$ since the numerator is the same in both fractions and the denominator is smaller and positive. Hence, Statement (2) alone answers the question. The answer to the question is "Yes. Percentage increase was greater in first decade than in second decade."

The answer is (B).

9. What is the average speed of the car during its entire trip?

   (1) The car traveled at 75 mph for the first half (by time) of the trip and at 40 mph for the second half of the trip.

   (2) The car would have taken 5 hrs to complete the trip if it traveled at 75 mph for the entire trip.

Let t be the entire time of the trip.

Then from Statement (1) alone, we have that the car traveled at 75 mph for $t/2$ hours and at 40 mph for the remaining $t/2$ hours. Remember that *Distance = Speed × Time*. Hence, the net distance traveled during the two periods equals $75 \times t/2 + 40 \times t/2$. Now, remember that

$$Average\ Speed =$$

$$Net\ Distance\ /\ Time\ Taken =$$

$$\frac{75 \times t/2 + 40 \times t/2}{t} =$$

$$75 \times 1/2 + 40 \times 1/2$$

Hence, Statement (1) alone is sufficient.

Now, from Statement (2) alone, we have that if the car had constantly traveled at 75 mph, it would have needed 5 hrs to complete the trip. But, we do not know how much time it has actually taken to complete the trip. Hence, we cannot find the average speed. So, Statement (2) alone is not sufficient.

The answer is (A).

10. The cost of production of a certain instrument increases with the number of units produced. What is the cost of production for 270 units?

   (1) The cost of production for 300 units is $300.

   (2) The cost of production is directly proportional to the number of units produced.

From Statement (1) alone, we have that the cost of production for 300 units is $300. Suppose the cost of production (in dollars) is calculated as $100 + 2/3 \times$ quantity. Then the cost of production of 300 units equals 300 dollars, and the cost of production of 270 units equals $100 + 2/3 \times 270 = 100 + 180 = 280$.

Now, suppose it were calculated as $200 + 1/3 \times$ quantity, then the cost of production for 270 units would equal $200 + 1/3 \times 270 = 200 + 90 = 290$ dollars.

Since we do not have a unique value, Statement (1) alone is not sufficient.

From Statement (2) alone, the cost of production is proportional to the number of units produced. Hence, we have the equation *The Cost of Production* = k × *Quantity*, where k is some constant. The *Cost of Production* of 270 units equals k × 270. But we do not know the value of k. So, Statement (2) alone is not sufficient.

Now, from the statements together, we have that 300 units cost 300 dollars. Putting this in the proportionality equation yields 300 = k × 300. Solving the equation for k yields k = 300/300 = 1. Since we now know the value of k, we can evaluate the cost of production of 270 items. Hence, the statements together answer the question. Hence, the answer is (C). The answer is the cost = k × 270 = 1 × 270 = 270 dollars.

11.   A worker is hired for 7 days. Each day, he is paid 11 dollars more than what he is paid for the preceding day of work. How much was he paid in total for the 7 days of work?

   (1)   The total amount he was paid in the first 4 days of work equaled the total amount he was paid in the last 3 days.

   (2)   The total amount he was paid in the last 3 days of work equaled \$132 more than the total amount he was paid in the first 3 days of work.

This problem can be solved with a series. Let the payments for the 7 continuous days be a_1, a_2, a_3, ..., a_7. Since each day's pay was 11 dollars more than the previous day's pay, the rule for the series is $a_{n+1} = a_n + 11$.

If we are able to find all 11 numbers in the sequence, we can add the numbers and answer the question. In order to find all the numbers, we need at least one element in the series.

By the rule, let the payments for each consecutive day be listed as

a_1

$a_2 = a_1 + 11$

$a_3 = a_2 + 11 = (a_1 + 11) + 11 = a_1 + 22$

$a_4 = a_3 + 11 = (a_1 + 22) + 11 = a_1 + 33$

$a_5 = a_4 + 11 = (a_1 + 33) + 11 = a_1 + 44$

$a_6 = a_5 + 11 = (a_1 + 44) + 11 = a_1 + 55$

$a_7 = a_6 + 11 = (a_1 + 55) + 11 = a_1 + 66$

Statement (1):

Statement (2) not available here.

So do not use:

From Statement (1) alone, we have that the net pay for the first 4 days equals the net pay for the last 3 days.

The net pay for the first 4 days is $a_1 + (a_1 + 11) + (a_1 + 22) + (a_1 + 33) = 4a_1 + 11(1 + 2 + 3)$.

The net pay for last (next) 3 days is $(a_1 + 44) + (a_1 + 55) + (a_1 + 66) = 3a_1 + 11(4 + 5 + 6)$.

Equating the two yields

$$4a_1 + 11(1 + 2 + 3) = 3a_1 + 11(4 + 5 + 6)$$

This equation can be solved for a_1. Then all the numbers in the series (a_1 through a_7) can be calculated based on rules we know, and all the results are summed to evaluate his net pay. Hence, Statement (1) alone is sufficient.

Statement (2):

Statement (1) not available here.

So do not use:

Now, from Statement (2) alone, we have that he was paid 330 dollars more for his last 3 days of work than that for his first 3 days.

The net pay for first 3 days is $a_1 + (a_1 + 11) + (a_1 + 22) = 3a_1 + 11(1 + 2)$.

The net pay for the last 3 days is $(a_1 + 44) + (a_1 + 55) + (a_1 + 66) = 3a_1 + 11(4 + 5 + 6)$.

The difference between the two is

$$3a_1 + 11(4 + 5 + 6) - [3a_1 + 11(1 + 2)] =$$

$$3a_1 + 11(4 + 5 + 6) - 3a_1 - 11(1 + 2) =$$

$11(4 + 5 + 6) - 11(1 + 2)$, and this equals 132 dollars.

Hence, Statement (2) is an inference from the information given in the question description and is not new information. So, the statement is not needed and we can straight away treat such statements as not necessary.

The answer is (A).

12. Which one is greater on Richard's farm: the total number of pigs and horses, or the number of chickens?

   (1) The ratio of the number of chickens to the number of pigs to the number of horses on his farm is $33 : 17 : 21$.

   (2) The total number of chickens, pigs, and horses on his farm is 142.

Let the number of chickens, pigs and horses on Richard's farm be c, p, and h. From Statement (1), we have that the ratio of the three is $c : p : h = 33 : 17 : 21$. So, let c equal $33k$, p equal $17k$, and h equal $21k$, where k is some positive integer (such that $c : p : h = 33 : 17 : 21$). Then the total number of pigs and horses is $17k + 21k = 38k$; and since this is greater than $33k$, the number of chickens, the answer to the question is "The total number of pigs and horses is greater than the number of chickens." Hence, Statement (1) alone is sufficient to answer the question.

Next, Statement (2) alone gives the total number of the three species available, which is of no use. Hence, Statement (2) alone is not sufficient.

Hence, the answer is (A).

13.   Train X leaves Los Angeles at 10:00AM and travels East at a constant speed of x miles per hour. If another Train Y leaves Los Angeles at 11:30AM and travels East along the same tracks at speed y, then at what time will Train Y catch Train X ?

(1) $y = 4x/3$

(2) $x = 60$ miles per hour

Train X started at 10:00AM. Let the time it has been traveling be t. Since Train Y started at 11:30AM, it has been traveling for an hour and a half lesser period which equals $t - 1\ 1/2 = t - 3/2$.

Train X travels at speed x miles per hour, and Train Y travels at speed y miles per hour. By the formula *Distance = Speed · Time*, the respective distances they travel before meeting equals xt and $y(t - 3/2)$. Since the trains started from same point and traveled in the same direction, they will have traveled the same distance when they meet. Hence, we have

$$xt = y(t - 3/2)$$

$$xt/y = t - 3/2 \qquad \text{(by dividing both sides by } y\text{)}$$

$$xt/y - t = -3/2$$

$$t(x/y - 1) = -3/2 \qquad \text{(by factoring out the common factor } t\text{)}$$

$$t = -3/2 \div (x/y - 1) \qquad ...\ (1)$$

Statement (1):

Statement (2) not available here.

So do not use:

From Statement (1), we have $x/y = 3/4$. Substituting this in equation (1) yields

$$t = -3/2 \div (3/4 - 1)$$

Because this is a numerical answer, we do not need to calculate any further to determine that Statement (1) is sufficient. But it is illustrative to do so.

$$-3/2 \div (-1/4) =$$

$$(-3)/(-1/2) =$$

6 hours

Hence, Train Y will catch Train X at 4PM (10AM plus 6 hours is 4PM), so Statement (1) alone is sufficient.

Statement (2):

Statement (1) not available here.

So do not use:

From Statement (2), we have $x = 60$. Substituting this in the equation (1) yields

$$t = -3/2 \div (60/y - 1)$$

Since we do not know the value of y, Statement (2) alone is not sufficient.

Hence, the answer is (A), Statement (1) alone is sufficient and Statement (2) alone is not.

14.   If Ms. Ana and Mr. Mathew are children of Mrs. Smith, how many brothers and sisters are there in Mrs. Smith's family?

(1)   Ms. Ana has the same number of brothers and sisters.

(2)   Mr. Mathew has twice as many sisters as brothers.

From Statement (1) alone, we have that Ms. Anna has the same number of brothers as sisters. If m is the number of male children Mrs. Smith has (so Anna has this many brothers), then she must have m sisters also. Hence, including Ms. Anna, Mrs. Smith must have $m + 1$ female children. Now, the number of children Mrs. Smith has equals $m + (m + 1) = 2m + 1$. But, we still do not know the value of m. Hence, Statement (1) alone is not sufficient.

From Statement (2) alone, we have that Mr. Mathew has twice as many sisters as brothers. Hence, if Mathew has, say, $m - 1$ brothers, then he must have $2(m - 1)$ sisters. Hence, the total number of children of Mrs. Smith equals $m - 1$ brothers of Mathew + 1 (Mathew himself) + $2(m - 1)$ sisters = $m + 2(m - 1) = 3m - 2$. Since we do not know the value m, Statement (2) alone is not sufficient.

Equating the number of children from both statements yields $2m + 1 = 3m - 2$. Solving this equation for m yields $m = 3$. Hence, the number of children of Mrs. Smith is $2m + 1 = 2 \cdot 3 + 1 = 7$. Hence, the statements together answer the question.

The answer is (C).

15.   An off-season discount of x percent is being offered at a store for any purchase with list price above $500. No other discounts are offered at the store. John purchased a computer from the store. Did he get the discount offer?

(1)   John paid $459 for the computer.

(2) $x = 10\%$

Suppose John did not get the discount. Then he might have paid exactly the list price amount, which would have been $459 [from Statement (1)]. This is a feasible case where the discount was not received.

Now, suppose John actually got the discount. Let l be the list price of the computer. Then after the 10% discount [from Statement (2)], the cost of the computer would be (List Price)(1 − Discount Percent/100) = $l(1 - 10/100) = 9l/10$ and this equals 459 dollars (from Statement (1)). Hence, we have the equation:

$$9l/10 = 459$$

$$l = 459 \cdot 10/9 = 510$$

Hence, it is certainly possible that the list price of the computer is $510; and since this is greater than $500, he got the discount offer and paid only $459.

We are still not sure if he got the discount offer. So, the question could not be answered. The answer is (E): the statements together could not answer the question.

16.   The profit earned by selling a commodity is generally given by the selling price of the commodity minus the cost of the commodity. Each year, both the price and the cost increase for commodity A. By what percentage will the profit on commodity A grow next year?

   (1)   Next year, the cost of the commodity to retailers will increase by 9%.

   (2)   Next year, the selling price of the commodity by retailers will increase by 10%.

Let c and s be the cost and the selling price of the commodity, respectively. Then the profit on the commodity equals the selling price – the cost = $s - c$.

From statements (1) and (2) together, we have that the cost increases by 9% and the selling price increases by 10% the next year. Hence, the new cost is $c(1 + 9/100) = 1.09c$, and the new selling price is $s(1 + 10/100) = 1.1s$. Hence, the new profit is New Selling Price – New Cost = $1.1s - 1.09c$. Hence, the percentage growth in profit is

$$\frac{\text{New Profit} - \text{Old Profit}}{\text{Old Profit}} \cdot 100 =$$

$$\frac{(1.1s - 1.09c) - (s - c)}{s - c} \cdot 100 =$$

$$\frac{0.1s - 0.09c}{s - c} \cdot 100 =$$

$$\frac{0.1\left(\dfrac{s}{c}\right) - 0.09}{\dfrac{s}{c} - 1} \cdot 100$$

We need at least the ratio of the cost and the selling price of the current year to evaluate the growth in profit. Since we do not have the information, the two statements are not sufficient. The answer is (E).

17.   An old man distributed his estate worth x dollars to his three sons Allen, Tommy, and Peter. Who received the smallest part of the estate?

   (1)   Allen got 4/5 of what Tommy got and 3/5 of what Peter got.

   (2)   Peter got 5/4 of what Tommy got and Tommy got 100 dollars more than what Allen got.

Let A, T, and P be the parts of the estate obtained by Allen, Tommy, and Peter, respectively.

From Statement (1), Allen got 4/5 of what Tommy got. Hence, we have $A = 4T/5$. Also, from Statement (1), Allen got 3/5 of what Peter got. Hence, $A = 3P/5$. Since both 3/5 and 4/5 are less than 1, we have $A < P$ and $A < T$. So, Allen got the smallest part. Hence, Statement (1) is sufficient to answer the question.

From Statement (2), Peter got 5/4 of what Tommy got. Hence, $P = 5T/4$. Since 5/4 is greater than 1, we have $P > T$ (or $T < P$). Also, from Statement (2), Tommy got 100 dollars more than what Allen got. Hence, $T = A + 100$, from which we have $A < T$. Now, combining this inequality with inequality $T < P$ yields $A < T < P$. Hence, Statement (2) alone is also sufficient. Hence, both statements are individually sufficient to answer the question, and the answer is (D).

18. A bank compounds interest for its customers annually. How much interest is earned in one year on $300?

   (1)   Interest rate per annum is 20%.

   (2)   Interest earned in two years on $300 is $132.

The formula for the interest earned in 1 year is *Interest = Principal × Interest Rate*. We have the principal ($300) in the question and the interest rate per annum (20%) in Statement (1). Hence, the two determine the interest earned, and Statement (1) alone is sufficient. The interest earned on the amount in 1 year is 300 × Interest Rate = 300 × 20% = 300 × 20/100 = 60. Hence, Statement (1) alone is sufficient.

From Statement (2) alone, we have that the interest earned in two years on $300 is $132. Hence, the principal after the 2 years equals 300 + 132 = 432 dollars. Since the interest is compounded annually, after 1 year, the principal should grow to *Principal* (1 + *Interest Rate*) = 300(1 + *Interest Rate*); and after 1 more year, it should grow over this to [300(1 + *Interest Rate*)](1 + *Interest Rate*). Equating this to 432 yields

$$300(1 + \textit{Interest Rate})(1 + \textit{Interest Rate}) = 432$$

$$(1 + \textit{Interest Rate})^2 = 432/300$$

$$1 + \textit{Interest Rate} = \sqrt{\frac{432}{300}}$$

$$\textit{Interest Rate} = 100\left(\sqrt{\frac{432}{300}} - 1\right)$$ equals some numeric value. Evaluating this is not necessary.

Hence, Statement (2) alone is sufficient.

The answer is (D).

19. Brand *A* bike costs twice as much as the Brand *B* bike. The monthly maintenance cost of the Brand B bike is twice the monthly maintenance cost of Brand A. John purchased a Brand A bike, and Peter purchased a Brand B bike. If at any time the total expenditure on a bike is calculated as the purchase cost plus the maintenance cost up to that time, then after how many months would John and Peter have spent equal amounts on their bikes?

   (1)   The monthly maintenance cost of the Brand A bike is 5% of the cost of the bike.

   (2)   John and Peter purchased their bikes on the same day.

Suppose the Brand B bike costs *x* dollars. Then the cost of the Brand A bike must be 2*x* dollars (as given).

Now, the total expenditure after time *t* is defined as the (Purchase Cost) + (Maintenance cost till the time *t*).

From Statement (1) alone, we have that the monthly maintenance cost of the Brand A bike is 5% of its purchase cost. 5% of 2*x* = (5/100)2*x* = *x*/10. Hence, monthly maintenance cost is *x*/10.

Since we are given that the monthly maintenance cost of Brand B bike equals two times the monthly maintenance cost of the Brand A bike, the former equals 2(*x*/10) = *x*/5.

Now, we are required to find the time when the total expenditure (includes purchase cost and maintenance cost) on bike A equals the expenditure on bike B. But, we still do not have the time difference between the two purchases. Hence, we cannot evaluate when the two brands would yield equal costs. Hence, Statement (1) alone is not sufficient.

From Statement (2) alone, we have the required time difference, but we do not have the relation between the maintenance costs of the two bikes. Hence, Statement (2) alone is not sufficient.

With the statements together, we have the required costs in terms of x and, say, the total expenditures equal after n months.

Then the total expenditure on bike A equals

$$(\text{Purchase cost}) + (\text{Maintenance cost}) =$$

$$2x + (x/10)n$$

And the total expenditure on the bike B equals

$$(\text{Purchase cost}) + (\text{Maintenance cost}) =$$

$$x + (x/5)n$$

The two are equal when $2x + xn/10 = x + xn/5$. Dividing both sides by x yields $2 + n/10 = 1 + n/5$. Solving the equation for n yields $n = 10$. Hence, the statements together answer the question. The answer is (C).

20.   A father distributed his total wealth to his two sons. How much wealth did the father have?

   (1)   The elder son received 3/5 of the wealth.

   (2)   The younger son received $30,000.

Suppose x and y are the amounts received in dollars by the elder and the younger son, respectively. Then the amount the father had is $x + y$.

From Statement (1), we have "The elder son received 3/5 of the amount." Expressing this as an equation yields $x = (3/5)(x + y)$, or $x = 3x/5 + 3y/5$, or $2x/5 = 3y/5$, or $x = 3y/2$.

From Statement (2), we have that the younger son received $30,000. Expressing this as an equation yields $y = 30,000$.

Hence, the question can now be modified as:

   What is the value of $x + y$?

   (1) $x = 3y/2$

   (2) $y = 30,000$

From Statement (1) alone, we have that $x = 3y/2$. Hence, $x + y = 3y/2 + y = 5y/2$. Since the value of y is unknown, Statement (1) alone is not sufficient.

From Statement (2) alone, we have that $y = 30,000$. Hence, $x + y = x + 30,000$. Since the value of x is unknown, Statement (2) alone is not sufficient.

From the statements together, we have that $x + y = 5y/2$ and $y = 30,000$. Hence, $x + y = 5/2 \times 30,000 = 75,000$. Hence, the statements together are sufficient, and the answer is (C).

21.   Chelsea traveled from point A to point B and then from point B to point C. If she took 1 hour to complete the trip, what is the total distance she traveled?

   (1)   From A to B, her average speed was 40 mph, and from B to C her average speed was 60 mph.

   (2)   Her average speed for the complete trip was 50 mph.

Let t hours be the time taken by Chelsea to travel from A to B. Then since the total time taken by her to travel from A to C is 1 hour, the time taken by Chelsea to travel from B to C should be $1 - t$ in hours.

From Statement (1) alone, we have that from A to B, her average speed was 40 mph and from B to C her average speed was 60 mph. Remember that *Distance = Rate × Time*. Hence, the distance between A and B = 40 mph $\times t$ hours, and distance between B and C = 60 mph $\times (1 - t)$ hours = $40t + 60 - 60t = 60 - 20t$. So, the distance traveled depends on t, which is unknown. Hence, Statement (1) alone is not sufficient.

From Statement (2) alone, we have that her average speed is 50 mph. The formula for the *Average Speed* is *Total Distance Traveled ÷ Time Taken*. Hence, we have the equation 50 mph = *Distance Traveled ÷ 1* hour. Solving this equation yields *Distance Traveled* = 50 miles. Hence, Statement (2) alone is sufficient.

The answer is (B).

22.   The total income of Mr. Teng in the years 2003, 2004, and 2005 was \$36,400. What was his income in 2005?

   (1)   His income increased by 20% each year.

   (2)   His income in 2004 was \$2000 more than in 2003.

Let p be the income of Mr. Teng in the year 2003.

From Statement (1) alone, we have that his income increased by 20% each year. So, the income in the second year, 2004, must be $p(1 + 20/100) = p(1 + 0.2) = 1.2p$. The income in the third year, 2005, must be $1.2p(1 + 20/100) = 1.2p(1 + 0.2) = 1.2p(1.2) = 1.44p$. Hence, the total income in the three years equals $p + 1.2p + 1.44p$. Since the total income is 36,400, we have $p + 1.2p + 1.44p = 36,400$, or $3.64p = 36,400$, or $p = 36,400/3.64 = 10,000$. Hence, the income in the third year equals $1.44p = 1.44 \times 10,000 = 14,400$. Hence, Statement (1) alone is sufficient to answer the question.

From Statement (2) alone, we have that his income in 2004 was \$2000 more than that in 2003. Now, suppose q is the income in 2004. Then we have $q - p = 2000$, or $q = p + 2000$. Also, the income in 2005 is unknown to us and let it be r. Then the total income $p + q + r$ equals 36,400, or $p + q + r = 36,400$. Substituting this in the equation yields $p + (p + 2000) + r = 36,400$, or $2p + 2000 + r = 36,400$. Solving the equation for r yields $r = 36,400 - 2p - 2000 = 34,400 - 2p$. Since the value of r depends on the value of p, which is unknown, the value of r cannot be calculated. Hence, Statement (2) alone is not sufficient.

The answer is (A).

23.   In a country, 65% of male citizen and 68% of female citizen are eligible to vote. What fraction of the citizens voted during the election?

(1)   68% of male citizens eligible to vote voted.

(2)   65% of female citizens eligible to vote voted.

Let the number of male and female citizens in the country be m and f, respectively.

Now, 65% of the male citizens are eligible to vote, and 65% of m is $\dfrac{65m}{100}$.

68% of female citizens are eligible to vote, and 68% of f is $\dfrac{68f}{100}$.

From statements (1) and (2) together, we have

68% of male citizens eligible to vote voted, and 68% of $\dfrac{65m}{100}$ is $\dfrac{68}{100} \cdot \dfrac{65m}{100} = \dfrac{65 \cdot 68m}{10,000}$.

65% of female citizens eligible to vote voted, and 65% of $\dfrac{68f}{100}$ is $\dfrac{65}{100} \cdot \dfrac{68f}{100} = \dfrac{65 \cdot 68f}{10,000}$.

So, out of the total $m + f$ citizens, the total number of voters who voted is

$$\frac{65 \cdot 68m}{10,000} + \frac{65 \cdot 68f}{10,000} = \frac{(65 \cdot 68)(m + f)}{10,000}$$

Hence, the required fraction is

$$\frac{\dfrac{(65 \cdot 68)(m + f)}{10,000}}{m + f} = \frac{65 \cdot 68}{10,000}$$

Hence, the statements together answer the question; and from the lack of the crucial details, the statements individually are not sufficient. Hence, the answer is (C).

24.   In a country, 65% of male citizen and 68% of female citizen are eligible to vote. What percentage of the voters voted during the election?

(1)   65% of eligible male citizens voted.

(2)   68% of eligible female citizens voted.

Let the number of male and female citizens in the country be m and f, respectively.

Now, 65% of male citizens are eligible to vote, and 65% of m is $\dfrac{65m}{100}$.

68% of female citizens are eligible to vote, and 68% of f is $\dfrac{68f}{100}$.

From statements (1) and (2) together, we have

65% of male citizens eligible for voting voted, and 65% of $\dfrac{65m}{100}$ is $\dfrac{65}{100} \cdot \dfrac{65m}{100} = \dfrac{65 \cdot 65m}{10,000}$.

68% of female citizens eligible for voting voted, and 68% of $\dfrac{68f}{100}$ is $\dfrac{68}{100} \cdot \dfrac{68f}{100} = \dfrac{68 \cdot 68f}{10,000}$.

So, out of the total $m + f$, the total number of voters who voted is

$$\dfrac{65 \cdot 65m}{10,000} + \dfrac{68 \cdot 68f}{10,000}$$

Hence, the required fraction is

$$\dfrac{\dfrac{65 \cdot 65m}{10,000} + \dfrac{68 \cdot 68f}{10,000}}{m + f}$$

Dividing the numerator and the denominator by f, we get the fraction

$$\dfrac{\dfrac{65 \cdot 65 \dfrac{m}{f}}{10,000} + \dfrac{68 \cdot 68}{10,000}}{\dfrac{m}{f} + 1}$$

This fraction cannot be reduced further. Hence, the value of the fraction depends on the ratio m to f, which is unknown. Hence, the statements together cannot answer the question. The answer is (E).

25.   The price of a car was m dollars. It then depreciated by $x\%$. Later, it appreciated by $y\%$ to n dollars. If there are no other changes in the price, is $m > n$?

(1) $y = \dfrac{x}{1 - \dfrac{x}{100}}$

(2) $y = \dfrac{3x}{4}$

After a depreciation of $x\%$ on the m dollars, the depreciated price of the car is $m\left(1 - \dfrac{x}{100}\right)$.

After an appreciation of $y\%$ on this price, the appreciated price is $m\left(1 - \dfrac{x}{100}\right)\left(1 + \dfrac{y}{100}\right)$, which equals n (given).

m is the price and is therefore positive. Now, if $m > n$, dividing by m yields $\dfrac{n}{m} < 1$.

Since $n = m\left(1 - \dfrac{x}{100}\right)\left(1 + \dfrac{y}{100}\right)$, $\dfrac{n}{m} = \left(1 - \dfrac{x}{100}\right)\left(1 + \dfrac{y}{100}\right)$. Hence, the question can be changed to

$$\text{“Is } \left(1 - \frac{x}{100}\right)\left(1 + \frac{y}{100}\right) < 1 \text{?”}$$

From Statement (1) alone, we have $y = \dfrac{x}{1 - \dfrac{x}{100}} = \dfrac{100x}{100 - x}$. Hence, $\dfrac{y}{100} = \dfrac{x}{100 - x}$. Also, $1 + \dfrac{y}{100} =$

$$1 + \frac{x}{100 - x} = \frac{(100 - x) + x}{100 - x} = \frac{100}{100 - x}.$$

Hence, $\left(1 - \dfrac{x}{100}\right)\left(1 + \dfrac{y}{100}\right) =$

$$\left(\frac{100 - x}{100}\right)\left(\frac{100}{100 - x}\right) = \qquad \text{by getting a common denominator in both terms}$$

$$1$$

Hence, the answer to the question “Is $\left(1 - \dfrac{x}{100}\right)\left(1 + \dfrac{y}{100}\right) < 1$” is “No. They are equal.”

Hence, Statement (1) alone is sufficient.

Now, from Statement (2) alone, we have $y = 3x/4$. Substituting this in the expression $\left(1 - \dfrac{x}{100}\right)\left(1 + \dfrac{y}{100}\right)$

yields

$$\left(1 - \frac{x}{100}\right)\left(1 + \frac{3x/4}{100}\right) =$$

$$\left(\frac{100 - x}{100}\right)\left(\frac{100 + 3x/4}{100}\right) =$$

$$\frac{(100 - x)(100 + 3x/4)}{10,000}$$

Since the value of this expression depends on the value of x, we cannot determine whether the expression is greater than 1 or not. Hence, Statement (2) alone is insufficient.

The answer is (A).

26.   The costs of equities of type A and type B (in dollars) are two different positive integers. What is the total cost of 2 equities of type A and 3 equities of type B?

   (1)   4 type A equities and 5 type B equities together cost 27 dollars.

   (2)   Cost of a type A equity plus the Cost of a type B equity is 6 dollars.

Let m and n be the costs of each equity of type A and each equity of type B equity, respectively. Since the costs are integers (given), m and n must be positive integers.

Now, the cost of 2 equities of type A and 3 equities of type B is $2m + 3n$. Hence, the question is “What is the value of $2m + 3n$?”

From Statement (1) alone, we have that 4 equities of type A and 5 equities of type B together costs 27 dollars. Hence, we have the equation $4m + 5n = 27$. Since m is a positive integer, $4m$ is positive integer; and since n is a positive integer, $5n$ is a positive integer. Let $p = 4m$ and $q = 5n$. So, p is a multiple of 4 and q is a multiple of 5 and $p + q = 27$. Subtracting q from both sides yields $p = 27 - q$ [(a positive multiple of 4) equals 27 − (a positive multiple of 5)]. Let's look at how many such solutions exist:

If $q = 5$, $p = 27 - 5 = 22$, not a multiple of 4. Reject.

If $q = 10$, $p = 27 - 10 = 17$, not a multiple of 4. Reject.

If $q = 15$, $p = 27 - 15 = 12$, a multiple of 4. Acceptable.

If $q = 20$, $p = 27 - 20 = 7$, not a multiple of 4. Reject.

If $q = 25$, $p = 27 - 25 = 2$, not a multiple of 4. Reject.

If $q \geq 30$, $p \leq 27 - 30 = -3$, not positive. Reject.

Hence, only one solution exists and that is $p = 15$ or $q = 12$ or $n = q/5 = 15/5 = 3$ and $m = 12/4 = 3$. Hence, $2m + 3n = 2 \times 3 + 3 \times 3 = 15$, a unique solution. Hence, Statement (1) alone is sufficient.

Now, from Statement (2) alone, we have that the cost of an equity of type A plus the cost of an equity of type B is 6. Hence, we have $m + n = 6$. But, there are multiple solutions, m and n, of the equation: $(m, n) = (1, 5), (2, 4), (3, 3), (4, 2), (5, 1)$. Not all the cases have the same value for the expression $2m + 3n$ varies. Hence, Statement (2) alone is *not* sufficient.

Hence, the answer is (A).

27. Station B is to the East of Station A. A train starts from Station A at 12 noon, traveling at a constant speed of x miles per hour toward Station B. At 12:30 PM, a train starts from Station B at a constant speed of y miles per hour toward Station A. When will they meet each other?

(1) $y = 4x/3$

(2) $x = 60$ miles per hour

The first train started at 12 noon. Let the time it has been traveling be t. Since the second train started at 12:30 PM, it has been traveling a half-hour less. So, represent its time as $t - 1/2$.

The first train travels at x miles per hour, and the second train travels at y miles per hour. By the formula *Distance = Speed · Time*, the respective distances they travel before meeting equals xt and $y(t - 1/2)$. Since the trains started at different stations and traveled towards each other, they meet when the distances traveled by them sum to the distance between their starting stations (let that distance be d). Then we have

$$xt + y(t - 1/2) = d$$

$$xt + yt - y/2 = d \qquad \text{(by distributing the } y\text{)}$$

$$xt + yt = y/2 + d$$

$$t(x + y) = y/2 + d \qquad \text{(by factoring out the common factor } t\text{)}$$

$$t = (y/2 + d)/(x + y)$$

$$t = (y/2x + d/x)/(1 + y/x) \qquad \text{... (A)}$$

From Statement (1), we can determine the value of y/x; but even with both statements, we cannot determine the value of d and thereby the value of d/x in equation (A). Hence, we cannot determine the value of t. Therefore, the statements together are *not* sufficient, and the answer is (E).

28.   How much time does Mr. Richards take to reach his office from home?

    (1)   One day, he started 30 minutes late from home and reached his office 50 minutes late, while driving 25% slower than his regular speed.

    (2)   He needs to drive at a constant speed of 25 miles per hour to reach his office just in time if he is 30 minutes late from home.

If d miles is the distance to his office from home, v miles per minute his usual speed, and t minutes the time he usually takes in minutes, then, by the formula *Time = Distance ÷ Speed*, the time taken on a regular day is $t = d/v$. Now, the question is "How much is d/v?" or "What is t?"

From Statement (1) alone, we have an instance when he started 30 minutes late and drove 25% slower [i.e., at speed $(1 - 25/100)v = 0.75v$]. Then he reached his office exactly 50 minutes late.

In this case, there are two delays. One is the "30 minute delay in starting from home" and the other one is the delay caused by driving slower than the regular speed, which equals $d/(0.75v) - d/v = 0.25d/0.75v = d/3v$. The total delay is 50 minutes. Hence, summing the delays to 50 minutes yields $d/3v + 30 = 50$; $d/3v = 20$ minutes; $d/v = 60$. Hence, Statement (1) alone is sufficient.

Now, using Statement (2) alone, we have that after a delay of 30 minutes he traveled at a speed of $s = 25$ miles per hour = 25/60 miles per minute to exactly make up (compensate) for the delay. So, the time taken in this instance is $d/s = d/(25/60)$. The time taken is 30 minutes (as given) less than the time taken regularly. Hence, we have the equation $d/(25/60) = t - 30$ minutes or $t = d/(25/60) + 30$. Since we do not know the value of d, the value of t cannot be determined and Statement (2) alone is *not* sufficient.

Hence, the answer is (A).

29.   Mr. David usually starts at 9:00AM and reaches his office just in time, driving at his regular speed. Last Wednesday, he started at 9:30AM and drove 25% faster than his regular speed. Did he reach the office in time?

    (1)   Last Monday, he started to his office 20 minutes early, drove 20% slower than his regular speed, and reached his office just in time.

    (2)   Last Tuesday, he started to his office 10 minutes early, and reached the office 10 minutes early driving at his regular speed.

Let d be the distance to his office from home, and let v be the regular speed. Then the time David takes to travel to his office equals d/v (by the formula *Time = Distance ÷ Speed*).

Now, if he started half an hour late (started at 9:30AM instead of 9:00AM), then he would have driven $d/v - 30$ minutes to reach his office in time. If he drove 25% faster, his speed is $v(1 + 25/100) = 1.25v$. Hence, by the formula *Time = Distance/Speed*, the time taken for the trip is $d/1.25v$.

Hence, to reach his office in time he should have saved at least 30 minutes of the travel time, lest he did not reach it in time. By driving 25% faster, the travel time he saved equals $d/v - d/(1.25v) = d/5v$. Hence, the question is "Is $d/5v < 30$" which if true, says, David did not reach his office in time on Wednesday. Multiplying the inequality in the question by 5 yields "Is $d/v < 150$?".

Now, from Statement (1) alone, we have that on Monday he started to his office 20 minutes late but was just in time (So, he traveled 20 minutes longer) and drove 20% slower than usual.

Hence, the speed on Monday (20% slower) equals $v(1 - 20/100) = 0.8v$. Hence, by the formula *Time = Distance/Speed*, the time taken to reach the office now equals $d/0.8v$. This is greater than the regular time d/v by $d/(0.8v) - d/v = (d/v)(1/0.8 - 1)$. Since we know that he drove 20 minutes longer, we have the equation $(d/v)(1/0.8 - 1) = 20$; $d/v = 20/(1/0.8 - 1) = 20 \cdot 0.8/(1 - 0.8) = 20 \cdot 0.8/0.2 = 80$. Hence, Statement (1) alone answers that "No. d/v is less than 150." So, David did not reach his office in time last Wednesday.

Now, from Statement (2) alone, we have that last Tuesday he started to his office 10 minutes early and reached the office 10 minutes early driving at regular speed. This is an automatic inference since starting 10 minutes early and traveling at regular speed, one would always reach the office 10 minutes early. Hence, this statement alone is not sufficient.

Hence, the answer is (A).

30.   Did the seller earn a profit?

   (1)   The selling price of 20 items equals the cost of 15 items.

   (2)   The cost of 10 items is $55 greater than the selling price of 8 items.

Let c and s be the cost and the selling price, respectively, for the seller on each item.

Statement (1): The selling price of 20 items equals the cost of 15 items.

Statement (2) not available here, so do not use.

From Statement (1) alone, we have that the selling price of 20 items equals the cost of 15 items. Hence, we have $20s = 15c$, or $s = (15/20)c = 3c/4$. Now, profit = selling price – cost = $s - c = 3c/4 - c = -c/4$, a negative value (c is price and therefore is positive. Hence, $-c/4$ is negative). A negative profit here indicates loss. Hence, Statement (1) alone is sufficient to determine that the seller did not earn a profit.

Statement (2): The cost of 10 items is $55 greater than the selling price of 8 items.

Statement (1) not available here, so do not use.

From Statement (2) alone, we have that the cost of 10 items is $55 more than the selling price of 8 items. The cost of 10 items is $10c$, and the selling price of 8 items is $8s$. Hence, we have $10c - 8s = 55$. Subtracting $2s$ from both sides yields

$$10c - 10s = 55 - 2s$$

$$10(c - s) = 55 - 2s$$

$$c - s = (55 - 2s)/10$$

Here, if $55 - 2s$ is positive, $c - s$ is positive and Cost > Selling Price. In this case, the seller did not make a profit. However, if $55 - 2s$ is negative (which occurs when $s < 55/2$), $c - s$ is negative and Cost < Selling Price. In this case, the seller did make a profit. Hence, we have a double case and Statement (2) alone is *not* sufficient.

The answer is (A).

Sequences & Series

A sequence is an ordered list of numbers. The following is a sequence of odd numbers:

$$1, 3, 5, 7, \ldots$$

A term of a sequence is identified by its position in the sequence. In the above sequence, 1 is the first term, 3 is the second term, etc. The ellipsis symbol (. . .) indicates that the sequence continues forever.

Example 1: What is the 1st term in sequence S?

   (1) In sequence S, the 3rd term is 4, and the 2nd term is three times the 1st.

   (2) The 3rd term is four times the 2nd.

We know *"the 3rd term of S is 4,"* and that *"the 3rd term is four times the 2nd."* This is equivalent to saying the 2nd term is 1/4 the 3rd term: $\frac{1}{4} \cdot 4 = 1$. Further, we know *"the 2nd term is three times the 1st."* This is equivalent to saying the 1st term is $\frac{1}{3}$ the 2nd term: $\frac{1}{3} \cdot 1 = \frac{1}{3}$. Hence, the first term of the sequence is fully determined:

$$\frac{1}{3}, 1, 4$$

The answer is (C), the statements together answer the question.

Example 2: How many numbers of this sequence of 342 numbers are odd?

   (1) The sequence starts with $-1, 3, -3, \ldots$

   (2) Except for the first two numbers, every number in the sequence is the product of the two immediately preceding numbers.

Since *"every number in the sequence $-1, 3, -3, \ldots$ is the product of the two immediately preceding numbers,"* the forth term of the sequence is $-9 = 3(-3)$. Calculating like this, the first 6 terms of this sequence are

$$-1, 3, -3, -9, 27, -243, \ldots$$

$$\text{odd, odd, odd} \times \text{odd} = \text{odd, odd} \times \text{odd} = \text{odd}, \ldots$$

Thus, all the numbers in the sequence are odd. There are 342 numbers in the sequence. So, there are 342 odd numbers in the sequence. The answer is (C), the statements together are sufficient.

Arithmetic Progressions

An arithmetic progression is a sequence in which the difference between any two consecutive terms is the same. This is the same as saying: each term exceeds the previous term by a fixed amount. For example, 0, 6, 12, 18, . . . is an arithmetic progression in which the common difference is 6. The sequence 8, 4, 0, –4, . . . is arithmetic with a common difference of –4.

A problem based on a linear rule can be calculated given the minimum number of initial values from anywhere in the sequence.

Example 3: Each number after the first number in the sequence is 4 less than the number immediately preceding it. What is the fourth number in the sequence?

    (1)   The seventh number in the sequence is 31.

    (2)   The first number in the sequence is 55.

Since each number *"in the sequence is 4 less than the number immediately preceding it,"* the sixth term is 31 + 4 = 35; the fifth number in the sequence is 35 + 4 = 39; and the fourth number in the sequence is 39 + 4 = 43. Following is the sequence written out:

$$55, 51, 47, 43, 39, 35, 31, 27, 23, 19, 15, 11, \ldots$$

We have a fixed sequence, and all the additional terms can be written at will. Therefore, the statements together are sufficient. The answer is (C).

Advanced concepts: (Sequence Formulas)

Students with strong backgrounds in mathematics may prefer to solve sequence problems by using formulas. Note, none of the formulas in this section are necessary to answer questions about sequences on the GMAT.

Since each term of an arithmetic progression *"exceeds the previous term by a fixed amount,"* we get the following:

first term $a + 0d$ where a is the first term and d is the common difference

second term $a + 1d$

third term $a + 2d$

fourth term $a + 3d$

. . .   . . .

nth term $a + (n-1)d$ This formula generates the nth term

The sum of the first n terms of an arithmetic sequence is

$$\frac{n}{2}\left[2a + (n-1)d\right]$$

Geometric Progressions

A geometric progression is a sequence in which the ratio of any two consecutive terms is the same. Thus, each term is generated by multiplying the preceding term by a fixed number. For example, $-3, 6, -12, 24, \ldots$ is a geometric progression in which the common ratio is -2. The sequence $32, 16, 8, 4, \ldots$ is geometric with common ratio $1/2$.

Example 4:   What is the sixth term of the sequence $90, -30, 10, -10/3, \ldots$?

(A) $1/3$ (B) 0 (C) $-10/27$ (D) -3 (E) $-100/3$

Since the common ratio between any two consecutive terms is $-\dfrac{1}{3}$, the fifth term is $\dfrac{10}{9} = \left(-\dfrac{1}{3}\right) \cdot \left(-\dfrac{10}{3}\right)$.

Hence, the sixth number in the sequence is $-\dfrac{10}{27} = \left(-\dfrac{1}{3}\right) \cdot \left(\dfrac{10}{9}\right)$. The answer is (C).

Advanced concepts: (Sequence Formulas)

Note, none of the formulas in this section are necessary to answer questions about sequences on the GMAT.

Since each term of a geometric progression *"is generated by multiplying the preceding term by a fixed number,"* we get the following:

first term	a	
second term	ar^1	where r is the common ratio
third term	ar^2	
fourth term	ar^3	
. . .	. . .	
nth term	$a_n = ar^{n-1}$	This formula generates the nth term

The sum of the first n terms of an geometric sequence is

$$\frac{a\left(1 - r^n\right)}{1 - r}$$

SERIES

A series is simply the sum of the terms of a sequence. The following is a series of even numbers formed from the sequence $2, 4, 6, 8, \ldots$:

$$2 + 4 + 6 + 8 + \cdots$$

A term of a series is identified by its position in the series. In the above series, 2 is the first term, 4 is the second term, etc. The ellipsis symbol (. . .) indicates that the series continues forever.

Example 5:   The sum of the squares of the first n positive integers $1^2 + 2^2 + 3^2 + \ldots + n^2$ is $\dfrac{n(n+1)(2n+1)}{6}$.

What is the sum of the squares of the first 9 positive integers?

(A) 90 (B) 125 (C) 200 (D) 285 (E) 682

We are given a formula for the sum of the squares of the first n positive integers. Plugging $n = 9$ into this formula yields

$$\frac{n(n+1)(2n+1)}{6} = \frac{9(9+1)(2\cdot 9+1)}{6} = \frac{9(10)(19)}{6} = 285$$

The answer is (D).

Example 6:   For all integers $x > 1$, $\langle x \rangle = 2x + (2x-1) + (2x-2) + \dots + 2 + 1$. What is the value of $\langle 3 \rangle \cdot \langle 2 \rangle$?

(A) 60   (B) 116   (C) 210   (D) 263   (E) 478

$\langle 3 \rangle = 2(3) + (2\cdot 3 - 1) + (2\cdot 3 - 2) + (2\cdot 3 - 3) + (2\cdot 3 - 4) + (2\cdot 3 - 5) = 6 + 5 + 4 + 3 + 2 + 1 = 21$

$\langle 2 \rangle = 2(2) + (2\cdot 2 - 1) + (2\cdot 2 - 2) + (2\cdot 2 - 3) = 4 + 3 + 2 + 1 = 10$

Hence, $\langle 3 \rangle \cdot \langle 2 \rangle = 21 \cdot 10 = 210$, and the answer is (C).

Problem Set Q: Sequences & Series

Question adequately defined but statements under-defined:

1. Does the Set A contain only odd prime numbers?

    (1)   *A* contains only odd numbers.

    (2)   *A* contains only prime numbers.

Adequately defined question and under-defined statements:

2. Does Set A contain only odd prime numbers?

    (1)   *A* contains odd numbers.

    (2)   *A* contains prime numbers.

Adequately defined question and under-defined statements:

3. Does Set A contain at least one odd prime number?

    (1)   *A* contains odd numbers.

    (2)   *A* contains prime numbers.

Under-defined question and fully defined statements:

4. The first four elements of Series *A* are 0, 1, 1, and 2. Two series are equal when the corresponding elements of the two series exist and are the same. Is Series *B* equal to Series *A*?

    (1)   The first and the second terms of Series *B* are 0 and 1, respectively, and each remaining term equals the sum of the preceding two terms.

    (2)   The first four terms of Series *B* are 0, 1, 1, and 2, respectively.

5. Any term in the series (except for the first and last terms) is the average of the two adjacent terms in the series. What is the 8th term in the series?

    (1)   First term is 2.

    (2)   Third term is 6.

Under-defined question - under-defined statement:

6. What is Set *A*?

    (1)   Set *A* contains only even numbers.

    (2)   Set *A* contains all the even numbers.

Under-defined statements:

7. What is the sum of numbers in the series?

    (1)   All the numbers in the series are 3-digit numbers.

    (2)   All the numbers in the series leave a remainder of 2 when divided by 3.

Answers and Solutions to Problem Set Q: Sequences & Series

Question adequately defined but statements under-defined:

1. Does the Set A contain only odd prime numbers?

    (1) *A* contains only odd numbers.

    (2) *A* contains only prime numbers.

Statement (1) says that *A* contains only odd numbers, which does not mean it contains all the odd numbers.

Statement (2) says that *A* contains only prime numbers, which does not mean it contains all the prime numbers.

Thus, both statements are under-determined in the sense that they do not fully define (list the elements in) *A*.

The question is adequately defined in the sense that it asks us to check whether all the elements (one by one) are odd and prime. This requirement is clearly defined.

The difference is that the statements are about listing while the question is about checking requirements. That's why the question is adequately defined and the statements are under-defined.

Now, joining the statements, we get *A* is a set of odd prime numbers only. The answer is "Yes." The answer is (C).

Adequately defined question and under-defined statements:

2. Does Set A contain only odd prime numbers?

    (1) *A* contains odd numbers.

    (2) *A* contains prime numbers.

Statement (1) allows odd numbers, and Statement (2) allows prime numbers. So, the statements together allow odd and prime numbers in Set A. This, of course, means there *could* be other numbers (not just odd or prime or both). If there are other numbers in Set A, the answer is "No"; and if there are not, the answer is "Yes." Hence, the answer to the question is "Can't say" and therefore the answer is (E).

Adequately defined question and under-defined statements:

3. Does Set A contain at least one odd prime number?

    (1) *A* contains odd numbers.

    (2) *A* contains prime numbers.

Statement (1) allows odd numbers but could contain other numbers that are not odd.

Statement (2) allows prime numbers but could contain other numbers that are not prime.

Statements (1) and (2) contain odd numbers and prime numbers. This does not necessarily mean that Set *A* contains at least a one odd prime number. 2 is a prime that is not odd. The set may contain only odd number and only prime number. For example, in the set $A = \{2, 9, 15\}$, both statements are satisfied and still not necessarily a single odd prime number is there. But if $A = \{3, 9, 15\}$, then both statements are satisfied and we have at least one odd-prime number, 3. Thus, we have a double case, and the answer is (E).

Under-defined question and fully defined statements:

4.   The first four elements of Series *A* are 0, 1, 1, and 2. Two series are equal when the corresponding elements of the two series exist and are the same. Is Series *B* equal to Series *A*?

   (1)   The first and the second terms of Series *B* are 0 and 1, respectively, and each remaining term equals the sum of the preceding two terms.

   (2)   The first four terms of Series *B* are 0, 1, 1, and 2, respectively.

Note here that only the first four elements of Series *A* are given. The series may or may not have more elements. Since nothing is said about whether it has more elements and if yes, what are the elements, the *question* is under-defined.

Now, whether or not we have *B* in hand, we can say not all corresponding terms between the two series exist.

Note that Statement (1) defines the series completely as *A* = 0, 1, 1, 2, 3, 5, 8, ..., and so on. At least the statements together do. So, we have Series *B*, which is fully defined, but we are not in position to compare it with Series *A*, which is not defined fully. Clearly, regardless of whether the statements together define *B* successfully or not, since the statements do not define *A*, the statements are *not* sufficient.

More insight: We can draw multiple rules to define a series without all the elements given. Hence, such a series is never completely defined.

For example, Series *A* in the problem above could be 0, 1, 1, 2, 2, 2, 3, 3, 3, 3, ... as well. (The rule that generates a series may not always be algebraic like here. But given a complete series, we can sure map out the algebraic rule for the series — at least one of the algebraic rules for the series.)

However, the statements together find certain initial terms that match with Series *A*. So, *A* could equal *B* if it contains all the remaining elements in *B* in order, or *A* may not equal *B* in case it does not contains all the remaining elements. Thus, we have a double case and the statements together are not sufficient.

In other words, Series *A* could be either of the following two sample series:

   0, 1, 1, 2, 3, 5, ... (The rule could be each element equals the sum of the preceding two elements, just like the Fibonacci series.)

   0, 1, 1, 2, 2, 2, 3, 3, 3, 3, ...

These two series are *not* equal.

Suppose Series A equals the first series, then it wouldn't equal the second and vice versa. So, our answer would be "Can't say." The answer is (C).

Summary: Two series cannot be said to be equal (or not equal) unless both are completely defined.

Two series cannot be compared unless both have the same set of corresponding numbers.

5. Any term in the series (except for the first and last terms) is the average of the two adjacent terms in the series. What is the 8th term in the series?

   (1) First term is 2.

   (2) Third term is 6.

Each term in the series is the average of the two adjacent terms. So, to calculate each term, we need at least two numbers. But to start calculating the terms, we need at least two initial values, and we have them only with the statements together. Hence, both statements are required, and the answer is (C).

The rule is $F_n = \dfrac{F_{n-1} + F_{n+1}}{2}$, and the initial values are $F_1 = 2$ and $F_3 = 6$.

$$F_2 = \frac{F_{2-1} + F_{2+1}}{2} = \frac{F_1 + F_3}{2} = \frac{2 + 6}{2} = \frac{8}{2} = 4$$

$$F_3 = \frac{F_{3-1} + F_{3+1}}{2} = \frac{F_2 + F_4}{2}, \text{ or } 6 = \frac{4 + F_4}{2}, \text{ or } F_4 = 2 \cdot 6 - 4 = 8$$

This is how we can proceed to calculate F_8. Note that we do not need to calculate it; we just need to know that we can calculate it and will get a unique value for the 8th term in the calculation.

No question will contain "could" in a Data Sufficiency problem.

Under-defined question - under-defined statement:

6. What is Set *A*?

   (1) Set *A* contains only even numbers.

   (2) Set *A* contains all the even numbers.

Clearly, the question is asking for the listing of the series or the definition of the series that can be used to list the series.

Statement (1): Set *A* contains only even numbers.

Here, Set *A* could be {2, 4}, or {6, 10}, or {4, 8, 18}, etc. We do not have a unique solution and therefore the statement is *not* sufficient.

Statement (2): Set *A* contains all the even numbers.

Here, Set *A* must have the elements …, –4, –2, 0, 2, 4, 6, …. But the statement does not prevent Set *A* from containing elements that are not even. It just says that it contains all the even numbers. Thus, we could also have non-even integers and literally the series is not adequately defined. The statement is *not* sufficient.

Considering both statements, we derive that *A* contains all the even numbers and only even numbers. Thus, the statements together are sufficient.

The answer is (C).

Under-defined statements:

7.   What is the sum of numbers in the series?

   (1)   All the numbers in the series are 3-digit numbers.

   (2)   All the numbers in the series leave a remainder of 2 when divided by 3.

Let the given series be represented by *A*.

Combining the two statements yields "All the numbers in the series are 3-digit numbers that leave a remainder of 2 when divided by 3." (Note: We need to be careful not to change the language while combining the statements.) The list of all such numbers is {101, 104, 107, ..., 998}. From the language of the problem, we are still not sure whether Set *A* contains all of these numbers {101, 104, 107, ..., 998}. So, the sum cannot be calculated, nor the average. The answer is (E).

If the statements adequately define the series, adding an extra condition will not violate or slice the already calculated Set *A*.

For example, adding Statement (3) "The numbers in the series are all even," which is a possibly valid statement, further reduces the Set *A* to {~~101~~, 104, ~~107~~, ..., ~~995~~, 998} = {104, 110,..., 992, 998}.

So, if Statement (2) were "The series is the set of all numbers and only the numbers that are 3-digited and leave a remainder of 2 when divided by 3," then no other kind of statement such as Statement (3) can slice the Set *A* further. If Statement (3) is slicing or adding new elements to the already fully defined set, the statement is invalid.

Counting

Counting may have been one of humankind's first thought processes; nevertheless, counting can be deceptively hard. In part, because we often forget some of the principles of counting, but also because counting can be inherently difficult.

 When counting elements that are in overlapping sets, the total number will equal the number in one group plus the number in the other group minus the number common to both groups. Venn diagrams are very helpful with these problems.

Example 1: How many students are taking either math or history?

    (1)   In a certain school, 20 students are taking math and 10 are taking history.

    (2)   7 are taking both.

Solution:

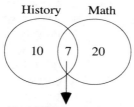

"Either math or history" means math alone or history alone or BOTH.

By the principle stated above, we add 10 and 20 and then subtract 7 from the result. Thus, there are $(10 + 20) - 7 = 23$ students. The answer is (C).

 The number of integers between two integers <u>inclusive</u> is one more than their difference.

Example 2: How many integers are there between 49 and 101, inclusive?

    (A) 50   (B) 51   (C) 52   (D) 53   (E) 54

By the principle stated above, the number of integers between 49 and 101 inclusive is $(101 - 49) + 1 = 53$. The answer is (D). To see this more clearly, choose smaller numbers, say, 9 and 11. The difference between 9 and 11 is 2. But there are three numbers between them inclusive—9, 10, and 11—one more than their difference.

Fundamental Principle of Counting: **If an event occurs *m* times, and each of the *m* events is followed by a second event which occurs *k* times, then the first event follows the second event *m · k* times.**

The following diagram illustrates the fundamental principle of counting for an event that occurs 3 times with each occurrence being followed by a second event that occurs 2 times for a total of 3 · 2 = 6 events:

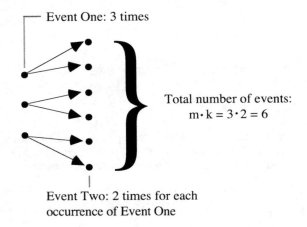

Event One: 3 times

Total number of events:
m · k = 3 · 2 = 6

Event Two: 2 times for each occurrence of Event One

Example 3:   A drum contains 3 to 5 jars each of which contains 30 to 40 marbles. If 10 percent of the marbles are flawed, what is the greatest possible number of flawed marbles in the drum?

(A) 51   (B) 40   (C) 30   (D) 20   (E) 12

There is at most 5 jars each of which contains at most 40 marbles; so by the fundamental counting principle, there is at most 5 · 40 = 200 marbles in the drum. Since 10 percent of the marbles are flawed, there is at most 20 = 10% · 200 flawed marbles. The answer is (D).

MISCELLANEOUS COUNTING PROBLEMS

Example 4:   In a legislative body of 200 people, the number of Democrats is 50 less than 4 times the number of Republicans. If one fifth of the legislators are neither Republican nor Democrat, how many of the legislators are Republicans?

(A) 42   (B) 50   (C) 71   (D) 95   (E) 124

Let *D* be the number of Democrats and let *R* be the number of Republicans. "One fifth of the legislators are neither Republican nor Democrat," so there are $\frac{1}{5} \cdot 200 = 40$ legislators who are neither Republican nor Democrat. Hence, there are 200 – 40 = 160 Democrats and Republicans, or $D + R = 160$. Translating the clause "the number of Democrats is 50 less than 4 times the number of Republicans" into an equation yields $D = 4R - 50$. Plugging this into the equation $D + R = 160$ yields

$$4R - 50 + R = 160$$

$$5R - 50 = 160$$

$$5R = 210$$

$$R = 42$$

The answer is (A).

Example 5: Speed bumps are being placed at 20-foot intervals along a road 1015 feet long. If the first speed bump is placed at one end of the road, how many speed bumps are needed?

(A) 49   (B) 50   (C) 51   (D) 52   (E) 53

Since the road is 1015 feet long and the speed bumps are 20 feet apart, there are $\frac{1015}{20} = 50.75$, or 50 full sections in the road. If we ignore the first speed bump and associate the speed bump at the end of each section with that section, then there are 50 speed bumps (one for each of the fifty full sections). Counting the first speed bump gives a total of 51 speed bumps. The answer is (C).

Problem Set R: Counting

1. If $x + y + z = 6$, then do any two of the three numbers x, y, and z sum to 3?

    (1) x, y, and z are different positive integers.

    (2) x, y, and z are consecutive integers.

2. A church C is on a hilltop at a height 300 feet from the ground and is reached only through stairs of steps of width 1/3 foot. How many steps must be climbed to reach the entrance of church C from the bottom A of the stairs?

    (1) The height of each step is 1/2 foot.

    (2) Church C is located at a horizontal distance of 300 feet from the bottom of the stairs A.

3. How many students aged between 21 and 23 scored between 70 and 90?

    (1) 17 students are aged between 21 and 23.

    (2) 17 students scored between 70 and 90.

Answers and Solutions to Problem Set R: Counting

1.   If $x + y + z = 6$, then do any two of the three numbers x, y, and z sum to 3?

    (1) x, y, and z are different positive integers.

    (2) x, y, and z are consecutive integers.

Statement (1): x, y, and z are different positive integers.

If the sum of the three different positive integers is 6, then the numbers must be 1, 2, and 3. Now, check whether any two of the three numbers sum to 3. The statement alone is sufficient: 1 and 2 sum to 3.

Statement (2): x, y, and z are consecutive integers.

Suppose a, $a + 1$, and $a + 2$ are the three consecutive integers x, y, and z. Since their sum is 6, we have

$$a + (a + 1) + (a + 2) = 6$$

$$3a + 3 = 6$$

$$3a = 3$$

$$a = 1$$

So, the other two numbers are $a + 1 = 1 + 1 = 2$, and $a + 2 = 1 + 2 = 3$. Now, check whether any two of the three numbers sum to 2. The statement is alone is sufficient: 1 and 2 sum to 3.

The answer is (D).

2.   A church C is on a hilltop at a height 300 feet from the ground and is reached only through stairs of steps of width 1/3 foot. How many steps must be climbed to reach the entrance of church C from the bottom A of the stairs?

    (1)   The height of each step is 1/2 foot.

    (2)   Church C is located at a horizontal distance of 300 feet from the bottom of the stairs A.

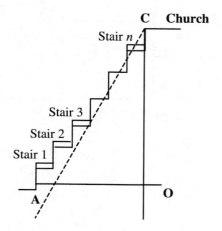

We know the height (vertical length) of the hilltop from the question setup and the height (vertical length) of each step from Statement (1). Dividing the former by the later, gives the number of steps that you need to get from the bottom to the top of the hill. So, Statement (1) alone is sufficient.

The same type of analysis applies to the horizontal lengths. Given the horizontal lengths alone the number of steps can be calculated as

The horizontal length of the hilltop/The horizontal length of each step

This is the number of steps, which gives us the horizontal displacement required to get from the bottom to the top of the hill. The numerator in the fraction above is given in Statement (2), and the denominator is given in the question setup. So, Statement (2) alone can calculate the number of steps required. The statement is sufficient.

The answer is (D), either statement alone is sufficient.

3.   How many students aged between 21 and 23 scored between 70 and 90?

   (1)   17 students are aged between 21 and 23.

   (2)   17 students scored between 70 and 90.

Let each student be represented by his age and score in the graph by a single crossed dot per student as shown below. Let's for example, use an *xy* – plotter graph.

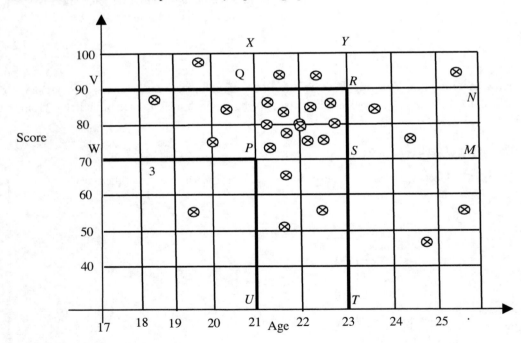

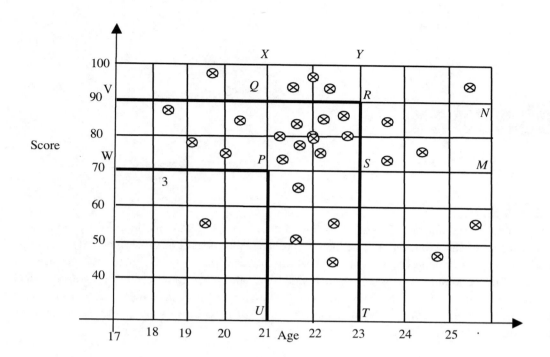

The students aged between 21 and 23 can be found in the region *UXYT*. The students who scored between 70 and 90 can be found in the region *WMNV*. The students aged between 21 and 23 and scoring between 70 and 90 can be found in the region *QRSP*. This is same as "Aged between 21 and 23 who scored between 70 and 90" or "Scored between 70 and 90 who are aged between 21 and 23." Now, the question can be reworded as

How many crossed dots does the region *QRSP* have?

(1)   There are 17 dots in the region *UXYT*.

(2)   There are 17 dots in the region *WMNV*.

From the figure, the counts of the regions follow the equations

$$UXYT = UPST + QRSP + QXYR \text{ and } WMNV = VQPW + QRSP + RNMS$$

There are 17 dots in *UXYT* and *WMNV*. Plugging 17 for the same yields

$$17 = UPST + QRSP + QXYR \text{ and } 17 = VQPW + QRSP + RNMS$$

Thus, we have two equations in 5 unknowns: *UPST*, *QXYR*, *QRSP*, *VQPW*, and *RNMS*. So, we have $5 - 2 = 3$ degrees of freedom for its unknowns, which means changing any one of the unknowns would change the other unknown, for example *QRSP*. Hence, we do not have a fixed value for *QRSP* and therefore the statements together are *not* sufficient. The answer is (E).

Method II: The two graphs present a possible double case (In the first figure, *QRSP* has 12 dots; and in the second one, there are 10 dots) with the statements together and therefore the statements together are *not* sufficient.

Probability

We know what probability means, but what is its formal definition? Let's use our intuition to define it. If there is no chance that an event will occur, then its probability of occurring should be 0. On the other extreme, if an event is certain to occur, then its probability of occurring should be 100%, or 1. Hence, our *probability* should be a number between 0 and 1, inclusive. But what kind of number? Suppose your favorite actor has a 1 in 3 chance of winning the Oscar for best actor. This can be measured by forming the fraction 1/3. Hence, a *probability* is a fraction where the top is the number of ways an event can occur and the bottom is the total number of possible events:

$$P = \frac{Number\ of\ ways\ an\ event\ can\ occur}{Number\ of\ total\ possible\ events}$$

Example: *Flipping a coin*

What's the probability of getting heads when flipping a coin?

There is only one way to get heads in a coin toss. Hence, the top of the probability fraction is 1. There are two possible results: heads or tails. Forming the probability fraction gives 1/2.

Example: *Tossing a die*

What's the probability of getting a 3 when tossing a die?

A die (a cube) has six faces, numbered 1 through 6. There is only one way to get a 3. Hence, the top of the fraction is 1. There are 6 possible results: 1, 2, 3, 4, 5, and 6. Forming the probability fraction gives 1/6.

Example: *Drawing a card from a deck*

What's the probability of getting a king when drawing a card from a deck of cards?

A deck of cards has four kings, so there are 4 ways to get a king. Hence, the top of the fraction is 4. There are 52 total cards in a deck. Forming the probability fraction gives 4/52, which reduces to 1/13. Hence, there is 1 chance in 13 of getting a king.

Example: *Drawing marbles from a bowl*

What's the probability of drawing a blue marble from a bowl containing 4 red marbles, 5 blue marbles, and 5 green marbles?

There are five ways of drawing a blue marble. Hence, the top of the fraction is 5. There are 14 (= 4 + 5 + 5) possible results. Forming the probability fraction gives 5/14.

Example: *Drawing marbles from a bowl (second drawing)*

What's the probability of drawing a red marble from the same bowl, given that the first marble drawn was blue and was not placed back in the bowl?

There are four ways of drawing a red marble. Hence, the top of the fraction is 4. Since the blue marble from the first drawing was not replaced, there are only 4 blue marbles remaining. Hence, there are 13 (= 4 + 4 + 5) possible results. Forming the probability fraction gives 4/13.

Consecutive Probabilities

What's the probability of getting heads twice in a row when flipping a coin twice? Previously we calculated the probability for the first flip to be 1/2. Since the second flip is not affected by the first (these are called *mutually exclusive* events), its probability is also 1/2. Forming the product yields the probability of two heads in a row: $\frac{1}{2} \times \frac{1}{2} = \frac{1}{4}$.

What's the probability of drawing a blue marble and then a red marble from a bowl containing 4 red marbles, 5 blue marbles, and 5 green marbles? (Assume that the marbles are not replaced after being selected.) As calculated before, there is a 5/14 likelihood of selecting a blue marble first and a 4/13 likelihood of selecting a red marble second. Forming the product yields the probability of a blue marble immediately followed by a red marble: $\frac{5}{14} \times \frac{4}{13} = \frac{20}{182} = \frac{10}{91}$.

These two examples can be generalized into the following rule for calculating consecutive probabilities:

> **To calculate consecutive probabilities, multiply the individual probabilities.**

This rule applies to two, three, or any number of consecutive probabilities.

Either-Or Probabilities

What's the probability of getting either heads or tails when flipping a coin once? Since the only possible outcomes are heads or tails, we expect the probability to be 100%, or 1: $\frac{1}{2} + \frac{1}{2} = 1$. Note that the events heads and tails are mutually exclusive. That is, if heads occurs, then tails cannot (and vice versa).

What's the probability of drawing a red marble or a green marble from a bowl containing 4 red marbles, 5 blue marbles, and 5 green marbles? There are 4 red marbles out of 14 total marbles. So, the probability of selecting a red marble is 4/14 = 2/7. Similarly, the probability of selecting a green marble is 5/14. So, the probability of selecting a red or green marble is $\frac{2}{7} + \frac{5}{14} = \frac{9}{14}$. Note again that the events are mutually exclusive. For instance, if a red marble is selected, then neither a blue marble nor a green marble is selected.

These two examples can be generalized into the following rule for calculating *either-or* probabilities:

> **To calculate *either-or* probabilities, add the individual probabilities (only if the events are mutually exclusive).**

The probabilities in the two immediately preceding examples can be calculated more naturally by adding up the events that occur and then dividing by the total number of possible events. For the coin example, we get 2 events (heads or tails) divided by the total number of possible events, 2 (heads and tails): 2/2 = 1. For the marble example, we get 9 (= 4 + 5) ways the event can occur divided by 14 (= 4 + 5 + 5) possible events: 9/14.

If it's more natural to calculate the *either-or* probabilities above by adding up the events that occur and then dividing by the total number of possible events, why did we introduce a second way of calculating the probabilities? Because in some cases, you may have to add the individual probabilities. For example, you may be given the individual probabilities of two mutually exclusive events and be asked for the probability that either could occur. You now know to merely add their individual probabilities.

Geometric Probability

In this type of problem, you will be given two figures, with one inside the other. You'll then be asked what is the probability that a randomly selected point will be in the smaller figure. These problems are solved with the same principle we have been using: $Probability = \dfrac{desired\ outcome}{possible\ outcomes}$.

Example: In the figure, the smaller square has sides of length 2 and the larger square has sides of length 4. If a point is chosen at random from the large square, what is the probability that it will be from the small square?

Applying the probability principle, we get $Probability = \dfrac{\text{area of the small square}}{\text{area of the large square}} = \dfrac{2^2}{4^2} = \dfrac{4}{16} = \dfrac{1}{4}$.

Strategy

How to set the probability fraction.

In any probability statement, we have two candidates for the fraction, one for the denominator and one for the numerator.

Typically, the two candidates are separated in a probability statement by verbs such as "is," "has," and "have," etc., or by a comma. It is always easy to choose a candidate for the denominator and a candidate for the numerator.

The candidate for the denominator is the one with the bigger scope, and the candidate for numerator is the one with the smaller scope.

For example, if we are asked, "what is the probability that a woman selected randomly from the women in a group of people is wearing pink attire?" then separate the candidates as

a woman selected randomly from <u>the women in a group of people</u>

"is"

<u>wearing pink attire</u>?

The top candidate is the group of all the women including the ones in pink attire. The bottom candidate has the smaller scope: it contains only the women in pink attire. So, the scope of the top candidate is bigger than the scope of the bottom candidate. So, the probability ratio is

(women wearing pink attire)/(women in a group of people)

The numerator has a smaller scope because it is constrained by the denominator. This is why the numerator is less than the denominator in the fraction and the fraction itself is less than 1. The probability is this! It tests the fraction to which certain quantities reduced after the constraining.

Finally, before choosing the candidates, prune the words that do not contribute to the selection criteria. Do this to both candidates. This greatly simplifies the effort to analyze the probability fraction.

We will see all this in the following example:

Example 1: What is the probability that a woman selected randomly from the women in a group of people is wearing pink attire?

    (1)   Of the women in the group, 7 percent are wearing pink attire.

    (2)   Of the people in the group, 40 percent are women.

Let's divide the numerator candidate and the denominator by the verb. We are asked for the probability that

[a woman selected randomly from the women in a group of people] <u>has</u> [pink attire].

The candidate with the bigger scope is

[*a woman* to be selected randomly <u>from</u> the women in a group of people]

And the candidate with the smaller scope is

[a woman selected randomly <u>from</u> the women in a group of people] <u>and</u> [wearing pink attire]

The constraint over the bigger candidate is to choose a women only from the group of people.

But apart from this, the "wearing pink attire" is the additional constraint of the smaller candidate over the bigger one.

We prune words such as "selected," "randomly," etc., which do not contribute to the selection criterion of the bigger candidate. This reduces the phrase

"a woman ~~selected randomly~~ from the women in a group ~~of people~~"

to

"a woman from the women in the group"

So, effectively the selection criterion is "Woman in Pink from the women in the group." We need to find the probability of this.

Summary of the Tip: Verbs such as "is," "has," and "have," etc., are words that separate the numerator and the denominator in the probability fraction. For example, in the above probability, the condition (a woman from a group of people) to the left of the verb "has" forms the denominator and this condition plus the condition to the right (pink attire) forms the numerator. So, the probability fraction is

(Women in pink attire)/(Women in the group)

And this is what is given in Statement (1). It says, "Of the women in the group, 7 percent of the women are wearing pink attire." So, the answer is $7\% = 7/100 = 0.07$. The statement alone is sufficient.

Statement (2) is not necessary since regardless of the number of people in the group, we are only going to pick women from the group.

Hence, the answer is (A).

Problem Set S: Probability

1. What is the probability that a person selected randomly from a group of people is a woman in pink attire?

    (1)   Of the women in the group, 4% are wearing pink attire.

    (2)   Of the people in the group, 40% are women.

2. What is the probability that on a given workday Mr. Jonathan dresses in formals, travels by car to his office, and drinks a coffee there?

    (1)   Jonathan dresses in formals on alternate days, and drinks coffee each day he wears formals.

    (2)   Jonathan goes to his office by car 3 of every 5 days.

3. In a factory, there are workers, executives, and clerks. What is the probability that a person randomly selected from the employees is an executive?

    (1)   41% of the employees are workers, 460 are executives, and the remaining 720 employees are clerks.

    (2)   460 of the employees are executives and account for 23% of the employees in the factory.

4. If each student gets at least one pencil in the exam hall, what is the probability that a student gets exactly one pencil in the exam hall?

    (1)   110 students are expected to get at least one pencil.

    (2)   60 students are expected to get at least two pencils.

5. In a country, 45% of male citizen and 47% of female citizen are eligible to vote. What is the probability that a citizen voted in the election?

    (1)   47% of male citizens eligible to vote voted.

    (2)   45% of female citizens eligible to vote voted.

6. In a country, 45% of male citizen and 47% of female citizen are eligible to vote. What is the probability that a citizen voted in the election?

    (1)   45% of eligible male citizens voted.

    (2)   47% of eligible female citizens voted.

Answers and Solutions to Problem Set S: Probability

1.   What is the probability that a person selected randomly from a group of people is a woman in pink attire?

   (1)   Of the women in the group, 4% are wearing pink attire.

   (2)   Of the people in the group, 40% are women.

In the question setup, the condition to the left of "is" is "a person selected randomly from a group of people."

So, the required ratio is

The number of women in pink/The number of people in the group =

(The number of women in pink/The number of women in the group) **×**

(The number of women in the group/The number of people in the group)

The first fraction is 4% [from Statement (1)], and the second fraction is 40% [from Statement (2)]. So, the probability equals

4% × 40% = 4/100 × 40/100 = 160/10,000 = 16/1,000 = 2/125

Hence, both statements are required, and the answer is (C).

2.   What is the probability that on a given workday Mr. Jonathan dresses in formals, travels by car to his office, and drinks a coffee there?

   (1)   Jonathan dresses in formals on alternate days, and drinks coffee each day he wears formals.

   (2)   Jonathan goes to his office by car 3 of every 5 days.

Statement (1): Jonathan dresses in formals on alternate days, and drinks coffee each day he wears formals.

Note: It is alternate days, not just alternate workdays. Jonathan dresses in formals on alternate days; so not on each alternate workday. In other words, we are not sure which set of alternate days of the week; so we are not sure about the schedule of working days; So, we cannot get the probability of Jonathan being dressed in formals on a given workday. So, we cannot get the probability of dressing in formals … blah, blah, blah … on a given workday.

On each day, he wears formals, and he drinks coffee, but we are not given "Where?" whether it is in his office or not. So, the statement is *not* sufficient.

Statement (2): Jonathan goes to office by car 3 of every 5 days.

Jonathan goes by car (not sure if it is his car; we need the probability of traveling by his car.)

The statement is *not* sufficient.

The answer is (E).

3.   In a factory, there are workers, executives, and clerks. What is the probability that a person randomly selected from the employees is an executive?

  (1)   41% of the employees are workers, 460 are executives, and the remaining 720 employees are clerks.

  (2)   460 of the employees are executives and account for 23% of the employees in the factory.

Let E represent the total number of employees. Let w represent the number of workers, x the number of executives, and c the number of clerks. Hence, the probability fraction is $\dfrac{x}{E}$, and the question is "What is

$\dfrac{x}{E}$?"

Then we have

$$E = w + x + c \qquad\qquad (1)$$

Now, the probability fraction is $\dfrac{x}{E} = \dfrac{x}{w + x + c}$. Dividing both the numerator and denominator by x yields

$\dfrac{x/x}{w/x + x/x + c/x} = \dfrac{1}{w/x + 1 + c/x} = \dfrac{1}{(w/x + c/x) + 1}$. So, the question can be transformed as "What is $(w/x + c/x)$?"

From Statement (1) alone, we have that 41% of the employees E are workers (w), 460 are executives (x), and the remaining 720 employees are clerks (c). Hence, we have the equations

$$w = 41/100 \times E \qquad\qquad (2)$$

$$x = 460 \qquad\qquad (3)$$

$$c = 720 \qquad\qquad (4)$$

With equations (1), (2), (3), and (4), we have four different linear equations in four unknowns E, w, x, and c. Hence, a unique solution must be possible for x, w, c, and E and therefore we have a unique value for the ratio x/E, which is the probability fraction. Hence, Statement (1) alone is sufficient. The answer to the question is "$E = 2000$."

From Statement (2) alone, we have that the number of executives (x) is 460, and this is 23% of the total number of employees (E). Hence, we have the probability fraction equals $23\% = 23/100 = 0.23$. The statement is sufficient.

Since either statement (1) or (2) is sufficient, the answer is (D).

4.   If each student gets at least one pencil in the exam hall, what is the probability that a student gets exactly one pencil in the exam hall?

   (1)   110 students are expected to get at least one pencil.

   (2)   60 students are expected to get at least two pencils.

Let *A* be the set of students having exactly one pencil. Then the question is how many students are there in set *A*.

Next, let *B* be the set of students having exactly two pencils, and let *C* be the set of students having more than two pencils.

Probability fraction is

$$\frac{\text{Number of students in A}}{\text{Number of students in A, B, and C together}}$$

Since each student gets at least one pencil (given), *A*, *B*, and *C* together is the set of all the students in the exam hall.

Statement (1) gives the same and nothing else. So, we have the denominator of the probability fraction but not the numerator. The statement alone is not sufficient.

Next, the set of students having at least two pencils is the collection of the two sets *B* and *C*. Since Statement (2) does not have any information about set *A*, Statement (2) alone is not sufficient.

Now, from the statements together we have that

   The number of students in all three sets *A*, *B*, and *C* together = 110 [from Statement (1)]

and

   The number of students in the two sets *B* and *C* together = 60 [from Statement (2)]

Since set *A* is the difference between a set containing the students of *A*, *B*, and *C* and a set of students of *B* and *C* only, The number of students in set *A* equals

   The number of students in sets *A*, *B*, and *C* together – the number of students in sets *B* and *C* =

$$110 - 60 =$$

$$50$$

Hence, both statements are required to answer the question, and the answer is (C). The answer is 50/110 = 5/11.

5.   In a country, 45% of male citizen and 47% of female citizen are eligible to vote. What is the probability that a citizen voted in the election?

(1)   47% of male citizens eligible to vote voted.

(2)   45% of female citizens eligible to vote voted.

Let the number of male and female citizens in the country be m and f, respectively. The total number of citizens must be $m + f$. The probability fraction is

$$\text{(Number of people voted)} \div \text{(Number of citizens)}$$

Now, 45% of the male citizens are eligible to vote, and 45% of m is $\dfrac{45m}{100}$.

47% of female citizens are eligible to vote, and 47% of f is $\dfrac{47f}{100}$.

From statements (1) and (2) together, we have

47% of male citizens eligible to vote voted, and 47% of $\dfrac{45m}{100}$ is $\dfrac{47}{100} \cdot \dfrac{45m}{100} = \dfrac{45 \cdot 47m}{10,000}$.

45% of female citizens eligible to vote voted, and 45% of $\dfrac{47f}{100}$ is $\dfrac{45}{100} \cdot \dfrac{47f}{100} = \dfrac{45 \cdot 47f}{10,000}$.

So, out of the total $m + f$ citizens, the total number of voters who voted is

$$\frac{45 \cdot 47m}{10,000} + \frac{45 \cdot 47f}{10,000} = \frac{(45 \cdot 47)(m + f)}{10,000}$$

Hence, the probability fraction is

$$\frac{\dfrac{(45 \cdot 47)(m + f)}{10,000}}{m + f} = \frac{45 \cdot 47}{10,000}$$

Hence, the statements together answer the question; and from the lack of the crucial details, the statements individually are not sufficient. Hence, the answer is (C).

6.   In a country, 45% of male citizen and 47% of female citizen are eligible to vote. What is the probability that a citizen voted in the election?

(1)   45% of eligible male citizens voted.

(2)   47% of eligible female citizens voted.

Let the number of male and female citizens in the country be m and f, respectively. The total number of citizens must be $m + f$. The probability fraction is

$$\text{Number of people who voted} \div \text{Number of citizens}$$

Now, 45% of male citizens are eligible to vote, and 45% of m is $\dfrac{45m}{100}$.

47% of female citizens are eligible to vote, and 47% of f is $\dfrac{47f}{100}$.

From statements (1) and (2) together, we have

45% of male citizens eligible for voting voted, and 45% of $\dfrac{45m}{100}$ is $\dfrac{45}{100} \cdot \dfrac{45m}{100} = \dfrac{45 \cdot 45m}{10,000}$.

47% of female citizens eligible for voting voted, and 47% of $\dfrac{47f}{100}$ is $\dfrac{47}{100} \cdot \dfrac{47f}{100} = \dfrac{47 \cdot 47f}{10,000}$.

So, out of the total $m + f$, the total number of voters who voted is

$$\frac{45 \cdot 45m}{10,000} + \frac{47 \cdot 47f}{10,000}$$

Hence, the required probability fraction is

$$\frac{\dfrac{45 \cdot 45m}{10,000} + \dfrac{47 \cdot 47f}{10,000}}{m + f}$$

Dividing the numerator and the denominator by f, we get the fraction

$$\frac{\dfrac{45 \cdot 45 \dfrac{m}{f}}{10,000} + \dfrac{47 \cdot 47}{10,000}}{\dfrac{m}{f} + 1}$$

This fraction cannot be reduced further. Hence, the value of the fraction depends on the ratio m to f, which is unknown. Hence, the statements together cannot answer the question. The answer is (E).

Permutations & Combinations

Suppose you must seat 3 of 5 delegates in 3 chairs. And suppose you are interested in the order in which they sit. You will first select 3 of the 5 delegates, and then choose the order in which they sit. The first act is a combination, the second is a permutation. Effectively, the permutation comes after the combination. The delegates in each combination can be ordered in different ways, which can be called permutations of the combination.

Now, if you can select 3 of the 5 delegates in m ways and each selection can be ordered in n ways, then the total number of possible arrangements (permutations) is $m \cdot n$.

Now, let's count the number of permutations of 3 objects taken from a set of 4 objects {A, B, C, D}. Let's call the set {A, B, C, D} a base set.

We must first choose 3 objects from the base set, which yields the following selections:

$$\{A, B, C\}, \{B, C, D\}, \{A, C, D\}, \{A, B, D\}$$

These are combinations. We have 4 selections (combinations) here.

If {E1, E2, E3} represents one of the four combinations above, then the following are its possible permutations:

E1	E2	E3
E1	E3	E2
E2	E1	E3
E2	E3	E1
E3	E1	E2
E3	E2	E1

You can use this scheme to find the permutations of each of the 4 selections (combinations) we formed above. For example, for the selection {A, B, C}, the following are the six permutations:

$$A - B - C$$
$$A - C - B$$
$$B - A - C$$
$$B - C - A$$
$$C - A - B$$
$$C - B - A$$

Thus, we have 6 permutations for each selection. For practice, you may wish to list the permutations for the remaining 3 selections: {B, C, D}, {A, C, D}, and {A, B, D}.

Summary:

Here, {A, B, C, D} is the base set. We formed 4 combinations that use 3 elements each. Then we formed 6 permutations for each of the 4 combinations. Hence, the problem has in total 6 + 6 + 6 + 6 = 4 × 6 = 24 permutations.

Note 1: A combination might have multiple permutations. The reverse is never true.

Note 2: A permutation is an ordered combination.

Note 3: With combinations, AB = BA. With permutations, AB ≠ BA.

Combinations and their Permutations

Here is another discussion of the distinction between permutations and combinations. The concept is repeated here because it forms the basis for the rest of the chapter.

Combinations are the selections (subsets) of a base set.

For example, the possible combinations of two elements each of the set {A, B} are

A, B or B, A

(Both are the same combination)

The permutations (the combination ordered in different ways) of the combination are

A – B and B – A

(The permutations are different)

How to distinguish between a Combination and a Permutation

At the risk of redundancy, here is yet another discussion of the distinction between permutations and combinations.

As combinations, {A, B, C} and {B, A, C} are the same because each has the same number of each type of object: A, B, and C as in the base set.

But, as permutations, A – B – C and B – A – C are not the same because the ordering is different, though each has the same number of each type of object: A, B, and C as in the base set In fact, no two arrangements that are not identical are ever the same permutation.

Hence, with combinations, look for selections, while with permutations, look for arrangements.

The following definitions will help you distinguish between Combinations and Permutations

Permutations are *arrangements* (order is important) of objects formed from an original set (base set) such that each new arrangement has an order different from the original set. So, the positions of objects is important.

Combinations are sets of objects formed by *selecting* (order not important) objects from an original set (base set).

To help you remember, think "**Permutation** ... **Position**."

Combinations with Repetitions: Permutations with Repetitions

Here, repetition of objects is allowed in selections or the arrangements.

Suppose you have the base set {A, B, C}. Allowing repetitions, the objects can repeat in the combinations (selections).

Hence, the allowed *selections* of 2 elements are {A, A}, {A, B} or {B, A}, {B, B}, {B, C} or {C, B}, {C, C}, {C, A} or {A, C} in total 6.

The corresponding *permutations* are

$$A - A \text{ for } \{A, A\}$$
$$A - B \text{ and } B - A \text{ for } \{A, B\}$$
$$B - B \text{ for } \{B, B\}$$
$$B - C \text{ and } C - B \text{ for } \{B, C\}$$
$$C - C \text{ for } \{C, C\}$$
$$C - A \text{ and } A - C \text{ for } \{C, A\}$$

The total number of combinations is 6, and the total number of permutations is 9. We have 3 objects to choose for 2 positions; allowing repetitions, the calculation is $3^2 = 9$.

Note that {A, B} and {B, A} are the same combination because each has an equal number of A's and B's.

By allowing repetitions, you can chose the same object more than once and therefore can have the same object occupying different positions.

In general, *permutation* means "permutation without repetition," unless stated otherwise.

Indistinguishable Objects

Suppose we replace C in the base set {A, B, C} with A. Then, we have {A, B, A}. Now the A's in the first and third positions of the set are indistinguishable and make some of the combinations and permutations formed earlier involving C redundant (because some identical combinations and permutations will be formed). Hence, replacing distinguishable objects with indistinguishable ones reduces the number of combinations and permutations.

Combinations (repetition not allowed) with Indistinguishable Objects

Consider the set {A, B, A}. Here, for example, ABA (2 A's and 1 B as in the base set) is an allowed combination but ABB (containing 2 B's not as in base set) is not because B occurs only once in the base set.

All the allowed permutations are listed in Table IV.

Permutations (repetition not allowed) with Indistinguishable Objects

The corresponding permutations are listed in Table IV.

Observe that {A, B, C} has permutations ABC, ACB, BAC, BCA, CAB, and CBA (6 permutations); and {A, B, A} has permutations ABA, AAB, BAA, ~~BAA~~, ~~AAB~~, and ~~ABA~~ (we crossed out the last three permutations because they are identical to the first three). So, there are 3 permutations.

Combinations (repetition allowed) with Indistinguishable Objects

Again, consider the set {A, B, A}. Here, for example, ABA is an allowed combination and ABB is an allowed combination.

All the allowed permutations are listed in Table III.

Permutations (repetition allowed) with Indistinguishable Objects

The corresponding permutations are listed in Table III.

Summary:

> ➤ Repetition problems have the objects repeating in the combinations or permutations that are formed from a base set.

> ➤ Problems with indistinguishable objects, instead, have the objects repeating in the base set itself.

> ➤ Allowing repetition increases the number of selections (combinations) and therefore the number of permutations.

> ➤ Using indistinguishable objects in the base set reduces the number of selections (combinations) and the number of permutations.

Table I

The base set is {A, B, C}

Permutations with Repetitions allowed. [$n = 3$, $r = 3$]

First Position (3 ways allowed: A, B, C)	Second Position (3 ways allowed: A, B, C)	Third Position (3 ways allowed: A, B, C)	Word Formed	Count
A	A	A	AAA	1
		B	AAB	2
		C	AAC	3
	B	A	ABA	4
		B	ABB	5
		C	ABC	6
	C	A	ACA	7
		B	ACB	8
		C	ACC	9
B	A	A	BAA	10
		B	BAB	11
		C	BAC	12
	B	A	BBA	13
		B	BBB	14
		C	BBC	15
	C	A	BCA	16
		B	BCB	17
		C	BCC	18
C	A	A	CAA	19
		B	CAB	20
		C	CAC	21
	B	A	CBA	22
		B	CBB	23
		C	CBC	24
	C	A	CCA	25
		B	CCB	26
		C	CCC	27

Total number of ways: 27

Table II

The base set is {A, B, C}

The Permutations (not allowing Repetitions) are as follows [n = 3, r = 3].
Shaded entries are redundant and therefore not counted. (That is, we pick
only the entries in which no object is repeated.) Shaded entries the ones
having the same object repeating and therefore not counted.

First Position (3 ways allowed: A, B, C)	Second Position (3 ways allowed: A, B, C)	Third Position (3 ways allowed: A, B, C)	Word Formed	Count
A	A	A	AAA	A repeat
		B	AAB	A repeat
		C	AAC	A repeat
	B	A	ABA	A repeat
		B	ABB	B repeat
		C	ABC	1
	C	A	ACA	A repeat
		B	ACB	2
		C	ACC	C repeat
B	A	A	BAA	A repeat
		B	BAB	B repeat
		C	BAC	3
	B	A	BBA	B repeat
		B	BBB	B repeat
		C	BBC	B repeat
	C	A	BCA	4
		B	BCB	B repeat
		C	BCC	C repeat
C	A	A	CAA	A repeat
		B	CAB	5
		C	CAC	C repeat
	B	A	CBA	6
		B	CBB	B repeat
		C	CBC	C repeat
	C	A	CCA	C repeat
		B	CCB	C repeat
		C	CCC	C repeat

Total number of ways: 6

There is only 1 combination (without repetition), because any of the 6 words (ABC or ACB or BAC or BCA or CAB or CBA) formed in the above table is the same combination (is a single combination).

Permutations (repetition allowed) using Indistinguishable Objects

By replacing C with A in the base set {A, B, C}, we get {A, B, A}. Reducing the repetitive permutations yields

Table III

The Permutations (allowing Repetitions) are as follows [n = 3, r = 3], and two of the three objects are indistinguishable. The table is derived by replacing C with A in Table I and eliminating the repeating entries. Shaded entries are redundant and therefore not counted. (That is, we pick only one of the indistinguishable permutations.)

First Position (3 ways allowed: A, B, C)	Second Position (3 ways allowed: A, B, C)	Third Position (3 ways allowed: A, B, C)	Word Formed	Count
A	A	A	AAA	1
		B	AAB	2
		A	AAA	already counted
	B	A	ABA	3
		B	ABB	4
		A	ABA	already counted
	A	A	AAA	already counted
		B	AAB	already counted
		A	AAA	already counted
B	A	A	BAA	5
		B	BAB	6
		A	BAA	already counted
	B	A	BBA	7
		B	BBB	8
		A	BBA	already counted
	A	A	BAA	already counted
		B	BAB	already counted
		A	BAA	already counted
A	A	A	AAA	already counted
		B	AAB	already counted
		A	AAA	already counted
	B	A	ABA	already counted
		B	ABB	already counted
		A	ABA	already counted
	A	A	AAA	already counted
		B	AAB	already counted
		A	AAA	already counted

Total number of ways: 8

Permutations (repetition not allowed) with Indistinguishable Objects

Indistinguishable objects are items that repeat in the original set. For example, replace C in the above set with A. Then the new base set would be {A, B, A}. Hence, if we replace C with A in the Table II, we get the repetitions in the permutations. Reducing the repetitive permutations yields

Table IV

The Permutations (not allowing Repetitions) with Indistinguishable objects are as follows [$n = 3$, $r = 3$]. The table is derived by replacing C with A in Table II and eliminating the repeating entries. Shaded entries are redundant and therefore not counted. (That is, we pick only one of the indistinguishable permutations)

First Position (3 ways allowed: A, B, C)	Second Position (3 ways allowed: A, B, C)	Third Position (3 ways allowed: A, B, C)	Word Formed	Count
A	B	A	ABA	1
	A	B	AAB	2
B	A	A	BAA	3
	A	A	BAA	already counted
A	A	B	AAB	already counted
	A	A	ABA	already counted

Total number of ways: 3

So far, we have discussed the types of the problems. When trying to solve a problem, it is very helpful to identify its type. Once this is done, we need to count the number of possibilities.

Distinction between Indistinguishable Objects Problems and Repetition Problems

Suppose you are to arrange the letters of the word SUCCESS.

The base set is {S, U, C, C, E, S, S}. There are 3 S's, which are indistinguishable objects. Hence, the letter S, can be used a maximum of 3 times in forming a new word if repetition is not allowed. So, SSSSUCE is not a possible arrangement.

If repetition is allowed, you can use S as many times as you wish, regardless of the number of S's in the base word (for example, even if there is only 1 S, you can use it up to maximum allowed times). Hence, SSSSSSS is a possible arrangement.

Counting

There are three models of counting we can use.

We already discussed that if there are m combinations possible from a base set and if there are n permutations possible for each combination, then the total number of permutations possible is $m \cdot n$.

This is also clear from the *Fundamental Principle of Counting*.

Model 1:

The Fundamental Principle of Counting:

Construct a tree diagram (we used tables above) to keep track of all possibilities. Each decision made produces a new branch. Finally, count all the allowed possibilities.

The previous tables are examples of tree diagrams. They can represent possibilities as trees. The possibilities are also counted in the tables.

Model 2:

Divide a work into mutually independent jobs and multiply the number of ways of doing each job to find the total number of ways the work can be done. For example, if you are to position three letters in 3 slots, you can divide the work into the jobs as

1) Choose one of three letters A, B, and C for the first position

2) Choose one of the remaining 2 letters for the second position

3) Choose the only remaining letter for the third position

This can be done in $3 \times 2 \times 1 = 6$ ways. The model is a result of the Fundamental Principle of Counting.

Model 3:

Models 1 and 2 are fundamental. Model 3 uses at least one of the first two models. Here, we use the following formula:

Total Number of Permutations = Number of Combinations × Number of Permutations of Each Combination

Predominantly, we use the model for calculating combinations. The total number of permutations and the number of permutations for each combination can be calculated using either or both models 1 and 2 in many cases.

Cyclic Permutations

A *cyclic permutation* is a permutation that shifts all elements of a given ordered set by a certain amount, with the elements that are shifted off the end inserted back at the beginning in the same order, i.e., cyclically. In other words, a rotation.

For example, {A, B, C, D}, {B, C, D, A}, {C, D, A, B}, and {D, A, B, C} are different linear permutations but the same cyclic permutation. The permutations when arranged in cyclic order, starting from, say, A and moving clockwise, yield the same arrangement {A, B, C, D}. The following figure helps visualize this.

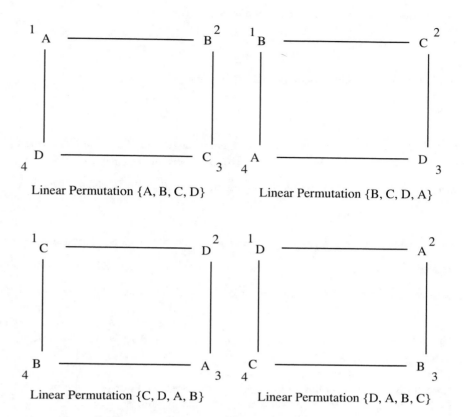

Cyclic arrangements of the cyclic permutations.

For the r placement positions (for the example in the figure, r equals 4), we get r permutations, each is an equivalent cyclic permutation. Hence, the number of cyclic permutations equals

(The number of ordinary permutations) $\div r$

Hence, for $_nP_r$ permutations, $_nP_r \div r$ cyclic permutations exist. Simply said, r linear permutations would be same cyclic permutation.

Also, {A, B, C, D} and {A, C, B, D} are different linear permutations and different cyclic permutations, because arranging them in cyclic order yields different sequences.

Factorial

The **factorial** of a non-negative integer n, denoted by n!, is the product of all positive integers less than or equal to n. That is, $n! = n(n-1)(n-2) \cdots 3 \cdot 2 \cdot 1$. For example, $4! = 4 \cdot 3 \cdot 2 \cdot 1 = 24$. Note: 0! is defined to be 1.

Formulas

Verify that the following formulas apply to the scenarios mentioned above. These formulas should be memorized.

Formula 1: If you have n items to choose from and you choose r of them, then the number of permutations *with repetitions allowed* is

$$n \cdot n \cdot \ldots n = n^r$$

(r times)

Formula 2: The formula for permutations *with repetitions not allowed* is

$$_nP_r = \frac{n!}{(n-r)!}$$

Formula 3: The formula for combinations *with repetitions not allowed* is

$$_nC_r = \frac{n!}{r!(n-r)!}$$

Formula 4: We know that *k distinguishable* objects have *k! different* arrangements (permutations). But a set of *k indistinguishable* objects, will have only 1 *indistinguishable* permutation. Hence, if we have *P* permutations for *k distinguishable* objects, we will have $\frac{P}{k!}$ permutations for *k indistinguishable* objects because we now treat the earlier *k!* arrangements as one.

The case is similar when we have more than one set of indistinguishable objects. Suppose the word ABCDEF has $_nP_r$ permutations (not allowing repetitions); then the word AAABBC will have $\frac{_nP_r}{3! \cdot 2!}$ permutations because here we have a set of 3 indistinguishable objects A and a set of 2 indistinguishable objects B.

There are formulas for the other problem models, but they are not needed for the test. We can always use the Fundamental Principal of Counting for them.

Formula 5: For *r* linear positions (for the example in the figure, *r* equals 4), we get *r* permutations, each of which is an equivalent cyclic permutation. Hence, the number of cyclic permutations is

(The number of ordinary permutations) ÷ *r*

The formulas in this section will be referenced while we solve the problems.

Problem Solving Strategy

In permutation and combination problems, it is very important to recognize the type of problem. Many students mistakenly approach a combination problem as a permutation, and vice versa. The steps below will help you determine the problem type.

Solving a permutation or combination problem involves two steps:

1)   Recognizing the problem type: permutation vs. combination.

2)   Using formulas or models to count the possibilities.

We have three questions to ask ourselves in order to identify the problem type:

1)   **Is it a permutation or combination?**

Check any two typical arrangements with the same combination. If the two arrangements are counted only once, it is a combination problem. Otherwise, it is a permutation.

For example, if you are asked for a lock code, then 321 and 123 could be two possibilities, and the two numbers are formed from the same combination (Same number of 1's, 2's, and 3's). So, lock codes must be permutations.

For another example, suppose you have 5 balls numbering 1 through 5. If you are asked to select 3 out of the 5 balls and you are only interested in the numbers on the balls, not the order in which they are taken, then you have a combination problem.

Problems that by definition connote ordering (though not directly stated) are permutations. For example, 3 digits form a 3-digit number. Here, the 3-digit number connotes ordering. For another example, if you are to answer 3 questions, you probably would not be asked to answer a particular question more than once. So, you would not allow repetition in the calculations. Though not often needed, such logical assumptions are allowed and sometimes expected.

If the problem itself defines slots for the arrangements, it is a permutation problem. Words like "arrange" define slots for the arrangements. We will explain this in more detail later in the problems.

Generally, "arrangements" refer to permutations, and "selections" refer to combinations. These words often flag the problem type.

Other words indicating permutations are "alteration," "shift," "transformation," and "transmutation," all of which connote ordering.

For example:

In how many ways can the letters of the word XYZ be *transformed* to form new words?

In how many ways can the letters of the word XYZ be *altered* to form new words?

Some words indicating combinations are "aggregation," "alliance," "association," "coalition," "composition," "confederation," "gang," "league," and "union," (all of which have nothing to do with arrangements but instead connote selections.)

For example:

In how many ways can a coalition of 2 countries be formed from 4 countries?

(Here, a coalition is the same whether you say country A and B are a coalition or country B and country A are a coalition.)

2) **Are repetitions allowed?**

Check whether, based on the problem description, the results of a permutation/combination can have repetitions.

For example:

If you are to list countries in a coalition, you can hardly list a country twice.

(Here, repetition automatically is not allowed unless specified otherwise.)

If you have 3 doors to a room, you could use the same door for both entering and exiting.

(Here, repetition is automatically allowed.)

3) **Are there any indistinguishable objects in the base set?**

Check the base set: the objects from which a permutation or a combination are drawn. If any indistinguishable objects (repetitions at base set level) are available, collect them. This is easy since it only requires finding identical objects in a base set, which is usually given.

For example, if the original question is to find the words formed from the word GARGUNTUNG, then, in this step, you collect the information: G exists thrice, U exists twice, and so on.

Once the problem type is recognized, use the corresponding formula or model to solve it.

Problem Set T: Permutations & Combinations

1. In how many ways can n different balls be arranged in r slots?

    (1)   Given r balls and n slots to arrange the balls in, the balls can be arranged in 210 ways.

    (2)   If we only need to select and not arrange n balls for r slots, we can do it in 35 ways.

2. $$A = \{2, 4, 7, 8\}$$

    $$B = \{3, 6, 7, 8\}$$

    A and B are the sets shown above. Another set C also has a total of 4 elements. Exactly two elements are shared by sets A and C. Exactly two elements are shared by sets B and C, and these could be the elements shared by A and C. If none of the elements in the sets appears more than once in the same set, how many elements do the three sets share?

    (1)   6 is *not* in set C.

    (2)   3 is in set C.

3. $$A = \{2, 4, 7, 8\}$$

    $$B = \{3, 6, 7, 8\}$$

    A and B are the sets shown above. Another set C also has a total of 4 elements. Exactly two elements are shared by sets A and C. Exactly two elements are shared by sets B and C, and these could be the elements shared by A and C. If none of the elements in the sets appear more than once in the same set and if x is the only common element of all three sets, then what is x?

    (1)   6 is *not* in set C.

    (2)   3 is in set C.

4. $$A = \{3, 9, 10, 15\}$$

    $$B = \{5, 12, 15, 21\}$$

    x is one of the elements in set A, and y is one of the elements in set B. What is the value of $x + y$?

    (1)   Exactly one of x and y is odd.

    (2)   Exactly one of x and y is prime.

Answers and Solutions to Problem Set T: Permutations & Combinations

1. In how many ways can n different balls be arranged in r slots?

    (1) Given r balls and n slots to arrange the balls in, the balls can be arranged in 210 ways.

    (2) If we only need to select and not arrange n balls for r slots, we can do it in 35 ways.

An arrangement is a permutation problem. n different balls can be arranged in r slots in $_nP_r$ ways. So, the question is "What is $_nP_r$?"

Statement (1): Given r balls and n slots to arrange the balls in, the balls can be arranged in 210 ways.

Again, r balls can be arranged in n slots in $_nP_r$ ways [the first ball can be placed in n slots, second one in $n - 1$ slots, and so on … the rth ball can be placed in the final slot in $n - r - 1$ slots. Multiplying all the possibilities (of all slots) yields $_nP_r$ ways.]. We are given that this can be done in 210 ways. Hence, Statement (1) directly determines the answer, $_nP_r$. The statement alone is sufficient.

Statement (2): If we only need to select and not arrange n balls for r slots, we can do it in 35 ways.

$_nP_r$ is the product of n through $n - r - 1$.

Clearly, the smaller the value of r, the greater the value of $_nP_r$.

Now, we know that $_nC_r$ always equals $_nC_{n-r}$ while $_nP_r$ might not equal $_nP_{n-r}$ unless $n - r = r$ (then $_nP_r$ equals $_nP_{n-r}$). So, unless $n = n - r$, we have a double case. The following calculations demonstrate this.

Given: $_nC_{n-r} = n!/[r!(n-r)!] = 35 = 5 \times 7 = 5 \times 6 \times 7/6 = 1 \times 2 \times 3 \times 4 \times 5 \times 6 \times 7/6 = 7!/3!(1 \times 2 \times 3 \times 4) = 7!/3!4! = 7!/3!(7 - 4)! = {_7C_3}$. Here r equals 3.

Or

$= 7!/4!(7 - 3)! = {_7C_4}$. Here r equals 4.

Since $_7P_3 \neq {_7P_4}$, we have a double case and therefore the statement is *not* sufficient.

The answer is (A).

2.
$$A = \{2, 4, 7, 8\}$$
$$B = \{3, 6, 7, 8\}$$

A and B are the sets shown above. Another set C also has a total of 4 elements. Exactly two elements are shared by sets A and C. Exactly two elements are shared by sets B and C, and these could be the elements shared by A and C. If none of the elements in the sets appears more than once in the same set, how many elements do the three sets share?

    (1) 6 is *not* in set C.

    (2) 3 is in set C.

Let's use compartments for the <u>selections</u> of the elements of set C. Let the compartments be $\{\_,\_,\_,\_\}$.

Any element common to sets A, B, and C must be common to any two of them. There are 2 common elements in sets A and B, which are 7 and 8. So, the common elements of all three sets could be none, one of 7 and 8, or both 7 and 8. So, the answer to the question could be none, one, or two.

In summary, C contains two the numbers from $\{2, 4, 7, 8\}$ and two numbers from $\{3, 6, 7, 8\}$.

Statement (1): 6 is *not* in set *C*.

First, let's see how we can choose 2 elements from Set *B* to fill the compartments.

Since Set *C* shares exactly two elements with Set *B* (given in the question), *C* must share two of the elements from Set *B* minus 6 (the statement says 6 is not in *C*), which is {3, 6̶, 7, 8}. Combinations of two of the three possible are 3 and 7, 3 and 8, and 7 and 8. Let's fill them in the compartments of *C* as follows:

$$\left\{\begin{array}{|c|c|} \hline \multirow{2}{*}{3} & 7 \\ \cline{2-2} & 8 \\ \hline 7 & \\ \hline \end{array}, \_,\_\right\}$$

The cell 3 in the first column is adjacent to both 7 and 8 in the second column. Hence, 3-7 and 3-8 are possible pairs. The cell 7 in the first column is adjacent to only 8 in the second column: 7-8 is a possible pair.

So, *C* = {3,7,_,_}, {3,8,_,_} or {7,8,_,_}. We have fully used Set *B*. Now, the blanks in *C* must be filled with elements in set *A* that are not in set *B* (so that no more than 2 elements from *C* are shared with *B*). Elements in *A* that are and not in *B* are {2, 4, 7̶, 8̶} = {2, 4}. So, *C* =

$$\left\{\begin{array}{|c|c|} \hline \multirow{2}{*}{3} & 7 \\ \cline{2-2} & 8 \\ \hline 7 & \\ \hline \end{array}, 2,4\right\}$$

So, the possible selections are {3, 7, 2, 4}, {3, 8, 2, 4}, and {7, 8, 2, 4}. The first two selections have exactly 1 number in common with *A* and *B*, while the third set has 2 such elements. So, the answer is 1 or 2. Since we do not have a unique answer, the statement is *not* sufficient.

Statement(2): 3 is in set *C*.

Sets *B* and *C* share exactly 2 elements (given in the question), and one of them must be 3 (because given in the statement that 3 is an element in *C* and this is already in Set *B*). Hence, the other element must be one of the remaining elements in Set *B*, which are 6, 7, and 8. Let's allot one compartment to allow one of these and one compartment to allow 3. We get *C* equals

$$\left\{\_,\_,\begin{array}{|c|} \hline 6 \\ \hline 7 \\ \hline 8 \\ \hline \end{array},3\right\}$$

Note: The remaining two blanks cannot be filled by any of these numbers 6, 7, 8, and 3 because then *C* would have more than two elements from *B* (while we are given it's just two.)

The remaining two blank compartments in *C* must be filled by two elements in A, but not in B. They are none other than 2 and 4. Filling the compartments yields

$$\left\{2,4,\begin{array}{|c|} \hline 6 \\ \hline 7 \\ \hline 8 \\ \hline \end{array},3\right\}$$

Now, if the filling can be done as {2, 4, 6, 3} such that the number of common elements in all the sets is zero, or the filling can be done as {2, 4, 7, 3} or as {2, 4, 8, 3} such that there is one common element in all the sets, then the number of common elements is 1. So, the answer could be zero or one and *not* two (because we can use either 7 or 8 and not both).

We have more than one answer and therefore the statement is *not* sufficient.

The only common answer of the two statements together is 1, and since Data Sufficiency problems must have at least one solution that must be 1. So, the statements together are sufficient. The answer is (C).

{3, 7, 2, 4}, {3, 8, 2, 4}, and {7, 8, 2, 4} are the short-listed selections from Statement (1), and applying Statement (2) that "3 is in the set" eliminates the third selection {7, 8, 2, 4} since it does not have 3. The two omitted solutions {3, 7, 2, 4} and {3, 8, 2, 4} share only one element with *A* and *B* (the first one shares 7 and the second one shares 8.) Either way, the answer is 1 only.

3. $A = \{2, 4, 7, 8\}$

                     $B = \{3, 6, 7, 8\}$

A and *B* are the sets shown above. Another set *C* also has a total of 4 elements. Exactly two elements are shared by sets *A* and *C*. Exactly two elements are shared by sets *B* and *C*, and these could be the elements shared by *A* and *C*. If none of the elements in the sets appear more than once in the same set and if *x* is the only common element of all three sets, then what is *x*?

(1)   6 is *not* in set *C*.

(2)   3 is in set *C*.

This problem is just like the one above.

From the Problem 3, with the statements together, we shortlist the possible sets as {3, 7, 2, 4} and {3, 8, 2, 4}. These sets share exactly one element with *A* and *B*, but not the same element. The first set shares 7, and the second set shares 8. So, both are feasible answers. Since we have more than one answer, the statements together are *not* sufficient. The answer is (E).

4. $A = \{3, 9, 10, 15\}$

                     $B = \{5, 12, 15, 21\}$

x is one of the elements in set *A*, and *y* is one of the elements in set *B*. What is the value of *x* + *y* ?

(1)   Exactly one of *x* and *y* is odd.

(2)   Exactly one of *x* and *y* is prime.

The number *x* could be any of the numbers in set *A*, and the number *y* could be any of the numbers in set *B* as listed in the figure. Each arrow between the two indicates a combination that can be made for the set {*x*, *y*}. You might as well calculate and write the sum of *x* and *y* for each combination on the respective lines which we will do later only for allowed combinations.

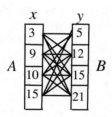

Statement (1): Exactly one of x and y is odd.

Since exactly one of x and y is odd, $x + y$ must be odd + even = odd. Let's delete all the links which represent combinations that do not sum to an odd number. For example, $3 + 5 = 8 \neq$ odd, so remove the link $3 - 5$. Then we get

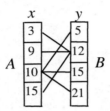

Writing the sums on the lines yields

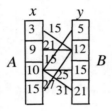

The sums on the lines are the solutions; and since there is more than one sum, the statement is *not* sufficient.

Statement(2): Exactly one of x and y is prime.

3 and 5 are the only primes in either set. Since at least one of x and y is prime, delete every line not through 3 and 5. Since exactly one of the numbers x or y is prime, delete the link $3 - 5$ also. So, the links now look like

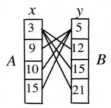

Writing the sums on the line yields

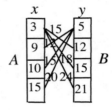

The sums in on the lines are the solutions; and since there is more than one sum, the statement is *not* sufficient.

Pick the output from Statement (1) and cleanse it with Statement (2), or pick the output from Statement (2) and cleanse it with (1).

The values for $x + y$ that Statement (2) allows are {12, 15, 18, 20, 24}. Statement (1) says the sum $x + y$ is odd. Cleansing the set {12, 15, 18, 20, 24} of even numbers yields {~~12~~, 15, ~~18~~, ~~20~~, ~~24~~} = {15}. So, there is only one value for $x + y$ (= 15) that both statements allow. Hence, the statements together are sufficient, and the answer is (C). The answer to the question is 15. The allowed values for $x - y$ are $3 - 12$ and $10 - 5$.

Functions

A function is a special relationship (correspondence) between two sets such that for each element x in its domain there is assigned one and <u>only one</u> element y in its range.

Notice that the correspondence has two parts:

1) For each x there is assigned *one y*. (This is the ordinary part of the definition.)

2) For each x there is assigned *only one y*. (This is the special part of the definition.)

The second part of the definition of a function creates the uniqueness of the assignment: There cannot be assigned two values of y to one x. In mathematics, uniqueness is very important. We know that $2 + 2 = 4$, but it would be confusing if $2 + 2$ could also equal something else, say 5. In this case, we could never be sure that the answer to a question was the *right* answer.

The correspondence between x and y is usually expressed with the function notation: $y = f(x)$, where y is called the dependent variable and x is called the independent variable. In other words, the value of y depends on the value of x plugged into the function. For example, the square root function can be written as $y = f(x) = \sqrt{x}$. To calculate the correspondence for $x = 4$, we get $y = f(4) = \sqrt{4} = 2$. That is, the square root function assigns the unique y value of 2 to the x value of 4. Most expressions can be turned into functions. For example, the expression $2^x - \dfrac{1}{x}$ becomes the function

$$f(x) = 2^x - \frac{1}{x}$$

DOMAIN AND RANGE

We usually identify a function with its correspondence, as in the example above. However, a function consists of three parts: a domain, a range, and correspondence between them.

➤ **The *domain* of a function is the set of *x* values for which the function is defined.**

For example, the function $f(x) = \dfrac{1}{x-1}$ is defined for all values of $x \neq 1$, which causes division by zero. There is an infinite variety of functions with restricted domains, but only two types of restricted domains appear on the GMAT: division by zero and even roots of negative numbers. For example, the function $f(x) = \sqrt{x-2}$ is defined only if $x - 2 \geq 0$, or $x \geq 2$. The two types of restrictions can be combined. For example, $f(x) = \dfrac{1}{\sqrt{x-2}}$. Here, $x - 2 \geq 0$ since it's under the square root symbol. Further $x - 2 \neq 0$, or $x \neq 2$, because that would cause division by zero. Hence, the domain is all $x > 2$.

➤ **The *range* of a function is the set of *y* values that are assigned to the *x* values in the domain.**

For example, the range of the function $y = f(x) = x^2$ is $y \geq 0$ since a square is never negative. The range of the function $y = f(x) = x^2 + 1$ is $y \geq 1$ since $x^2 + 1 \geq 1$. You can always calculate the range of a function algebraically, but is usually better to graph the function and read off its range from the y values of the graph.

GRAPHS

The graph of a function is the set of ordered pairs $(x, f(x))$, where x is in the domain of f and $y = f(x)$.

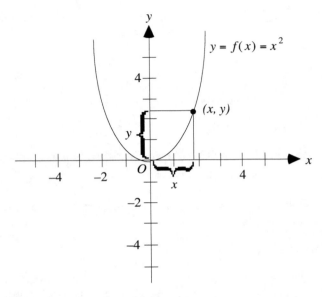

For this function, the domain is all x and the range is all $y \geq 0$ (since the graph touches the x-axis at the origin and is above the x-axis elsewhere).

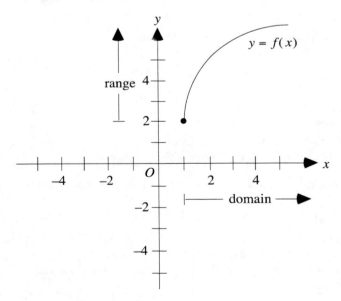

For this function, the domain is all $x \geq 1$ and the range is all $y \geq 2$.

TRANSLATIONS OF GRAPHS

Many graphs can be obtained by shifting a base graph around by adding positive or negative numbers to various places in the function. Take for example, the absolute value function $y = |x|$. Its graph is

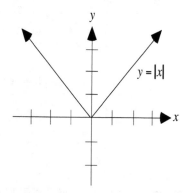

(Notice that sometimes an arrow is added to a graph to indicate the graph continues indefinitely and sometimes nothing is used. To indicate that a graph stops, a dot is added to the terminal point of the graph. Also, notice that the domain of the absolute value function is all x because you can take the absolute value of any number. The range is $y \geq 0$ because the graph touches the x-axis at the origin, is above the x-axis elsewhere, and increases indefinitely.)

To shift this base graph up one unit, we add 1 outside the absolute value symbol, $y = |x| + 1$:

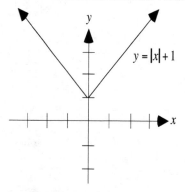

(Notice that the range is now $y \geq 1$.)

To shift the base graph down one unit, we subtract 1 outside the absolute value symbol, $y = |x| - 1$:

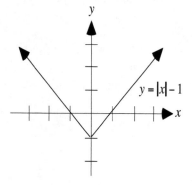

(Notice that the range is now $y \geq -1$.)

To shift the base graph to the right one unit, we subtract 1 inside the absolute value symbol, $y = |x - 1|$:

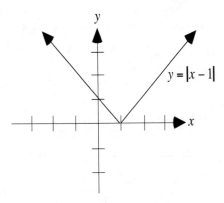

(Notice that the range did not change; it's still $y \geq 0$. Notice also that subtracting 1 moved the graph to right. Many students will mistakenly move the graph to the left because that's where the negative numbers are.)

To shift the base graph to the left one unit, we add 1 inside the absolute value symbol, $y = |x + 1|$:

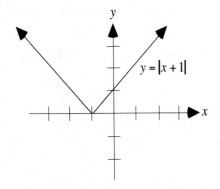

(Notice that the range did not change; it's still $y \geq 0$. Notice also that adding 1 moved the graph to left. Many students will mistakenly move the graph to the right because that's where the positive numbers are.)

The pattern of the translations above holds for all functions. So, to move a function $y = f(x)$ up c units, add the positive constant c to the exterior of the function: $y = f(x) + c$. To move a function $y = f(x)$ to the right c units, subtract the constant c in interior of the function: $y = f(x - c)$. To summarize, we have

To shift up c units:	$y = f(x) + c$
To shift down c units:	$y = f(x) - c$
To shift to the right c units:	$y = f(x - c)$
To shift to the left c units:	$y = f(x + c)$

REFLECTIONS OF GRAPHS

Many graphs can be obtained by reflecting a base graph by multiplying various places in the function by negative numbers. Take for example, the square root function $y = \sqrt{x}$. Its graph is

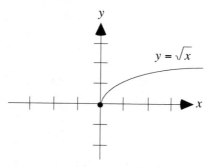

(Notice that the domain of the square root function is all $x \geq 0$ because you cannot take the square root of a negative number. The range is $y \geq 0$ because the graph touches the x-axis at the origin, is above the x-axis elsewhere, and increases indefinitely.)

To reflect this base graph about the x-axis, multiply the exterior of the square root symbol by negative one, $y = -\sqrt{x}$:

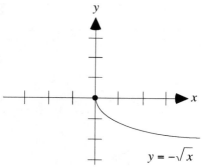

(Notice that the range is now $y \leq 0$ and the domain has not changed.)

To reflect the base graph about the y-axis, multiply the interior of the square root symbol by negative one, $y = \sqrt{-x}$:

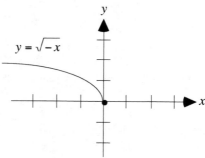

(Notice that the domain is now $x \leq 0$ and the range has not changed.)

The pattern of the reflections above holds for all functions. So, to reflect a function $y = f(x)$ about the x-axis, multiply the exterior of the function by negative one: $y = -f(x)$. To reflect a function $y = f(x)$ about the y-axis, multiply the exterior of the function by negative one: $y = f(-x)$. To summarize, we have

To reflect about the x-axis: $y = -f(x)$

To reflect about the y-axis: $y = f(-x)$

Reflections and translations can be combined. Let's reflect the base graph of the square root function $y = \sqrt{x}$ about the *x*-axis, the *y*-axis and then shift it to the right 2 units and finally up 1 unit:

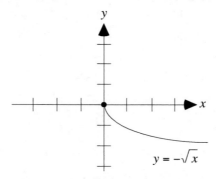

(Notice that the domain is still $x \geq 0$ and the range is now $y \leq 0$.)

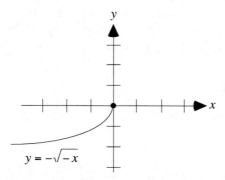

(Notice that the domain is now $x \leq 0$ and the range is still $y \leq 0$.)

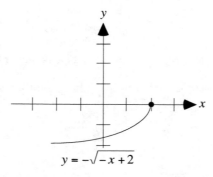

(Notice that the domain is now $x \leq 2$ and the range is still $y \leq 0$.)

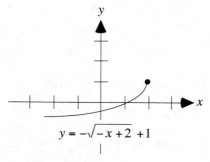

(Notice that the domain is still $x \leq 2$ and the range is now $y \leq 1$.)

EVALUATION AND COMPOSITION OF FUNCTIONS

EVALUATION

We have been using the function notation $f(x)$ intuitively; we also need to study what it actually means. You can think of the letter f in the function notation $f(x)$ as the name of the function. Instead of using the equation $y = x^3 - 1$ to describe the function, we can write $f(x) = x^3 - 1$. Here, f is the name of the function and $f(x)$ is the value of the function at x. So, $f(2) = 2^3 - 1 = 8 - 1 = 7$ is the value of the function at 2. As you can see, this notation affords a convenient way of prompting the evaluation of a function for a particular value of x.

Any letter can be used as the independent variable in a function. So, the above function could be written $f(p) = p^3 - 1$. This indicates that the independent variable in a function is just a "placeholder." The function could be written without a variable as follows:

$$f(\ ) = (\ )^3 - 1$$

In this form, the function can be viewed as an input/output operation. If 2 is put into the function $f(2)$, then $2^3 - 1$ is returned.

In addition to plugging numbers into functions, we can plug expressions into functions. Plugging $y + 1$ into the function $f(x) = x^2 - x$ yields

$$f(y + 1) = (y + 1)^2 - (y + 1)$$

You can also plug other expressions in terms of x into a function. Plugging $2x$ into the function $f(x) = x^2 - x$ yields

$$f(2x) = (2x)^2 - 2x$$

This evaluation can be troubling to students because the variable x in the function is being replaced by the same variable. But the x in function is just a placeholder. If the placeholder were removed from the function, the substitution would appear more natural. In $f(\ ) = (\ )^2 - (\ )$, we plug $2x$ into the left side $f(2x)$ and it returns the right side $(2x)^2 - 2x$.

COMPOSITION

We have plugged numbers into functions and expressions into functions; now let's plug in other functions. Since a function is identified with its expression, we have actually already done this. In the example above with $f(x) = x^2 - x$ and $2x$, let's call $2x$ by the name $g(x)$. In other words, $g(x) = 2x$. Then the composition of f with g (that is plugging g into f) is

$$f(g(2x)) = f(2x) = (2x)^2 - 2x$$

You probably won't see the notation $f(g(x))$ on the test. But you probably will see one or more problems that ask you perform the substitution. For another example, let $f(x) = \dfrac{1}{x + 1}$ and let $g(x) = x^2$. Then $f(g(x)) = \dfrac{1}{x^2 + 1}$ and $g(f(x)) = \left(\dfrac{1}{x + 1}\right)^2$. Once you see that the composition of functions merely substitutes one function into another, these problems can become routine. Notice that the composition operation $f(g(x))$ is performed from the inner parentheses out, not from left to right. In the operation $f(g(2))$, the number 2 is first plugged into the function g and then that result is plugged in the function f.

A function can also be composed with itself. That is, substituted into itself. Let $f(x) = \sqrt{x} - 2$. Then $f(f(x)) = \sqrt{\sqrt{x} - 2} - 2$.

Example: The graph of $y = f(x)$ is shown. If $f(-1) = v$, then which one of the following could be the value of $f(v)$?

(A)   0
(B)   1
(C)   2
(D)   2.5
(E)   3

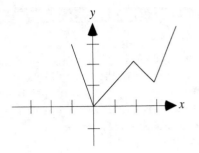

Since we are being asked to evaluate $f(v)$ and we are told that $v = f(-1)$, we are just being asked to compose $f(x)$ with itself. That is, we need to calculate $f(f(-1))$. From the graph, $f(-1) = 3$. So, $f(f(-1)) = f(3)$. Again, from the graph, $f(3) = 1$. So, $f(f(-1)) = f(3) = 1$. The answer is (B).

QUADRATIC FUNCTIONS

Quadratic functions (parabolas) have the following form:

$$y = f(x) = ax^2 + bx + c$$

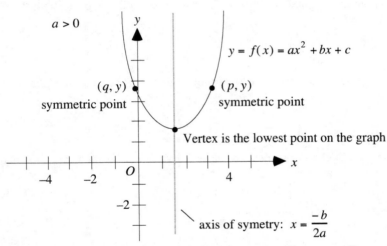

The lowest or highest point on a quadratic graph is called the vertex. The x–coordinate of the vertex occurs at $x = \dfrac{-b}{2a}$. This vertical line also forms the axis of symmetry of the graph, which means that if the graph were folded along its axis, the left and right sides of the graph would coincide.

In graphs of the form $y = f(x) = ax^2 + bx + c$ if $a > 0$, then the graph opens up.

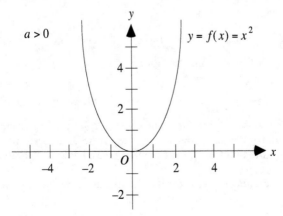

If $a < 0$, then the graph opens down.

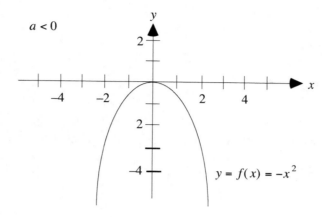

By completing the square, the form $y = ax^2 + bx + c$ can be written as $y = a(x - h)^2 + k$. You are not expected to know this form on the test. But it is a convenient form since the vertex occurs at the point (h, k) and the axis of symmetry is the line $x = h$.

We have been analyzing quadratic functions that are vertically symmetric. Though not as common, quadratic functions can also be horizontally symmetric. They have the following form:

$$x = g(y) = ay^2 + by + c$$

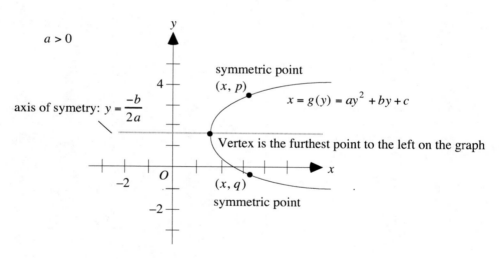

The furthest point to the left on this graph is called the vertex. The y-coordinate of the vertex occurs at $y = \dfrac{-b}{2a}$. This horizontal line also forms the axis of symmetry of the graph, which means that if the graph were folded along its axis, the top and bottom parts of the graph would coincide.

In graphs of the form $x = ay^2 + by + c$ if $a > 0$, then the graph opens to the right and if $a < 0$ then the graph opens to the left.

Example: The graph of $x = -y^2 + 2$ and the graph of the line k intersect at $(0, \ p)$ and $(1, \ q)$. Which one of the following is the smallest possible slope of line k ?

(A) $-\sqrt{2} - 1$
(B) $\quad -\sqrt{2} + 1$
(C) $\quad \sqrt{2} - 1$
(D) $\quad \sqrt{2} + 1$
(E) $\quad \sqrt{2} + 2$

Let's make a rough sketch of the graphs. Expressing $x = -y^2 + 2$ in standard form yields $x = -1y^2 + 0 \cdot y + 2$. Since $a = -1$, $b = 0$, and $c = 2$, the graph opens to the left and its vertex is at $(2, 0)$.

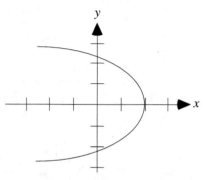

Since p and q can be positive or negative, there are four possible positions for line k (the y-coordinates in the graphs below can be calculated by plugging $x = 0$ and $x = 1$ into the function $x = -y^2 + 2$):

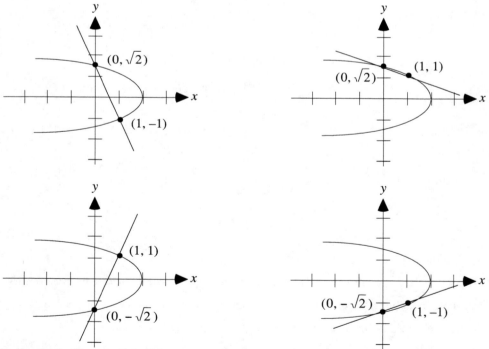

Since the line in the first graph has the steepest negative slope, it is the smallest possible slope. Calculating the slope yields

$$m = \frac{\sqrt{2} - (-1)}{0 - 1} = \frac{\sqrt{2} + 1}{-1} = -\left(\sqrt{2} + 1\right) = -\sqrt{2} - 1$$

The answer is (A).

QUALITATIVE BEHAVIOR OF GRAPHS AND FUNCTIONS

In this rather vague category, you will be asked how a function and its graph are related. You may be asked to identify the zeros of a function based on its graph. The zeros, or roots, of a function are the *x*-coordinates of where it crosses the *x*-axis. Or you may be given two graphs and asked for what *x* values are their functions equal. The functions will be equal where they intersect.

Example: The graphs of $y = f(x)$ and $y = 1$ are shown. For how many *x* values does $f(x)$ equal 1?

(A) 0
(B) 1
(C) 2
(D) 3
(E) 4

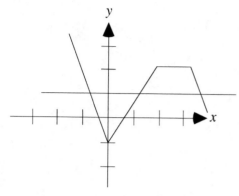

The figure shows that the graphs intersect at three points. At each of these points, both graphs have a height, or *y*-coordinate, of 1. The points are approximately (–.8, 1), (1.2, 1), and (4, 1). Hence, $f(x) = 1$ for three *x* values. The answer is (D).

FUNCTIONS AS MODELS OF REAL-LIFE SITUATIONS

Functions can be used to predict the outcomes of certain physical events or real-life situations. For example, a function can predict the maximum height a projectile will reach when fired with an initial velocity, or the number of movie tickets that will be sold at a given price.

Example: The graph shows the number of music CDs sold at various prices. At what price should the CDs be marked to sell the maximum number of CDs?

(A) 0
(B) 5
(C) 10
(D) 15
(E) 20

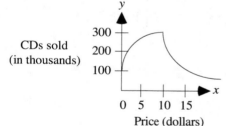

CDs sold
(in thousands)

Price (dollars)

As you read the graph from left to right, it shows that sales initially increase rapidly and then slow to a maximum of about 300,000. From there, sales drop precipitously and then slowly approach zero as the price continues to increase. From the graph, sales of 300,000 units on the *y*-axis correspond to a price of about $10 on the *x*-axis. The answer is (C).

Problem Set U: Functions

Two functions are equal only in their common domain.

1.

$$f(x) = x^2 \qquad \text{for } |x| \le 1$$

$$f(x) = 1/x^2 \qquad \text{for } |x| > 1$$

The above equations define how the function f varies with x. Is $-0.9 < a < 0.9$?

    (1) $f(-a) = 1/f(b)$

    (2) $a = 1/b$

Table to evaluate $f(x, y)$

y x	-1	0	1
-1	$-2m + n$	$m - n$	m
0	$6m + n$	0	$3m + 5n$
1	$m + n$	$-m + 2n$	$2m + n$

2.   If $f(x, y)$ is a function defined on x and y as shown in the table above, what is the value of $f(-1, 1) + f(1, -1)$?

    (1) $f(0, -1) + f(-1, -1) = 8$

    (2) $f(1, -1) + f(-1, 0) = 9$

3. The possible arguments of the functions $f(x, y)$ and $g(x, y)$ are $x = 0$ or 1 and $y = 0$ or 1 and are defined by the following tables:

Table for $g(x, y)$

$g(x, y)$	0	1
0	0	1
1	1	1

Table for $f(x, y)$

$f(x, y)$	0	1
0	0	0
1	0	1

What is the value of $f(a, b) + g(a, b)$?

    (1) $f(a, b) = 0$

    (2) $g(a, b) = 0$

4.   A function is expressed as $f(x) = mx + c$. Does $f(p) - f(q)$ equal $p - q$?

(1) $m = 1$

(2) $c = 1$

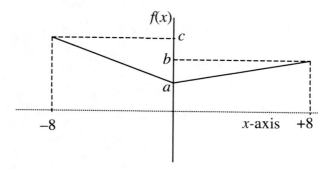

5.   The graph above shows two lines, one on the left of the *y*-axis and one on the right, that represent the curve $f(x)$. What is the value of $f(4) \cdot f(-4)$?

(1) $a = 3$

(2) $b = 5$

Answers and Solutions to Problem Set U: Functions

Two functions are equal only in their common domain.

1. $f(x) = x^2$ for $|x| \le 1$

        $f(x) = 1/x^2$ for $|x| > 1$

The above equations define how the function f varies with x. Is $-0.9 < a < 0.9$?

(1) $f(-a) = 1/f(b)$

(2) $a = 1/b$

When x is in the range $-1 < x < 1$ (here $|x| < 1$), $f(x) = x^2$ is less than 1.

When x equals 1 or -1, $f(x) = x^2$ equals 1.

When $|x| > 1$ (i.e., when $x > 1$ or $x < -1$), $f(x) = 1/x^2$ is less than 1. Thus, when $|x| > 1$, $f(x)$ lies between 0 and 1, inclusive of 1 and not inclusive of 0 ($0 < f(x) \le 1$). So, $1/f(x) \ge 1$.

If you thought $f(x) = 1/x^2$ so $1/f(x) = x^2$ and equals 0 when x is 0 [$1/f(0) = 0^2$] you are mistaken. This is because for $x = 0$, $f(x) = 1/x^2 = 1/0^2$ [$f(x)$ is not defined].

In summary, $0 < f(x) \le 1$ and $1/f(x) \ge 1$. Now, the common region of $f(x)$ and $1/f(x)$ is none other than $\{1\}$ alone. Therefore, if $f(a) = 1/f(b)$, both must be equal to 1. So, $f(a) = 1/f(b) = 1$. This means $a^2 = 1/b^2 = 1$, or $a = \pm 1$ and $b = \pm 1$. Clearly, "Is $-0.9 < a < 0.9$" is false. Statement (1) alone which says $f(a) = 1/f(b)$ is sufficient.

The statement sure gives the relation between a and b, while b is completely new information. Clearly, the statement is irrelevant. In other words, the statement is not required; Statement is not sufficient.

The answer is (A).

Table to evaluate $f(x, y)$

y \ x	-1	0	1
-1	$-2m + n$	$m - n$	m
0	$6m + n$	0	$3m + 5n$
1	$m + n$	$-m + 2n$	$2m + n$

2.   If $f(x, y)$ is a function defined on x and y as shown in the table above, what is the value of $f(-1, 1) + f(1, -1)$?

(1) $f(0, -1) + f(-1, -1) = 8$

(2) $f(1, -1) + f(-1, 0) = 9$

From the table, $f(-1, 1) + f(1, -1) = m + (m + n) = 2m + n$.

Statement (1): $f(0, -1) + f(-1, -1) = 8$

We know $f(0, -1) = 6m + n$ and $f(-1, -1) = -2m + n$. Hence,

$$f(0, -1) + f(-1, -1) = 8$$

$$(6m + n) + (-2m + n) = 8$$

$$4m + 2n = 8$$

$$2(2m + n) = 8$$

Dividing both sides by 2 yields $2m + n = 4$; Data Sufficient.

The answer is (A).

Statement (2): $f(1, -1) + f(-1, 0) = 9$

We know $f(1, -1) = m + n$ and $f(-1, 0) = m - n$. Hence,

$$f(1, -1) + f(-1, 0) = 9$$

$$(m + n) + (m - n) = 9$$

$$2m = 9$$

$$m = 9/2$$

Since we do not know what n is, the statement is not sufficient.

3. The possible arguments of the functions $f(x, y)$ and $g(x, y)$ are $x = 0$ or 1 and $y = 0$ or 1 and are defined by the following tables:

Table for $g(x, y)$

$g(x, y)$	0	1
0	0	1
1	1	1

Table for $f(x, y)$

$f(x, y)$	0	1
0	0	0
1	0	1

What is the value of $f(a, b) + g(a, b)$?

(1)　$f(a, b) = 0$

(2)　$g(a, b) = 0$

Statement (1): $f(a, b) = 0$

From the table, $f(a, b)$ equals 0 in three cases:

    1. $\{a, b\} = \{0, 0\}$, then $g(a, b) = 0$
    2. $\{a, b\} = \{0, 1\}$, then $g(a, b) = 1$
    3. $\{a, b\} = \{1, 0\}$, then $g(a, b) = 1$

In the corresponding cases, $f(a, b) + g(a, b)$ equals

    $0 + 0 = 0$ when $\{a, b\} = \{0, 0\}$
    $0 + 1 = 1$ when $\{a, b\} = \{0, 1\}$
    $0 + 1 = 1$ when $\{a, b\} = \{1, 0\}$

This is a double case and therefore the statement alone is not sufficient.

The answer is (B).

Statement (2): $g(a, b) = 0$

From the table, $g(a, b)$ equals 0 only when $\{a, b\} = \{0, 0\}$, the unique solution for a and b. Hence we have a unique value for $f(a, b) + g(a, b)$ (we do not need to calculate any further and can say the statement is sufficient) $= f(0, 0) = 0$ [from it's table] $+ g(a, b)$ [from it's table] $= 0 + 0 = 0$. The statement is sufficient.

4.   A function is expressed as $f(x) = mx + c$. Does $f(p) - f(q)$ equal $p - q$?

   (1) $m = 1$

   (2) $c = 1$

From the rule, $f(p) = mp + c$ and $f(q) = mq + c$. Their difference is

$$f(p) - f(q) = (mp + c) - (mq + c)$$

$$= mp - mq$$

$$= m(p - q)$$

$$= 1(p - q) \qquad \text{from Statement (1), } m = 1$$

$$= p - q$$

Hence, Statement (1) alone is sufficient.

The parameter m is independent of the parameter c. So, knowing c does not determine m. Regardless of the value of c, if m equals 1, the objective $f(p) - f(q) = p - q$ is achieved. Hence, Statement (2) is not needed. So, Statement (2) is not sufficient.

The answer is (A).

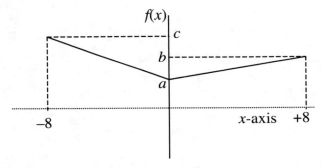

5.   The graph above shows two lines, one on the left of the y-axis and one on the right, that represent the curve $f(x)$. What is the value of $f(4) \cdot f(-4)$?

   (1) $a = 3$

   (2) $b = 5$

Draw the xy-axes. On the x-axis, plot two points one on either side of the y-axis that are 8 units from the y-axis.

Now, using Statements (1) and (2), we can plot the points $A(0, a)$ and $B(8, b)$. Thus, the positive side of the curve can be constructed and thereby the value of $f(4)$ can be evaluated.

But since we still do not know what c is, we cannot construct the negative side of the curve. So, $f(-4)$ can vary; it is not fixed. Hence, $f(4) \cdot f(-4)$ cannot be calculated. Data is not sufficient.

The answer is (E).

Miscellaneous Problems

Example 1:   Is CAB a code word in Language Q?

    (1)   ABC is the base word.

    (2)   If C immediately follows B, then C can be moved to the front of the code word to generate another word.

From (1), ABC is a code word.

From (2), the C in the code word ABC can be moved to the front of the word: CAB.

Hence, CAB is a code word and the answer is (C), both statements needed to answer the question.

Example 2:   How many marbles are in bowl S?

    (1)   If 1/4 of the marbles were removed, the bowl would be filled to 1/2 of its capacity.

    (2)   If 100 marbles were added, the bowl would be full.

To determine the number of marbles in the bowl, we need at least the fraction that the particular number of marbles in the bowl makes.

Statement (1) gives only fractions no quantity, and Statement (2) gives quantity and no fraction. So, neither statement alone is sufficient.

Now, let's analyze the statements together:

Statement (1):

If 1/4 of the marbles were removed, the bowl would be filled to 1/2 of its capacity. So, originally, there were 1/2 + 1/4 = 3/4 marbles. The bowl is short 1/4 of its capacity of marbles.

Statement (2):

If 100 marbles were added, the bowl would be full. So, originally the bowl was short 100 marbles needed to be full. So, 1/4 capacity of marbles corresponds to 100 marbles. So, 1 capacity of the marbles corresponds to what? Forming the proportion yields

Number of marbles in 1 capacity ÷ the fraction 1 = 100 marbles ÷ (1/4)

(1/4 is the fraction that 100 marbles make)

Number of marbles in 1 capacity = 100 · 4 = 400.

The answer is 100 and therefore the statements together are sufficient. The answer is (C).

Problem Set V: Miscellaneous Problems

1.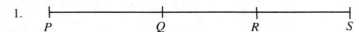

    On the segment *PS* above, *PS* = 10. What is the length of the middle segment *QR*?

    (1)   *PR* = 7

    (2)   *QS* = 6

2. Is $x + y = 7$?

    (1)   The sentence "$x = 3$ and $y = 4$" is incorrect.

    (2)   Either *x* equals 3 or *y* equals 4.

3. If $pq \neq 0$ and $q = -|m|p + c$, then is the product of *p* and *q* negative?

    (1) $c = 0$

    (2) $m = 4$

4. For any increase in *x*, the value of *y* decreases by double the value. Also, for any decrease in *x*, the value of *y* increases by double the value. What is the value of *x* when *y* is 2?

    (1)   When *x* is 1, $y = 5$.

    (2)   When *x* is 3, $y = 1$.

$a/2 + b$	$a/2 + c/2$	$c/2$
b	$4/3\, d$	$d/3 + (3/5)e$
$a + d$	$d + e/5$	$a + d/3$

5. If the sum of the rows and columns of the table are equal, then what is the sum?

    (1)   The sum of the diagonal elements from the top left through the bottom right is 10.

    (2)   The diagonal elements on both diagonals sum to same number.

				Row Sum
	1	x	$x + y$	--
	x	$2x$	--	--
	$x + y$	3	y	10
Column Sum	--	--	--	

6. In the table above, the symbol "--" means the expression in the respective cell is not known. What is the sum of the diagonal elements from the top left through the bottom right in the table ?

    (1)   The sum of the elements in each row is the same.

    (2)   The sum of the elements in each column is the same.

7. A changing system in x and y is such that y never equals 0 and x always equals a constant K. What is the constant K equal to?

    (1) $x + y$ equals either 3 or 5.

    (2) $x - y$ equals either 3 or 5.

8. Jennifer is upset because she confused the two close readings that she took for the period of a simple pendulum. She needs to find the average of the two readings. What is the exact average of the two readings?

    (1) She knows that the second reading is one of the numbers 3.02 and 3.2.

    (2) She knows that the greater reading is one of the numbers 3.01 and 3.11.

Answers and Solutions to Problem Set V: Miscellaneous Problems

1.

On the segment PS above, $PS = 10$. What is the length of the middle segment QR?

   (1) $PR = 7$

   (2) $QS = 6$

From the figure, $PS = PQ + QR + RS$. Since we are given that $PS = 10$, we have the equation

$$PQ + QR + RS = 10$$

So, $QR = 10 - PQ - RS$. Hence, to find QR, we need the segments PQ and RS.

Now, let's also express the statements in the basic segments.

Statement (1): $PR = 7$	Statement (2): $QS = 6$
$PR = 7$. Now, PR equals $PQ + QR$ (from the figure). So, we have	$QS = 6$. Now, QS equals $QR + RS$ (from the figure). So, we have

<table>
<tr><td>$PQ + QR = 7$</td><td></td><td>$QR + RS = 6$</td><td></td></tr>
<tr><td>$PQ + 10 - PQ - RS = 7$</td><td>(Since $QR =$
$10 - PQ - RS$)</td><td>$10 - PQ - RS + RS = 6$</td><td>(Since $QR =$
$10 - PQ - RS$)</td></tr>
<tr><td>$10 - RS = 7$</td><td></td><td>$10 - PQ = 6$</td><td></td></tr>
<tr><td>$RS = 10 - 7 = 3$</td><td></td><td>$PQ = 10 - 6 = 4$</td><td></td></tr>
</table>

We still do not have the length of the basic segment PQ. So, we cannot find QR. The statement is *not* sufficient.	We still do not have the length of the basic segment RS. So, we cannot find QR. The statement is *not* sufficient.

With the two statements together, we have both RS and PQ. So, QR can be evaluated. The answer is (C). $QR = 10 - PQ - RS = 10 - 4 - 3 = 3$.

2.   Is $x + y = 7$?

   (1)   The sentence "$x = 3$ and $y = 4$" is incorrect.

   (2)   Either x equals 3 or y equals 4.

If you interpreted the question setup as "Is x equal to 3 and y equal to 4?", you are mistaken: $x = 3$ and $y = 4$ is not the only instance when $x + y = 7$. So, transformation fails.

Drawing a table for the situation yields

&	$y = 4$ is true.	$y = 4$ is false.
$x = 3$ is true.	$x + y = 7$	$x + y \neq 7$
$x = 3$ is false.	$x + y \neq 7$	$x + y = 7$ could be 7 or not 7.

Statement (1): The sentence "x = 3 and y = 4" is incorrect.

Modifying the table correspondingly yields

&	y = 4 is true.	y = 4 is false.
x = 3 is true.	x + y = 7	x + y ≠ 7
x = 3 is false.	x + y ≠ 7	✖ x + y = 7 could be 7 or not 7.

We see that the possible cases column 1, row 1, column 1, row 2, and column 2, row 1 have conflicting results about x + y equaling 7.

We have a double case and therefore the statement is not sufficient.

Statement (2): Either x equals 3 or y equals 4.

So, x = 3 and y = 4 is possible, x = 3 and y ≠ 4 is possible, and x ≠ 3 and y = 4 is possible, while x ≠ 3 and y ≠ 4 is impossible. Modifying the table correspondingly yields

&	y = 4 is true.	y = 4 is false.
x = 3 is true.	x + y = 7	x + y ≠ 7
x = 3 is false.	x + y ≠ 7	✖ x + y = 7 could be 7 or not 7.

The table is the same as the one in Statement (1). So, effectively, Statements (1) and (2) mean the same thing.

Statement (2) is not sufficient just as Statement (1).

Since Statements (1) and (2) mean the same thing and each individually is not sufficient, the statements together are not sufficient. The answer is (E).

3. If $pq \neq 0$ and $q = -|m|p + c$, then is the product of p and q negative?

   (1) $c = 0$

   (2) $m = 4$

Method I (Coordinate Geometry):

Suppose $p = x$ and $q = y$ are coordinates on the line.

The question can now be changed as

   If $xy \neq 0$, then is the product of the x-and y-coordinates on the line $y = -|m|x + c$ negative?

   (1) $c = 0$

   (2) $m = 4$

Since $xy \neq 0$, neither x nor y are 0.

Multiplying both sides of the equation $y = -|m|x + c$ by x yields $xy = -|m|x^2 + cx$. So, the product of the x-and y-coordinates of a given point (x, y) on line $y = -|m|x + c$ is given by $-|m|x^2 + cx$. So, the question is "Is $-|m|x^2 + cx$ negative?"

Statement (1): $c = 0$

Substituting $c = 0$ in the expression $-|m|x^2 + cx$ yields

$$-|m|x^2 + (0)x$$
$$-|m|x^2$$

For all values of x (negative or positive [we know x is not zero]), x^2 is positive.

Also because $xy \neq 0$, $-|m|x^2 + cx$, which equals $-|m|x^2$, is not zero. So, $|m|$ and therefore m must not be zero.

So, for any value of m (negative or positive), $|m|$ is positive.

Now, the product of -1, $|m|$, and x^2 is

negative · positive · positive = negative

The statement is sufficient.

The answer is (A).
Method II:

Statement (2): $m = 4$

Substituting $m = 4$ in the expression $-|m|x^2 + cx$ yields

$$-|4|x^2 + cx$$
$$-4x^2 + cx$$

Now, the value of the expression depends upon x and c which are free to take any value. The expression can be negative (for example when $x = 1$ and $c = 0$) or zero (for example when $x = c = 0$) or positive (for example when $x = 1$ and $c = 5$).

We do not have sufficient data with the statement alone.

Since the product xy is not zero (given), neither x nor y are 0 and therefore the point (x, y) does not lie on the x- or y-axis.

The product of the x-and y-coordinates is negative only when the point (x, y) is in quadrants II or IV. So, the question can be transformed as "Is (x, y) in the quadrants I or III?"

Statement (1): $c = 0$

Substituting $c = 0$ in the equation $y = -|m|x + c$ yields

$$y = -|m|x + 0$$
$$y = -|m|x$$

Since $|m|$, the slope of the line, is negative and $(0, 0)$ is one point on the line $y = -|m|x$ (Regardless, we know that $(x, y) = (0, 0)$ is not a feasible solution). So, the line should look like the line l in the coordinate system below.

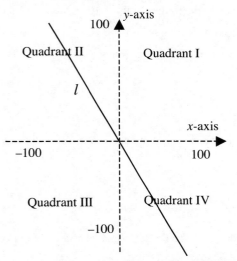

Clearly, the line passes through only quadrants II and IV. So, the product of x and y is negative.

The statement is sufficient.

The answer is (A).

Statement (2): $m = 4$

Substituting $m = 4$ in the equation $y = -|m|x + c$ yields

$$y = -|4|x + c$$
$$y = -4x + c$$

If c is 0, $(0, 0)$ is a solution of the equation.

If not, $(0, 0)$ is not a solution to the equation. Hence, the line does not pass through the origin.

The coefficients of x and y are not zero. So, the line is not horizontal or vertical.

A line not passing through origin and not horizontal or vertical passes through exactly three of the quadrants. So, at least one of the three quadrants is quadrant II or IV (xy is negative in this case) and at least one of the three quadrants is not quadrant II or IV (xy is positive in this case). Thus, we have a double case and therefore the statement is not sufficient.

4.   For any increase in x, the value of y decreases by double the value. Also, for any decrease in x, the value of y increases by double the value. What is the value of x when y is 2?

   (1)   When x is 1, $y = 5$.

   (2)   When x is 3, $y = 1$.

Either detail "For any increase in x, the value of y decreases by double the value" and "For any decrease in x, the value of y increases by double the value." indicates the same thing: that the slope of the curve is negative and the numeric value is 2. In short, the slope is -2 (this applies for any value of x, so the curve becomes a straight line) or 2. So, we indicate the curve in the form $y = mx + c$ as $y = -2x + c$. If we find c, we have the line and we can find any point on the line for example, $(x, 2)$. Now, substituting the point in either statement in the line yields

Statement (1):

When x is 1, $y = 5$. Substituting in the curve $y = -2x + c$ yields $5 = -2 \cdot 1 + c$, or $c = 5 + 2 = 7$. So, the line is $y = -2x + 7$ and the point $(x, 2)$ can be evaluated by substitution as $2 = -2x + 7$, or $-2x = -5$, or $x = 5/2$.

Statement (2):

When x is 3, $y = 1$. Substituting in the curve $y = -2x + c$ yields $1 = -2 \cdot 3 + c$, or $c = 1 + 6 = 7$. So, the line is $y = -2x + 7$ and the point $(x, 2)$ can be evaluated by substitution as $2 = -2x + 7$, or $-2x = 7 - 2$, or $-2x = 5$, or $x = -5/-2 = 5/2$.

Either statement is sufficient, and the answer is (D).

$a/2 + b$	$a/2 + c/2$	$c/2$
b	$4/3\ d$	$d/3 + (3/5)e$
$a + d$	$d + e/5$	$a + d/3$

5. If the sum of the rows and columns of the table are equal, then what is the sum?

    (1) The sum of the diagonal elements from the top left through the bottom right is 10.

    (2) The diagonal elements on both diagonals sum to same number.

Since the sum of the rows and columns in the table are equal, we have the following rules:

> Row 1 Sum = Row 2 Sum [*]

> Row 2 Sum = Row 3 Sum

Row 1 Sum = Row 3 Sum follows from the above two rules, so we do not consider it a different or new rule.

> Column 1 Sum = Column 2 Sum

> Column 2 Sum = Column 3 Sum

Column 1 Sum = Column 3 Sum follows from the above two rules, so we do not consider it a different or new rule.

> Column 1 Sum = Row 1 Sum

We have these 5 different new rules in 5 unknowns in the system.

The expected degree of freedom is 5 unknowns minus 5 rules = 0. But, here, this is a special case, where the resultant degree of freedom being 0 doesn't mean we have a solution. The reason is we do not have a non-zero constant at least not with Statement (2), which is again a ratio rule. Statement (2) is a non-ratio rule, so a solution is possible. We will see.

Statement (1) gives a rule that gives a non-zero constant. "Sum of diagonal elements top left through bottom right is 10." So, we have a fixed solution. Hence, the statement is sufficient.

Statement (2) gives yet again a ratio rule and no non-zero constant. "The diagonal elements on both diagonals sum to the same number." So, we already have a ratio solution, and here we have no fixed solution still. The statement is not sufficient.

The answer is (A).

---

[*] (Note: Neither row 1 nor row 2 have a non-zero constant. So, we get a ratio rule as shown at the end of the solution. Row 1 Sum = Row 2 Sum indicates $(a/2 + b) + (a/2 + c/2) + (c/2) = (b) + (4/3\ d) + (d/3 + 3/5\ e)$. In this rule, there is no non-zero constant term. So, this is a ratio rule. Any number of such rules do not yield a specific solution. To derive a specific solution, we would need at least one non-zero constant rule (a rule which has a non-zero constant solution) which Statement (1) gives and Statement (2) does not.)

				Row Sum
	1	x	$x + y$	--
	x	$2x$	--	--
	$x + y$	3	y	10
Column Sum	--	--	--	

6. In the table above, the symbol "--" means the expression in the respective cell is not known. What is the sum of the diagonal elements from the top left through the bottom right in the table ?

(1) The sum of the elements in each row is the same.

(2) The sum of the elements in each column is the same.

The sum of the elements from the top left through the bottom right is $1 + 2x + y$.

Column 1 Sum: $1 + x + (x + y) = 1 + 2x + y$.

Row 1 Sum: $1 + x + (x + y) = 1 + 2x + y$.

Hence, the sum of the elements from the top left through the bottom right is Column 1 Sum = Row 1 Sum = $1 + 2x + y$.

Statement (1): The sum of the elements in each row is same.

So, the question can be changed to "What is Row 1 sum?"

The sum of the numbers in each row is same.

So, Row 1 Sum = Row 2 Sum = Row 3 Sum, while Row 3 Sum is given to be 10.

So, Row 1 Sum is 10. The statement is sufficient.

Statement (2): The sum of the elements in each column is same.

So, the question can be changed to "What is Column 1 sum?"

The sum of the numbers in each column is same.

So,

Col 1 Sum = Col 2 Sum
$1 + x + x + y = x + 2x + 3$
$1 + 2x + y = 3x + 3$
$y = x + 2$

There is no other derivation possible from the statement. The derivation alone cannot evaluate the Column 1 Sum, so the statement is *not* sufficient.

The answer is (A).

Method II: To evaluate ratios of unknowns, rules with no constants are sufficient. But to evaluate exact values of the unknowns, rules with non-zero constant are a must. So, rows equal [Statement (1)] gives non-zero constant rules with Row 3 Sum = 10. So, the statement is sufficient. Statement (2) gives only rules with no constant. So, exact values cannot be found and therefore the statement is *not* sufficient.

7.   A changing system in *x* and *y* is such that *y* never equals 0 and *x* always equals a constant *K*. What is the constant *K* equal to?

   (1) $x + y$ equals either 3 or 5.

   (2) $x - y$ equals either 3 or 5.

A possible mistake: With the statements together, both $x + y$ *and* $x - y$ have a double case. So, if you thought *x* would also have a double case and answered (E), you are mistaken.

With Statement (1), $x + y$ has a double case; and with Statement (2), we have $x - y$ but this will not help us evaluate $x + y$. Hence, neither statement is sufficient.

Now, $x + y$ equals $x - y$ only when *y* equals 0, which we get by adding $-x - y$ to both sides of the assumed equation $x + y = x - y$. But we are given that *y* is not zero. Hence, $x + y$ and $x - y$ are different. Hence, if $x + y = 3$, $x - y$ would rather equal 5; and if $x + y$ equals 5, $x - y$ would rather equal 3. The sum of $(x + y)$ and $(x - y)$ would equal $3 + 5$ and $5 + 3$ in respective cases. Hence,

$$(x + y) + (x - y) = 3 + 5 \text{ or } 5 + 3$$

$$x + y + x - y = 8 \text{ or } 8$$

$$2x = 8$$

$$x = 4$$

The statements together are sufficient and therefore the answer is (C).

8.   Jennifer is upset because she confused the two close readings that she took for the period of a simple pendulum. She needs to find the average of the two readings. What is the exact average of the two readings?

   (1)   She knows that the second reading is one of the numbers 3.02 and 3.2.

   (2)   She knows that the greater reading is one of the numbers 3.01 and 3.11.

Let's analyze both statements. Since the second reading is 3.02 or 3.2, either of which is greater than 3.01, the greatest reading is not 3.01. So, the greatest reading is 3.11. Since 3.2 is greater than 3.11, 3.2 is not the second reading. Hence, 3.02 is the second reading. So, the other reading (first reading) must be 3.11. Their average is $(3.02 + 3.11)/2$. Both statements are sufficient. The answer is (C).